Football League Tables

1889 to the Present

D1098724

Collins

Glasgow and London

Editor: Jim Mallory
Assistant Editor: Jeanette Tannock

First published 1977
© William Collins Sons and Company Limited
Printed in Great Britain
ISBN 0 00 435009 10

Cover photos

Acknowledgements: Radio Times, Hilton Picture
Library, Syndication International, Mary Evans Picture
Library

Players pictured: (front) Stanley Matthews Alex James,
Kevin Keegan: (back) R. Gardener

Foreword

All football supporters keep track of the fortunes over the years of their home side. Most also relish the opportunity to look back and compare the results of the current team with those of its forerunners. There are a great many who take this interest still further, assiduously noting the relative rise and fall of all the clubs in the Football League or the Scottish League.

This book has been compiled for two reasons: first, to bring together all the league tables since the formation of the leagues and the final rounds of the FA and Scottish FA Cups, making it possible to compare league and cup successes year by year. The second reason is to make all this information readily available in a pocket-size form, handy for settling arguments on the terrace or in the pub.

In compilation, all the records have been thoroughly checked, and in several instances mistakes were uncovered, particularly in the years prior to 1919, which has led to minor adjustments in the club sequence.

Key

P indicates games played
W wins
D draws
L losses
F goals for
A goals against
Pts points

Contents

1888–89
Football League

	P	W	D	L	F	A	Pts
1 Preston	22	18	4	0	74	15	40
2 Aston Villa	22	12	5	5	61	43	29
3 Wolves	22	12	4	6	50	37	28
4 Blackburn	22	10	6	6	66	45	26
5 Bolton	22	10	2	10	63	59	22
6 WBA	22	10	2	10	40	46	22
7 Accrington	22	6	8	8	48	48	20
8 Everton	22	9	2	11	35	46	20
9 Burnley	22	7	3	12	42	62	17
10 Derby	22	7	2	13	41	60	16
11 Notts County	22	5	2	15	39	73	12
12 Stoke	22	4	4	14	26	51	12

FA Cup

Third Round

Preston North End v Birmingham St George's	2-0
Chatham v West Bromwich Albion	1-10
Wolverhampton Wanderers v The Wednesday	5-0
Blackburn Rovers v Aston Villa	8-1

Semi-Final

Preston North End v West Bromwich Albion	1-0
Wolverhampton Wanderers v Blackburn Rovers	1-1, 3-1

Final at Kennington Oval

Preston North End v Wolverhampton Wanderers	3-0

Scottish FA Cup

Fifth Round

Third Lanark v Abercorn	2-2, 2-2, 3-1
Renton v Arbroath	3-3, 4-0
Celtic v Clyde	9-2
Dumbarton v Mossend Swifts	3-1
St Mirren v Queen of the South Wanderers	3-1
Campsie	bye
Dumbarton Athletic	bye
East Stirlingshire	bye

Sixth Round

Third Lanark v Campsie	6-0
Dumbarton v St Mirren	1-1, 2-2, 2-2, 3-1
Dumbarton Athletic v Renton	1-2
East Stirlingshire v Celtic	1-2

Semi-Final

Dumbarton v Celtic	1-4
Third Lanark v Renton	2-0

Final at Hampden Park

Third Lanark v Celtic	2-1

1889–90
Football League

	P	W	D	L	F	A	Pts
1 Preston	22	15	3	4	71	30	33
2 Everton	22	14	3	5	65	40	31
3 Blackburn	22	12	3	7	78	41	27
4 Wolves	22	10	5	7	51	38	25
5 WBA	22	11	3	8	47	50	25
6 Accrington	22	9	6	7	53	56	24
7 Derby	22	9	3	10	43	55	21
8 Aston Villa	22	7	5	10	43	51	19
9 Bolton	22	9	1	12	54	65	19
10 Notts County	22	6	5	11	43	51	17
11 Burnley	22	4	5	13	36	65	13
12 Stoke	22	3	4	15	27	69	10

FA Cup

Third Round

Preston North End v Bolton Wanderers	2-3
The Wednesday v Notts County	2-1
Bootle v Blackburn Rovers	0-7
Wolverhampton Wanderers v Stoke	3-2

Semi-Final

Bolton Wanderers v The Wednesday	1-2
Blackburn Rovers v Wolverhampton Wanderers	1-0

Final at Kennington Oval

Blackburn Rovers v The Wednesday	6-1

Scottish FA Cup

Fourth Round

Aberdeen v Queen's Park	1-13
Airdrieonians v Abercorn	2-3
Grangemouth v Vale of Leven	1-7
Third Lanark v Linthouse	2-0

Lanemark v St Mirren   2-8
Moffat v Carfin Shamrock   4-2
Ayr v Leith Athletic   1-4
Cowdenbeath v Dunblane   †
Hibernian v Queen of the South
    Wanderers   †
Kilbirnie v East Stirlingshire   †
Heart of Midlothian v Alloa Athletic   †
East End v Cambuslang   †
†No scores are available. The first named team won in each case.

Fifth Round

Queen's Park v St Mirren   1-0
Cowdenbeath v Abercorn   2-8
Vale of Leven v Heart of Midlothian   3-1
East End v Moffat*   2-2
Third Lanark   bye
Hibernian   bye
Leith Athletic   bye
Kilbirnie   bye
*East End won the replay

Sixth Round

Queen's Park v Leith Athletic   1-0
Abercorn v Hibernian   6-2
Vale of Leven v East End   4-0
Third Lanark v Kilbirnie   4-1

Semi-Final

Vale of Leven v Third Lanark   3-0
Queen's Park v Abercorn   2-0

Final at Ibrox Park

Queen's Park v Vale of Leven   1-1, 2-1

1890–91
Football League

	P	W	D	L	F	A	Pts
1 Everton	22	14	1	7	63	29	29
2 Preston	22	12	3	7	44	23	27
3 Notts County	22	11	4	7	52	35	26
4 Wolves	22	12	2	8	39	50	26
5 Bolton	22	12	1	9	47	34	25
6 Blackburn	22	11	2	9	52	43	24
7 Sunderland*	22	10	5	7	51	31	23
8 Burnley	22	9	3	10	52	63	21
9 Aston Villa	22	7	4	11	45	58	18
10 Accrington	22	6	4	12	28	50	16
11 Derby	22	7	1	14	47	81	15
12 WBA	22	5	2	15	34	57	12

*Two points deducted for fielding un-registered player.

Scottish League

	P	W	D	L	F	A	Pts
1 Dumbarton†	18	13	3	2	61	21	29
1 Rangers†	18	13	3	2	58	25	29
3 Celtic*	18	11	3	4	48	21	21
4 Cambuslang	18	8	4	6	47	42	20
5 Third Lanark*	18	8	3	7	38	39	15
6 Hearts	18	6	2	10	31	37	14
7 Abercorn	18	5	2	11	36	47	12
8 St Mirren	18	5	1	12	39	62	11
9 Vale of Leven	18	5	1	12	27	65	11
10 Cowlairs*	18	3	4	11	24	50	6

†Dumbarton and Rangers drew 2-2 in a play-off and were declared joint Champions.
*Each had four points deducted for infringements.

FA Cup

Third Round

Blackburn Rovers v Wolverhampton
    Wanderers   2-0
The Wednesday v West Bromwich
    Albion   0-2
Sunderland v Nottingham Forest   4-0
Notts County v Stoke   1-0

Semi-Final

Blackburn Rovers v West Bromwich
    Albion   3-2
Sunderland v Notts County   3-3, 0-2

Final at Kennington Oval

Blackburn Rovers v Notts County   3-1

Scottish FA Cup

Fifth Round

Dumbarton v 5th KRV   8-0
Heart of Midlothian v Morton   5-1
Royal Albert v Celtic   0-2
St Mirren v Queen's Park   2-3
Abercorn   bye
Third Lanark   bye
East Stirlingshire   bye
Leith Athletic   bye

Sixth Round

Dumbarton v Celtic	3-0
Heart of Midlothian v East Stirlingshire	3-1
Third Lanark v Queen's Park	1-1, 2-2, 4-1
Leith Athletic v Abercorn	2-3

Semi-Final

Dumbarton v Abercorn	3-1
Heart of Midlothian v Third Lanark	4-1

Final at Hampden Park

Heart of Midlothian v Dumbarton	1-0

1891-92
Football League

	P	W	D	L	F	A	Pts
1 Sunderland	26	21	0	5	93	36	42
2 Preston	26	18	1	7	61	31	37
3 Bolton	26	17	2	7	51	37	36
4 Aston Villa	26	15	0	11	89	56	30
5 Everton	26	12	4	10	49	49	28
6 Wolves	26	11	4	11	59	46	26
7 Burnley	26	11	4	11	49	45	26
8 Notts County	26	11	4	11	55	51	26
9 Blackburn	26	10	6	10	58	65	26
10 Derby	26	10	4	12	46	52	24
11 Accrington	26	8	4	14	40	78	20
12 WBA	26	6	6	14	51	58	18
13 Stoke	26	5	4	17	38	61	14
14 Darwen	26	4	3	19	38	112	11

Scottish League

	P	W	D	L	F	A	Pts
1 Dumbarton	22	18	1	3	81	26	37
2 Celtic	22	16	3	3	64	19	35
3 Hearts	22	15	4	3	64	36	34
4 Rangers	22	12	2	8	57	49	26
5 Leith	22	12	1	9	52	38	25
6 Third Lanark	22	9	4	9	44	38	22
7 Clyde	22	8	4	10	64	60	20
8 Renton	22	8	4	10	43	41	20
9 Abercorn	22	6	5	11	45	59	17
10 St Mirren	22	4	5	13	43	56	13
11 Cambuslang	22	2	6	14	21	79	10
12 Vale of Leven	22	0	5	17	24	101	5

FA Cup

Third Round

West Bromwich Albion v The Wednesday	2-1
Nottingham Forest v Preston North End	2-0
Wolverhampton Wanderers v Aston Villa	1-3
Sunderland v Stoke	2-2, 4-0

Semi-Final

West Bromwich Albion v Nottingham Forest	1-1, 1-1, 6-2
Aston Villa v Sunderland	4-1

Final at Kennington Oval

West Bromwich Albion v Aston Villa	3-0

Scottish FA Cup

Third Round

Celtic v Cowlairs	4-1
Rangers v Annbank	2-0
Renton v Heart of Midlothian	4-4, 1-1, 3-2
Dumbarton v Queen's Park	2-2, 1-4

Semi-Final

Renton v Queen's Park	1-1, 0-3
Celtic v Rangers	5-3

Final at Ibrox Park

Celtic v Queen's Park	5-1

1892-93
First Division

	P	W	D	L	F	A	Pts
1 Sunderland	30	22	4	4	100	36	48
2 Preston	30	17	3	10	57	39	37
3 Everton	30	16	4	10	74	51	36
4 Aston Villa	30	16	3	11	73	62	35
5 Bolton	30	13	6	11	56	55	32
6 Burnley	30	13	4	13	51	44	30
7 Stoke	30	12	5	13	58	48	29
8 WBA	30	12	5	13	58	69	29
9 Blackburn	30	8	13	9	47	56	29
10 Nottm Forest	30	10	8	12	48	52	28
11 Wolves	30	12	4	14	47	68	28

12 Wednesday	30	12	3	15	55	65	27
13 Derby	30	9	9	12	52	64	27
14 Notts County	30	10	4	16	53	61	24
15 Accrington	30	6	11	13	57	81	23
16 Newton Heath	30	6	6	18	50	85	18

Second Division

	P	W	D	L	F	A	Pts
1 Small Heath	22	17	2	3	90	35	36
2 Sheff United	22	16	3	3	62	19	35
3 Darwen	22	14	2	6	60	36	30
4 Grimsby	22	11	1	10	42	41	23
5 Ardwick	22	9	3	10	45	40	21
6 Burton Swifts	22	9	2	11	47	47	20
7 Northwich Vic	22	9	2	11	42	58	20
8 Bootle	22	8	3	11	49	63	19
9 Lincoln	22	7	3	12	45	51	17
10 Crewe	22	6	3	13	42	69	15
11 Burslem PV	22	6	3	13	30	57	15
12 Walsall TS	22	5	3	14	37	75	13

Scottish League

	P	W	D	L	F	A	Pts
1 Celtic	18	14	1	3	54	25	29
2 Rangers	18	12	4	2	41	27	28
3 St Mirren	18	9	2	7	40	39	20
4 Third Lanark	18	9	1	8	53	39	19
5 Hearts	18	8	2	8	39	42	18
6 Leith	18	8	1	9	36	31	17
7 Dumbarton	18	8	1	9	35	35	17
8 Renton	18	5	5	8	31	44	15
9 Abercorn	18	5	1	12	35	52	11
10 Clyde	18	2	2	14	25	55	6

FA Cup

Third Round
Everton v The Wednesday	3-0
Preston North End v Middlesbrough	
Ironopolis	2-2, 7-0
Wolverhampton Wanderers v	
Darwen	5-0
Blackburn Rovers v Sunderland	3-0

Semi-Final
Everton v Preston North End 2-2, 0-0,	2-1
Wolverhampton Wanderers v	
Blackburn Rovers	2-1

Final at Fallowfield (Manchester)
Wolverhampton Wanderers v	
Everton	1-0

Scottish FA Cup

Third Round
Heart of Midlothian v Queen's	
Park	1-1, 2-5
Celtic v Third Lanark	5-1
St Bernard's v Rangers	3-2
Broxburn Shamrock v St Mirren	4-3

Semi-Final
Queen's Park v Broxburn Shamrock	4-2
Celtic v St Bernard's	5-0

Final at Ibrox Park
Queen's Park v Celtic	2-1

1893–94
First Division

	P	W	D	L	F	A	Pts
1 Aston Villa	30	19	6	5	84	42	44
2 Sunderland	30	17	4	9	72	44	38
3 Derby	30	16	4	10	73	62	36
4 Blackburn	30	16	2	12	69	53	34
5 Burnley	30	15	4	11	61	51	34
6 Everton	30	15	3	12	90	57	33
7 Nottm Forest	30	14	4	12	57	48	32
8 WBA	30	14	4	12	66	59	32
9 Wolves	30	14	3	13	52	63	31
10 Sheff United	30	13	5	12	47	61	31
11 Stoke	30	13	3	14	65	79	29
12 Wednesday	30	9	8	13	48	57	26
13 Bolton	30	10	4	16	38	52	24
14 Preston	30	10	3	17	44	56	23
15 Darwen	30	7	5	18	37	83	19
16 Newton Heath	30	6	2	22	36	72	14

Second Division

	P	W	D	L	F	A	Pts
1 Liverpool	28	22	6	0	77	18	50
2 Small Heath	28	21	0	7	103	44	42
3 Notts County	28	18	3	7	70	31	39
4 Newcastle	28	15	6	7	66	39	36
5 Grimsby	28	15	2	11	71	58	32
6 Burton Swifts	28	14	3	11	79	61	31
7 Burslem PV	28	13	4	11	66	64	30
8 Lincoln	28	11	6	11	59	58	28

	P	W	D	L	F	A	Pts
9 Woolwich A	28	12	4	12	52	55	28
10 Walsall TS	28	10	3	15	51	61	23
11 Md Ironopolis	28	8	4	16	37	72	20
12 Crewe	28	6	7	15	42	73	19
13 Ardwick	28	8	2	18	47	71	18
14 Rotherham Tn	28	6	3	19	44	91	15
15 Northwich Vic	28	3	3	22	30	98	9

Scottish First Division

	P	W	D	L	F	A	Pts
1 Celtic	18	14	1	3	53	32	29
2 Hearts	18	11	4	3	46	32	26
3 St Bernard's	18	11	1	6	53	39	23
4 Rangers	18	8	4	6	44	30	20
5 Dumbarton	18	7	5	6	32	35	19
6 St Mirren	18	7	3	8	49	47	17
7 Third Lanark	18	7	3	8	38	44	17
8 Dundee	18	6	3	9	47	59	15
9 Leith	18	4	2	12	36	46	10
10 Renton	18	1	2	15	23	57	4

Scottish Second Division

	P	W	D	L	F	A	Pts
1 Hibernian	18	13	3	2	72	27	29
2 Cowlairs	18	13	1	4	73	32	27
3 Clyde	18	11	2	5	50	37	24
4 Motherwell	18	11	1	6	63	46	23
5 Partick	18	10	0	8	58	59	20
6 Port Glasgow*	18	9	2	7	52	53	13
7 Abercorn	18	5	2	11	42	60	12
8 Morton	18	4	1	13	36	63	9
9 Northern	18	3	3	12	34	62	9
10 Thistle	18	2	3	13	32	73	7

*Port Glasgow Athletic had 7 points deducted for fielding an ineligible player

FA Cup

Third Round

Nottingham Forest v Notts County	1-1, 1-4
Derby County v Blackburn Rovers	1-4
Bolton Wanderers v Liverpool	3-0
The Wednesday v Aston Villa	3-2

Semi-Final

Notts County v Blackburn Rovers	1-0
Bolton Wanderers v The Wednesday	2-1

Final at Goodison Park

Notts County v Bolton Wanderers	4-1

Scottish FA Cup

Third Round

Third Lanark v Port Glasgow Athletic	2-1
Celtic v St Bernard's	8-1
Clyde v Rangers	0-5
Abercorn v Queen's Park	3-3, 3-3, 0-2

Semi-Final

Third Lanark v Celtic	3-5
Rangers v Queen's Park	1-1, 3-1

Final at Hampden Park

Rangers v Celtic	3-1

1894-95
First Division

	P	W	D	L	F	A	Pts
1 Sunderland	30	21	5	4	80	37	47
2 Everton	30	18	6	6	82	50	42
3 Aston Villa	30	17	5	8	82	43	39
4 Preston	30	15	5	10	62	46	35
5 Blackburn	30	11	10	9	59	49	32
6 Sheff United	30	14	4	12	57	55	32
7 Nottm Forest	30	13	5	12	50	56	31
8 Wednesday	30	12	4	14	50	55	28
9 Burnley	30	11	4	15	44	56	26
10 Bolton	30	9	7	14	61	62	25
11 Wolves	30	9	7	14	43	63	25
12 Small Heath	30	9	7	14	50	74	25
13 WBA	30	10	4	16	51	66	24
14 Stoke	30	9	6	15	50	67	24
15 Derby	30	7	9	14	45	68	23
16 Liverpool	30	7	8	15	51	70	22

Second Division

	P	W	D	L	F	A	Pts
1 Bury	30	23	2	5	78	33	48
2 Notts County	30	17	5	8	75	45	39
3 Newton Heath	30	15	8	7	78	44	38
4 Leicester Fosse	30	15	8	7	72	53	38
5 Grimsby	30	18	1	11	79	52	37
6 Darwen	30	16	4	10	74	43	36
7 Burton Wand	30	14	7	9	67	39	35
8 Woolwich A	30	14	6	10	75	58	34
9 Man City	30	14	3	13	82	72	31
10 Newcastle	30	12	3	15	72	84	27
11 Burton Swifts	30	11	3	16	52	74	25
12 Rotherham Tn	30	11	2	17	55	62	24
13 Lincoln	30	10	0	20	52	92	20
14 Walsall TS	30	10	0	20	47	92	20
15 Burslem PV	30	7	4	19	39	77	18
16 Crewe	30	3	4	23	26	103	10

Scottish First Division

	P	W	D	L	F	A	Pts
1 Hearts	18	15	1	2	50	18	31
2 Celtic	18	11	4	3	50	29	26
3 Rangers	18	10	2	6	41	26	22
4 Third Lanark	18	10	1	7	51	39	21
5 St Mirren	18	9	1	8	34	34	19
6 St Bernard's	18	8	1	9	37	40	17
7 Clyde	18	8	0	10	38	47	16
8 Dundee	18	6	2	10	28	33	14
9 Leith	18	3	1	14	32	64	7
10 Dumbarton	18	3	1	14	27	58	7

Scottish Second Division

	P	W	D	L	F	A	Pts
1 Hibernian	18	14	2	2	92	28	30
2 Motherwell	18	10	2	6	56	39	22
3 Port Glasgow	18	8	4	6	62	56	20
4 Renton*	17	10	0	7	46	44	20
5 Morton	18	9	1	8	59	63	19
6 Airdrieonians	18	8	2	8	68	45	18
7 Partick	18	8	2	8	51	59	18
8 Abercorn	18	7	3	8	48	66	17
9 Dundee Wand*	17	3	1	13	44	86	9
10 Cowlairs	18	2	3	13	37	77	7

*Dundee Wanderers and Renton played each other once. Dundee awarded two points when Renton failed to turn up for the return fixture.

FA Cup

Third Round

Aston Villa v Nottingham Forest	6–2
Sunderland v Bolton Wanderers	2–1
West Bromwich Albion v Wolverhampton Wanderers	1–0
The Wednesday v Everton	2–0

Semi-Final

Aston Villa v Sunderland	2–1
West Bromwich Albion v The Wednesday	2–0

Final at Crystal Palace

Aston Villa v West Bromwich Albion	1–0

Scottish FA Cup

Third Round

St Bernard's v Clyde	2–1

Ayr Parkhouse v Renton	2–3
Dundee v Celtic	1–0
Heart of Midlothian v King's Park	4–2

Semi-Final

Dundee v Renton	1–1, 3–3, 0–3
Heart of Midlothian v St Bernard's	0–0, 0–1

Final at Ibrox Park

St Bernard's v Renton	2–1

1895-96
First Division

	P	W	D	L	F	A	Pts
1 Aston Villa	30	20	5	5	78	45	45
2 Derby	30	17	7	6	68	35	41
3 Everton	30	16	7	7	66	43	39
4 Bolton	30	16	5	9	49	37	37
5 Sunderland	30	15	7	8	52	41	37
6 Stoke	30	15	0	15	56	47	30
7 Wednesday	30	12	5	13	44	53	29
8 Blackburn	30	12	5	13	40	50	29
9 Preston	30	11	6	13	44	48	28
10 Burnley	30	10	7	13	48	44	27
11 Bury	30	12	3	15	50	54	27
12 Sheff United	30	10	6	14	40	50	26
13 Nottm Forest	30	11	3	16	42	57	25
14 Wolves	30	10	1	19	51	65	21
15 Small Heath	30	8	4	18	39	79	20
16 WBA	30	6	7	17	30	59	19

Second Division

	P	W	D	L	F	A	Pts
1 Liverpool	30	22	2	6	106	32	46
2 Man City	30	21	4	5	63	38	46
3 Grimsby	30	20	2	8	82	38	42
4 Burton Wand	30	19	4	7	69	40	42
5 Newcastle	30	16	2	12	73	50	34
6 Newton Heath	30	15	3	12	66	57	33
7 Woolwich A	30	14	4	12	59	42	32
8 Leicester Fosse	30	14	4	12	57	44	32
9 Darwen	30	12	6	12	72	67	30
10 Notts County	30	12	2	16	57	54	26
11 Burton Swifts	30	10	4	16	39	69	24
12 Loughborough	30	9	5	16	40	67	23
13 Lincoln	30	9	4	17	53	75	22
14 Burslem PV	30	7	4	19	43	78	18
15 Rotherham Tn	30	7	3	20	34	97	17

16 Crewe   30 5 3 22 30 95 13

Scottish First Division

	P	W	D	L	F	A	Pts
1 Celtic	18	15	0	3	64	25	30
2 Rangers	18	11	4	3	57	39	26
3 Hibernian	18	11	2	5	58	39	24
4 Hearts	18	11	0	7	67	36	22
5 Dundee	18	7	2	9	33	40	16
6 Third Lanark	18	7	1	10	47	51	15
7 St Bernard's	18	7	1	10	36	53	15
8 St Mirren	18	5	3	10	31	51	13
9 Clyde	18	4	3	11	39	59	11
10 Dumbarton	18	4	0	14	36	75	8

Scottish Second Division

	P	W	D	L	F	A	Pts
1 Abercorn	18	12	3	3	53	31	27
2 Leith	18	11	1	6	55	37	23
3 Renton	18	9	3	6	40	28	21
4 Kilmarnock	18	10	1	7	51	45	21
5 Airdrieonians	18	7	4	7	48	44	18
6 Partick	18	8	2	8	46	54	18
7 Port Glasgow	18	6	4	8	40	41	16
8 Motherwell	18	5	3	10	31	52	13
9 Morton	18	4	4	10	42	50	12
10 Linthouse	18	5	1	12	25	49	11

FA Cup

Third Round

Wolverhampton Wanderers v Stoke	3-0
Derby County v West Bromwich Albion	1-0
The Wednesday v Everton	4-0
Bolton Wanderers v Bury	2-0

Semi-Final

Wolverhampton Wanderers v Derby County	2-1
The Wednesday v Bolton Wanderers	1-1, 3-1

Final at Crystal Palace

The Wednesday v Wolverhampton Wanderers	2-1

Scottish FA Cup

Third Round

Heart of Midlothian v Arbroath	4-0

Hibernian v Rangers	3-2
St Bernard's v Queen's Park	3-2
Renton v Third Lanark	3-3, 2-0

Semi-Final

Heart of Midlothian v St Bernard's	1-0
Hibernian v Renton	2-1

Final at Logie Green, Edinburgh

Heart of Midlothian v Hibernian	3-1

1896–97
First Division

	P	W	D	L	F	A	Pts
1 Aston Villa	30	21	5	4	73	38	47
2 Sheff United	30	13	10	7	42	29	36
3 Derby	30	16	4	10	70	50	36
4 Preston	30	11	12	7	55	40	34
5 Liverpool	30	12	9	9	46	38	33
6 Wednesday	30	10	11	9	42	37	31
7 Everton	30	14	3	13	62	57	31
8 Bolton	30	12	6	12	40	43	30
9 Bury	30	10	10	10	39	44	30
10 Wolves	30	11	6	13	45	41	28
11 Nottm Forest	30	9	8	13	44	49	26
12 WBA	30	10	6	14	33	56	26
13 Stoke	30	11	3	16	48	59	25
14 Blackburn	30	11	3	16	35	62	25
15 Sunderland	30	7	9	14	34	47	23
16 Burnley	30	6	7	17	43	61	19

Second Division

	P	W	D	L	F	A	Pts
1 Notts County	30	19	4	7	92	43	42
2 Newton Heath	30	17	5	8	56	34	39
3 Grimsby	30	17	4	9	66	45	38
4 Small Heath	30	16	5	9	69	47	37
5 Newcastle	30	17	1	12	56	52	35
6 Man City	30	12	8	10	58	50	32
7 Gainsborough	30	12	7	11	50	47	31
8 Blackpool	30	13	5	12	59	56	31
9 Leicester Fosse	30	13	4	13	59	56	30
10 Woolwich A	30	13	4	13	68	70	30
11 Darwen	30	14	0	16	67	61	28
12 Walsall	30	11	4	15	53	69	26
13 Loughborough	30	12	1	17	50	64	25
14 Burton Swifts	30	9	6	15	46	61	24
15 Burton Wand	30	9	2	19	31	67	20
16 Lincoln	30	5	2	23	27	85	12

Scottish First Division

	P	W	D	L	F	A	Pts
1 Hearts	18	13	2	3	47	22	28
2 Hibernian	18	12	2	4	50	20	26
3 Rangers	18	11	3	4	64	30	25
4 Celtic	18	10	4	4	42	18	24
5 Dundee	18	10	2	6	38	30	22
6 St Mirren	18	9	1	8	38	29	19
7 St Bernard's	18	7	0	11	32	40	14
8 Third Lanark	18	5	1	12	29	46	11
9 Clyde	18	4	0	14	27	65	8
10 Abercorn	18	1	1	16	21	88	3

Scottish Second Division

	P	W	D	L	F	A	Pts
1 Partick	18	14	3	1	61	28	31
2 Leith	18	13	1	4	54	27	27
3 Kilmarnock	18	10	1	7	44	35	21
4 Airdrieonians	18	10	1	7	48	40	21
5 Morton	18	7	2	9	38	40	16
6 Renton	18	6	2	10	35	40	14
7 Linthouse*	18	8	2	8	44	52	14
8 Port Glasgow	18	4	5	9	39	50	13
9 Motherwell	18	6	1	11	40	55	13
10 Dumbarton	18	2	2	14	27	63	6

*Four points deducted for fielding an ineligible player.

FA Cup

Third Round

Aston Villa v Preston North End	1-1, 0-0, 3-2
Nottingham Forest v Liverpool	1-1, 0-1
Everton v Blackburn Rovers	2-0
Derby County v Newton Heath	2-0

Semi-Final

Aston Villa v Liverpool	3-0
Everton v Derby County	3-2

Final at Crystal Palace

Aston Villa v Everton	3-2

Scottish FA Cup

Third Round

Dumbarton v St Bernard's	2-0
Morton v Abercorn	2-2, 3-2
Dundee v Rangers	0-4
Kilmarnock v Third Lanark	3-1

Semi-Final

Morton v Rangers	2-7
Dumbarton v Kilmarnock	4-3

Final at Hampden Park

Rangers v Dumbarton	5-1

1897–98
First Division

	P	W	D	L	F	A	Pts
1 Sheff United	30	17	8	5	56	31	42
2 Sunderland	30	16	5	9	43	30	37
3 Wolves	30	14	7	9	57	41	35
4 Everton	30	13	9	8	48	39	35
5 Wednesday	30	15	3	12	51	42	33
6 Aston Villa	30	14	5	11	61	51	33
7 WBA	30	11	10	9	44	45	32
8 Nottm Forest	30	11	9	10	47	49	31
9 Liverpool	30	11	6	13	48	45	28
10 Derby	30	11	6	13	57	61	28
11 Bolton	30	11	4	15	28	41	26
12 Preston NE	30	8	8	14	35	43	24
13 Notts County	30	8	8	14	36	46	24
14 Bury	30	8	8	14	39	51	24
15 Blackburn	30	7	10	13	39	54	24
16 Stoke	30	8	8	14	35	55	24

Second Division

	P	W	D	L	F	A	Pts
1 Burnley	30	20	8	2	80	24	48
2 Newcastle	30	21	3	6	64	32	45
3 Man City	30	15	9	6	66	36	39
4 Newton Heath	30	16	6	8	64	35	38
5 Woolwich A	30	16	5	9	69	49	37
6 Small Heath	30	16	4	10	58	50	36
7 Leicester Fosse	30	13	7	10	46	35	33
8 Luton	30	13	4	13	68	50	30
9 Gainsborough	30	12	6	12	50	54	30
10 Walsall	30	12	5	13	58	58	29
11 Blackpool	30	10	5	15	49	61	25
12 Grimsby	30	10	4	16	52	62	24
13 Burton Swifts	30	8	5	17	38	69	21
14 Lincoln	30	6	5	19	43	82	17
15 Darwen	30	6	2	22	31	76	14
16 Loughborough	30	6	2	22	24	87	14

Scottish First Division

	P	W	D	L	F	A	Pts
1 Celtic	18	15	3	0	56	13	33
2 Rangers	18	13	3	2	71	15	29
3 Hibernian	18	10	2	6	47	29	22
4 Hearts	18	8	4	6	54	33	20
5 Third Lanark	18	9	1	8	39	41	19
6 St Mirren	18	8	2	8	30	37	18
7 Dundee*	18	5	3	10	29	36	13
8 Partick*	18	6	1	11	34	62	13
9 St Bernard's	18	4	1	13	35	67	9
10 Clyde	18	1	3	14	21	83	5

*Partick Thistle and Dundee played a test match to decide the bottom three and Dundee won 2-0.

Scottish Second Division

	P	W	D	L	F	A	Pts
1 Kilmarnock	18	14	1	3	64	29	29
2 Port Glasgow	18	12	1	5	66	36	25
3 Morton	18	9	4	5	47	38	22
4 Leith	18	9	2	7	45	41	20
5 Linthouse	18	6	4	8	38	39	16
6 Abercorn	18	6	4	8	33	41	16
7 Ayr	18	7	2	9	36	45	16
8 Airdrieonians	18	6	2	10	44	56	14
9 Hamilton	18	5	2	11	28	51	12
10 Motherwell	18	3	4	11	31	56	10

FA Cup

Third Round

Southampton St Mary's v Bolton Wanderers	0-0, 4-0
West Bromwich Albion v Nottingham Forest	2-3
Liverpool v Derby County	1-1, 1-5
Burnley v Everton	1-3

Semi-Final

Southampton St Mary's v Nottingham Forest	1-1, 0-2
Derby county v Everton	3-1

Final at Crystal Palace

Nottingham Forest v Derby County   3-1

Scottish FA Cup

Third Round

Queen's Park v Rangers   1-3

Third Lanark v Hibernian	2-0
Ayr Parkhouse v Kilmarnock	2-7
Dundee v Heart of Midlothian	3-0

Semi-Final

Rangers v Third Lanark	1-1, 2-2, 2-0
Kilmarnock v Dundee	3-2

Final at Hampden Park

Rangers v Kilmarnock   2-0

1898-99
First Division

	P	W	D	L	F	A	Pts
1 Aston Villa	34	19	7	8	76	40	45
2 Liverpool	34	19	5	10	49	33	43
3 Burnley	34	15	9	10	45	47	39
4 Everton	34	15	8	11	48	41	38
5 Notts County	34	12	13	9	47	51	37
6 Blackburn	34	14	8	12	60	52	36
7 Sunderland	34	15	6	13	41	41	36
8 Wolves	34	14	7	13	54	48	35
9 Derby	34	12	11	11	62	57	35
10 Bury	34	14	7	13	48	49	35
11 Nottm Forest	34	11	11	12	42	42	33
12 Stoke	34	13	7	14	47	52	33
13 Newcastle	34	11	8	15	49	48	30
14 WBA	34	12	6	16	42	57	30
15 Preston	34	10	9	15	44	47	29
16 Sheff United	34	9	11	14	45	51	29
17 Bolton	34	9	7	18	37	51	25
18 Wednesday	34	8	8	18	32	61	24

Second Division

	P	W	D	L	F	A	Pts
1 Man City	34	23	5	6	92	35	52
2 Glossop NE	34	20	6	8	76	38	46
3 Leicester Fosse	34	18	9	7	64	42	45
4 Newton Heath	34	19	5	10	67	43	43
5 New Brighton	34	18	7	9	71	52	43
6 Walsall	34	15	12	7	79	36	42
7 Woolwich A	34	18	5	11	72	41	41
8 Small Heath	34	17	7	10	85	50	41
9 Burslem PV	34	17	5	12	56	34	39
10 Grimsby	34	15	5	14	71	60	35
11 Barnsley	34	12	7	15	52	56	31
12 Lincoln	34	12	7	15	51	56	31
13 Burton Swifts	34	10	8	16	51	70	28
14 Gainsborough	34	10	5	19	56	72	25

15 Luton	34	10	3	21	51	95	23
16 Blackpool	34	8	4	22	49	90	20
17 Loughborough	34	6	6	22	38	92	18
18 Darwen	34	2	5	27	22	141	9

Scottish First Division

	P	W	D	L	F	A	Pts
1 Rangers	18	18	0	0	79	18	36
2 Hearts	18	12	2	4	56	30	26
3 Celtic	18	11	2	5	51	33	24
4 Hibernian	18	10	3	5	42	43	23
5 St Mirren	18	8	4	6	46	32	20
6 Third Lanark	18	7	3	8	33	38	17
7 St Bernard's	18	4	4	10	30	37	12
8 Clyde	18	4	4	10	23	48	12
9 Partick	18	2	2	14	19	58	6
10 Dundee	18	1	2	15	23	65	4

Scottish Second Division

	P	W	D	L	F	A	Pts
1 Kilmarnock	18	14	4	0	73	25	32
2 Leith	18	12	3	3	63	38	27
3 Port Glasgow	18	12	1	5	75	51	25
4 Motherwell	18	7	6	5	40	30	20
5 Hamilton	18	7	1	10	48	58	15
6 Airdrieonians	18	6	3	9	36	46	15
7 Morton	18	6	1	11	36	42	13
8 Ayr	18	5	3	10	35	51	13
9 Linthouse	18	5	1	12	20	62	11
10 Abercorn	18	4	1	13	42	65	9

FA Cup

Third Round

Nottingham Forest v Sheffield United	0-1
West Bromwich Albion v Liverpool	0-2
Southampton v Derby County	1-2
Stoke v Tottenham Hotspur	4-1

Semi-Final

Sheffield United v Liverpool 2-2, 4-4,	1-0
Derby County v Stoke	3-1

Final at Crystal Palace

Sheffield United v Derby County	4-1

Scottish FA Cup

Third Round

Celtic v Queen's Park	4-2*, 2-1
Port Glasgow Athletic v Partick Thistle	7-3

Kilmarnock v St Mirren	1-2
Rangers v Clyde	4-0
*abandoned	

Semi-Final

Celtic v Port Glasgow Athletic	4-2
St Mirren v Rangers	1-2

Final at Hampden Park

Celtic v Rangers	2-0

1899–1900
First Division

	P	W	D	L	F	A	Pts
1 Aston Villa	34	22	6	6	77	35	50
2 Sheff United	34	18	12	4	63	33	48
3 Sunderland	34	19	3	12	50	35	41
4 Wolves	34	15	9	10	48	37	39
5 Newcastle	34	13	10	11	53	43	36
6 Derby	34	14	8	12	45	43	36
7 Man City	34	13	8	13	50	44	34
8 Nottm Forest	34	13	8	13	56	55	34
9 Stoke	34	10	10	14	37	45	34
10 Liverpool	34	14	5	15	49	45	33
11 Everton	34	13	7	14	47	49	33
12 Bury	34	13	6	15	40	44	32
13 WBA	34	11	8	15	43	51	30
14 Blackburn	34	13	4	17	49	61	30
15 Notts County	34	9	11	14	46	60	29
16 Preston	34	12	4	18	38	48	28
17 Burnley	34	11	5	18	34	54	27
18 Glossop NE	34	4	10	20	31	74	18

Second Division

	P	W	D	L	F	A	Pts
1 Wednesday	34	25	4	5	84	22	54
2 Bolton	34	22	8	4	79	25	52
3 Small Heath	34	20	6	8	78	38	46
4 Newton Heath	34	20	4	10	63	27	44
5 Leicester Fosse	34	17	9	8	53	36	43
6 Grimsby	34	17	6	11	67	46	40
7 Chesterfield	34	16	6	12	65	60	38
8 Woolwich A	34	16	4	14	61	43	36
9 Lincoln	34	14	8	12	46	43	36
10 New Brighton	34	13	9	12	66	58	35
11 Burslem PV	34	14	6	14	39	49	34
12 Walsall	34	12	8	14	50	55	32
13 Gainsborough	34	9	7	18	47	75	25
14 Middlesbrough	34	8	8	18	39	69	24

	P	W	D	L	F	A	Pts
15 Burton Swifts	34	9	6	19	43	84	24
16 Barnsley	34	8	7	19	46	79	23
17 Luton	34	5	8	21	40	75	18
18 Loughborough	34	1	6	27	18	100	8

Scottish First Division

	P	W	D	L	F	A	Pts
1 Rangers	18	15	2	1	68	27	32
2 Celtic	18	9	7	2	46	27	25
3 Hibernian	18	9	6	3	43	24	24
4 Hearts	18	10	3	5	41	24	23
5 Kilmarnock	18	6	6	6	30	37	18
6 Dundee	18	4	7	7	36	40	15
7 Third Lanark	18	5	5	8	31	37	15
8 St Mirren	18	3	6	9	30	46	12
9 St Bernard's	18	4	4	10	29	47	12
10 Clyde	18	2	0	16	25	70	4

Scottish Second Division

	P	W	D	L	F	A	Pts
1 Partick	18	14	1	3	56	26	29
2 Morton*	17	13	0	4	63	25	26
3 Port Glasgow	18	10	0	8	50	41	20
4 Motherwell*	17	9	1	7	38	33	19
5 Leith	18	9	1	8	33	37	19
6 Abercorn	18	7	2	9	46	39	16
7 Hamilton	18	7	1	10	33	47	15
8 Ayr	18	6	2	10	39	48	14
9 Airdrieonians	18	4	3	11	27	49	11
10 Linthouse	18	2	5	11	28	68	9

*Played each other once.

FA Cup

Third Round

Preston North End v Nottingham Forest	0-0, 0-1
Sheffield United v Bury	2-2, 0-2
Southampton v West Bromwich Albion	2-1
Milwall Athletic v Aston Villa	1-1, 0-0, 2-1

Semi-Final

Nottingham Forest v Bury	1-1, 2-3
Southampton v Millwall Athletic	0-0, 3-0

Final at Crystal Palace

Bury v Southampton	4-0

Scottish FA Cup

Third Round

Rangers v Partick Thistle	6-1
Celtic v Kilmarnock	4-0
Queen's Park v Dundee	1-0
Third Lanark v Heart of Midlothian	1-2

Semi-Final

Rangers v Celtic	1-1, 0-4
Queen's Park v Heart of Midlothian	2-1

Final at Ibrox Park

Celtic v Queen's Park	4-3

1900–01
First Division

	P	W	D	L	F	A	Pts
1 Liverpool	34	19	7	8	59	35	45
2 Sunderland	34	15	13	6	57	26	43
3 Notts County	34	18	4	12	54	46	40
4 Nottm Forest	34	16	7	11	53	36	39
5 Bury	34	16	7	11	53	37	39
6 Newcastle	34	14	10	10	42	37	38
7 Everton	34	16	5	13	55	42	37
8 Wednesday	34	13	10	11	52	42	36
9 Blackburn	34	12	9	13	39	47	33
10 Bolton	34	13	7	14	39	55	33
11 Man City	34	13	6	15	48	58	32
12 Derby	34	12	7	15	55	42	31
13 Wolves	34	9	13	12	39	55	31
14 Sheff United	34	12	7	15	35	52	31
15 Aston Villa	34	10	10	14	45	51	30
16 Stoke	34	11	5	18	46	57	27
17 Preston	34	9	7	18	49	75	25
18 WBA	34	7	8	19	35	62	22

Second Division

	P	W	D	L	F	A	Pts
1 Grimsby	34	20	9	5	60	33	49
2 Small Heath	34	19	10	5	57	24	48
3 Burnley	34	20	4	10	53	29	44
4 New Brighton	34	17	8	9	57	38	42
5 Glossop NE	34	15	8	11	51	33	38
6 Middlesbrough	34	15	7	12	50	40	37
7 Woolwich A	34	15	6	13	39	35	36
8 Lincoln	34	13	7	14	43	39	33
9 Burslem PV	34	11	11	12	45	47	33
10 Newton Heath	34	14	4	16	42	38	32
11 Leicester Fosse	34	11	10	13	39	37	32
12 Blackpool	34	12	7	15	33	58	31
13 Gainsborough	34	10	10	14	45	60	30
14 Chesterfield	34	9	10	15	46	58	28
15 Barnsley	34	11	5	18	47	60	27

		P	W	D	L	F	A	
16	Walsall	34	7	13	14	40	56	27
17	Stockport	34	11	3	20	38	68	25
18	Burton Swifts	34	8	4	22	34	66	20

Scottish First Division

		P	W	D	L	F	A	Pts
1	Rangers	20	17	1	2	60	25	35
2	Celtic	20	13	3	4	49	28	29
3	Hibernian	20	9	7	4	29	22	25
4	Morton	20	9	3	8	40	40	21
5	Kilmarnock	20	7	4	9	35	47	18
6	Third Lanark	20	6	6	8	20	29	18
7	Dundee	20	6	5	9	36	35	17
8	Queen's Park	20	7	3	10	33	37	17
9	St Mirren	20	5	6	9	33	43	16
10	Hearts	20	5	4	11	22	30	14
11	Partick	20	4	2	14	28	49	10

Scottish Second Division

		P	W	D	L	F	A	Pts
1	St Bernard's	18	11	4	3	43	26	26
2	Airdrieonians	18	11	1	6	43	32	23
3	Abercorn	18	9	3	6	37	33	21
4	Port Glasgow*	17	9	0	8	42	41	18
5	Clyde*	16	8	1	7	38	31	17
6	Ayr*	14	8	0	6	27	26	16
7	Leith*	17	5	2	10	21	29	12
8	E Stirlingshire*	14	5	2	7	19	29	12
9	Motherwell	18	4	3	11	26	42	11
10	Hamilton*	16	3	4	9	36	43	10

*No record available of these clubs having completed their fixtures

FA Cup

Third Round

Reading v Tottenham Hotspur	1-1, 0-3
Middlesbrough v West Bromwich Albion	0-1
Wolverhampton Wanderers v Sheffield United	0-4
Small Heath v Aston Villa	0-0, 0-1

Semi-Final

Tottenham Hotspur v West Bromwich Albion	4-0
Sheffield United v Aston Villa	2-2, 3-0

Final at Crystal Palace

Tottenham Hotspur v Sheffield United	2-2, 3-1*

*replay at Bolton

Scottish FA Cup

Third Round

Dundee v Celtic	0-1
St Mirren v Third Lanark	0-0, 1-1, 3-3, 1-0
Port Glasgow Athletic v Heart of Midlothian	1-5
Hibernian v Morton	2-0

Semi-Final

Heart of Midlothian v Hibernian	1-1, 2-1
St Mirren v Celtic	0-1

Final at Ibrox Park

Heart of Midlothian v Celtic	4-3

1901–02
First Division

		P	W	D	L	F	A	Pts
1	Sunderland	34	19	6	9	50	35	44
2	Everton	34	17	7	10	53	35	41
3	Newcastle	34	14	9	11	48	34	37
4	Blackburn	34	15	6	13	52	48	36
5	Nottm Forest	34	13	9	12	43	43	35
6	Derby	34	13	9	12	39	41	35
7	Bury	34	13	8	13	44	38	34
8	Aston Villa	34	13	8	13	42	40	34
9	Wednesday	34	13	8	13	48	52	34
10	Sheff United	34	13	7	14	53	48	33
11	Liverpool	34	10	12	12	42	38	32
12	Bolton	34	12	8	14	51	56	32
13	Notts County	34	14	4	16	51	57	32
14	Wolves	34	13	6	15	46	57	32
15	Grimsby	34	13	6	15	44	60	32
16	Stoke	34	11	9	14	45	55	31
17	Small Heath	34	11	8	15	47	45	30
18	Man City	34	11	6	17	42	58	28

Second Division

		P	W	D	L	F	A	Pts
1	WBA	34	25	5	4	82	29	55
2	Middlesbrough	34	23	5	6	90	24	51
3	Preston NE	34	18	6	10	71	32	42
4	Woolwich A	34	18	6	10	50	26	42
5	Lincoln	34	14	13	7	45	35	41
6	Bristol City	34	17	6	11	52	35	40
7	Doncaster	34	13	8	13	49	58	34
8	Glossop NE	34	10	12	12	36	40	32
9	Burnley	34	10	10	14	41	45	30

10 Burton United	34	11	8	15	46	54	30
11 Barnsley	34	12	6	16	51	63	30
12 Burslem PV	34	10	9	15	43	59	29
13 Blackpool	34	11	7	16	40	56	29
14 Leicester Fosse	34	12	5	17	38	56	29
15 Newton Heath	34	11	6	17	38	53	28
16 Chesterfield	34	11	6	17	47	68	28
17 Stockport	34	8	7	19	36	72	23
18 Gainsborough	34	4	11	19	30	80	19

Scottish First Division

	P	W	D	L	F	A	Pts
1 Rangers	18	13	2	3	43	29	28
2 Celtic	18	11	4	3	38	28	26
3 Hearts	18	10	2	6	32	21	22
4 Third Lanark	18	7	5	6	30	26	19
5 St Mirren	18	8	3	7	29	28	19
6 Hibernian	18	6	4	8	36	23	16
7 Kilmarnock	18	5	6	7	21	25	16
8 Queen's Park	18	5	4	9	21	32	14
9 Dundee	18	4	5	9	15	31	13
10 Morton	18	1	5	12	18	40	7

Scottish Second Division

	P	W	D	L	F	A	Pts
1 Port Glasgow	22	14	4	4	70	31	32
2 Partick	22	14	3	5	56	26	31
3 Motherwell	22	12	2	8	50	44	26
4 Airdrieonians	22	10	5	7	41	32	25
5 Hamilton	22	11	3	8	46	40	25
6 St Bernard's	22	10	2	10	30	31	22
7 Leith	22	9	3	10	33	39	21
8 Ayr	22	8	5	9	27	33	21
9 E Stirlingshire	22	8	3	11	36	45	19
10 Arthurlie	22	6	5	11	32	42	17
11 Abercorn	22	4	5	13	27	57	13
12 Clyde	22	5	3	14	22	50	13

FA Cup

Third Round

Bury v Southampton	2-3
Nottingham Forest v Stoke	2-0
Newcastle United v Sheffield United	1-1, 1-2
Derby County v Portsmouth	0-0, 6-3

Semi-Final

Southampton v Nottingham Forest	3-1
Sheffield United v Derby County	1-1, 1-1, 1-0

Final at Crystal Palace

Sheffield United v Southampton 1-1, 2-1†
†replay at Crystal Palace

Scottish FA Cup

Third Round

Falkirk v St Mirren	0-1
Heart of Midlothian v Celtic	1-1, 1-2
Hibernian v Queen's Park	7-1
Rangers v Kilmarnock	2-0

Semi-Final

Rangers v Hibernian	0-2
St Mirren v Celtic	2-3

Final at Celtic Park

Hibernian v Celtic	1-0

1902–03
First Division

	P	W	D	L	F	A	Pts
1 Wednesday	34	19	4	11	54	36	42
2 Aston Villa	34	19	3	12	61	40	41
3 Sunderland	34	16	9	9	51	36	41
4 Sheff United	34	17	5	12	58	44	39
5 Liverpool	34	17	4	13	68	49	38
6 Stoke	34	15	7	12	46	38	37
7 WBA	34	16	4	14	54	53	36
8 Bury	34	16	3	15	54	43	35
9 Derby	34	16	3	15	50	47	35
10 Nottm Forest	34	14	7	13	49	47	35
11 Wolves	34	14	5	15	48	57	33
12 Everton	34	13	6	15	45	47	32
13 Middlesbrough	34	14	4	16	41	50	32
14 Newcastle	34	14	4	16	41	51	32
15 Notts County	34	12	7	15	41	49	31
16 Blackburn	34	12	5	17	44	63	29
17 Grimsby	34	8	9	17	43	62	25
18 Bolton	34	8	3	23	37	73	19

Second Division

	P	W	D	L	F	A	Pts
1 Man City	34	25	4	5	95	29	54
2 Small Heath	34	24	3	7	74	36	51
3 Woolwich A	34	20	8	6	66	30	48
4 Bristol City	34	17	8	9	59	38	42
5 Man United	34	15	8	11	53	38	38
6 Chesterfield	34	14	9	11	67	40	37

	P	W	D	L	F	A	Pts
7 Preston	34	13	10	11	56	40	36
8 Barnsley	34	13	8	13	55	51	34
9 Burslem PV	34	13	8	13	57	62	34
10 Lincoln	34	12	6	16	46	53	30
11 Glossop NE	34	11	7	16	43	58	29
12 Gainsborough	34	11	7	16	41	59	29
13 Burton United	34	11	7	16	39	59	29
14 Blackpool	34	9	10	15	44	59	28
15 Leicester Fosse	34	10	8	16	41	65	28
16 Doncaster	34	9	7	18	35	72	25
17 Stockport	34	7	6	21	39	74	20
18 Burnley	34	6	8	20	30	77	20

Scottish First Division

	P	W	D	L	F	A	Pts
1 Hibernian	22	16	5	1	49	19	37
2 Dundee	22	13	5	4	31	12	31
3 Rangers	22	12	5	5	56	30	29
4 Hearts	22	11	6	5	46	28	28
5 Celtic	22	8	10	4	36	30	26
6 St Mirren	22	7	8	7	39	39	22
7 Third Lanark	22	8	5	9	34	27	21
8 Partick	22	6	7	9	34	50	19
9 Kilmarnock	22	6	4	12	24	43	16
10 Queen's Park	22	5	5	12	33	48	15
11 Port Glasgow	22	3	5	14	26	49	11
12 Morton	22	2	5	15	22	55	9

Scottish Second Division

	P	W	D	L	F	A	Pts
1 Airdrieonians	22	15	5	2	43	19	35
2 Motherwell	22	12	4	6	44	35	28
3 Ayr	22	12	3	7	34	24	27
4 Leith	22	11	5	6	43	42	27
5 St Bernard's	22	12	2	8	45	32	26
6 Hamilton	22	11	1	10	45	35	23
7 Falkirk	22	8	7	7	39	37	23
8 E Stirlingshire	22	9	3	10	46	41	21
9 Arthurlie	22	6	8	8	34	46	20
10 Abercorn	22	5	2	15	35	58	12
11 Raith	22	3	5	14	34	55	11
12 Clyde	22	2	7	13	22	40	11

FA Cup

Third Round

Tottenham Hotspur v Aston Villa	2-3
Bury v Notts County	1-0
Derby County v Stoke	3-0
Milwall Athletic v Everton	1-0

Semi-Final

Aston Villa v Bury	0-3
Derby County v Millwall Athletic	3-0

Final at Crystal Palace

Bury v Derby County	6-0

Scottish FA Cup

Third Round

Celtic v Rangers		0-3
Dundee v Hibernian	0-0, 0-0,	1-0
Heart of Midlothian v Third Lanark		2-1
Stenhousemuir v Partick Thistle		3-0

Semi-Final

Stenhousemuir v Rangers		1-4
Dundee v Heart of Midlothian	0-0,	0-1

Final at Celtic Park

Rangers v Heart of Midlothian
1-1, 0-0, 2-0

1903–04
First Division

	P	W	D	L	F	A	Pts
1 Wednesday	34	20	7	7	48	28	47
2 Man City	34	19	6	9	71	45	44
3 Everton	34	19	5	10	59	32	43
4 Newcastle	34	18	6	10	58	45	42
5 Aston Villa	34	17	7	10	70	48	41
6 Sunderland	34	17	5	12	63	49	39
7 Sheff United	34	15	8	11	62	57	38
8 Wolves	34	14	8	12	44	66	36
9 Nottm Forest	34	11	9	14	57	57	31
10 Middlesbrough	34	9	12	13	46	47	30
11 Small Heath	34	11	8	15	39	52	30
12 Bury	34	7	15	12	40	53	29
13 Notts County	34	12	5	17	37	61	29
14 Derby	34	9	10	15	58	60	28
15 Blackburn	34	11	6	17	48	60	28
16 Stoke	34	10	7	17	54	57	27
17 Liverpool	34	9	8	17	49	62	26
18 WBA	34	7	10	17	36	60	24

Second Division

	P	W	D	L	F	A	Pts
1 Preston	34	20	10	4	62	24	50
2 Woolwich A	34	21	7	6	91	22	49

3 Man United	34 20	8	6 65 33 48
4 Bristol City	34 18	6 10 73 41 42	
5 Burnley	34 15	9 10 50 55 39	
6 Grimsby	34 14	8 12 50 49 36	
7 Bolton	34 12 10 12 59 41 34		
8 Barnsley	34 11 10 13 38 57 32		
9 Gainsborough	34 14	3 17 53 60 31	
10 Bradford City	34 12	7 15 45 59 31	
11 Chesterfield	34 11	8 15 37 45 30	
12 Lincoln	34 11	8 15 41 58 30	
13 Burslem PV	34 10	9 15 54 52 29	
14 Burton United	34 11	7 16 45 61 29	
15 Blackpool	34 11	5 18 40 67 27	
16 Stockport	34	8 11 15 40 72 27	
17 Glossop NE	34 10	6 18 57 64 26	
18 Leicester Fosse	34	6 10 18 42 82 22	

Scottish First Division

	P W D L F A Pts
1 Third Lanark	26 20 3 3 61 26 43
2 Hearts	26 18 3 5 63 35 39
3 Celtic	26 18 2 6 69 28 38
4 Rangers	26 16 6 4 80 33 38
5 Dundee	26 13 2 11 54 45 28
6 St Mirren	26 11 5 10 45 38 27
7 Partick	26 10 7 9 43 40 27
8 Queen's Park	26 6 9 11 28 47 21
9 Port Glasgow	26 8 4 14 33 49 20
10 Hibernian	26 7 5 14 31 42 19
11 Morton	26 7 4 15 31 51 18
12 Airdrieonians	26 7 4 15 32 62 18
13 Motherwell	26 6 3 17 26 61 15
14 Kilmarnock	26 4 5 17 26 65 13

Scottish Second Division

	P W D L F A Pts
1 Hamilton	22 16 5 1 56 19 37
2 Clyde	22 12 5 5 51 36 29
3 Ayr	22 11 5 6 33 29 28
4 Falkirk	22 11 4 7 50 36 26
5 Raith	22 8 5 9 40 38 21
6 E Stirlingshire	22 8 5 9 33 40 21
7 Leith	22 8 4 10 42 40 20
8 St Bernard's	22 9 2 11 31 43 20
9 Albion*	22 8 5 9 41 37 19
10 Abercorn	22 6 4 12 40 54 16
11 Arthurlie	22 5 5 12 37 50 15
12 Ayr Parkhouse	22 3 4 15 22 54 10

*Two points deducted for fielding an unregistered player

FA Cup

Third Round

Manchester City v Middlesbrough	
	0-0, 3-1
Tottenham Hotspur v The Wednesday	
	1-1, 0-2
Sheffield United v Bolton Wanderers	0-2
Derby County v Blackburn Rovers	2-1

Semi-Final

Manchester City v The Wednesday	3-0
Bolton Wanderers v Derby County	1-0

Final at Crystal Palace

Manchester City v Bolton Wanderers	1-0

Scottish FA Cup

Third Round

Celtic v Dundee	1-1, 0-0, 5-0
Third Lanark v Kilmarnock	3-0
St Mirren v Rangers	0-1
Leith Athletic v Morton	1-3

Semi-Final

Celtic v Third Lanark	2-1
Rangers v Morton	3-0

Final at Hampden Park

Celtic v Rangers	3-2

1904–05
First Division

	P W D L F A Pts
1 Newcastle	34 23 2 9 72 33 48
2 Everton	34 21 5 8 63 36 47
3 Man 'City	34 20 6 8 66 37 46
4 Aston Villa	34 19 4 11 63 43 42
5 Sunderland	34 16 8 10 60 44 40
6 Sheff United	34 19 2 13 64 56 40
7 Small Heath	34 17 5 12 54 38 39
8 Preston	34 13 10 11 42 37 36
9 Wednesday	34 14 5 15 61 57 33
10 Woolwich A	34 12 9 13 36 40 33
11 Derby	34 12 8 14 37 48 32
12 Stoke	34 13 4 17 40 58 30
13 Blackburn	34 11 5 18 40 51 27
14 Wolves	34 11 4 19 47 73 26
15 Middlesbrough	34 9 8 17 36 56 26

	P	W	D	L	F	A	Pts
16 Nottm Forest	34	9	7	18	40	61	25
17 Bury	34	10	4	20	47	67	24
18 Notts County	34	5	8	21	36	69	18

Second Division

	P	W	D	L	F	A	Pts
1 Liverpool	34	27	4	3	93	25	58
2 Bolton	34	27	2	5	87	32	56
3 Man United	34	24	5	5	81	30	53
4 Bristol City	34	19	4	11	66	45	42
5 Chesterfield	34	14	11	9	44	35	39
6 Gainsborough	34	14	8	12	61	58	36
7 Barnsley	34	14	5	15	38	56	33
8 Bradford City	34	12	8	14	45	49	32
9 Lincoln	34	12	7	15	42	40	31
10 WBA	34	13	4	17	56	48	30
11 Burnley	34	12	6	16	43	52	30
12 Glossop NE	34	10	10	14	37	46	30
13 Grimsby	34	11	8	15	33	46	30
14 Leicester Fosse	34	11	7	16	40	55	29
15 Blackpool	34	9	10	15	36	48	28
16 Burslem PV	34	10	7	17	47	72	27
17 Burton United	34	8	4	22	30	84	20
18 Doncaster	34	3	2	29	23	81	8

Scottish First Division

	P	W	D	L	F	A	Pts
1 Celtic*	26	19	3	4	83	28	41
2 Rangers	26	18	5	3	68	31	41
3 Third Lanark	26	14	7	5	60	28	35
4 Airdrieonians	26	11	5	10	38	45	27
5 Hibernian	26	9	8	9	39	39	26
6 Partick	26	12	2	12	36	56	26
7 Dundee	26	10	5	11	38	32	25
8 Hearts	26	11	3	12	46	44	25
9 Kilmarnock	26	9	5	12	29	45	23
10 St Mirren	26	9	4	13	33	36	22
11 Port Glasgow	26	8	5	13	30	51	21
12 Queen's Park	26	6	8	12	28	45	20
13 Morton	26	7	4	15	27	50	18
14 Motherwell	26	6	2	18	28	53	14

*Celtic won a deciding match against Rangers

Scottish Second Division

	P	W	D	L	F	A	Pts
1 Clyde	22	13	6	3	38	22	32
2 Falkirk	22	12	4	6	31	25	28
3 Hamilton	22	12	3	7	40	22	27
4 Leith	22	10	4	8	36	26	24
5 Ayr	22	11	1	10	46	37	23
6 Arthurlie	22	9	5	8	37	42	23
7 Aberdeen	22	7	7	8	36	26	21
8 Albion	22	8	4	10	38	53	20
9 E Stirlingshire	22	7	5	10	38	38	19
10 Raith	22	9	1	12	30	34	19
11 Abercorn	22	8	1	13	31	45	17
12 St Bernard's	22	3	5	14	23	54	11

FA Cup

Third Round

Bolton Wanderers v Newcastle United	0–2
Preston North End v The Wednesday	1–1, 0–3
Everton v Southampton	4–0
Aston Villa v Fulham	5–0

Semi-Final

Newcastle United v The Wednesday	1–0
Everton v Aston Villa	1–1, 1–2

Final at Crystal Palace

Aston Villa v Newcastle United	2–0

Scottish FA Cup

Third Round

St Mirren v Airdrieonians	0–0, 1–3
Rangers v Beith	5–1
Celtic v Partick Thistle	3–0
Third Lanark v Aberdeen	4–1

Semi-Final

Celtic v Rangers	0–2
Airdrieonians v Third Lanark	1–2

Final at Hampden Park

Third Lanark v Rangers	0–0, 3–1

1905–06
First Division

	P	W	D	L	F	A	Pts
1 Liverpool	38	23	5	10	79	46	51
2 Preston NE	38	17	13	8	54	39	47
3 Wednesday	38	18	8	12	63	52	44
4 Newcastle	38	18	7	13	74	48	43
5 Man City	38	19	5	14	73	54	43
6 Bolton	38	17	7	14	81	67	41

	P	W	D	L	F	A	Pts
7 Birmingham	38	17	7	14	65	59	41
8 Aston Villa	28	17	6	15	72	56	40
9 Blackburn	38	16	8	14	54	52	40
10 Stoke	38	16	7	15	54	55	39
11 Everton	38	15	7	16	70	66	37
12 Woolwich A	38	15	7	16	62	64	37
13 Sheff United	38	15	6	17	57	62	36
14 Sunderland	38	15	5	18	61	70	35
15 Derby	38	14	7	17	39	58	35
16 Notts County	38	11	12	15	55	71	34
17 Bury	38	11	10	17	57	74	32
18 Middlesbrough	38	10	11	17	56	71	31
19 Nottm Forest	38	13	5	20	58	79	31
20 Wolves	38	8	7	23	58	99	23

Second Division

	P	W	D	L	F	A	Pts
1 Bristol City	38	30	6	2	83	28	66
2 Man United	38	28	6	4	90	28	62
3 Chelsea	38	22	9	7	90	37	53
4 WBA	38	22	8	8	79	36	52
5 Hull	38	19	6	13	67	54	44
6 Leeds City	38	17	9	12	59	47	43
7 Leicester Fosse	38	15	12	11	53	48	42
8 Grimsby	38	15	10	13	46	46	40
9 Burnley	38	15	8	15	42	53	38
10 Stockport	38	13	9	16	44	56	35
11 Bradford City	38	13	8	17	46	60	34
12 Barnsley	38	12	9	17	60	62	33
13 Lincoln	38	12	6	20	69	72	30
14 Blackpool	38	10	9	19	37	62	29
15 Gainsborough	38	12	4	22	44	57	28
16 Glossop NE	38	10	8	20	49	71	28
17 Burslem PV	38	12	4	22	49	82	28
18 Chesterfield	38	10	8	20	40	72	28
19 Burton United	38	10	6	22	34	67	26
20 Clapton Orient	38	7	7	24	35	78	21

Scottish First Division

	P	W	D	L	F	A	Pts
1 Celtic	30	24	1	5	76	19	49
2 Hearts	30	18	7	5	64	27	43
3 Airdrieonians	30	15	8	7	53	31	38
4 Rangers	30	15	7	8	58	48	37
5 Partick	30	15	6	9	44	40	36
6 Third Lanark	30	16	2	12	62	37	34
7 Dundee	30	11	12	7	40	34	34
8 St Mirren	30	13	5	12	41	37	31
9 Motherwell	30	9	8	13	50	64	26
10 Morton	30	10	6	14	35	54	26
11 Hibernian	30	10	5	15	34	40	25

	P	W	D	L	F	A	Pts
12 Aberdeen	30	8	8	14	37	49	24
13 Falkirk	30	9	5	16	54	69	23
14 Kilmarnock	30	8	4	18	46	68	20
15 Port Glasgow	30	6	8	16	38	68	20
16 Queen's Park	30	5	4	21	41	88	14

Scottish Second Division

	P	W	D	L	F	A	Pts
1 Leith	22	15	4	3	46	22	34
2 Clyde	22	11	9	2	38	21	31
3 Albion	22	12	3	7	48	33	27
4 Hamilton	22	12	2	8	45	33	26
5 St Bernard's	22	9	4	9	42	34	22
6 Arthurlie	22	10	2	10	45	45	22
7 Ayr	22	9	3	10	44	51	21
8 Raith	22	6	7	9	38	42	19
9 Cowdenbeath	22	7	3	12	27	39	17
10 Abercorn	22	6	5	11	31	46	17
11 Vale of Leven	22	6	4	12	33	50	16
12 E Stirlingshire	22	1	10	11	26	47	12

FA Cup

Third Round

Woolwich Arsenal v Sunderland	5-0
Manchester United v Aston Villa	5-1
Newcastle United v Blackpool	5-0
Tottenham Hotspur v Birmingham	1-1, 0-2
Everton v Bradford City	1-0
The Wednesday v Nottingham Forest	4-1
Liverpool v Brentford	2-0
Southampton v Middlesbrough	6-1

Fourth Round

Manchester United v Woolwich Arsenal	2-3
Birmingham v Newcastle United	2-2, 0-3
Everton v The Wednesday	4-3
Liverpool v Southampton	3-0

Semi-Final

Woolwich Arsenal v Newcastle United	0-2
Everton v Liverpool	2-0

Final at Crystal Palace

Everton v Newcastle United	1-0

Scottish FA Cup

Third Round

Celtic v Heart of Midlothian	1-2

Airdrieonians v St Mirren   0–0, 0–2
Port Glasgow Athletic v Rangers   1–0
Hibernian v Third Lanark   1–2

Semi-Final
St Mirren v Third Lanark   1–1, 0–0, 0–1
Port Glasgow Athletic v Heart of
     Midlothian   0–2

Final at Ibrox Park
Heart of Midlothian v Third Lanark   1–0

1906–07
First Division

	P	W	D	L	F	A	Pts
1 Newcastle	38	22	7	9	74	46	51
2 Bristol City	38	20	8	10	66	47	48
3 Everton	38	20	5	13	70	46	45
4 Sheff United	38	17	11	10	57	55	45
5 Aston Villa	38	19	6	13	78	52	44
6 Bolton	38	18	8	12	59	47	44
7 Woolwich A	38	20	4	14	66	59	44
8 Man United	38	17	8	13	53	56	42
9 Birmingham	38	15	8	15	52	52	38
10 Sunderland	38	14	9	15	65	66	37
11 Middlesbrough	38	15	6	17	56	63	36
12 Blackburn	38	14	7	17	56	59	35
13 Wednesday	38	12	11	15	49	60	35
14 Preston	38	14	7	17	44	57	35
15 Liverpool	38	13	7	18	64	65	33
16 Bury	38	13	6	19	58	68	32
17 Man City	38	10	12	16	53	77	32
18 Notts County	38	8	15	15	46	50	31
19 Derby	38	9	9	20	41	59	27
20 Stoke	38	8	10	20	41	64	26

Second Division

	P	W	D	L	F	A	Pts
1 Nottm Forest	38	28	4	6	74	36	60
2 Chelsea	38	26	5	7	80	34	57
3 Leicester Fosse	38	20	8	10	62	39	48
4 WBA	38	21	5	12	83	45	47
5 Bradford City	38	21	5	12	70	53	47
6 Wolves	38	17	7	14	66	53	41
7 Burnley	38	17	6	15	62	47	40
8 Barnsley	38	15	8	15	73	55	38
9 Hull	38	15	7	16	65	57	37
10 Leeds City	38	13	10	15	55	63	36

11 Grimsby	38	16	3	19	57	62	35
12 Stockport	38	12	11	15	42	52	35
13 Blackpool	38	11	11	16	33	51	33
14 Gainsborough	38	14	5	19	45	72	33
15 Glossop NE	38	13	6	19	53	79	32
16 Burslem PV	38	12	7	19	60	83	31
17 Clapton Orient	38	11	8	19	45	67	30
18 Chesterfield	38	11	7	20	50	66	29
19 Lincoln	38	12	4	22	46	73	28
20 Burton United	38	8	7	23	34	68	23

Scottish First Division

	P	W	D	L	F	A	Pts
1 Celtic	34	23	9	2	80	30	55
2 Dundee	34	18	12	4	53	26	48
3 Rangers	34	19	7	8	69	33	45
4 Airdrieonians	34	18	6	10	60	43	42
5 Falkirk	34	17	7	10	73	58	41
6 Third Lanark	34	15	9	10	57	48	39
7 St Mirren	34	12	13	9	50	44	37
8 Clyde	34	15	6	13	47	52	36
9 Hearts	34	11	13	10	46	43	35
10 Motherwell	34	12	9	13	45	48	33
11 Hibernian	34	11	9	14	40	49	31
12 Aberdeen	34	10	10	14	50	55	30
13 Morton	34	11	6	17	41	50	28
14 Partick Thistle	34	9	8	17	40	61	26
15 Queen's Park	34	9	6	19	51	66	24
16 Hamilton	34	8	5	21	40	64	21
17 Kilmarnock	34	8	5	21	40	72	21
18 Port Glasgow	34	7	7	20	30	67	21

Scottish Second Division

	P	W	D	L	F	A	Pts
1 St Bernard's†	21	13	4	4	39	25	30
2 Vale of Leven	22	13	1	8	54	35	27
3 Arthurlie	22	12	3	7	51	39	27
4 Dumbarton	22	11	3	8	52	35	25
5 Leith	22	10	4	8	40	35	24
6 Albion	22	10	3	9	43	37	23
7 Cowdenbeath†*	21	10	5	6	36	37	23
8 Ayr†	21	7	5	9	33	35	19
9 Raith	22	6	4	12	40	48	16
10 E Stirlingshire	22	6	4	12	36	49	16
11 Abercorn†	21	5	6	10	29	46	16
12 Ayr Parkhouse	22	5	2	15	31	63	12

*Two points deducted for an irregularity
†No record of these clubs having completed their fixtures

FA Cup

Third Round

Notts County v Tottenham Hotspur	4-0
West Bromwich Albion v Derby County	2-0
Crystal Palace v Brentford	1-1, 1-0
Everton v Bolton Wanderers	0-0, 3-0
Woolwich Arsenal v Bristol Rovers	1-0
Barnsley v Bury	1-0
Liverpool v Bradford City	1-0
The Wednesday v Sunderland	0-0, 1-0

Fourth Round

West Bromwich Albion v Notts County	3-1
Crystal Palace v Everton	1-1, 0-4
Barnsley v Woolwich Arsenal	1-2
The Wednesday v Liverpool	1-0

Semi-Final

West Bromwich Albion v Everton	1-2
Woolwich Arsenal v The Wednesday	1-3

Final at Crystal Palace

The Wednesday v Everton	2-1

Scottish FA Cup

Third Round

Rangers v Celtic	0-3
St Mirren v Hibernian	1-1, 0-2
Queen's Park v Renton	4-1
Heart of Midlothian v Raith Rovers	2-2, 1-0

Semi-Final

Celtic v Hibernian	0-0, 0-0, 3-0
Heart of Midlothian v Queen's Park	1-0

Final at Hampden Park

Celtic v Heart of Midlothian	3-0

1907-08
First Division

	P	W	D	L	F	A	Pts
1 Man United	38	23	6	9	81	48	52
2 Aston Villa	38	17	9	12	77	59	43
3 Man City	38	16	11	11	62	54	43
4 Newcastle	38	15	12	11	65	54	42
5 Wednesday	38	19	4	15	73	64	42
6 Middlesbrough	38	17	7	14	54	45	41
7 Bury	38	14	11	13	58	61	39
8 Liverpool	38	16	6	16	68	61	38
9 Nottm Forest	38	13	11	14	59	62	37
10 Bristol City	38	12	12	14	58	61	36
11 Everton	38	15	6	17	58	64	36
12 Preston	38	12	12	14	47	53	36
13 Chelsea	38	14	8	16	53	62	36
14 Blackburn	38	12	12	14	51	63	36
14 Woolwich A	38	12	12	14	51	63	36
16 Sunderland	38	16	3	19	78	75	35
17 Sheff United	38	12	11	15	52	58	35
18 Notts County	38	13	8	17	39	51	34
19 Bolton	38	14	5	19	52	58	33
20 Birmingham	38	9	12	17	40	60	30

Second Division

	P	W	D	L	F	A	Pts
1 Bradford City	38	24	6	8	90	42	54
2 Leicester Fosse	38	21	10	7	72	47	52
3 Oldham	38	22	6	10	76	42	50
4 Fulham	38	22	5	11	82	49	49
5 WBA	38	19	9	10	61	39	47
6 Derby	38	21	4	13	77	45	46
7 Burnley	38	20	6	12	67	59	46
8 Hull	38	21	4	13	73	62	46
9 Wolves	38	15	7	16	50	45	37
10 Stoke	38	16	5	17	57	52	37
11 Gainsborough	38	14	7	17	47	71	35
12 Leeds City	38	12	8	18	53	65	32
13 Stockport	38	12	8	18	48	67	32
14 Clapton Orient	38	11	10	17	40	65	32
15 Blackpool	38	11	9	18	51	58	31
16 Barnsley	38	12	6	20	54	68	30
17 Glossop NE	38	11	8	19	54	74	30
18 Grimsby	38	11	8	19	43	71	30
19 Chesterfield	38	6	11	21	46	92	23
20 Lincoln	38	9	3	26	46	83	21

Scottish First Division

	P	W	D	L	F	A	Pts
1 Celtic	34	24	7	3	86	27	55
2 Falkirk	34	22	7	5	103	41	51
3 Rangers	34	21	8	5	74	40	50
4 Dundee	34	20	8	6	71	28	48
5 Hibernian	34	17	8	9	55	42	42
6 Airdrieonians	34	18	5	11	58	41	41
7 St Mirren	34	13	10	11	50	59	36
8 Aberdeen	34	13	9	12	45	44	35

	P	W	D	L	F	A	Pts
9 Third Lanark	34	13	7	14	44	50	33
10 Motherwell	34	12	7	15	61	53	31
11 Hamilton	34	10	8	16	54	65	28
12 Hearts	34	11	6	17	50	61	28
13 Morton	34	9	9	16	43	66	27
14 Kilmarnock	34	6	13	15	38	61	25
15 Partick	34	8	9	17	43	69	25
16 Queen's Park	34	7	8	19	54	84	22
17 Clyde	34	5	8	21	37	75	18
18 Port Glasgow	34	5	7	22	39	99	17

Scottish Second Division

	P	W	D	L	F	A	Pts
1 Raith	22	14	2	6	37	23	30
2 Dumbarton*	22	12	5	5	49	32	27
3 Ayr	22	11	5	6	39	33	27
4 Abercorn	22	9	5	8	33	30	23
5 E Stirlingshire	22	9	5	8	30	31	23
6 Ayr Parkhouse	22	11	0	11	38	37	22
7 Leith	22	8	5	9	41	40	21
8 St Bernard's	22	8	5	9	31	32	21
9 Albion	22	7	5	10	36	48	19
10 Vale of Leven	22	5	8	9	25	31	18
11 Arthurlie	22	6	5	11	33	46	17
12 Cowdenbeath	22	5	4	13	26	35	14

* Two points deducted for registration irregularity

FA Cup

Third Round

Wolverhampton Wanderers v Swindon Town	2–0
Portsmouth v Stoke	0–1
Bolton Wanderers v Everton	3–3, 1–3
Southampton v Bristol Rovers	2–0
Newcastle United v Liverpool	3–1
Grimsby Town v Crystal Palace	1–0
Manchester City v Fulham	1–1, 1–3
Aston Villa v Manchester United	0–2

Fourth Round

Stoke v Wolverhampton Wanderers	0–1
Everton v Southampton	0–0, 2–3
Newcastle United v Grimsby Town	5–1
Fulham v Manchester United	2–1

Semi-Final

Wolverhampton Wanderers v Southampton	2–0
Newcastle United v Fulham	6–0

Final at Crystal Palace

Wolverhampton Wanderers v Newcastle United	3–1

Scottish FA Cup

Third Round

Aberdeen v Queen's Park	3–1
Raith Rovers v Celtic	0–3
Hibernian v Kilmarnock	0–1
St Mirren v Heart of Midlothian	1–0*, 3–1

*abandoned

Semi-Final

Aberdeen v Celtic	0–1
Kilmarnock v St Mirren	0–0, 0–2

Final at Hampden Park

Celtic v St Mirren	5–1

1908–09
First Division

	P	W	D	L	F	A	Pts
1 Newcastle	38	24	5	9	65	41	53
2 Everton	38	18	10	10	82	57	46
3 Sunderland	38	21	2	15	78	63	44
4 Blackburn	38	14	13	11	61	50	41
5 Wednesday	38	17	6	15	67	61	40
6 Woolwich A	38	14	10	14	52	49	38
7 Aston Villa	38	14	10	14	58	56	38
8 Bristol City	38	13	12	13	45	58	38
9 Middlesbrough	38	14	9	15	59	53	37
10 Preston	38	13	11	14	48	44	37
11 Chelsea	38	14	9	15	56	61	37
12 Sheff United	38	14	9	15	51	59	37
13 Man United	38	15	7	16	58	68	37
14 Nottm Forest	38	14	8	16	66	57	36
15 Notts County	38	14	8	16	51	48	36
16 Liverpool	38	15	6	17	57	65	36
17 Bury	38	14	8	16	63	77	36
18 Bradford City	38	12	10	16	47	47	34
19 Man City	38	15	4	19	67	69	34
20 Leicester Fosse	38	8	9	21	54	102	25

Second Division

	P	W	D	L	F	A	Pts
1 Bolton	38	24	4	10	59	28	52
2 Tottenham	38	20	11	7	67	32	51
3 WBA	38	19	13	6	56	27	51
4 Hull	38	19	6	13	63	39	44

	P	W	D	L	F	A	Pts
5 Derby	38	16	11	11	55	41	43
6 Oldham	38	17	6	15	55	43	40
7 Wolves	38	14	11	13	56	48	39
8 Glossop NE	38	15	8	15	57	53	38
9 Gainsborough	38	15	8	15	49	70	38
10 Fulham	38	13	11	14	58	48	37
11 Birmingham	38	14	9	15	58	61	37
12 Leeds City	38	14	7	17	43	53	35
13 Grimsby	38	14	7	17	41	54	35
14 Burnley	38	13	7	18	51	58	33
15 Clapton Orient	38	12	9	17	37	49	33
16 Bradford PA	38	13	6	19	51	59	32
17 Barnsley	28	11	10	17	48	57	32
18 Stockport	38	14	3	21	39	71	31
19 Chesterfield	38	11	8	19	37	67	30
20 Blackpool	38	9	11	18	46	68	29

Scottish First Division

	P	W	D	L	F	A	Pts
1 Celtic	34	23	5	6	71	24	51
2 Dundee	34	22	6	6	70	33	50
3 Clyde	34	21	6	7	61	37	48
4 Rangers	34	19	7	8	90	37	45
5 Airdrieonians	34	16	9	9	67	46	41
6 Hibernian	34	16	7	11	41	32	39
7 St Mirren	34	15	6	13	53	45	36
8 Aberdeen	34	15	6	13	61	53	36
9 Falkirk	34	13	7	14	58	56	33
10 Kilmarnock	34	13	7	14	47	61	33
11 Third Lanark	34	11	10	13	56	49	32
12 Hearts	34	12	8	14	54	49	32
13 Port Glasgow	34	10	8	16	39	52	28
14 Motherwell	34	11	6	17	47	73	28
15 Queen's Park	34	6	13	15	41	64	25
16 Hamilton	34	6	12	16	42	74	24
17 Morton	34	8	7	19	39	90	23
18 Partick	34	2	4	28	38	102	8

Scottish Second Division

	P	W	D	L	F	A	Pts
1 Abercorn	22	13	5	4	39	16	31
2 Raith	22	11	6	5	46	21	28
3 Vale of Leven	22	12	4	6	38	25	28
4 Dumbarton	22	10	5	7	34	34	25
5 Leith	22	10	3	9	38	33	23
6 Ayr	22	10	3	9	40	36	23
7 Ayr Parkhouse	22	8	5	9	29	31	21
8 St Bernard's	22	9	3	10	34	37	21
9 E Stirlingshire	22	9	3	10	27	33	21
10 Albion	22	9	2	11	36	46	20
11 Cowdenbeath	22	4	4	14	19	43	12
12 Arthurlie	22	5	1	16	30	55	11

FA Cup

Third Round

Manchester United v Blackburn Rovers	6-1
Tottenham Hotspur v Burnley	0-0, 1-3
West Ham United v Newcastle United	0-0, 1-2
Bradford City v Sunderland	0-1
Bristol City v Norwich City	2-0
The Wednesday v Glossop North End	0-1
Derby County v Plymouth Argyle	1-0
Nottingham Forest v Millwall Athletic	3-1

Fourth Round

Burnley v Manchester United	1-0*, 2-3
Newcastle United v Sunderland	2-2, 3-0
Glossop North End v Bristol City	0-0, 0-1
Derby County v Nottingham Forest	3-0

*abandoned

Semi-Final

Manchester United v Newcastle United	1-0
Bristol City v Derby County	1-1, 2-1

Final at Crystal Palace

Manchester United v Bristol City	1-0

Scottish FA Cup

Third Round

Celtic v Airdrieonians	3-1
Third Lanark v Falkirk	1-2
Clyde v St Mirren	3-1
Rangers v Queen's Park	1-0

Semi-Final

Falkirk v Rangers	0-1
Celtic v Clyde	0-0, 2-0

Final at Hampden Park

Rangers v Celtic	2-2, 1-1†

† Rangers and Celtic both refused to play a third game as a result of the crowd rioting at the end of the second drawn match threatening that one or other would scratch. The Scottish FA agreed that the Cup would be withheld.

1909-10
First Division

	P	W	D	L	F	A	Pts
1 Aston Villa	38	23	7	8	84	42	53
2 Liverpool	38	21	6	11	78	57	48
3 Blackburn	38	18	9	11	73	55	45
4 Newcastle	38	19	7	12	70	56	45
5 Man United	38	19	7	12	69	61	45
6 Sheff United	38	16	10	12	62	41	42
7 Bradford City	38	17	8	13	64	47	42
8 Sunderland	38	18	5	15	66	51	41
9 Notts County	38	15	10	13	67	59	40
10 Everton	38	16	8	14	51	56	40
11 Wednesday	38	15	9	14	60	63	39
12 Preston	38	15	5	18	52	58	35
13 Bury	38	12	9	17	62	66	33
14 Nottm Forest	38	11	11	16	54	72	33
15 Tottenham	38	11	10	17	53	69	32
16 Bristol City	38	12	8	18	45	60	32
17 Middlesbrough	38	11	9	18	56	73	31
18 Woolwich A	38	11	9	18	37	67	31
19 Chelsea	38	11	7	20	47	70	29
20 Bolton	38	9	6	23	44	71	24

Second Division

	P	W	D	L	F	A	Pts
1 Man City	38	23	8	7	81	40	54
2 Oldham	38	23	7	8	79	39	53
3 Hull City	38	23	7	8	80	46	53
4 Derby	38	22	9	7	72	47	53
5 Leicester Fosse	38	20	4	14	79	58	44
6 Glossop NE	38	18	7	13	64	57	43
7 Fulham	38	14	13	11	51	43	41
8 Wolves	38	17	6	15	64	63	40
9 Barnsley	38	16	7	15	62	59	39
10 Bradford PA	38	17	4	17	64	59	38
11 WBA	38	16	5	17	58	56	37
12 Blackpool	38	14	8	16	50	52	36
13 Stockport	38	13	8	17	50	47	34
14 Burnley	38	14	6	18	62	61	34
15 Lincoln	38	10	11	17	42	69	31
16 Clapton Orient	38	12	6	20	37	60	30
17 Leeds City	38	10	7	21	46	80	27
18 Gainsborough	38	10	6	22	33	75	26
19 Grimsby	38	9	6	23	50	77	24
20 Birmingham	38	8	7	23	42	78	23

Scottish First Division

	P	W	D	L	F	A	Pts
1 Celtic	34	24	6	4	63	22	54
2 Falkirk	34	22	8	4	71	28	52
3 Rangers	34	20	6	8	70	35	46
4 Aberdeen	34	16	8	10	44	29	40
5 Clyde	34	14	9	11	47	33	37
6 Dundee	34	14	8	12	52	44	36
7 Third Lanark	34	13	8	13	62	44	34
8 Hibernian	34	14	6	14	33	40	34
9 Airdrieonians	34	12	9	13	46	57	33
10 Motherwell	34	12	8	14	59	60	32
11 Kilmarnock	34	12	8	14	53	59	32
12 Hearts	34	12	7	15	59	57	31
13 St Mirren	34	13	5	16	48	58	31
14 Queen's Park	34	12	6	16	54	74	30
15 Hamilton	34	11	6	17	50	67	28
16 Partick	34	8	10	16	45	59	26
17 Morton	34	11	3	20	38	60	25
18 Port Glasgow	34	3	5	26	25	93	11

Scottish Second Division

	P	W	D	L	F	A	Pts
1 Leith	22	13	7	2	41	18	33
2 Raith	22	14	5	3	35	20	33
3 St Bernard's	22	12	3	7	43	31	27
4 Dumbarton	22	9	5	8	44	37	23
5 Abercorn	22	7	8	7	38	39	22
6 Ayr	22	9	3	10	37	40	21
7 Vale of Leven	22	8	5	9	35	39	21
8 E Stirlingshire	22	9	2	11	38	43	20
9 Albion	22	7	5	10	34	39	19
10 Arthurlie	22	6	5	11	34	45	17
11 Cowdenbeath	22	7	3	12	22	34	17
12 Ayr Parkhouse	22	4	3	15	27	43	11

FA Cup

Third Round

Newcastle United v Blackburn Rovers	3-1
Leicester Fosse v Leyton	1-0
Swindon Town v Tottenham Hotspur	3-2
Aston Villa v Manchester City	1-2
Barnsley v West Bromwich Albion	1-0
Queen's Park Rangers v West Ham United	1-1, 1-0
Everton v Sunderland	2-0
Coventry City v Nottingham Forest	3-1

Fourth Round

Newcastle United v Leicester Fosse	3-0

Swindon Town v Manchester City		2-0
Barnsley v Queen's Park Rangers		1-0
Coventry City v Everton		0-2

Semi-Final

Newcastle United v Swindon Town	2-0
Barnsley v Everton	0-0, 3-0

Final at Crystal Palace

Newcastle United v Barnsley	1-1, 2-0*

* Replay at Goodison Park

Scottish FA Cup

Third Round

Hibernian v Heart of Midlothian	0-1*, 1-0
Celtic v Aberdeen	2-1
Queen's Park v Clyde	2-2, 2-2, 1-2
Motherwell v Dundee	1-3

*abandoned

Semi-Final

Clyde v Celtic	3-1
Hibernian v Dundee	0-0, 0-0, 0-1

Final at Ibrox Park

Dundee v Clyde	2-2,0-0, 2-1

1910–11
First Division

	P	W	D	L	F	A	Pts
1 Man United	38	22	8	8	72	40	52
2 Aston Villa	38	22	7	9	69	41	51
3 Sunderland	38	15	15	8	67	48	45
4 Everton	38	19	7	12	50	36	45
5 Bradford City	38	20	5	13	51	42	45
6 Wednesday	38	17	8	13	47	48	42
7 Oldham	38	16	9	13	44	41	41
8 Newcastle	38	15	10	13	61	43	40
9 Sheff United	38	15	8	15	49	43	38
10 Woolwich A	38	13	12	13	41	49	38
11 Notts County	38	14	10	14	37	45	38
12 Blackburn	38	13	11	14	62	54	37
13 Liverpool	38	15	7	16	53	53	37
14 Preston	38	12	11	15	40	49	35
15 Tottenham	38	13	6	19	52	63	32
16 Middlesbrough	38	11	10	17	49	63	32
17 Man City	38	9	13	16	43	58	31
18 Bury	38	9	11	18	43	71	29
19 Bristol City	38	11	5	22	43	66	27
20 Nottm Forest	38	9	7	22	55	75	25

Second Division

	P	W	D	L	F	A	Pts
1 WBA	38	22	9	7	67	41	53
2 Bolton	38	21	9	8	69	40	51
3 Chelsea	38	20	9	9	71	35	49
4 Clapton Orient	38	19	7	12	44	35	45
5 Hull	38	14	16	8	55	39	44
6 Derby	38	17	8	13	73	52	42
7 Blackpool	38	16	10	12	49	38	42
8 Burnley	38	13	15	10	45	45	41
9 Wolves	38	15	8	15	51	52	38
10 Fulham	38	15	7	16	52	48	37
11 Leeds City	38	15	7	16	58	56	37
12 Bradford PA	38	14	9	15	53	55	37
13 Huddersfield	38	13	8	17	57	58	34
14 Glossop NE	38	13	8	17	48	62	34
15 Leicester Fosse	38	14	5	19	52	62	33
16 Birmingham	38	12	8	18	42	64	32
17 Stockport	38	11	8	19	47	79	30
18 Gainsborough	38	9	11	18	37	55	29
19 Barnsley	38	7	14	17	52	62	28
20 Lincoln	38	7	10	21	28	72	24

Scottish First Division

	P	W	D	L	F	A	Pts
1 Rangers	34	23	6	5	90	34	52
2 Aberdeen	34	19	10	5	53	28	48
3 Falkirk	34	17	10	7	65	42	44
4 Partick	34	17	8	9	50	41	42
5 Celtic	34	15	11	8	48	18	41
6 Dundee	34	18	5	11	54	42	41
7 Clyde	34	14	11	9	45	36	39
8 Third Lanark	34	16	7	11	59	53	39
9 Hibernian	34	15	6	13	44	48	36
10 Kilmarnock	34	12	10	12	42	45	34
11 Airdrieonians	34	12	9	13	49	53	33
12 St Mirren	34	12	7	15	46	57	31
13 Morton	34	9	11	14	49	51	29
14 Hearts	34	8	8	18	42	59	24
15 Raith	34	7	10	17	36	55	24
16 Hamilton	34	8	5	21	31	60	21
17 Motherwell	34	8	4	22	37	66	20
18 Queen's Park	34	5	4	25	28	80	14

Scottish Second Division

	P	W	D	L	F	A	Pts
1 Dumbarton	22	15	1	6	52	30	31
2 Ayr	22	12	3	7	54	36	27

3 Albion	22	10	5	7	26	21	25
4 Leith	22	9	6	7	43	43	24
5 Cowdenbeath	22	9	5	8	33	28	23
6 St Bernard's	22	10	2	10	36	41	22
7 E Stirlingshire	22	7	6	9	28	34	20
8 Dundee Hibs	22	7	5	10	29	36	19
9 Port Glasgow	22	8	3	11	27	32	19
10 Arthurlie	22	7	5	10	27	35	19
11 Abercorn	22	9	1	12	39	50	19
12 Vale of Leven	22	4	8	10	21	29	16

FA Cup

Third Round

Bradford City v Grimsby Town	1-0
Burnley v Coventry City	5-0
Middlesbrough v Blackburn Rovers	0-3
West Ham United v Manchester United	2-1
Newcastle United v Hull City	3-2
Derby County v Everton	5-0
Wolverhampton Wanderers v Chelsea	0-2
Darlington v Swindon Town	0-3

Fourth Round

Bradford City v Burnley	1-0
West Ham United v Blackburn Rovers	2-3
Newcastle United v Derby County	4-0
Chelsea v Swindon Town	3-1

Semi-Final

Bradford City v Blackburn Rovers	3-0
Newcastle United v Chelsea	3-0

Final at Crystal Palace

Bradford City v Newcastle United	0-0, 1-0*

*Replay at Old Trafford

Scottish FA Cup

Third Round

Aberdeen v Forfar Athletic	6-0
Celtic v Clyde	1-0
Dundee v Rangers	2-1
Hamilton Academicals v Motherwell	2-1

Semi-Final

Celtic v Aberdeen	1-0
Hamilton Academicals v Dundee	3-2

Final at Ibrox Park

Celtic v Hamilton Academicals	0-0, 2-1

1911-12
First Division

	P	W	D	L	F	A	Pts
1 Blackburn	38	20	9	9	60	43	49
2 Everton	38	20	6	12	46	42	46
3 Newcastle	38	18	8	12	64	50	44
4 Bolton	38	20	3	15	54	43	43
5 Wednesday	38	16	9	13	69	49	41
6 Aston Villa	38	17	7	14	76	63	41
7 Middlesbrough	38	16	8	14	56	45	40
8 Sunderland	38	14	11	13	58	51	39
9 WBA	38	15	9	14	43	47	39
10 Woolwich A	38	15	8	15	55	59	38
11 Bradford City	38	15	8	15	46	50	38
12 Tottenham	38	14	9	15	53	53	37
13 Man United	38	13	11	14	45	60	37
14 Sheff United	38	13	10	15	63	56	36
15 Man City	38	13	9	16	56	58	35
16 Notts County	38	14	7	17	46	63	35
17 Liverpool	38	12	10	16	49	55	34
18 Oldham	38	12	10	16	46	54	34
19 Preston	38	13	7	18	40	57	33
20 Bury	38	6	9	23	32	59	21

Second Division

	P	W	D	L	F	A	Pts
1 Derby	38	23	8	7	74	28	54
2 Chelsea	38	24	6	8	64	34	54
3 Burnley	38	22	8	8	77	41	52
4 Clapton Orient	38	21	3	14	61	44	45
5 Wolves	38	16	10	12	57	33	42
6 Barnsley	38	15	12	11	45	42	42
7 Hull	38	17	8	13	54	51	42
8 Fulham	38	16	7	15	66	58	39
9 Grimsby	38	15	9	14	48	55	39
10 Leicester Fosse	38	15	7	16	49	66	37
11 Bradford PA	38	13	9	16	44	45	35
12 Birmingham	38	14	6	18	55	59	34
13 Bristol City	38	14	6	18	41	60	34
14 Blackpool	38	13	8	17	32	52	34
15 Nottm Forest	38	13	7	18	46	48	33
16 Stockport	38	11	11	16	47	54	33
17 Huddersfield	38	13	6	19	50	64	32
18 Glossop NE	38	8	12	18	42	56	28

	P	W	D	L	F	A	Pts
19 Leeds City	38	10	8	20	50	78	28
20 Gainsborough	38	5	13	20	30	64	23

Scottish First Division

	P	W	D	L	F	A	Pts
1 Rangers	34	24	3	7	86	34	51
2 Celtic	34	17	11	6	58	33	45
3 Clyde	34	19	4	11	56	32	42
4 Hearts	34	16	8	10	54	40	40
5 Partick	34	16	8	10	47	40	40
6 Morton	34	14	9	11	44	44	37
7 Falkirk	34	15	6	13	46	43	36
8 Dundee	34	13	9	12	52	41	35
9 Aberdeen	34	14	7	13	44	44	35
10 Airdrieonians	34	12	8	14	31	41	32
11 Third Lanark	34	12	7	15	40	57	31
12 Hamilton	34	11	8	15	32	44	30
13 Hibernian	34	12	5	17	44	47	29
14 Raith	34	9	9	16	48	59	27
15 Motherwell	34	11	5	18	34	44	27
16 Kilmarnock	34	11	4	19	38	60	26
17 Queen's Park	34	8	9	17	29	53	25
18 St Mirren	34	7	10	17	32	59	24

Scottish Second Division

	P	W	D	L	F	A	Pts
1 Ayr	22	16	3	3	54	24	35
2 Abercorn	22	13	4	5	43	23	30
3 Dumbarton	22	13	1	8	47	31	27
4 Cowdenbeath	22	12	2	8	39	31	26
5 St Johnstone	22	10	4	8	29	27	24
6 St Bernard's	22	9	5	8	39	36	23
7 Leith	22	9	4	9	31	34	22
8 Arthurlie	22	7	5	10	30	30	19
9 E Stirlingshire	22	7	3	12	22	31	17
10 Dundee Hibs	22	5	5	12	21	41	15
11 Vale of Leven	22	6	1	15	26	51	13
12 Albion	22	6	1	15	19	41	13

FA Cup

Third Round

Reading v Manchester United	1-1, 0-3
Blackburn Rovers v Wolverhampton Wanderers	3-2
Sunderland v West Bromwich Albion	1-2
Fulham v Northampton Town	2-1
West Ham United v Swindon Town	1-1, 0-4
Oldham Athletic v Everton	0-2
Bradford Park Avenue v Bradford City	0-1
Bolton Wanderers v Barnsley	1-2

Fourth Round

Manchester United v Blackburn Rovers	1-1, 2-4
West Bromwich Albion v Fulham	3-0
Swindon Town v Everton	2-1
Barnsley v Bradford City 0-0, 0-0, 0-0, 3-2	

Semi-Final

Blackburn Rovers v West Bromwich Albion	0-0, 0-1
Swindon Town v Barnsley	0-0, 0-1

Final at Crystal Palace

Barnsley v West Bromwich Albion	0-0, 1-0*

*Replay at Bramall Lane

Scottish FA Cup

Third Round

Aberdeen v Celtic	2-2, 0-2
Kilmarnock v Clyde	1-6
Morton v Heart of Midlothian	0-1
Third Lanark v Motherwell	3-1

Semi-Final

Celtic v Heart of Midlothian	3-0
Clyde v Third Lanark	3-1

Final at Ibrox Park

Celtic v Clyde	2-0

1912-13
First Division

	P	W	D	L	F	A	Pts
1 Sunderland	38	25	4	9	86	43	54
2 Aston Villa	38	19	12	7	86	52	50
3 Wednesday	38	21	7	10	75	55	49
4 Man United	38	19	8	11	69	43	46
5 Blackburn	38	16	13	9	79	43	45
6 Man City	38	18	8	12	53	37	44
7 Derby	38	17	8	13	69	66	42
8 Bolton	38	16	10	12	62	63	42
9 Oldham	38	14	14	10	50	55	42
10 WBA	38	13	12	13	57	50	38
11 Everton	38	15	7	16	48	54	37
12 Liverpool	38	16	5	17	61	71	37
13 Bradford City	38	12	11	15	50	60	35

	P	W	D	L	F	A	Pts
14 Newcastle	38	13	8	17	47	47	34
15 Sheff United	38	14	6	18	56	70	34
16 Middlesbrough	38	11	10	17	55	69	32
17 Tottenham	38	12	6	20	45	72	30
18 Chelsea	38	11	6	21	51	73	28
19 Notts County	38	7	9	22	28	56	23
20 Woolwich A	38	3	12	23	26	74	18

Second Division

	P	W	D	L	F	A	Pts
1 Preston	38	19	15	4	56	33	53
2 Burnley	38	21	8	9	88	53	50
3 Birmingham	38	18	10	10	59	44	46
4 Barnsley	38	19	7	12	57	47	45
5 Huddersfield	38	17	9	12	66	40	43
6 Leeds City	38	15	10	13	70	64	40
7 Grimsby	38	15	10	13	51	50	40
8 Lincoln	38	15	10	13	50	52	40
9 Fulham	38	17	5	16	65	55	39
10 Wolves	38	14	10	14	56	54	38
11 Bury	38	15	8	15	53	57	38
12 Hull	38	15	6	17	60	56	36
13 Bradford PA	38	14	8	16	60	60	36
14 Clapton Orient	38	10	14	14	34	47	34
15 Leicester Fosse	38	13	7	18	50	65	33
16 Bristol City	38	9	15	14	46	72	33
17 Nottm Forest	38	12	8	18	58	59	32
18 Glossop NE	38	12	8	18	49	68	32
19 Stockport	38	8	10	20	56	78	26
20 Blackpool	38	9	8	21	39	69	26

Scottish First Division

	P	W	D	L	F	A	Pts
1 Rangers	34	24	5	5	76	41	53
2 Celtic	34	22	5	7	53	28	49
3 Hearts	34	17	7	10	71	43	41
4 Airdrieonians	34	15	11	8	64	46	41
5 Falkirk	34	14	12	8	56	38	40
6 Motherwell	34	12	13	9	47	39	37
7 Aberdeen	34	14	9	11	47	40	37
8 Hibernian	34	16	5	13	63	54	37
9 Clyde	34	13	9	12	41	44	35
10 Hamilton	34	12	8	14	44	47	32
11 Kilmarnock	34	10	11	13	37	54	31
12 St Mirren	34	10	10	14	50	60	30
13 Morton	34	11	7	16	50	59	29
14 Dundee	34	8	13	13	33	46	29
15 Third Lanark	34	8	12	14	31	41	28
16 Raith	34	8	10	16	46	60	26
17 Partick	34	10	4	20	40	55	24
18 Queen's Park	34	5	3	26	34	88	13

Scottish Second Division

	P	W	D	L	F	A	Pts
1 Ayr	26	13	8	5	45	19	34
2 Dunfermline	26	13	7	6	45	27	33
3 E Stirlingshire	26	12	8	6	43	27	32
4 Abercorn	26	12	7	7	33	31	31
5 Cowdenbeath	26	12	6	8	36	27	30
6 Dumbarton	26	12	5	9	38	30	29
7 St Bernard's	26	12	3	11	36	34	27
8 Johnstone	26	9	6	11	31	43	24
9 Albion	26	10	3	13	38	40	23
10 Dundee Hibs	26	6	10	10	34	43	22
11 St Johnstone	26	7	7	12	29	38	21
12 Vale of Leven	26	8	5	13	28	45	21
13 Arthurlie	26	7	5	14	38	49	19
14 Leith	26	5	8	13	26	47	18

FA Cup

Third Round

Aston Villa v Crystal Palace	5-0
Bradford Park Avenue v The Wednesday	2-1
Oldham Athletic v Manchester United	0-0, 2-1
Bristol Rovers v Everton	0-4
Sunderland v Swindon Town	4-2
Liverpool v Newcastle United	1-1, 0-1
Burnley v Middlesbrough	3-1
Reading v Blackburn Rovers	1-2

Fourth Round

Bradford Park Avenue v Aston Villa	0-5
Everton v Oldham Athletic	0-1
Sunderland v Newcastle United	0-0, 2-2, 3-0
Blackburn Rovers v Burnley	0-1

Semi-Final

Aston Villa v Oldham Athletic	1-0
Sunderland v Burnley	0-0, 3-2

Final at Crystal Palace

Aston Villa v Sunderland	1-0

Scottish FA Cup

Third Round

Celtic v Peebles Rovers	3-0
Clyde v Queen's Park	1-0

Dumbarton v St Johnstone	1-0
Partick Thistle v Dundee	0-1
Ranger v Falkirk	1-3
Kilmarnock v Heart of Midlothian	0-2
Raith Rovers v Hibernian	2-2, 1-0
St Mirren v Airdrieonians	1-0

Fourth Round

Clyde v Dundee	1-1, 0-0, 2-1
Falkirk v Dumbarton	1-0
Celtic v Heart of Midlothian	0-1
Raith Rovers v St Mirren	2-1

Semi-Final

Falkirk v Heart of Midlothian	1-0
Raith Rovers v Clyde	1-1, 1-0

Final at Celtic Park

Falkirk v Raith Rovers	2-0

1913–14
First Division

	P	W	D	L	F	A	Pts
1 Blackburn	38	20	11	7	78	42	51
2 Aston Villa	38	19	6	13	65	50	44
3 Oldham	38	17	9	12	55	45	43
4 Middlesbrough	38	19	5	14	77	60	43
5 WBA	38	15	13	10	46	42	43
6 Bolton	38	16	10	12	65	52	42
7 Sunderland	38	17	6	15	63	52	40
8 Chelsea	38	16	7	15	46	55	39
9 Bradford City	38	12	14	12	40	40	38
10 Sheff United	38	16	5	17	63	60	37
11 Newcastle	38	13	11	14	39	48	37
12 Burnley	38	12	12	14	61	53	36
13 Man City	38	14	8	16	51	53	36
14 Man United	38	15	6	17	52	62	36
15 Everton	38	12	11	15	46	55	35
16 Liverpool	38	14	7	17	46	62	35
17 Tottenham	38	12	10	16	50	62	34
18 Wednesday	38	13	8	17	53	70	34
19 Preston	38	12	6	20	52	69	30
20 Derby	38	8	11	19	55	71	27

Second Division

	P	W	D	L	F	A	Pts
1 Notts County	38	23	7	8	77	36	53
2 Bradford PA	38	23	3	12	71	47	49
3 Arsenal	38	20	9	9	54	38	49
4 Leeds City	38	20	7	11	76	46	47

	P	W	D	L	F	A	Pts
5 Barnsley	38	19	7	12	51	45	45
6 Clapton Orient	38	16	11	11	47	35	43
7 Hull	38	16	9	13	53	37	41
8 Bristol City	38	16	9	13	52	50	41
9 Wolves	38	18	5	15	51	52	41
10 Bury	38	15	10	13	39	40	40
11 Fulham	38	16	6	16	46	43	38
12 Stockport	38	13	10	15	55	57	36
13 Huddersfield	38	13	8	17	47	53	34
14 Birmingham	38	12	10	16	48	60	34
15 Grimsby	38	13	8	17	42	58	34
16 Blackpool	38	9	14	15	33	44	32
17 Glossop NE	38	11	6	21	51	67	28
18 Leicester Fosse	38	11	4	23	45	61	26
19 Lincoln	38	10	6	22	36	66	26
20 Nottm Forest	38	7	9	22	37	76	23

Scottish First Division

	P	W	D	L	F	A	Pts
1 Celtic	38	30	5	3	81	14	65
2 Rangers	38	27	5	6	79	31	59
3 Hearts	38	23	8	7	70	39	54
4 Morton	38	26	2	10	76	51	54
5 Falkirk	38	20	9	9	69	51	49
6 Airdrieonians	38	18	12	8	71	43	48
7 Dundee	38	19	5	14	65	53	43
8 Third Lanark	38	13	10	15	42	51	36
9 Clyde	38	11	11	16	44	44	33
10 Ayr	38	13	7	18	56	72	33
11 Raith	38	13	6	19	56	57	32
12 Kilmarnock	38	11	9	18	48	68	31
13 Aberdeen	38	10	10	18	47	55	30
14 Hibernian	38	12	6	20	58	75	30
15 Partick	38	10	9	19	37	51	29
16 Queen's Park	38	10	9	19	52	84	29
17 Motherwell	38	11	6	21	49	65	28
18 Hamilton	38	11	6	21	46	65	28
19 Dumbarton	38	10	7	21	45	87	27
20 St. Mirren	38	8	6	24	38	73	22

Scottish Second Division

	P	W	D	L	F	A	Pts
1 Cowdenbeath	22	13	5	4	34	17	31
2 Albion	22	10	7	5	38	33	27
3 Dunfermline	22	11	4	7	46	28	26
4 Dundee Hibs	22	11	4	7	36	31	26
5 St Johnstone	22	9	5	8	48	38	23
6 Abercorn	22	10	3	9	32	32	23
7 St Bernard's	22	8	6	8	39	31	22
8 E Stirlingshire	22	7	8	7	40	36	22

9 Arthurlie	22	8	4	10	35	37	20
10 Leith	22	5	9	8	31	37	19
11 Vale of Leven	22	5	3	14	23	47	13
12 Johnstone	22	4	4	14	20	55	12

FA Cup

Third Round

Millwall Athletic v Sheffield United	0-4
Blackburn Rovers v Manchester City	1-2
Burnley v Bolton Wanderers	3-0
Sunderland v Preston North End	2-0
Aston Villa v West Bromwich Albion	2-1
The Wednesday v Brighton	3-0
West Ham United v Liverpool	1-1, 1-5
Birmingham v Queen's Park Rangers	1-2

Fourth Round

Manchester City v Sheffield United	0-0, 0-0, 0-1
Sunderland v Burnley	0-0, 1-2
The Wednesday v Aston Villa	0-1
Liverpool v Queen's Park Rangers	2-1

Semi-Final

Sheffield United v Burnley	0-0, 0-1
Aston Villa v Liverpool	0-2

Final at Crystal Palace

Burnley v Liverpool	1-0

Scottish FA Cup

Third Round

Forfar Athletic v Celtic	0-5
Hibernian v Rangers	2-1
Broxburn United v Motherwell	0-2
Kilmarnock v Partick Thistle	1-4
Airdrieonians v Queen's Park	1-1, 1-2
Aberdeen v St Mirren	1-2
Stevenston United v Peebles Rovers	3-2
Third Lanark v Raith Rovers	4-1

Fourth Round

Motherwell v Celtic	1-3
Queen's Park v Hibernian	1-3
St Mirren v Partick Thistle	1-0
Third Lanark v Stevenston United	1-1, 0-0, 1-0

Semi-Final

Celtic v Third Lanark	2-0
Hibernian v St Mirren	3-1

Final at Ibrox Park

Celtic v Hibernian	0-0, 4-1

1914–15
First Division

	P	W	D	L	F	A	Pts
1 Everton	38	19	8	11	76	47	46
2 Oldham	38	17	11	10	70	56	45
3 Blackburn	38	18	7	13	83	61	43
4 Burnley	38	18	7	13	61	47	43
5 Man City	38	15	13	10	49	39	43
6 Sheff United	38	15	13	10	49	41	43
7 Wednesday	38	15	13	10	61	54	43
8 Sunderland	38	18	5	15	81	72	41
9 Bradford PA	38	17	7	14	69	65	41
10 Bradford City	38	13	14	11	55	49	40
11 WBA	38	15	10	13	49	43	40
12 Middlesbrough	38	13	12	13	62	74	38
13 Aston Villa	38	13	11	14	62	72	37
14 Liverpool	38	14	9	15	65	75	37
15 Newcastle	38	11	10	17	46	48	32
16 Notts County	38	9	13	16	41	57	31
17 Bolton	38	11	8	19	68	84	30
18 Man United	38	9	12	17	46	62	30
19 Chelsea	38	8	13	17	51	65	29
20 Tottenham	38	8	12	18	57	90	28

Second Division

	P	W	D	L	F	A	Pts
1 Derby	38	23	7	8	71	33	53
2 Preston	38	20	10	8	61	42	50
3 Barnsley	38	22	3	13	51	51	47
4 Wolves	38	19	7	12	77	52	45
5 Birmingham	38	17	9	12	62	39	43
6 Arsenal	38	19	5	14	69	41	43
7 Hull	38	19	5	14	65	54	43
8 Huddersfield	38	17	8	13	61	42	42
9 Clapton Orient	38	16	9	13	50	48	41
10 Blackpool	38	17	5	16	58	57	39
11 Bury	38	15	8	15	61	56	38
12 Fulham	38	15	7	16	53	47	37
13 Bristol City	38	15	7	16	62	56	37
14 Stockport	38	15	7	16	54	60	37
15 Leeds City	38	14	4	20	65	64	32
16 Lincoln	38	11	9	18	46	65	31
17 Grimsby	38	11	9	18	48	76	31
18 Nottm Forest	38	10	9	19	43	77	29
19 Leicester Fosse	38	10	4	24	47	88	24
20 Glossop NE	38	6	6	26	31	87	18

Scottish Division 'A'

	P	W	D	L	F	A	Pts
1 Celtic	38	30	5	3	91	25	65
2 Hearts	38	27	7	4	83	32	61
3 Rangers	38	23	4	11	74	47	50
4 Morton	38	18	12	8	74	48	48
5 Ayr	38	20	8	10	55	40	48
6 Falkirk	38	16	7	15	48	48	39
7 Hamilton	38	16	6	16	60	55	38
8 Partick	38	15	8	15	56	58	38
9 St Mirren	38	14	8	16	56	65	36
10 Airdrieonians	38	14	7	17	54	60	35
11 Hibernian	38	12	11	15	59	66	35
12 Dumbarton	38	13	8	17	51	66	34
13 Kilmarnock	38	15	4	19	55	59	34
14 Aberdeen	38	11	11	16	39	52	33
15 Dundee	38	12	9	17	43	61	33
16 Third Lanark	38	10	12	16	51	57	32
17 Clyde	38	12	6	20	44	59	30
18 Motherwell	38	10	10	18	49	66	30
19 Raith	38	9	10	19	53	68	28
20 Queen's Park	38	4	5	29	27	90	13

Scottish Division 'B'

	P	W	D	L	F	A	Pts
1 Cowdenbeath	26	16	5	5	49	17	37
2 St Bernard's	26	18	1	7	66	34	37
3 Leith	26	15	7	4	54	31	37
4 E Stirlingshire	26	13	5	8	51	37	31
5 Clydebank	26	13	4	9	67	37	30
6 Dunfermline	26	13	2	11	49	39	28
7 Johnstone	26	11	5	10	41	51	27
8 St Johnstone*	25	10	6	9	54	50	26
9 Albion	26	9	7	10	37	42	25
10 Lochgelly	26	9	3	14	37	59	21
11 Dundee Hibs	26	8	3	15	48	61	19
12 Abercorn	26	5	7	14	34	65	17
13 Arthurlie*	25	5	4	16	33	64	14
14 Vale of Leven	26	4	5	17	33	66	13

*No record of St Johnstone and Arthurlie playing each other more than once

FA Cup

Third Round

Sheffield United v Bradford Park Avenue	1-0
Birmingham v Oldham Athletic	2-3
Bolton Wanderers v Burnley	2-1
Southampton v Hull City	2-2, 0-4
Manchester City v Chelsea	0-1
The Wednesday v Newcastle United	1-2
Queen's Park Rangers v Everton	1-2
Bradford City v Norwich City	
	1-1*, 0-0*, 2-0

Fourth Round

Oldham Athletic v Sheffield United	0-0*, 0-3
Bolton Wanderers v Hull City	4-2
Chelsea v Newcastle United	1-1*, 1-0
Bradford City v Everton	0-2

Semi-Final

Sheffield United v Bolton Wanderers	2-1
Chelsea v Everton	2-0

Final at Old Trafford

Sheffield United v Chelsea	3-0

*Extra time played

1915–16
Scottish League

	P	W	D	L	F	A	Pts
1 Celtic	38	32	3	3	116	23	67
2 Rangers	38	25	6	7	87	39	56
3 Morton*	37	22	7	8	86	35	51
4 Ayr	38	20	8	10	72	45	48
5 Partick	38	19	8	11	65	41	46
6 Hearts*	37	20	6	11	66	45	46
7 Hamilton	38	19	3	16	68	76	41
8 Dundee	38	18	4	16	56	49	40
9 Dumbarton	38	13	11	14	53	64	37
10 Kilmarnock	38	12	11	15	46	49	35
11 Aberdeen	38	11	12	15	51	64	34
12 Falkirk	38	12	9	17	45	61	33
13 St Mirren	38	13	4	21	50	67	30
14 Motherwell	38	11	8	19	55	81	30
15 Airdrieonians	38	11	8	19	44	74	30
16 Clyde	38	11	7	20	49	71	29
17 Third Lanark	38	9	11	18	40	66	29
18 Queen's Park	38	11	6	21	53	100	28
19 Hibernian	38	9	7	22	44	71	25
20 Raith	38	9	5	24	30	65	23

*Morton and Hearts only played each other once

1916–17
Scottish League

	P	W	D	L	F	A	Pts
1 Celtic	38	27	10	1	79	17	64
2 Morton	38	24	6	8	72	39	54
3 Rangers	38	24	5	9	68	32	53
4 Airdrieonians	38	21	8	9	71	38	50
5 Third Lanark	38	19	11	8	53	37	49
6 Kilmarnock	38	18	7	13	69	45	43
7 St Mirren	38	15	10	13	49	43	40
8 Motherwell	38	16	6	16	57	59	38
9 Partick	38	14	7	17	44	43	35
10 Dumbarton	38	12	11	15	56	73	35
11 Hamilton	38	13	9	16	54	73	35
12 Falkirk	38	12	10	16	57	57	34
13 Clyde	38	10	14	14	41	53	34
14 Hearts	38	14	4	20	44	59	32
15 Ayr	38	12	7	19	47	59	31
16 Dundee	38	13	4	21	58	71	30
17 Hibernian	38	10	10	18	57	72	30
18 Queen's Park	38	11	7	20	56	81	29
19 Raith	38	8	7	23	42	91	23
20 Aberdeen	38	7	7	24	36	68	21

1917–18
Scottish League

	P	W	D	L	F	A	Pts
1 Rangers	34	25	6	3	66	24	56
2 Celtic	34	24	7	3	66	26	55
3 Kilmarnock	34	19	5	10	69	41	43
4 Morton	34	17	9	8	53	42	43
5 Motherwell	34	16	9	9	70	51	41
6 Partick	34	14	12	8	51	37	40
7 Queen's Park	34	14	6	14	64	63	34
8 Dumbarton	34	13	8	13	48	49	34
9 Clydebank	34	14	5	15	55	56	33
10 Hearts	34	14	4	16	41	58	32
11 St Mirren	34	11	7	16	42	50	29
12 Hamilton	34	11	6	17	52	63	28
13 Third Lanark	34	10	7	17	56	62	27
14 Falkirk	34	9	9	16	36	68	27
15 Airdrieonians	34	10	6	18	46	58	26
16 Hibernian	34	8	9	17	42	57	25
17 Clyde	34	9	2	23	37	72	20
18 Ayr	34	5	9	20	32	61	19

1918–19
Scottish League

	P	W	D	L	F	A	Pts
1 Celtic	34	26	6	2	71	22	58
2 Rangers	34	26	5	3	86	16	57
3 Morton	34	18	11	5	76	40	47
4 Partick	34	17	7	10	62	43	41
5 Motherwell	34	14	10	10	51	40	38
6 Ayr	34	15	8	11	62	53	38
7 Hearts	34	14	9	11	59	52	37
8 Queen's Park	34	15	5	14	59	57	35
9 Kilmarnock	34	14	7	13	61	59	35
10 Clydebank	34	12	8	14	54	65	32
11 St Mirren	34	10	12	12	43	55	32
12 Third Lanark	34	11	9	14	60	62	31
13 Airdrieonians	34	9	11	14	45	54	29
14 Hamilton	34	11	5	18	49	75	27
15 Dumbarton	34	7	8	19	31	58	22
16 Falkirk	34	6	8	20	46	73	20
17 Clyde	34	7	6	21	45	75	20
18 Hibernian	34	5	3	26	30	91	13

1919–20
First Division

	P	W	D	L	F	A	Pts
1 WBA	42	28	4	10	104	47	60
2 Burnley	42	21	9	12	65	59	51
3 Chelsea	42	22	5	15	56	51	49
4 Liverpool	42	19	10	13	59	44	48
5 Sunderland	42	22	4	16	72	59	48
6 Bolton	42	19	9	14	72	65	47
7 Man City	42	18	9	15	71	62	45
8 Newcastle	42	17	9	16	44	39	43
9 Aston Villa	42	18	6	18	75	73	42
10 Arsenal	42	15	12	15	56	58	42
11 Bradford PA	42	15	12	15	60	63	42
12 Man United	42	13	14	15	54	50	40
13 Middlesbrough	42	15	10	17	61	65	40
14 Sheff United	42	16	8	18	59	69	40
15 Bradford City	42	14	11	17	54	63	39
16 Everton	42	12	14	16	69	68	38
17 Oldham	42	15	8	19	49	52	38
18 Derby	42	13	12	17	47	57	38
19 Preston	42	14	10	18	57	73	38
20 Blackburn	42	13	11	18	64	77	37
21 Notts County	42	12	12	18	56	74	36
22 Wednesday	42	7	9	26	28	64	23

Second Division

	P	W	D	L	F	A	Pts
1 Tottenham	42	32	6	4	102	32	70
2 Huddersfield	42	28	8	6	97	38	64
3 Birmingham	42	24	8	10	85	34	56
4 Blackpool	42	21	10	11	65	47	52
5 Bury	42	20	8	14	60	44	48
6 Fulham	42	19	9	14	61	50	47
7 West Ham	42	19	9	14	47	40	47
8 Bristol City	42	13	17	12	46	43	43
9 South Shields	42	15	12	15	58	48	42
10 Stoke	42	18	6	18	60	54	42
11 Hull	42	18	6	18	78	72	42
12 Barnsley	42	15	10	17	61	55	40
13 Port Vale*	42	16	8	18	59	62	40
14 Leicester	42	15	10	17	41	61	40
15 Clapton Orient	42	16	6	20	51	59	38
16 Stockport	42	14	9	19	52	61	37
17 Rotherham Co	42	13	8	21	51	83	34
18 Nottm Forest	42	11	9	22	43	73	31
19 Wolves	42	10	10	22	55	80	30
20 Coventry	42	9	11	22	35	73	29
21 Lincoln	42	9	9	24	44	101	27
22 Grimsby	42	10	5	27	34	75	25

*Replaced Leeds City after 8 matches

Scottish League

	P	W	D	L	F	A	Pts
1 Rangers	42	31	9	2	106	25	71
2 Celtic	42	29	10	3	89	31	68
3 Motherwell	42	23	11	8	73	53	57
4 Dundee	42	22	6	14	79	65	50
5 Clydebank	42	20	8	14	78	54	48
6 Morton	42	16	13	13	71	48	45
7 Airdrieonians	42	17	10	15	57	43	44
8 Kilmarnock	42	20	3	19	59	74	43
9 Third Lanark	41	16	11	14	56	61	41
10 Ayr	42	15	10	17	72	69	40
11 Dumbarton	42	13	13	16	57	65	39
12 Queen's Park	42	14	10	18	67	73	38
13 Partick	42	13	12	17	51	62	38
14 St Mirren	42	15	8	19	63	81	38
15 Clyde	42	14	9	19	64	71	37
16 Hearts	42	14	9	19	57	72	37
17 Aberdeen	42	11	13	18	46	64	35
18 Hibernian	42	13	7	22	60	79	33
19 Raith	42	11	10	21	61	82	32
20 Falkirk	42	10	11	21	45	74	31
21 Hamilton	42	11	7	24	56	86	29
22 Albion	41	9	8	24	41	76	26

1919–20
FA Cup

Third Round
Aston Villa v Sunderland	1-0
Tottenham Hotspur v West Ham United	3-0
Chelsea v Leicester City	3-0
Notts County v Bradford Park Avenue	3-4
Bristol City v Cardiff City	2-1
Preston North End v Bradford City	0-3
Huddersfield Town v Plymouth Argyle	3-1
Liverpool v Birmingham	2-0

Fourth Round
Tottenham Hotspur v Aston Villa	0-1
Chelsea v Bradford Park Avenue	4-1
Bristol City v Bradford City	2-0
Huddersfield Town v Liverpool	2-1

Semi-Final
Aston Villa v Chelsea	3-1
Huddersfield Town v Bristol City	2-1

Final at Stamford Bridge
Aston Villa v Huddersfield Town	1-0

Scottish FA Cup

Third Round
Aberdeen v Heart of Midlothian	1-0
St Bernard's v Albion Rovers	1-1, 1-4
Ayr United v Armadale	1-1, 0-1
Celtic v Partick Thistle	2-0
Kilmarnock v Queen's Park	4-1
Raith Rovers v Morton	2-2, 0-3
Rangers v Broxburn United	3-0
Lochgelly United v Third Lanark	0-3

Fourth Round
Albion Rovers v Aberdeen	2-1
Morton v Third Lanark	3-0
Armadale v Kilmarnock	1-2
Rangers v Celtic	1-0

Semi-Final
Kilmarnock v Morton	3-2
Albion Rovers v Rangers	0-0, 1-1, 2-0

Final at Hampden Park
Kilmarnock v Albion Rovers	3-2

1920–21
First Division

	P	W	D	L	F	A	Pts
1 Burnley	42	23	13	6	79	36	59
2 Man City	42	24	6	12	70	50	54
3 Bolton	42	19	14	9	77	53	52
4 Liverpool	42	18	15	9	63	35	51
5 Newcastle	42	20	10	12	66	45	50
6 Tottenham	42	19	9	14	70	48	47
7 Everton	42	17	13	12	66	55	47
8 Middlesbrough	42	17	12	13	53	53	46
9 Arsenal	42	15	14	13	59	63	44
10 Aston Villa	42	18	7	17	63	70	43
11 Blackburn	42	13	15	14	57	59	41
12 Sunderland	42	14	13	15	57	60	41
13 Man United	42	15	10	17	64	68	40
14 WBA	42	13	14	15	54	58	40
15 Bradford City	42	12	15	15	61	63	39
16 Preston	42	15	9	18	61	65	39
17 Huddersfield	42	15	9	18	42	49	39
18 Chelsea	42	13	13	16	48	58	39
19 Oldham	42	9	15	18	49	86	33
20 Sheff United	42	6	18	18	42	68	30
21 Derby	42	5	16	21	32	58	26
22 Bradford PA	42	8	8	26	43	76	24

Second Division

	P	W	D	L	F	A	Pts
1 Birmingham	42	24	10	8	79	38	58
2 Cardiff	42	24	10	8	59	32	58
3 Bristol City	42	19	13	10	49	29	51
4 Blackpool	42	20	10	12	54	42	50
5 West Ham	42	19	10	13	51	30	48
6 Notts County	42	18	11	13	55	40	47
7 Clapton Orient	42	16	13	13	43	42	45
8 South Shields	42	17	10	15	61	46	44
9 Fulham	42	16	10	16	43	47	42
10 Wednesday	42	15	11	16	48	48	41
11 Bury	42	15	10	17	45	49	40
12 Leicester	42	12	16	14	39	46	40
13 Hull	42	10	20	12	43	53	40
14 Leeds	42	14	10	18	40	45	38
15 Wolves	42	16	6	20	49	66	38
16 Barnsley	42	10	16	16	48	50	36
17 Port Vale	42	11	14	17	43	49	36
18 Nottm Forest	42	12	12	18	48	55	36
19 Rotherham Co	42	12	12	18	37	53	36
20 Stoke	42	12	11	19	46	56	35
21 Coventry	42	12	11	19	39	70	35

22 Stockport	42	9	12	21	42	75	30

Third Division

	P	W	D	L	F	A	Pts
1 Crystal Palace	42	24	11	7	70	34	59
2 Southampton	42	19	16	7	64	28	54
3 QPR	42	22	9	11	61	32	53
4 Swindon	42	21	10	11	73	49	52
5 Swansea	42	18	15	9	56	45	51
6 Watford	42	20	8	14	59	44	48
7 Millwall Ath	42	18	11	13	42	30	47
8 Merthyr Town	42	15	15	12	60	49	45
9 Luton	42	16	12	14	61	56	44
10 Bristol Rovers	42	18	7	17	68	57	43
11 Plymouth	42	11	21	10	35	34	43
12 Portsmouth	42	12	15	15	46	48	39
13 Grimsby	42	15	9	18	49	59	39
14 Northampton	42	15	8	19	59	75	38
15 Newport	42	14	9	19	43	64	37
16 Norwich	42	10	16	16	44	53	36
17 Southend	42	14	8	20	44	61	36
18 Brighton	42	14	8	20	42	61	36
19 Exeter	42	10	15	17	39	54	35
20 Reading	42	12	7	23	42	59	31
21 Brentford	42	9	12	21	42	67	30
22 Gillingham	42	8	12	22	34	74	28

Scottish League

	P	W	D	L	F	A	Pts
1 Rangers	42	35	6	1	91	24	76
2 Celtic	42	30	6	6	86	35	66
3 Hearts	42	20	10	12	74	49	50
4 Dundee	42	19	11	12	54	48	49
5 Motherwell	42	19	10	13	75	51	48
6 Partick	42	17	12	13	53	39	46
7 Clyde	42	21	3	18	63	62	45
8 Third Lanark	42	19	6	17	74	61	44
9 Morton	42	15	14	13	66	58	44
10 Airdrieonians	42	17	9	16	71	64	43
11 Aberdeen	42	14	14	14	53	54	42
12 Kilmarnock	42	17	8	17	62	68	42
13 Hibernian	42	16	9	17	58	57	41
14 Ayr	42	14	12	16	62	69	40
15 Hamilton	42	14	12	16	44	57	40
16 Raith	42	16	5	21	54	58	37
17 Albion	42	11	12	19	57	68	34
18 Falkirk	42	11	12	19	54	72	34
19 Queen's Park	42	11	11	20	45	80	33
20 Clydebank	42	7	14	21	47	72	28
21 Dumbarton	42	10	4	28	41	89	24

22 St Mirren   42 7 4 31 43 92 18

FA Cup

Third Round
Southend United v Tottenham Hotspur
                                    1-4
Aston Villa v Huddersfield Town	2-0
Hull City v Burnley	3-0
Luton Town v Preston North End	2-3
Everton v Newcastle United	3-0
Fulham v Wolverhampton Wanderers
0-1
Southampton v Cardiff City	0-1
Plymouth Argyle v Chelsea 0-0, 0-0, 1-2

Fourth Round
| Tottenham Hotspur v Aston Villa | 1-0 |
| Hull City v Preston North End   0-0, 0-1 |
| Everton v Wolverhampton Wanderers 0-1 |
| Cardiff City v Chelsea | 1-0 |

Semi-Final
Tottenham Hotspur v Preston North End
                                    2-1
Wolverhampton Wanderers v Cardiff City
                                  0-0, 3-1

Final at Stamford Bridge
Tottenham Hotspur v Wolverhampton
     Wanderers   1-0

Scottish FA Cup

Third Round
Armadale v Albion Rovers
                         0-0, 0-0, 2-2, 0-2
| East Fife v Celtic | 1-3 |
| Dumbarton v Nithsdale Wanderers | 5-0 |
| Aberdeen v Dundee   1-1, 0-0, 0-2 |
Hamilton Academicals v Heart of Mid-
     lothian   0-1
| Motherwell v Ayr United   1-1, 1-1, 3-1 |
| East Stirlingshire v Partick Thistle | 1-2 |
| Rangers v Alloa Athletic   0-0, 4-1 |

Fourth Round
| Dundee v Albion Rovers | 0-2 |
| Celtic v Heart of Midlothian | 1-2 |
| Partick Thistle v Motherwell 0-0, 2-2, 2-1 |
| Dumbarton v Rangers | 0-3 |

Semi-Final
Partick v Heart of Midlothian 0-0, 0-0, 2-0

| Rangers v Albion Rovers | 4-1 |

Final at Celtic Park
Partick Thistle v Rangers   1-0

1921-22
First Division

	P	W	D	L	F	A	Pts
1 Liverpool	42	22	13	7	63	36	57
2 Tottenham	42	21	9	12	65	39	51
3 Burnley	42	22	5	15	72	54	49
4 Cardiff	42	19	10	13	61	53	48
5 Aston Villa	42	22	3	17	74	55	47
6 Bolton	42	20	7	15	68	59	47
7 Newcastle	42	18	10	14	59	45	46
8 Middlesbrough	42	16	14	12	79	69	46
9 Chelsea	42	17	12	13	40	43	46
10 Man City	42	18	9	15	65	70	45
11 Sheff United	42	15	10	17	59	54	40
12 Sunderland	42	16	8	18	60	62	40
13 WBA	42	15	10	17	51	63	40
14 Huddersfield	42	15	9	18	53	54	39
15 Blackburn	42	13	12	17	54	57	38
16 Preston	42	13	12	17	42	65	38
17 Arsenal	42	15	7	20	47	56	37
18 Birmingham	42	15	7	20	48	60	37
19 Oldham	42	13	11	18	38	50	37
20 Everton	42	12	12	18	57	55	36
21 Bradford City	42	11	10	21	48	72	32
22 Man United	42	8	12	22	41	73	28

Second Division

	P	W	D	L	F	A	Pts
1 Nottm Forest	42	22	12	8	51	30	56
2 Stoke	42	18	16	8	60	44	52
3 Barnsley	42	22	8	12	67	52	52
4 West Ham	42	20	8	14	52	39	48
5 Hull	42	19	10	13	51	41	48
6 South Shields	42	17	12	13	43	38	46
7 Fulham	42	18	9	15	57	38	45
8 Leeds	42	16	13	13	48	38	45
9 Leicester	42	14	17	11	39	34	45
10 Wednesday	42	15	14	13	47	50	44
11 Bury	42	15	10	17	54	55	40
12 Derby	42	15	9	18	60	64	39
13 Notts County	42	12	15	15	47	51	39
14 Crystal Palace	42	13	13	16	45	51	39
15 Clapton Orient	42	15	9	18	43	50	39
16 Rotherham Co	42	14	11	17	32	43	39

	P	W	D	L	F	A	Pts
17 Wolves	42	13	11	18	44	49	37
18 Port Vale	42	14	8	20	43	57	36
19 Blackpool	42	15	5	22	44	57	35
20 Coventry	42	12	10	20	51	60	34
21 Bristol City	42	12	9	21	37	58	33
22 Bradford PA	42	12	9	21	46	62	33

Third Division (North)

	P	W	D	L	F	A	Pts
1 Stockport	38	24	8	6	60	21	56
2 Darlington	38	22	6	10	81	37	50
3 Grimsby	38	21	8	9	72	47	50
4 Hartlepools	38	17	8	13	52	39	42
5 Accrington	38	19	3	16	73	57	41
6 Crewe	38	18	5	15	60	56	41
7 Stalybridge Cel	38	18	5	15	62	63	41
8 Walsall	38	18	3	17	66	65	39
9 Southport	38	14	10	14	55	44	38
10 Ashington	38	17	4	17	59	66	38
11 Durham City	38	17	3	18	68	67	37
12 Wrexham	38	14	9	15	51	56	37
13 Chesterfield	38	16	3	19	48	67	35
14 Lincoln	38	14	6	18	48	59	34
15 Barrow	38	14	5	19	42	54	33
16 Nelson	38	13	7	18	48	66	33
17 Wigan Borough	38	11	9	18	46	72	31
18 Tranmere	38	9	11	18	51	61	29
19 Halifax	38	10	9	19	56	76	29
20 Rochdale	38	11	4	23	52	77	26

Third Division (South)

	P	W	D	L	F	A	Pts
1 Southampton	42	23	15	4	68	21	61
2 Plymouth	42	25	11	6	63	24	61
3 Portsmouth	42	18	17	7	62	39	53
4 Luton	42	22	8	12	64	35	52
5 QPR	42	18	13	11	53	44	49
6 Swindon	42	16	13	13	72	60	45
7 Watford	42	13	18	11	54	48	44
8 Aberdare Ath	42	17	10	15	57	51	44
9 Brentford	42	16	11	15	52	43	43
10 Swansea	42	13	15	14	50	47	41
11 Merthyr Town	42	17	6	19	45	56	40
12 Millwall Ath	42	10	18	14	38	42	38
13 Reading	42	14	18	10	40	47	38
14 Bristol Rovers	42	14	10	18	52	67	38
15 Norwich	42	12	13	17	50	62	37
16 Charlton	42	13	11	18	43	56	37
17 Northampton	42	13	11	18	47	71	37
18 Gillingham	42	14	8	20	47	60	36

	P	W	D	L	F	A	Pts
19 Brighton	42	13	9	20	45	51	35
20 Newport	42	11	12	19	44	61	34
21 Exeter	42	11	12	19	38	59	34
22 Southend	42	8	11	23	34	74	27

Scottish First Division

	P	W	D	L	F	A	Pts
1 Celtic	42	27	13	2	83	20	67
2 Rangers	42	28	10	4	83	26	66
3 Raith	42	19	13	10	66	43	51
4 Dundee	42	19	11	12	57	40	49
5 Falkirk	42	16	17	9	48	38	49
6 Partick	42	20	8	14	57	53	48
7 Hibernian	42	16	14	12	55	44	46
8 St Mirren	42	17	12	13	71	61	46
9 Third Lanark	42	17	12	13	58	52	46
10 Clyde	42	16	12	14	60	51	44
11 Albion	42	17	10	15	55	51	44
12 Morton	42	16	10	16	58	57	42
13 Motherwell	42	16	7	19	63	58	39
14 Ayr	42	13	12	17	55	63	38
15 Aberdeen	42	13	9	20	48	54	35
16 Airdrieonians	42	12	11	19	46	56	35
17 Kilmarnock	42	13	9	20	56	83	35
18 Hamilton	42	9	16	17	51	62	34
19 Hearts	42	11	10	21	50	60	32
20 Dumbarton	42	10	10	22	46	81	30
21 Queen's Park	42	9	10	23	38	82	28
22 Clydebank	42	6	8	28	34	103	20

Scottish Second Division

	P	W	D	L	F	A	Pts
1 Alloa	38	26	8	4	81	32	60
2 Cowdenbeath	38	19	9	10	56	30	47
3 Armadale	38	20	5	13	64	49	45
4 Vale of Leven	38	17	10	11	56	43	44
5 Bathgate	38	16	11	11	56	41	43
6 Bo'ness	38	16	7	15	57	49	39
7 Broxburn	38	14	11	13	43	43	39
8 Dunfermline	38	14	10	14	56	42	38
9 St Bernard's	38	15	8	15	50	49	38
10 Stenhousemuir	38	14	10	14	50	51	38
11 Johnstone	38	14	10	14	46	59	38
12 East Fife	38	15	7	16	55	54	37
13 St Johnstone	38	12	11	15	41	52	35
14 Forfar	38	11	12	15	44	53	34
15 E Stirlingshire	38	12	10	16	43	60	34
16 Arbroath	38	11	11	16	45	56	33
17 King's Park	38	10	12	16	47	65	32
18 Lochgelly Utd	38	11	9	18	46	56	31

19 Dundee Hibs	38	10	8	20	47	65	28
20 Clackmannan	38	10	7	21	41	75	27

FA Cup

Third Round

Millwall Athletic v Swansea Town	4-0
Blackburn Rovers v Huddersfield Town	1-1, 0-5
Stoke v Aston Villa	0-0, 0-4
West Bromwich Albion v Notts County	1-1, 0-2
Arsenal v Leicester City	3-0
Barnsley v Preston North End	1-1, 0-3
Cardiff City v Nottingham Forest	4-1
Tottenham Hotspur v Manchester City	2-1

Fourth Round

Huddersfield Town v Millwall Athletic	3-0
Notts County v Aston Villa	2-2, 4-3
Arsenal v Preston North End	1-1, 1-2
Cardiff City v Tottenham Hotspur	1-1, 1-2

Semi-Final

Huddersfield Town v Notts County	3-1
Preston North End v Tottenham Hotspur	2-1

Final at Stamford Bridge

Huddersfield Town v Preston North End	1-0

Scottish FA Cup

Third Round

Aberdeen v Dundee	3-0
Morton v Clyde	4-1
Celtic v Hamilton Academicals	1-3
Motherwell v Alloa Athletic	1-0
Partick Thistle v Bathgate	3-0
Queen of the South v East Stirlingshire	2-0
Heart of Midlothian v Rangers	0-4
St Mirren v Airdrieonians	3-0

Fourth Round

Hamilton Academicals v Aberdeen	0-0, 0-2
Motherwell v Morton	1-2
Partick Thistle v Queen of the South	1-0
Rangers v St Mirren	1-1, 2-0

Semi-Final

Morton v Aberdeen	3-1
Rangers v Partick Thistle	2-0

Final at Hampden Park

Morton v Rangers	1-0

1922–23
First Division

	P	W	D	L	F	A	Pts
1 Liverpool	42	26	8	8	70	31	60
2 Sunderland	42	22	10	10	72	54	54
3 Huddersfield	42	21	11	10	60	32	53
4 Newcastle	42	18	12	12	45	37	48
5 Everton	42	20	7	15	63	59	47
6 Aston Villa	42	18	10	14	64	51	46
7 WBA	42	17	11	14	58	49	45
8 Man City	42	17	11	14	50	49	45
9 Cardiff	42	18	7	17	73	59	43
10 Sheff United	42	16	10	16	68	64	42
11 Arsenal	42	16	10	16	61	62	42
12 Tottenham	42	17	7	18	50	50	41
13 Bolton	42	14	12	16	50	58	40
14 Blackburn	42	14	12	16	47	62	40
15 Burnley	42	16	6	20	58	59	38
16 Preston	42	13	11	18	60	64	37
17 Birmingham	42	13	11	18	41	57	37
18 Middlesbrough	42	13	10	19	57	63	36
19 Chelsea	42	9	18	15	45	53	36
20 Nottm Forest	42	13	8	21	41	70	34
21 Stoke	42	10	10	22	47	67	30
22 Oldham	42	10	10	22	35	65	30

Second Division

	P	W	D	L	F	A	Pts
1 Notts County	42	23	7	12	46	34	53
2 West Ham	42	20	11	11	63	38	51
3 Leicester	42	21	9	12	65	44	51
4 Man United	42	17	14	11	51	36	48
5 Blackpool	42	18	11	13	60	43	47
6 Bury	42	18	11	13	55	46	47
7 Leeds	42	18	11	13	43	36	47
8 Wednesday	42	17	12	13	54	47	46
9 Barnsley	42	17	11	14	62	51	45
10 Fulham	42	16	12	14	43	32	44
11 Southampton	42	14	14	14	40	40	42
12 Hull	42	14	14	14	43	45	42
13 South Shields	42	15	10	17	35	44	40
14 Derby	42	14	11	17	46	50	39

15 Bradford City	42	12	13	17	41	45	37
16 Crystal Palace	42	13	11	18	54	62	37
17 Port Vale	42	14	9	19	39	51	37
18 Coventry	42	15	7	20	46	63	37
19 Clapton Orient	42	12	12	18	40	50	36
20 Stockport	42	14	8	20	43	58	36
21 Rotherham Co	42	13	9	20	44	63	35
22 Wolves	42	9	9	24	42	77	27

Third Division (North)

	P	W	D	L	F	A	Pts
1 Nelson	38	24	3	11	61	41	51
2 Bradford PA	38	19	9	10	67	38	47
3 Walsall	38	19	8	11	51	44	46
4 Chesterfield	38	19	7	12	68	52	45
5 Wigan Borough	38	18	8	12	64	39	44
6 Crewe	38	17	9	12	48	38	43
7 Halifax	38	17	7	14	53	46	41
8 Accrington	38	17	7	14	59	65	41
9 Darlington	38	15	10	13	59	46	40
10 Wrexham	38	14	10	14	38	48	38
11 Stalybridge Cel	38	15	6	17	42	47	36
12 Rochdale	38	13	10	15	42	53	36
13 Lincoln	38	13	10	15	39	55	36
14 Grimsby	38	14	5	19	55	52	33
15 Hartlepools	38	10	12	16	48	54	32
16 Tranmere	38	12	8	18	49	59	32
17 Southport	38	12	7	19	32	46	31
18 Barrow	38	13	4	21	50	60	30
19 Ashington	38	11	8	19	51	77	30
20 Durham City	38	9	10	19	43	59	28

Third Division (South)

	P	W	D	L	F	A	Pts
1 Bristol City	42	24	11	7	66	40	59
2 Plymouth	42	23	7	12	61	29	53
3 Swansea	42	22	9	11	78	45	53
4 Brighton	42	20	11	11	52	34	51
5 Luton	42	21	7	14	68	49	49
6 Portsmouth	42	19	8	15	58	52	46
7 Millwall Ath	42	14	18	10	45	40	46
8 Northampton	42	17	11	14	54	44	45
9 Swindon	42	17	11	14	62	56	45
10 Watford	42	17	10	15	57	54	44
11 QPR	42	16	10	16	54	49	42
12 Charlton	42	14	14	14	55	51	42
13 Bristol Rovers	42	13	16	13	35	36	42
14 Brentford	42	13	12	17	41	51	38
15 Southend	42	12	13	17	49	54	37
16 Gillingham	42	15	7	20	51	59	37
17 Merthyr Town	42	11	14	17	39	48	36

18 Norwich	42	13	10	19	51	71	36
19 Reading	42	10	14	18	36	55	34
20 Exeter	42	13	7	22	47	84	33
21 Aberdare Ath	42	9	11	22	42	70	29
22 Newport	42	8	11	23	40	70	27

Scottish First Division

	P	W	D	L	F	A	Pts
1 Rangers	38	23	9	6	67	29	55
2 Airdrieonians	38	20	10	8	58	38	50
3 Celtic	38	19	8	11	52	39	46
4 Falkirk	38	14	17	7	44	32	45
5 Aberdeen	38	15	12	11	46	34	42
6 St Mirren	38	15	12	11	54	44	42
7 Dundee	38	17	7	14	51	45	41
8 Hibernian	38	17	7	14	45	40	41
9 Raith	38	13	13	12	31	43	39
10 Ayr	38	13	12	13	43	44	38
11 Partick	38	14	9	15	51	48	37
12 Hearts	38	11	15	12	51	50	37
13 Motherwell	38	13	10	15	59	60	36
14 Morton	38	12	11	15	44	47	35
15 Kilmarnock	38	14	7	17	57	66	35
16 Clyde	38	12	9	17	36	44	33
17 Third Lanark	38	11	8	19	40	59	30
18 Hamilton	38	11	7	20	43	59	29
19 Albion	38	8	10	20	38	64	26
20 Alloa	38	6	11	21	27	52	23

Scottish Second Division

	P	W	D	L	F	A	Pts
1 Queen's Park	38	24	9	5	73	31	57
2 Clydebank	38	21	10	7	69	29	52
3 St Johnstone*	38	19	12	7	60	39	48
4 Dumbarton	38	17	8	13	61	40	42
5 Bathgate	38	16	9	13	67	55	41
6 Armadale	38	15	11	12	63	52	41
7 Bo'ness	38	12	17	9	48	46	41
8 Broxburn	38	14	12	12	40	43	40
9 East Fife	38	16	7	15	48	42	39
10 Lochgelly	38	16	5	17	41	64	37
11 Cowdenbeath*	38	16	6	16	56	52	36
12 King's Park	38	14	6	18	46	60	34
13 Dunfermline	38	11	11	16	47	44	33
14 Stenhousemuir	38	13	7	18	53	67	33
15 Forfar	38	13	7	18	51	73	33
16 Johnstone	38	13	6	19	41	62	32
17 Vale of Leven	38	11	8	19	50	59	30
18 St Bernard's*	38	8	15	15	39	50	29
19 E Stirlingshire	38	10	8	20	48	69	28

20 Arbroath   38   8 12 18 45 69 28
*Two points deducted for fielding an
ineligible player

FA Cup

Third Round
Huddersfield Town v Bolton Wanderers
                                1-1, 0-1
Charlton Athletic v West Bromwich
    Albion   1-0
Liverpool v Sheffield United   1-2
Queen's Park Rangers v South Shields 3-0
Bury v Southampton   0-0, 0-1
West Ham United v Plymouth Argyle
                                    2-0
Derby County v The Wednesday   1-0
Cardiff City v Tottenham Hotspur   2-3

Fourth Round
Charlton Athletic v Bolton Wanderers 0-1
Queen's Park Rangers v Sheffield United
                                    0-1
Southampton v West Ham United
                          1-1, 1-1, 0-1
Tottenham Hotspur v Derby County 0-1

Semi-Final
Bolton Wanderers v Sheffield United 1-0
West Ham United v Derby County   5-2

Final
Bolton Wanderers v West Ham United
                                    2-0

Scottish FA Cup

Third Round
Aberdeen v Peterhead   13-0
Bo'ness v Nithsdale Wanderers   2-0
Celtic v East Fife   2-1
Dundee v Hamilton Academicals 0-0, 1-0
Hibernian v Queen's Park   2-0
Motherwell v Falkirk   3-0
Dunfermline Athletic v Raith Rovers 0-3
Third Lanark v Ayr United   2-0

Fourth Round
Celtic v Raith Rovers   1-0
Hibernian v Aberdeen   2-0
Motherwell v Bo'ness   4-2
Dundee v Third Lanark   0-0, 1-1, 0-1

Semi-Final
Celtic v Motherwell   2-0
Hibernian v Third Lanark   1-0

Final at Hampden Park
Celtic v Hibernian   1-0

1923-24
First Division

	P	W	D	L	F	A	Pts
1 Huddersfield	42	23	11	8	60	33	57
2 Cardiff	42	22	13	7	61	34	57
3 Sunderland	42	22	9	11	71	54	53
4 Bolton	42	18	14	10	68	34	50
5 Sheff United	42	19	12	11	69	49	50
6 Aston Villa	42	18	13	11	52	37	49
7 Everton	42	18	13	11	62	53	49
8 Blackburn	42	17	11	14	54	50	45
9 Newcastle	42	17	10	15	60	54	44
10 Notts County	42	14	14	14	44	49	42
11 Man City	42	15	12	15	54	71	42
12 Liverpool	42	15	11	16	49	48	41
13 West Ham	42	13	15	14	40	43	41
14 Birmingham	42	13	13	16	41	49	39
15 Tottenham	42	12	14	16	50	56	38
16 WBA	42	12	14	16	51	62	38
17 Burnley	42	12	12	18	55	60	36
18 Preston	42	12	10	20	52	67	34
19 Arsenal	42	12	9	21	40	63	33
20 Nottm Forest	42	10	12	20	42	64	32
21 Chelsea	42	9	14	19	31	53	32
22 Middlesbrough	42	7	8	27	37	60	22

Second Division

	P	W	D	L	F	A	Pts
1 Leeds	42	21	12	9	61	35	54
2 Bury	42	21	9	12	63	35	51
3 Derby	42	21	9	12	75	42	51
4 Blackpool	42	18	13	11	72	47	49
5 Southampton	42	17	14	11	52	31	48
6 Stoke	42	14	18	10	44	42	46
7 Oldham	42	14	17	11	45	52	45
8 Wednesday	42	16	12	14	54	51	44
9 South Shields	42	17	10	15	49	50	44
10 Clapton Orient	42	14	15	13	40	36	43
11 Barnsley	42	16	11	15	57	61	43
12 Leicester	42	17	8	17	64	54	42
13 Stockport	42	13	16	13	44	52	42

	P	W	D	L	F	A	Pts
14 Man United	42	13	14	15	52	44	40
15 Crystal Palace	42	13	13	16	53	65	39
16 Port Vale	42	13	12	17	50	66	38
17 Hull	42	10	17	15	46	51	37
18 Bradford City	42	11	15	16	35	48	37
19 Coventry	42	11	13	18	52	68	35
20 Fulham	42	10	14	18	45	56	34
21 Nelson	42	10	13	19	40	74	33
22 Bristol City	42	7	15	20	32	65	29

	P	W	D	L	F	A	Pts
14 Charlton	42	11	15	16	38	45	37
15 Gillingham	42	12	13	17	43	58	37
16 Exeter	42	15	7	20	37	52	37
17 Brentford	42	14	8	20	54	71	36
18 Reading	42	13	9	20	51	57	35
19 Southend	42	12	10	20	53	84	34
20 Watford	42	9	15	18	45	54	33
21 Bournemouth	42	11	11	20	40	65	33
22 QPR	42	11	9	22	37	77	31

Third Division (North)

	P	W	D	L	F	A	Pts
1 Wolves	42	24	15	3	76	27	63
2 Rochdale	42	25	12	5	60	26	62
3 Chesterfield	42	22	10	10	70	39	54
4 Rotherham Co	42	23	6	13	70	43	52
5 Bradford PA	42	21	10	11	69	43	52
6 Darlington	42	20	8	14	70	53	48
7 Southport	42	16	14	12	44	42	46
8 Ashington	42	18	8	16	59	61	44
9 Doncaster	42	15	12	15	59	53	42
10 Wigan Borough	42	14	14	14	55	53	42
11 Grimsby	42	14	13	15	49	47	41
12 Tranmere	42	13	15	14	51	60	41
13 Accrington	42	16	8	18	48	61	40
14 Halifax	42	15	10	17	42	59	40
15 Durham City	42	15	9	18	59	60	39
16 Wrexham	42	10	18	14	37	44	38
17 Walsall	42	14	8	20	44	59	36
18 New Brighton	42	11	13	18	40	53	35
19 Lincoln	42	10	12	20	48	59	32
20 Crewe	42	7	13	22	32	58	27
21 Hartlepools	42	7	11	24	33	70	25
22 Barrow	42	8	9	25	35	80	25

Third Division (South)

	P	W	D	L	F	A	Pts
1 Portsmouth	42	24	11	7	87	30	59
2 Plymouth	42	23	9	10	70	34	55
3 Millwall Ath	42	22	10	10	64	38	54
4 Swansea	42	22	8	12	60	48	52
5 Brighton	42	21	9	12	68	37	51
6 Swindon	42	17	13	12	58	44	47
7 Luton	42	16	14	12	50	44	46
8 Northampton	42	17	11	14	64	47	45
9 Bristol Rovers	42	15	13	14	52	46	43
10 Newport	42	17	9	16	56	64	43
11 Norwich	42	16	8	18	60	59	40
12 Aberdare Ath	42	12	14	16	45	58	38
13 Merthyr Town	42	11	16	15	45	65	38

Scottish First Division

	P	W	D	L	F	A	Pts
1 Rangers	38	25	9	4	72	22	59
2 Airdrieonians	38	20	10	8	72	46	50
3 Celtic	38	17	12	9	56	33	46
4 Raith	38	18	7	13	56	38	43
5 Dundee	38	15	13	10	70	57	43
6 St Mirren	38	15	12	11	53	45	42
7 Hibernian	38	15	11	12	66	52	41
8 Partick	38	15	9	14	58	55	39
9 Hearts	38	14	10	14	61	50	38
10 Motherwell	38	15	7	16	58	63	37
11 Morton	38	16	5	17	48	54	37
12 Hamilton	38	15	6	17	52	57	36
13 Aberdeen	38	13	10	15	37	41	36
14 Ayr	38	12	10	16	38	60	34
15 Falkirk	38	13	6	19	46	53	32
16 Kilmarnock	38	12	8	18	48	65	32
17 Queen's Park	38	11	9	18	43	60	31
18 Third Lanark	38	11	8	19	54	78	30
19 Clyde	38	10	9	19	40	70	29
20 Clydebank	38	10	5	23	42	71	25

Scottish Second Division

	P	W	D	L	F	A	Pts
1 St Johnstone	38	22	12	4	79	33	56
2 Cowdenbeath	38	23	9	6	78	33	55
3 Bathgate	38	16	12	10	58	49	44
4 Stenhousemuir	38	16	11	11	58	45	43
5 Albion	38	15	12	11	67	53	42
6 King's Park	38	16	10	12	67	56	42
7 Dunfermline	38	14	11	13	52	45	39
8 Johnstone	38	16	7	15	60	56	39
9 Dundee United	38	12	15	11	41	41	39
10 Dumbarton	38	17	5	16	55	58	39
11 Armadale	38	16	6	16	56	63	38
12 Bo'ness	38	13	11	14	45	52	37
13 East Fife	38	14	9	15	54	47	37
14 Forfar	38	14	7	17	43	68	35
15 Broxburn	38	13	8	17	50	56	34

16 Alloa	38	14	6	18	44	53	34
17 Arbroath	38	12	8	18	49	51	32
18 St Bernard's	38	11	10	17	49	54	32
19 Vale of Leven	38	11	9	18	41	67	31
20 Lochgelly	38	4	4	30	20	86	12

FA Cup

Third Round

Watford v Newcastle United	0-1
Southampton v Liverpool	0-0, 0-2
Brighton v Manchester City	1-5
Cardiff City v Bristol City	3-0
Aston Villa v Leeds United	3-0
West Bromwich Albion v Wolver- hampton Wanderers	1-1, 2-0
Crystal Palace v Swindon Town	1-2
Burnley v Huddersfield Town	1-0

Fourth Round

Newcastle United v Liverpool	1-0
Manchester City v Cardiff City	0-0, 1-0
West Bromwich Albion v Aston Villa	0-2
Swindon Town v Burnley	1-1, 1-3

Semi-Final

Newcastle United v Manchester City	2-0
Aston Villa v Burnley	3-0

Final

Newcastle United v Aston Villa	2-0

Scottish FA Cup

Third Round

Motherwell v Airdrieonians	0-5
Clydebank v Ayr United	2-3
Falkirk v Queen's Park	0-0, 2-0
Heart of Midlothian v Clyde	3-1
Aberdeen v East Stirlingshire	2-0
Raith Rovers v St Bernard's	0-1
Rangers v Hibernian	1-2
Partick Thistle v Hamilton Academicals	1-1, 2-1

Fourth Round

Airdrieonians v Ayr United	1-1, 0-0, 1-0
Heart of Midlothian v Falkirk	1-2
Aberdeen v St Bernard's	3-0
Hibernian v Partick Thistle	2-2, 1-1, 2-1

Semi-Final

Airdrieonians v Falkirk	2-1
Aberdeen v Hibernian	0-0, 0-0, 0-1

Final at Ibrox Park

Airdrieonians v Hibernian	2-0

1924–25
First Division

	P	W	D	L	F	A	Pts
1 Huddersfield	42	21	16	5	69	28	58
2 WBA	42	23	10	9	58	34	56
3 Bolton	42	22	11	9	76	34	55
4 Liverpool	42	20	10	12	63	55	50
5 Bury	42	17	15	10	54	51	49
6 Newcastle	42	16	16	10	61	42	48
7 Sunderland	42	19	10	13	64	51	48
8 Birmingham	42	17	12	13	49	53	46
9 Notts County	42	16	13	13	42	31	45
10 Man City	42	17	9	16	76	68	43
11 Cardiff	42	16	11	15	56	51	43
12 Tottenham	42	15	12	15	52	43	42
13 West Ham	42	15	12	15	62	60	42
14 Sheff United	42	13	13	16	55	63	39
15 Aston Villa	42	13	13	16	58	71	39
16 Blackburn	42	11	13	18	53	66	35
17 Everton	42	12	11	19	40	60	35
18 Leeds	42	11	12	19	46	59	34
19 Burnley	42	11	12	19	46	75	34
20 Arsenal	42	14	5	23	46	58	33
21 Preston	42	10	6	26	37	74	26
22 Nottm Forest	42	6	12	24	29	65	24

Second Division

	P	W	D	L	F	A	Pts
1 Leicester	42	24	11	7	90	32	59
2 Man United	42	23	11	8	57	23	57
3 Derby	42	22	11	9	71	36	55
4 Portsmouth	42	15	18	9	58	50	48
5 Chelsea	42	16	15	11	51	37	47
6 Wolves	42	20	6	16	55	51	46
7 Southampton	42	13	18	11	40	36	44
8 Port Vale	42	17	8	17	48	56	42
9 South Shields	42	12	17	13	42	38	41
10 Hull	42	15	11	16	50	49	41
11 Clapton Orient	42	14	12	16	42	42	40
12 Fulham	42	15	10	17	41	56	40
13 Middlesbrough	42	10	19	13	36	44	39
14 Wednesday	42	15	8	19	50	56	38
15 Barnsley	42	13	12	17	46	59	38
16 Bradford City	42	13	12	17	37	50	38
17 Blackpool	42	14	9	19	65	61	37

18 Oldham	42 13 11 18 35 51 37
19 Stockport	42 13 11 18 37 57 37
20 Stoke	42 12 11 19 34 46 35
21 Crystal Palace	42 12 10 20 38 54 34
22 Coventry	42 11 9 22 45 84 31

Third Division (North)

	P W D L F A Pts
1 Darlington	42 24 10 8 78 33 58
2 Nelson	42 23 7 12 79 50 53
3 New Brighton	42 23 7 12 75 50 53
4 Southport	42 22 7 13 59 37 51
5 Bradford PA	42 19 12 11 84 42 50
6 Rochdale	42 21 7 14 75 53 49
7 Chesterfield	42 17 11 14 60 44 45
8 Lincoln	42 18 8 16 53 58 44
9 Halifax	42 16 11 15 56 52 43
10 Ashington	42 16 10 16 68 76 42
11 Wigan Borough	42 15 11 16 62 65 41
12 Grimsby	42 15 9 18 60 60 39
13 Durham City	42 13 13 16 50 68 39
14 Barrow	42 16 7 19 51 74 39
15 Crewe	42 13 13 16 53 78 39
16 Wrexham	42 15 8 19 53 61 38
17 Accrington	42 15 8 19 60 72 38
18 Doncaster	42 14 10 18 54 65 38
19 Walsall	42 13 11 18 44 53 37
20 Hartlepools	42 12 11 19 45 63 35
21 Tranmere	42 14 4 24 59 78 32
22 Rotherham Co	42 7 7 28 42 88 21

Third Division (South)

	P W D L F A Pts
1 Swansea	42 23 11 8 68 35 57
2 Plymouth	42 23 10 9 77 38 56
3 Bristol City	42 22 9 11 60 41 53
4 Swindon	42 20 11 11 66 38 51
5 Millwall Ath	42 18 13 11 58 38 49
6 Newport	42 20 9 13 62 42 49
7 Exeter	42 19 9 14 59 48 47
8 Brighton	42 19 8 15 59 45 46
9 Northampton	42 20 6 16 51 44 46
10 Southend	42 19 5 18 51 61 43
11 Watford	42 17 9 16 38 47 43
12 Norwich	42 14 13 15 53 51 41
13 Gillingham	42 13 14 15 35 44 40
14 Reading	42 14 10 18 37 38 38
15 Charlton	42 13 12 17 46 48 38
16 Luton	42 10 17 15 49 57 37
17 Bristol Rovers	42 12 13 17 42 49 37

18 Aberdare Ath	42 14 9 19 54 67 37
19 QPR	42 14 8 20 42 63 36
20 Bournemouth	42 13 8 21 40 58 34
21 Brentford	42 9 7 26 38 91 25
22 Merthyr Town	42 8 5 29 35 77 21

Scottish First Division

	P W D L F A Pts
1 Rangers	38 25 10 3 77 27 60
2 Airdrieonians	38 25 7 6 85 31 57
3 Hibernian	38 22 8 8 78 43 52
4 Celtic	38 18 8 12 76 43 44
5 Cowdenbeath	38 16 10 12 76 65 42
6 St Mirren	38 18 4 16 65 63 40
7 Partick	38 14 10 14 60 61 38
8 Dundee	38 14 8 16 48 55 36
9 Raith	38 14 8 16 52 60 36
10 Hearts	38 12 11 15 65 69 35
11 St Johnstone	38 12 11 15 56 71 35
12 Kilmarnock	38 12 9 17 53 64 33
13 Hamilton	38 15 3 20 50 63 33
14 Morton	38 12 9 17 46 69 33
15 Aberdeen	38 11 10 17 46 56 32
16 Falkirk	38 12 8 18 44 54 32
17 Queen's Park	38 12 8 18 50 71 32
18 Motherwell	38 10 10 18 55 64 30
19 Ayr	38 11 8 19 43 65 30
20 Third Lanark	38 11 8 19 53 84 30

Scottish Second Division

	P W D L F A Pts
1 Dundee United	38 20 10 8 58 44 50
2 Clydebank	38 20 8 10 65 42 48
3 Clyde	38 20 7 11 72 39 47
4 Alloa	38 17 11 10 57 33 45
5 Arbroath	38 16 10 12 47 46 42
6 Bo'ness	38 16 9 13 71 48 41
7 Broxburn	38 16 9 13 48 54 41
8 Dumbarton	38 15 10 13 45 44 40
9 East Fife	38 17 5 16 66 58 39
10 King's Park	38 15 8 15 54 46 38
11 Stenhousemuir	38 15 7 16 51 58 37
12 Arthurlie	38 14 8 16 56 60 36
13 Dunfermline	38 14 7 17 62 57 35
14 Armadale	38 15 5 18 55 62 35
15 Albion	38 15 5 18 46 61 35
16 Bathgate	38 12 10 16 58 74 34
17 St Bernard's	38 14 4 20 52 70 32
18 E Stirlingshire	38 11 8 19 58 72 30
19 Johnstone	38 12 4 22 53 85 28

20 Forfar   38 10 7 21 46 67 27

FA Cup

Third Round
Notts County v Cardiff City	0-2
Hull City v Leicester City	1-1, 1-3
West Ham United v Blackpool	1-1, 0-3
Tottenham Hotspur v Blackburn Rovers	2-2, 1-3
Southampton v Bradford City	2-0
Liverpool v Birmingham	2-1
West Bromwich Albion v Aston Villa	1-1, 2-1
Sheffield United v Everton	1-0

Fourth Round
Cardiff City v Leicester City	2-1
Blackburn Rovers v Blackpool	1-0
Southampton v Liverpool	1-0
Sheffield United v West Bromwich Albion	2-0

Semi-Final
Cardiff City v Blackburn Rovers	3-1
Sheffield United v Southampton	2-0

Final
Sheffield United v Cardiff City	1-0

Scottish FA Cup

Third Round
Celtic v Solway Star	2-0
St Mirren v Partick Thistle	2-0
Rangers v Arbroath	5-3
Kilmarnock v Dykehead	5-3
Dundee v Airdrieonians	3-1
Broxburn United v Falkirk	2-1
Hamilton Academicals v Raith Rovers	1-0
Aberdeen v Motherwell	0-0, 2-1

Fourth Round
St Mirren v Celtic	0-0, 1-1, 0-1
Kilmarnock v Rangers	1-2
Dundee v Broxburn United	1-0
Aberdeen v Hamilton Academicals	0-2

Semi-Final
Celtic v Rangers	5-0
Dundee v Hamilton Academicals	1-1, 2-0

Final
Celtic v Dundee	2-1

1925-26
First Division

	P	W	D	L	F	A	Pts
1 Huddersfield	42	23	11	8	92	60	57
2 Arsenal	42	22	8	12	87	63	52
3 Sunderland	42	21	6	15	96	80	48
4 Bury	42	20	7	15	85	77	47
5 Sheff United	42	19	8	15	102	82	46
6 Aston Villa	42	16	12	14	86	76	44
7 Liverpool	42	14	16	12	70	63	44
8 Bolton	42	17	10	15	75	76	44
9 Man United	42	19	6	17	66	73	44
10 Newcastle	42	16	10	16	84	75	42
11 Everton	42	12	18	12	72	70	42
12 Blackburn	42	15	11	16	91	80	41
13 WBA	42	16	8	18	79	78	40
14 Birmingham	42	16	8	18	66	81	40
15 Tottenham	42	15	9	18	66	79	39
16 Cardiff	42	16	7	19	61	76	39
17 Leicester	42	14	10	18	70	80	38
18 West Ham	42	15	7	20	63	76	37
19 Leeds	42	14	8	20	64	76	36
20 Burnley	42	13	10	19	85	108	36
21 Man City	42	12	11	19	89	100	35
22 Notts County	42	13	7	22	54	74	33

Second Division

	P	W	D	L	F	A	Pts
1 Wednesday	42	27	6	9	88	48	60
2 Derby	42	25	7	10	77	42	57
3 Chelsea	42	19	14	9	76	49	52
4 Wolves	42	21	7	14	84	60	49
5 Swansea	42	19	11	12	77	57	49
6 Blackpool	42	17	11	14	76	69	45
7 Oldham	42	18	8	16	74	62	44
8 Port Vale	42	19	6	17	79	69	44
9 South Shields	42	18	8	16	74	65	44
10 Middlesbrough	42	21	2	19	77	68	44
11 Portsmouth	42	17	10	15	79	74	44
12 Preston	42	18	7	17	71	84	43
13 Hull	42	16	9	17	63	61	41
14 Southampton	42	15	8	19	63	63	38
15 Darlington	42	14	10	18	72	77	38
16 Bradford City	42	13	10	19	47	66	36
17 Nottm Forest	42	14	8	20	51	73	36
18 Barnsley	42	12	12	18	58	84	36
19 Fulham	42	11	12	19	46	77	34
20 Clapton Orient	42	12	9	21	50	65	33

21 Stoke	42	12	8	22	54	77	32
22 Stockport	42	8	9	25	51	97	25

Third Division (North)

	P	W	D	L	F	A	Pts
1 Grimsby	42	26	9	7	91	40	61
2 Bradford PA	42	26	8	8	101	43	60
3 Rochdale	42	27	5	10	104	58	59
4 Chesterfield	42	25	5	12	100	54	55
5 Halifax	42	17	11	14	53	50	45
6 Hartlepools	42	18	8	16	82	73	44
7 Tranmere	42	19	6	17	73	83	44
8 Nelson	42	16	11	15	89	71	43
9 Ashington	42	16	11	15	70	62	43
10 Doncaster	42	16	11	15	80	72	43
11 Crewe	42	17	9	16	63	61	43
12 New Brighton	42	17	8	17	69	67	42
13 Durham City	42	18	6	18	63	70	42
14 Rotherham	42	17	7	18	69	92	41
15 Lincoln	42	17	5	20	66	82	39
16 Coventry	42	16	6	20	73	82	38
17 Wigan Borough	42	13	11	18	68	74	37
18 Accrington	42	17	3	22	81	105	37
19 Wrexham	42	11	10	21	63	92	32
20 Southport	42	11	10	21	62	92	32
21 Walsall	42	10	6	26	58	107	26
22 Barrow	42	7	4	31	50	98	18

Third Division (South)

	P	W	D	L	F	A	Pts
1 Reading	42	23	11	8	77	52	57
2 Plymouth	42	24	8	10	107	67	56
3 Millwall	42	21	11	10	73	39	53
4 Bristol City	42	21	9	12	72	51	51
5 Brighton	42	19	9	14	84	73	47
6 Swindon	42	20	6	16	69	64	46
7 Luton	42	18	7	17	80	75	43
8 Bournemouth	42	17	9	16	75	91	43
9 Aberdare	42	17	8	17	74	66	42
10 Gillingham	42	17	8	17	53	49	42
11 Southend	42	19	4	19	78	73	42
12 Northampton	42	17	7	18	82	80	41
13 Crystal Palace	42	19	3	20	75	79	41
14 Merthyr Town	42	14	11	17	69	75	39
15 Watford	42	15	9	18	73	89	39
16 Norwich	42	15	9	18	58	73	39
17 Newport	42	14	10	18	64	74	38
18 Brentford	42	16	6	20	69	94	38
19 Bristol Rovers	42	15	6	21	66	69	36
20 Exeter	42	15	5	22	72	70	35

21 Charlton	42	11	13	18	48	68	35
22 QPR	42	6	9	27	37	84	21

Scottish First Division

	P	W	D	L	F	A	Pts
1 Celtic	38	25	8	5	97	40	58
2 Airdrieonians	38	23	4	11	95	54	50
3 Hearts	38	21	8	9	87	56	50
4 St Mirren	38	20	7	11	62	52	47
5 Motherwell	38	19	8	11	67	46	46
6 Rangers	38	19	6	13	79	55	44
7 Cowdenbeath	38	18	6	14	87	68	42
8 Falkirk	38	14	14	10	61	57	42
9 Kilmarnock	38	17	7	14	79	77	41
10 Dundee	38	14	9	15	47	59	37
11 Aberdeen	38	13	10	15	49	54	36
12 Hamilton	38	13	9	16	68	79	35
13 Queen's Park	38	15	4	19	70	81	34
14 Partick	38	10	13	15	64	73	33
15 Morton	38	12	7	19	57	84	31
16 Hibernian	38	12	6	20	72	77	30
17 Dundee United	38	11	6	21	52	74	28
18 St Johnstone	38	9	10	19	43	78	28
19 Raith	38	11	4	23	46	81	26
20 Clydebank	38	7	8	23	55	92	22

Scottish Second Division

	P	W	D	L	F	A	Pts
1 Dunfermline	38	26	7	5	109	43	59
2 Clyde	38	24	5	9	87	51	53
3 Ayr	38	20	12	6	77	39	52
4 East Fife	38	20	9	9	98	73	49
5 Stenhousemuir	38	19	10	9	74	52	48
6 Third Lanark	38	19	8	11	72	47	46
7 Arthurlie	38	17	5	16	81	75	39
8 Bo'ness	38	17	5	16	65	70	39
9 Albion	38	16	6	16	78	71	38
10 Arbroath	38	17	4	17	80	73	38
11 Dumbarton	38	14	10	14	54	78	38
12 Nithsdale	38	15	7	16	79	82	37
13 King's Park	38	14	9	15	67	73	37
14 St Bernard's	38	15	5	18	86	82	35
15 Armadale	38	14	5	19	82	101	33
16 Alloa	38	11	8	19	54	63	30
17 Queen of the S	38	10	8	20	64	88	28
18 E Stirlingshire	38	10	7	21	59	89	27
19 Bathgate	38	7	6	25	60	105	20
20 Broxburn	38	4	6	28	55	126	14

FA Cup

Fourth Round

Bournemouth v Bolton Wanderers	
	2-2, 2-6
South Shields v Birmingham	2-1
Nottingham Forest v Swindon Town	2-0
Southend United v Derby County	4-1
Swansea Town v Stoke City	6-3
Bury v Millwall	3-3, 0-2
Arsenal v Blackburn Rovers	3-1
West Bromwich Albion v Aston Villa	1-2
Manchester City v Huddersfield Town	4-0
Crystal Palace v Chelsea	2-1
Clapton Orient v Middlesbrough	4-2
Cardiff City v Newcastle United	0-2
Tottenham Hotspur v Manchester United	
	2-2, 0-2
Sheffield United v Sunderland	1-2
Fulham v Liverpool	3-1
Notts County v New Brighton	2-0

Fifth Round

Bolton Wanderers v South Shields	3-0
Southend United v Nottingham Forest	0-1
Millwall v Swansea Town	0-1
Aston Villa v Arsenal	1-1, 0-2
Manchester City v Crystal Palace	11-4
Clapton Orient v Newcastle United	2-0
Sunderland v Manchester United	3-3, 1-2
Notts County v Fulham	0-1

Sixth Round

Nottingham Forest v Bolton Wanderers	
	2-2, 0-0, 0-1
Swansea Town v Arsenal	2-1
Clapton Orient v Manchester City	1-6
Fulham v Manchester United	1-2

Semi-Final

Bolton Wanderers v Swansea Town	3-0
Manchester City v Manchester United	
	3-0

Final

Bolton Wanderers v Manchester City	1-0

Scottish FA Cup

Third Round

St Mirren v Partick Thistle	2-1
Bathgate v Airdrieonians	2-5
Falkirk v Rangers	0-2
Morton v Albion Rovers	1-0
Heart of Midlothian v Celtic	0-4
Dumbarton v Clyde	3-0
Aberdeen v St Johnstone	2-2, 1-0
Third Lanark v Brechin City	4-0

Fourth Round

St Mirren v Airdrieonians	2-0
Morton v Rangers	0-4
Celtic v Dumbarton	6-1
Third Lanark v Aberdeen	1-1, 0-3

Semi-Final

St Mirren v Rangers	1-0
Celtic v Aberdeen	1-0

Final

St Mirren v Celtic	2-0

1926-27
First Division

	P	W	D	L	F	A	Pts
1 Newcastle	42	25	6	11	96	58	56
2 Huddersfield	42	17	17	8	76	60	51
3 Sunderland	42	21	7	14	98	70	49
4 Bolton	42	19	10	13	84	62	48
5 Burnley	42	19	9	14	91	80	47
6 West Ham	42	19	8	15	86	70	46
7 Leicester	42	17	12	13	85	70	46
8 Sheff United	42	17	10	15	74	86	44
9 Liverpool	42	18	7	17	69	61	43
10 Aston Villa	42	18	7	17	81	83	43
11 Arsenal	42	17	9	16	77	86	43
12 Derby	42	17	7	18	86	73	41
13 Tottenham	42	16	9	17	76	78	41
14 Cardiff	42	16	9	17	55	65	41
15 Man United	42	13	14	15	52	64	40
16 Wednesday	42	15	9	18	75	92	39
17 Birmingham	42	17	4	21	64	73	38
18 Blackburn	42	15	8	19	77	96	38
19 Bury	42	12	12	18	68	77	36
20 Everton	42	12	10	20	64	90	34
21 Leeds	42	11	8	23	69	88	30
22 WBA	42	11	8	23	65	86	30

Second Division

	P	W	D	L	F	A	Pts
1 Middlesbrough	42	27	8	7	122	60	62
2 Portsmouth	42	23	8	11	87	49	54
3 Man City	42	22	10	10	108	61	54

	P	W	D	L	F	A	Pts
4 Chelsea	42	20	12	10	62	52	52
5 Nottm Forest	42	18	14	10	80	55	50
6 Preston	42	20	9	13	74	72	49
7 Hull	42	20	7	15	63	52	47
8 Port Vale	42	16	13	13	88	78	45
9 Blackpool	42	18	8	16	95	80	44
10 Oldham	42	19	6	17	74	84	44
11 Barnsley	42	17	9	16	88	87	43
12 Swansea	42	16	11	15	68	72	43
13 Southampton	42	15	12	15	60	62	42
14 Reading	42	16	8	18	64	72	40
15 Wolves	42	14	7	21	73	75	35
16 Notts County	42	15	5	22	70	96	35
17 Grimsby	42	11	12	19	74	91	34
18 Fulham	42	13	8	21	58	92	34
19 South Shields	42	11	11	20	71	96	33
20 Clapton Orient	42	12	7	23	60	96	31
21 Darlington	42	12	6	24	79	98	30
22 Bradford City	42	7	9	26	50	88	23

Third Division (North)

	P	W	D	L	F	A	Pts
1 Stoke	42	27	9	6	92	40	63
2 Rochdale	42	26	6	10	105	65	58
3 Bradford PA	42	24	7	11	101	59	55
4 Halifax	42	21	11	10	70	53	53
5 Nelson	42	22	7	13	104	75	51
6 Stockport*	42	22	7	13	93	69	49
7 Chesterfield	42	21	5	16	92	68	47
8 Doncaster	42	18	11	13	81	65	47
9 Tranmere	42	19	8	15	85	67	46
10 New Brighton	42	18	10	14	79	67	46
11 Lincoln	42	15	12	15	90	78	42
12 Southport	42	15	9	18	80	85	39
13 Wrexham	42	14	10	18	65	73	38
14 Walsall	42	14	10	18	68	81	38
15 Crewe	42	14	9	19	71	81	37
16 Ashington	42	12	12	18	60	90	36
17 Hartlepools	42	14	6	22	66	81	34
18 Wigan Borough	42	11	10	21	66	83	32
19 Rotherham	42	10	12	20	70	92	32
20 Durham City	42	12	6	24	58	105	30
21 Accrington	42	10	7	25	62	98	27
22 Barrow	42	7	8	27	34	117	22

*Two points deducted for fielding unregistered player

Third Division (South)

	P	W	D	L	F	A	Pts
1 Bristol City	42	27	8	7	104	54	62
2 Plymouth	42	25	10	7	95	61	60
3 Millwall	42	23	10	9	89	51	56
4 Brighton	42	21	11	10	79	50	53
5 Swindon	42	21	9	12	100	85	51
6 Crystal Palace	42	18	9	15	84	81	45
7 Bournemouth	42	18	8	16	78	66	44
8 Luton	42	15	14	13	68	66	44
9 Newport	42	19	6	17	57	71	44
10 Bristol Rovers	42	16	9	17	78	80	41
11 Brentford	42	13	14	15	70	61	40
12 Exeter	42	15	10	17	76	73	40
13 Charlton	42	16	8	18	60	61	40
14 QPR	42	15	9	18	65	71	39
15 Coventry	42	15	7	20	71	86	37
16 Norwich	42	12	11	19	59	71	35
17 Merthyr Town	42	13	9	20	63	80	35
18 Northampton	42	15	5	22	59	87	35
19 Southend	42	14	6	22	64	77	34
20 Gillingham	42	11	10	21	54	72	32
21 Watford	42	12	8	22	57	87	32
22 Aberdare Ath	42	9	7	26	62	101	25

Scottish First Division

	P	W	D	L	F	A	Pts
1 Rangers	38	23	10	5	85	41	56
2 Motherwell	38	23	5	10	81	52	51
3 Celtic	38	21	7	10	101	55	49
4 Airdrieonians	38	18	9	11	97	64	45
5 Dundee	38	17	9	12	77	51	43
6 Falkirk	38	16	10	12	77	60	42
7 Cowdenbeath	38	18	6	14	74	60	42
8 Aberdeen	38	13	14	11	73	72	40
9 Hibernian	38	16	7	15	62	71	39
10 St Mirren	38	16	5	17	78	76	37
11 Partick	38	15	6	17	89	74	36
12 Queen's Park	38	15	6	17	74	84	36
13 Hearts	38	12	11	15	65	64	35
14 St Johnstone	38	13	9	16	55	69	35
15 Hamilton	38	13	9	16	60	85	35
16 Kilmarnock	38	12	8	18	54	71	32
17 Clyde	38	10	9	19	54	85	29
18 Dunfermline	38	10	8	20	53	85	28
19 Morton	38	12	4	22	56	101	28
20 Dundee United	38	7	8	23	56	101	22

Scottish Second Division

	P	W	D	L	F	A	Pts
1 Bo'ness	38	23	10	5	86	41	56
2 Raith	38	21	7	10	92	52	49
3 Clydebank	38	18	9	11	94	75	45
4 Third Lanark	38	17	10	11	67	48	44

5 E Stirlingshire	38 18 8 12 93 75 44	
6 East Fife	38 19 4 15103 91 42	
7 Arthurlie	38 18 5 15 90 83 41	
8 Ayr	38 13 15 10 67 68 41	
9 Forfar	38 15 7 16 66 79 37	
10 Stenhousemuir	38 12 12 14 69 75 36	
11 Queen of the S	38 16 4 18 72 80 36	
12 King's Park	38 13 9 16 76 75 35	
13 St Bernard's	38 14 6 18 70 77 34	
14 Armadale	38 12 10 16 69 78 34	
15 Alloa	38 11 11 16 70 78 33	
16 Albion	38 11 11 16 74 87 33	
17 Bathgate	38 13 7 18 76 98 33	
18 Dumbarton	38 13 6 19 69 84 32	
19 Arbroath	38 13 6 19 64 82 32	
20 Nithsdale	38 7 9 22 59100 23	

FA Cup

Fourth Round

Chelsea v Accrington Stanley	7-2
Fulham v Burnley	0-4
Leeds United v Bolton Wanderers	0-0, 0-3
Darlington v Cardiff City	0-2
The Wednesday v South Shields	1-1, 0-1
Barnsley v Swansea Town	1-3
Reading v Portsmouth	3-1
West Ham United v Brentford	1-1, 0-2
Port Vale v Arsenal	2-2, 0-1
Liverpool v Southport	3-1
Wolverhampton Wanderers v Nottingham Forest	2-0
Hull City v Everton	1-1, 2-2, 3-2
Derby County v Millwall	0-2
Preston North End v Middlesbrough	0-3
Southampton v Birmingham	4-1
Corinthians v Newcastle United	1-3

Fifth Round

Chelsea v Burnley	2-1
Bolton Wanderers v Cardiff City	0-2
South Shields v Swansea Town	2-2, 1-2
Reading v Brentford	1-0
Arsenal v Liverpool	2-0
Wolverhampton Wanderers v Hull City	1-0
Millwall v Middlesbrough	3-2
Southampton v Newcastle United	2-1

Sixth Round

Chelsea v Cardiff City	0-0, 2-3
Swansea Town v Reading	1-3
Arsenal v Wolverhampton Wanderers	2-1

Millwall v Southampton	0-0, 0-2

Semi-Final

Cardiff City v Reading	3-0
Arsenal v Southampton	2-1

Final

Cardiff City v Arsenal	1-0

Scottish FA Cup

Third Round

Buckie Thistle v Bo'ness	0-3
Dundee v Celtic	2-4
Falkirk v Mid Annandale	3-0
Rangers v Hamilton Academicals	4-0
Alloa Athletic v Arthurlie	0-0, 0-3
East Fife v Dunfermline Athletic	2-0
Clyde v Patrick Thistle	0-1
Dundee United v Montrose	2-2, 3-1

Fourth Round

Bo'ness v Celtic	2-5
Falkirk v Rangers	2-2, 1-0
Arthurlie v East Fife	0-3
Partick Thistle v Dundee United	5-0

Semi-Final

Celtic v Falkirk	1-0
East Fife v Partick Thistle	2-1

Final

Celtic v East Fife	3-1

1927–28
First Division

	P W D L F A Pts
1 Everton	42 20 13 9102 66 53
2 Huddersfield	42 22 7 13 91 68 51
3 Leicester	42 18 12 12 96 72 48
4 Derby	42 17 10 15 96 83 44
5 Bury	42 20 4 18 80 80 44
6 Cardiff	42 17 10 15 70 80 44
7 Bolton	42 16 11 15 81 66 43
8 Aston Villa	42 17 9 16 78 73 43
9 Newcastle	42 15 13 14 79 81 43
10 Arsenal	42 13 15 14 82 86 41
11 Birmingham	42 13 15 14 70 75 41
12 Blackburn	42 16 9 17 66 78 41
13 Sheff United	42 15 10 17 79 86 40
14 Wednesday	42 13 13 16 81 78 39

15 Sunderland	42	15	9	18	74 76	39
16 Liverpool	42	13	13	16	84 87	39
17 West Ham	42	14	11	17	81 88	39
18 Man United	42	16	7	19	72 80	39
19 Burnley	42	16	7	19	82 98	39
20 Portsmouth	42	16	7	19	66 90	39
21 Tottenham	42	15	8	19	74 86	38
22 Middlesbrough	42	11	15	16	81 88	37

Second Division

	P	W	D	L	F	A	Pts
1 Man City	42	25	9	8	100	59	59
2 Leeds	42	25	7	10	98	49	57
3 Chelsea	42	23	8	11	75	45	54
4 Preston	42	22	9	11	100	66	53
5 Stoke	42	22	8	12	78	59	52
6 Swansea	42	18	12	12	75	63	48
7 Oldham	42	19	8	15	75	51	46
8 WBA	42	17	12	13	90	70	46
9 Port Vale	42	18	8	16	68	57	44
10 Nottm Forest	42	15	10	17	83	84	40
11 Grimsby	42	14	12	16	69	83	40
12 Bristol City	42	15	9	18	76	79	39
13 Hull	42	12	15	15	41	54	39
14 Barnsley	42	14	11	17	65	85	39
15 Notts County	42	13	12	17	68	74	38
16 Wolves	42	13	10	19	63	91	36
17 Southampton	42	14	7	21	68	77	35
18 Reading	42	11	13	18	53	75	35
19 Blackpool	42	13	8	21	83	101	34
20 Clapton Orient	42	11	12	19	55	85	34
21 Fulham	42	13	7	22	68	89	33
22 South Shields	42	7	9	26	56	111	23

Third Division (North)

	P	W	D	L	F	A	Pts
1 Bradford PA	42	27	9	6	101	45	63
2 Lincoln	42	24	7	11	91	64	55
3 Stockport	42	23	8	11	89	51	54
4 Doncaster	42	23	7	12	80	44	53
5 Tranmere	42	22	9	11	105	72	53
6 Bradford City	42	18	12	12	85	60	48
7 Darlington	42	21	5	16	89	74	47
8 Southport	42	20	5	17	79	70	45
9 Accrington	42	18	8	16	76	67	44
10 New Brighton	42	14	14	14	72	62	42
11 Wrexham	42	18	6	18	64	67	42
12 Halifax	42	13	15	14	73	71	41
13 Rochdale	42	17	7	18	74	77	41
14 Rotherham	42	14	11	17	65	69	39
15 Hartlepools	42	16	6	20	69	81	38

16 Chesterfield	42	13	10	19	71 78	36
17 Crewe	42	12	10	20	77 86	34
18 Ashington	42	11	11	20	77 103	33
19 Barrow	42	10	11	21	54 102	31
20 Wigan Borough	42	10	10	22	56 97	30
21 Durham City	42	11	7	24	53 100	29
22 Nelson	42	10	6	26	76 136	26

Third Division (South)

	P	W	D	L	F	A	Pts
1 Millwall	42	30	5	7	127	50	65
2 Northampton	42	23	9	10	102	64	55
3 Plymouth	42	23	7	12	85	54	53
4 Brighton	42	19	10	13	81	69	48
5 Crystal Palace	42	18	12	12	79	72	48
6 Swindon	42	19	9	14	90	69	47
7 Southend	42	20	6	16	80	64	46
8 Exeter	42	17	12	13	70	60	46
9 Newport	42	18	9	15	81	84	45
10 QPR	42	17	9	16	72	71	43
11 Charlton	42	15	13	14	60	70	43
12 Brentford	42	16	8	18	76	74	40
13 Luton	42	16	7	19	94	87	39
14 Bournemouth	42	13	12	17	72	79	38
15 Watford	42	14	10	18	68	78	38
16 Gillingham	42	13	11	18	62	81	37
17 Norwich	42	10	16	16	66	70	36
18 Walsall	42	12	9	21	75	101	33
19 Bristol Rovers	42	14	4	24	67	93	32
20 Coventry	42	11	9	22	67	96	31
21 Merthyr Town	42	9	13	20	53	91	31
22 Torquay	42	8	14	20	53	103	30

Scottish First Division

	P	W	D	L	F	A	Pts
1 Rangers	38	26	8	4	109	36	60
2 Celtic	38	23	9	6	93	39	55
3 Motherwell	38	23	9	6	92	46	55
4 Hearts	38	20	7	11	89	50	47
5 St Mirren	38	18	8	12	77	76	44
6 Partick	38	18	7	13	85	67	43
7 Aberdeen	38	20	5	13	71	61	43
8 Kilmarnock	38	15	10	13	68	78	40
9 Cowdenbeath	38	16	7	15	66	68	39
10 Falkirk	38	16	5	17	76	69	37
11 St Johnstone	38	14	8	16	66	67	36
12 Hibernian	38	13	9	16	73	75	35
13 Airdrieonians	38	12	11	15	59	69	35
14 Dundee	38	14	7	17	65	80	35
15 Clyde	38	10	11	17	46	72	31

	P	W	D	L	F	A	Pts
16 Queen's Park	38	12	6	20	69	80	30
17 Raith	38	11	7	20	60	89	29
18 Hamilton	38	11	6	21	67	86	28
19 Bo'ness	38	9	8	21	48	86	26
20 Dunfermline	38	4	4	30	41	126	12

Scottish Second Division

	P	W	D	L	F	A	Pts
1 Ayr	38	24	6	8	117	60	54
2 Third Lanark	38	18	9	11	99	66	45
3 King's Park	38	16	12	10	84	68	44
4 East Fife	38	18	7	13	87	73	43
5 Forfar	38	18	7	13	83	73	43
6 Dundee United	38	17	9	12	81	73	43
7 Arthurlie	38	18	4	16	84	90	40
8 Albion	38	17	4	17	79	69	38
9 E Stirlingshire	38	14	10	14	84	76	38
10 Arbroath	38	16	4	18	84	86	36
11 Dumbarton	38	16	4	18	66	72	36
12 Queen of the S	38	15	6	17	92	106	36
13 Leith	38	13	9	16	76	71	35
14 Clydebank	38	16	3	19	78	80	35
15 Alloa	38	12	11	15	72	76	35
16 Stenhousemuir	38	15	5	18	75	81	35
17 St Bernard's	38	15	5	18	75	101	35
18 Morton	38	13	8	17	65	82	34
19 Bathgate	38	10	11	17	62	81	31
20 Armadale	38	8	8	22	53	112	24

FA Cup

Fourth Round

Exeter City v Blackburn Rovers	2-2, 1-3
Port Vale v New Brighton	3-0
Bury v Manchester United	1-1, 0-1
Wrexham v Birmingham	1-3
Arsenal v Everton	4-3
Aston Villa v Crewe Alexandra	3-0
Sunderland v Manchester City	1-2
Stoke City v Bolton Wanderers	4-2
Huddersfield Town v West Ham United	2-1
Southport v Middlesbrough	0-3
Reading v Leicester City	0-1
Tottenham Hotspur v Oldham Athletic	3-0
Sheffield United v Wolverhampton Wanderers	3-1
Swindon Town v The Wednesday	1-2
Derby County v Nottingham Forest	0-0, 0-2

Cardiff City v Liverpool	2-1

Fifth Round

Blackburn Rovers v Port Vale	2-1
Manchester United v Birmingham	1-0
Arsenal v Aston Villa	4-1
Manchester City v Stoke City	0-1
Huddersfield Town v Middlesbrough	4-0
Leicester City v Tottenham Hotspur	0-3
The Wednesday v Sheffield United	1-1, 1-4
Nottingham Forest v Cardiff City	2-1

Sixth Round

Blackburn Rovers v Manchester United	2-0
Arsenal v Stoke City	4-1
Huddersfield Town v Tottenham Hotspur	6-1
Sheffield United v Nottingham Forest	3-0

Semi-Final

Blackburn Rovers v Arsenal	1-0
Huddersfield Town v Sheffield United	2-2, 0-0, 1-0

Final

Blackburn Rovers v Huddersfield Town	3-1

Scottish FA Cup

Third Round

Rangers v King's Park	3-1
Albion Rovers v Airdrieonians	3-1
Hibernian v Falkirk	0-0, 1-0
Dundee v Dunfermline Athletic	1-2
Celtic v Alloa Athletic	2-0
Heart of Midlothian v Motherwell	1-2
Kilmarnock v Queen's Park	4-4, 0-1
St Mirren v Partick Thistle	0-5

Fourth Round

Albion Rovers v Rangers	0-1
Dunfermline Athletic v Hibernian	0-4
Motherwell v Celtic	0-2
Queen's Park v Partick Thistle	1-0

Semi-Final

Rangers v Hibernian	3-0
Celtic v Queen's Park	2-1

Final

Rangers v Celtic	4-0

1928-29
First Division

	P	W	D	L	F	A	Pts
1 Wednesday	42	21	10	11	86	62	52
2 Leicester	42	21	9	12	96	67	51
3 Aston Villa	42	23	4	15	98	81	50
4 Sunderland	42	20	7	15	93	75	47
5 Liverpool	42	17	12	13	90	64	46
6 Derby	42	18	10	14	86	71	46
7 Blackburn	42	17	11	14	72	63	45
8 Man City	42	18	9	15	95	86	45
9 Arsenal	42	16	13	13	77	72	45
10 Newcastle	42	19	6	17	70	72	44
11 Sheff United	42	15	11	16	86	85	41
12 Man United	42	14	13	15	66	76	41
13 Leeds	42	16	9	17	71	84	41
14 Bolton	42	14	12	16	73	80	40
15 Birmingham	42	15	10	17	68	77	40
16 Huddersfield	42	14	11	17	70	61	39
17 West Ham	42	15	9	18	86	96	39
18 Everton	42	17	4	21	63	75	38
19 Burnley	42	15	8	19	81	103	38
20 Portsmouth	42	15	6	21	56	80	36
21 Bury	42	12	7	23	62	99	31
22 Cardiff	42	8	13	21	43	59	29

Second Division

	P	W	D	L	F	A	Pts
1 Middlesbrough	42	22	11	9	92	57	55
2 Grimsby	42	24	5	13	82	61	53
3 Bradford PA	42	22	4	16	88	70	48
4 Southampton	42	17	14	11	74	60	48
5 Notts County	42	19	9	14	78	65	47
6 Stoke	42	17	12	13	74	51	46
7 WBA	42	19	8	15	80	79	46
8 Blackpool	42	19	7	16	92	76	45
9 Chelsea	42	17	10	15	64	65	44
10 Tottenham	42	17	9	16	75	81	43
11 Nottm Forest	42	15	12	15	71	70	42
12 Hull	42	13	14	15	58	63	40
13 Preston	42	15	9	18	78	79	39
14 Millwall	42	16	7	19	71	86	39
15 Reading	42	15	9	18	63	86	39
16 Barnsley	42	16	6	20	69	66	38
17 Wolves	42	15	7	20	77	81	37
18 Oldham	42	16	5	21	54	75	37
19 Swansea	42	13	10	19	62	75	36
20 Bristol City	42	13	10	19	58	72	36
21 Port Vale	42	15	4	23	71	86	34
22 Clapton Orient	42	12	8	22	45	72	32

Third Division (North)

	P	W	D	L	F	A	Pts
1 Bradford City	42	27	9	6	128	43	63
2 Stockport	42	28	6	8	111	58	62
3 Wrexham	42	21	10	11	91	69	52
4 Wigan Borough	42	21	9	12	82	49	51
5 Doncaster	42	20	10	12	76	66	50
6 Lincoln	42	21	6	15	91	67	48
7 Tranmere	42	22	3	17	79	77	47
8 Carlisle	42	19	8	15	86	77	46
9 Crewe	42	18	8	16	80	68	44
10 South Shields	42	18	8	16	83	74	44
11 Chesterfield	42	18	5	19	71	77	41
12 Southport	42	16	8	18	75	85	40
13 Halifax	42	13	13	16	63	62	39
14 New Brighton	42	15	9	18	64	71	39
15 Nelson	42	17	5	20	77	90	39
16 Rotherham	42	15	9	18	60	77	39
17 Rochdale	42	13	10	19	79	96	36
18 Accrington	42	13	8	21	68	82	34
19 Darlington	42	13	7	22	64	88	33
20 Barrow	42	10	8	24	64	93	28
21 Hartlepools	42	10	6	26	59	112	26
22 Ashington	42	8	7	27	45	115	23

Third Division (South)

	P	W	D	L	F	A	Pts
1 Charlton	42	23	8	11	86	60	54
2 Crystal Palace	42	23	8	11	81	67	54
3 Northampton	42	20	12	10	96	57	52
4 Plymouth	42	20	12	10	83	51	52
5 Fulham	42	21	10	11	101	71	52
6 QPR	42	19	14	9	82	61	52
7 Luton	42	19	11	12	89	73	49
8 Watford	42	19	10	13	79	74	48
9 Bournemouth	42	19	9	14	84	77	47
10 Swindon	42	15	13	14	75	72	43
11 Coventry	42	14	14	14	62	57	42
12 Southend	42	15	11	16	80	75	41
13 Brentford	42	14	10	18	56	60	38
14 Walsall	42	13	12	17	73	79	38
15 Brighton	42	16	6	20	58	76	38
16 Newport	42	13	9	20	69	86	35
17 Norwich	42	14	6	22	69	81	34
18 Torquay	42	14	6	22	66	84	34
19 Bristol Rovers	42	13	7	22	60	79	33
20 Merthyr Town	42	11	8	23	55	103	30
21 Exeter	42	9	11	22	67	88	29

22 Gillingham   42 10 9 23 43 83 29

Scottish First Division

	P	W	D	L	F	A	Pts
1 Rangers	38	30	7	1	107	32	67
2 Celtic	38	22	7	9	67	44	51
3 Motherwell	38	20	10	8	85	66	50
4 Hearts	38	19	9	10	91	57	47
5 Queen's Park	38	18	7	13	100	69	43
6 Partick	38	17	7	14	91	70	41
7 Aberdeen	38	16	8	14	81	69	40
8 St Mirren	38	16	8	14	78	74	40
9 St Johnstone	38	14	10	14	57	70	38
10 Kilmarnock	38	14	8	16	79	74	36
11 Falkirk	38	14	8	16	68	86	36
12 Hamilton	38	13	9	16	58	83	35
13 Cowdenbeath	38	14	5	19	55	69	33
14 Hibernian	38	13	6	19	54	62	32
15 Airdrieonians	38	12	7	19	56	65	31
16 Ayr	38	12	7	19	65	84	31
17 Clyde	38	12	6	20	47	71	30
18 Dundee	38	9	11	18	58	68	29
19 Third Lanark	38	10	6	22	71	102	26
20 Raith	38	9	6	23	52	105	24

Scottish Second Division

	P	W	D	L	F	A	Pts
1 Dundee United	36	24	3	9	99	55	51
2 Morton	36	21	8	7	85	49	50
3 Arbroath	36	19	9	8	90	60	47
4 Albion	36	18	8	10	95	67	44
5 Leith	36	18	7	11	78	56	43
6 St Bernard's	36	16	9	11	77	55	41
7 Forfar	35	14	10	11	69	75	38
8 East Fife	35	15	6	14	88	77	36
9 Queen of the S	36	16	4	16	86	79	36
10 Bo'ness	35	15	5	15	62	62	35
11 Dunfermline	36	13	7	16	66	72	33
12 E Stirlingshire	36	14	4	18	71	75	32
13 Alloa	36	12	7	17	64	77	31
14 Dumbarton	36	11	9	16	59	78	31
15 King's Park	36	8	13	15	60	84	29
16 Clydebank	36	11	5	20	70	86	27
17 Arthurlie*	32	9	7	16	51	73	25
18 Stenhousemuir	35	9	6	20	52	90	24
19 Armadale	36	8	7	21	47	99	23

*Arthurlie resigned towards the end of the season—but their record was allowed to stand

FA Cup
Fourth Round
Blackburn Rovers v Derby County
                                    1-1, 3-0
Manchester United v Bury   0-1
Leicester City v Swansea Town   1-0
Liverpool v Bolton Wanderers   0-0, 2-5
West Bromwich Albion v Middlesbrough
                                      1-0
Plymouth Argyle v Bradford Park
        Avenue   0-1
Huddersfield Town v Leeds United   3-0
Millwall v Crystal Palace   0-0, 3-5
Chelsea v Birmingham   1-0
Portsmouth v Bradford City   2-0
Bournemouth v Watford   6-4
West Ham United v Corinthians   3-0
Reading v The Wednesday   1-0
Aston Villa v Clapton Orient   0-0, 8-0
Burnley v Swindon Town   3-3, 2-3
Arsenal v Mansfield Town   2-0

Fifth Round
Blackburn Rovers v Bury   1-0
Leicester City v Bolton Wanderers   1-2
West Bromwich Albion v Bradford
        Park Avenue   6-0
Huddersfield Town v Crystal Palace   5-2
Chelsea v Portsmouth   1-1, 0-1
Bournemouth v West Ham United
                                 1-1, 1-3
Reading v Aston Villa   1-3
Swindon Town v Arsenal   0-0, 0-1

Sixth Round
Blackburn Rovers v Bolton Wanderers
                                 1-1, 1-2
West Bromwich Albion v Huddersfield
        Town   1-1, 1-2
Portsmouth v West Ham United   3-2
Aston Villa v Arsenal   1-0

Semi-Final
Bolton Wanderers v Huddersfield Town
                                      3-1
Portsmouth v Aston Villa   1-0

Final
Bolton Wanderers v Portsmouth   2-0

Scottish FA Cup
Third Round
Celtic v Arbroath   4-1

Airdrieonians v Motherwell	1-1, 1-3
Raith Rovers v Dumbarton	3-2
Albion Rovers v Kilmarnock	0-1
Clyde v Rangers	0-2
Dundee v Dundee United	1-1, 0-1
Falkirk v Aberdeen	3-5
Ayr United v St Mirren	0-2

Fourth Round

Celtic v Motherwell	0-0, 2-1
Raith Rovers v Kilmarnock	2-3
Rangers v Dundee United	3-1
St Mirren v Aberdeen	4-3

Semi-Final

| Celtic v Kilmarnock | 0-1 |
| Rangers v St Mirren | 3-2 |

Final

| Kilmarnock v Rangers | 2-0 |

1929-30
First Division

		P	W	D	L	F	A	Pts
1	Sheff Wed	42	26	8	8	105	57	60
2	Derby	42	21	8	13	90	82	50
3	Man City	42	19	9	14	91	81	47
4	Aston Villa	42	21	5	16	92	83	47
5	Leeds	42	20	6	16	79	63	46
6	Blackburn	42	19	7	16	99	93	45
7	West Ham	42	19	5	18	86	79	43
8	Leicester	42	17	9	16	86	90	43
9	Sunderland	42	18	7	17	76	80	43
10	Huddersfield	42	17	9	16	63	69	43
11	Birmingham	42	16	9	17	67	62	41
12	Liverpool	42	16	9	17	63	79	41
13	Portsmouth	42	15	19	17	66	62	40
14	Arsenal	42	14	11	17	78	66	39
15	Bolton	42	15	9	18	74	74	39
16	Middlesbrough	42	16	6	20	82	84	38
17	Man United	42	15	8	19	67	88	38
18	Grimsby	42	15	7	20	73	89	37
19	Newcastle	42	15	7	20	71	92	37
20	Sheff United	42	15	6	21	91	96	36
21	Burnley	42	14	8	20	79	97	36
22	Everton	42	12	11	19	80	92	35

Second Division

		P	W	D	L	F	A	Pts
1	Blackpool	42	27	4	11	98	67	58
2	Chelsea	42	22	11	9	74	46	55
3	Oldham	42	21	11	10	90	51	53
4	Bradford PA	42	19	12	11	91	70	50
5	Bury	42	22	5	15	78	67	49
6	WBA	42	21	5	16	105	73	47
7	Southampton	42	17	11	14	77	76	45
8	Cardiff	42	18	8	16	61	59	44
9	Wolves	42	16	9	17	77	79	41
10	Nottm Forest	42	13	15	14	55	69	41
11	Stoke	42	16	8	18	74	72	40
12	Tottenham	42	15	9	18	59	61	39
13	Charlton	42	14	11	17	59	63	39
14	Millwall	42	12	15	15	57	73	39
15	Swansea	42	14	9	19	57	61	37
16	Preston	42	13	11	18	65	80	37
17	Barnsley	42	14	8	20	56	71	36
18	Bradford City	42	12	12	18	60	77	36
19	Reading	42	12	11	19	54	67	35
20	Bristol City	42	13	9	20	61	83	35
21	Hull	42	14	7	21	51	78	35
22	Notts County	42	9	15	18	54	70	33

Third Division (North)

		P	W	D	L	F	A	Pts
1	Port Vale	42	30	7	5	103	37	67
2	Stockport	42	28	7	7	106	44	63
3	Darlington	42	22	6	14	108	73	50
4	Chesterfield	42	22	6	14	76	56	50
5	Lincoln	42	17	14	11	83	61	48
6	York	42	15	16	11	77	64	46
7	South Shields	42	18	10	14	77	74	46
8	Hartlepools	42	17	11	14	81	74	45
9	Southport	42	15	13	14	81	74	43
10	Rochdale	42	18	7	17	89	91	43
11	Crewe	42	17	8	17	82	71	42
12	Tranmere	42	16	9	17	83	86	41
13	New Brighton	42	16	8	18	69	79	40
14	Doncaster	42	15	9	18	62	69	39
15	Carlisle	42	16	7	19	90	101	39
16	Accrington	42	14	9	19	84	81	37
17	Wrexham	42	13	8	21	67	88	34
18	Wigan Borough	42	13	7	22	60	88	33
19	Nelson	42	13	7	22	51	80	33
20	Rotherham	42	11	8	23	67	113	30
21	Halifax	42	10	8	24	44	79	28
22	Barrow	42	11	5	26	41	98	27

Third Division (South)

		P	W	D	L	F	A	Pts
1	Plymouth	42	30	8	4	98	38	68
2	Brentford	42	28	5	9	94	44	61

3 QPR	42	21	9	12	80	68	51
4 Northampton	42	21	8	13	82	58	50
5 Brighton	42	21	8	13	87	63	50
6 Coventry	42	19	9	14	88	73	47
7 Fulham	42	18	11	13	87	83	47
8 Norwich	42	18	10	14	88	77	46
9 Crystal Palace	42	17	12	13	81	74	46
10 Bournemouth	42	15	13	14	72	61	43
11 Southend	42	15	13	14	69	59	43
12 Clapton Orient	42	14	13	15	55	62	41
13 Luton	42	14	12	16	64	78	40
14 Swindon	42	13	12	17	73	83	38
15 Watford	42	15	8	19	60	73	38
16 Exeter	42	12	11	19	67	73	35
17 Walsall	42	13	8	21	71	78	34
18 Newport	42	12	10	20	74	85	34
19 Torquay	42	10	11	21	64	94	31
20 Bristol Rovers	42	11	8	23	67	93	30
21 Gillingham	42	11	8	23	51	80	30
22 Merthyr Town	42	6	9	27	60	135	21

Scottish First Division

	P	W	D	L	F	A	Pts
1 Rangers	38	28	4	6	94	32	60
2 Motherwell	38	25	5	8	104	48	55
3 Aberdeen	38	23	7	8	85	61	53
4 Celtic	38	22	5	11	88	46	49
5 St Mirren	38	18	5	15	73	56	41
6 Partick	38	16	9	13	72	61	41
7 Falkirk	38	16	9	13	62	64	41
8 Kilmarnock	38	15	9	14	77	73	39
9 Ayr	38	16	6	16	70	92	38
10 Hearts	38	14	9	15	69	69	37
11 Clyde	38	13	11	14	64	69	37
12 Airdrieonians	38	16	4	18	60	66	36
13 Hamilton	38	14	7	17	76	81	35
14 Dundee	38	14	6	18	51	58	34
15 Queen's Park	38	15	4	19	67	80	34
16 Cowdenbeath	38	13	7	18	64	74	33
17 Hibernian	38	9	11	18	45	62	29
18 Morton	38	10	7	21	67	95	27
19 Dundee United	38	7	8	23	56	109	22
20 St Johnstone	38	6	7	25	48	96	19

Scottish Second Division

	P	W	D	L	F	A	Pts
1 Leith Athletic	38	23	11	4	92	42	57
2 East Fife	38	26	5	7	114	58	57
3 Albion	38	24	6	8	101	60	54
4 Third Lanark	38	23	6	9	92	53	52
5 Raith	38	18	8	12	94	67	44

6 King's Park	38	17	8	13	109	80	42
7 Queen of the S	38	18	6	14	65	63	42
8 Forfar	38	18	5	15	98	95	41
9 Arbroath	38	16	7	15	83	87	39
10 Dunfermline	38	16	6	16	99	85	38
11 Montrose	38	14	10	14	79	87	38
12 E Stirlingshire	38	16	4	18	83	75	36
13 Bo'ness	38	15	4	19	67	95	34
14 St Bernard's	38	13	6	19	65	65	32
15 Armadale	38	13	5	20	56	91	31
16 Dumbarton	38	14	2	22	77	95	30
17 Stenhousemuir	38	11	5	22	75	108	27
18 Clydebank	38	7	10	21	66	92	24
19 Alloa	38	9	6	23	55	104	24
20 Brechin	38	7	4	27	57	125	18

FA Cup

Fourth Round

West Ham United v Leeds United	4-1
Millwall v Doncaster Rovers	4-0
Arsenal v Birmingham	2-2, 1-0
Middlesbrough v Charlton Athletic	1-1, 1-1, 1-0
Hull City v Blackpool	3-1
Swindon Town v Manchester City	1-1, 1-10
Newcastle United v Clapton Orient	3-1
Portsmouth v Brighton	0-1
Aston Villa v Walsall	3-1
Blackburn Rovers v Everton	4-1
Huddersfield Town v Sheffield United	2-1
Wrexham v Bradford City	0-0, 1-2
Nottingham Forest v Fulham	2-1
Sunderland v Cardiff City	2-1
Oldham Athletic v Sheffield Wednesday	3-4
Derby County v Bradford Park Avenue	1-1, 1-2

Fifth Round

West Ham United v Millwall	4-1
Middlesbrough v Arsenal	0-2
Manchester City v Hull City	1-2
Newcastle United v Brighton	3-0
Aston Villa v Blackburn Rovers	4-1
Huddersfield Town v Bradford City	2-1
Sunderland v Nottingham Forest	2-2, 1-3
Sheffield Wednesday v Bradford Park Avenue	5-1

Sixth Round

West Ham United v Arsenal	0-3
Newcastle United v Hull City	1-1, 0-1

| Aston Villa v Huddersfield Town | 1-2 |
| Nottingham Forest v Sheffield Wednesday | 2-2, 1-3 |

Semi-Final

| Arsenal v Hull City | 2-2, 1-0 |
| Huddersfield Town v Sheffield Wednesday | 2-1 |

Final

| Arsenal v Huddersfield Town | 2-0 |

Scottish FA Cup

Third Round

Motherwell v Rangers	2-5
Albion Rovers v Montrose	2-2, 1-3
Dundee v Airdrieonians	0-0, 0-0, 1-0
Hibernian v Heart of Midlothian	1-3
Celtic v St Mirren	1-3
Hamilton Academicals v King's Park	4-0
Falkirk v Leith Athletic	0-0, 1-1, 1-1, 1-0
Partick Thistle v Aberdeen	3-2

Fourth Round

Rangers v Montrose	3-0
Dundee v Heart of Midlothian	2-2, 0-4
St Mirren v Hamilton Academicals	3-4
Partick Thistle v Falkirk	3-1

Semi-Final

| Rangers v Heart of Midlothian | 4-1 |
| Partick Thistle v Hamilton Academicals | 3-1 |

Final

| Rangers v Partick Thistle | 0-0, 2-1 |

1930–31
First Division

	P	W	D	L	F	A	Pts
1 Arsenal	42	28	10	4	127	59	66
2 Aston Villa	42	25	9	8	128	78	59
3 Sheff Wed	42	22	8	12	102	75	52
4 Portsmouth	42	18	13	11	84	67	49
5 Huddersfield	42	18	12	12	81	65	48
6 Derby	42	18	10	14	94	79	46
7 Middlesbrough	42	19	8	15	98	90	46
8 Man City	42	18	10	14	75	70	46
9 Liverpool	42	15	12	15	86	85	42
10 Blackburn	42	17	8	17	83	84	42
11 Sunderland	42	16	9	17	89	85	41
12 Chelsea	42	15	10	17	64	67	40
13 Grimsby	42	17	5	20	82	87	39
14 Bolton	42	15	9	18	68	81	39
15 Sheff United	42	14	10	18	78	84	38
16 Leicester	42	16	6	20	80	95	38
17 Newcastle	42	15	6	21	78	87	36
18 West Ham	42	14	8	20	79	94	36
19 Birmingham	42	13	10	19	55	70	36
20 Blackpool	42	11	10	21	71	125	32
21 Leeds	42	12	7	23	68	81	31
22 Man United	42	7	8	27	53	115	22

Second Division

	P	W	D	L	F	A	Pts
1 Everton	42	28	5	9	121	66	61
2 WBA	42	22	10	10	83	49	54
3 Tottenham	42	22	7	13	88	55	51
4 Wolves	42	21	5	16	84	67	47
5 Port Vale	42	21	5	16	67	61	47
6 Bradford PA	42	18	10	14	97	66	46
7 Preston	42	17	11	14	83	64	45
8 Burnley	42	17	11	14	81	77	45
9 Southampton	42	19	6	17	74	62	44
10 Bradford City	42	17	10	15	61	63	44
11 Stoke	42	17	10	15	64	71	44
12 Oldham	42	16	10	16	61	72	42
13 Bury	42	19	3	20	75	82	41
14 Millwall	42	16	7	19	71	80	39
15 Charlton	42	15	9	18	59	86	39
16 Bristol City	42	15	8	19	54	82	38
17 Nottm Forest	42	14	9	19	80	85	37
18 Plymouth	42	14	8	20	76	84	36
19 Barnsley	42	13	9	20	59	79	35
20 Swansea	42	12	10	20	51	74	34
21 Reading	42	12	6	24	72	96	30
22 Cardiff	42	8	9	25	47	87	25

Third Division (North)

	P	W	D	L	F	A	Pts
1 Chesterfield	42	26	6	10	102	57	58
2 Lincoln	42	25	7	10	102	59	57
3 Tranmere	42	24	6	12	111	74	54
4 Wrexham	42	21	12	9	94	62	54
5 Southport	42	22	9	11	88	56	53
6 Hull	42	20	10	12	99	55	50
7 Stockport	42	20	9	13	77	61	49
8 Carlisle	42	20	5	17	98	81	45
9 Gateshead	42	16	13	13	71	73	45
10 Wigan Borough	42	19	5	18	76	86	43
11 Darlington	42	16	10	16	71	59	42

		P	W	D	L	F	A	Pts
12	York	42	18	6	18	85	82	42
13	Accrington	42	15	9	18	84	108	39
14	Rotherham	42	13	12	17	81	83	38
15	Doncaster	42	13	11	18	65	65	37
16	Barrow	42	15	7	20	68	89	37
17	Halifax	42	13	9	20	55	89	35
18	Crewe	42	14	6	22	66	93	34
19	New Brighton	42	13	7	22	49	76	33
20	Hartlepools	42	12	6	24	67	86	30
21	Rochdale	42	12	6	24	62	107	30
22	Nelson	42	6	7	29	43	113	19

Third Division (South)

		P	W	D	L	F	A	Pts
1	Notts County	42	24	11	7	97	46	59
2	Crystal Palace	42	22	7	13	107	71	51
3	Brentford	42	22	6	14	90	64	50
4	Brighton	42	17	15	10	68	53	49
5	Southend	42	22	5	15	76	60	49
6	Northampton	42	18	12	12	77	59	48
7	Luton	42	19	8	15	76	51	46
8	QPR	42	20	3	19	82	75	43
9	Fulham	42	18	7	17	77	75	43
10	Bournemouth	42	15	13	14	72	73	43
11	Torquay	42	17	9	16	80	84	43
12	Swindon	42	18	6	18	89	94	42
13	Exeter	42	17	8	17	84	90	42
14	Coventry	42	16	9	17	75	65	41
15	Bristol Rovers	42	16	8	18	75	92	40
16	Gillingham	42	14	10	18	61	76	38
17	Walsall	42	14	9	19	78	95	37
18	Watford	42	14	7	21	72	75	35
19	Clapton Orient	42	14	7	21	63	91	35
20	Thames	42	13	8	21	54	93	34
21	Norwich	42	10	8	24	47	76	28
22	Newport	42	11	6	25	69	111	28

Scottish First Division

		P	W	D	L	F	A	Pts
1	Rangers	38	27	6	5	96	29	60
2	Celtic	38	24	10	4	101	34	58
3	Motherwell	38	24	8	6	102	42	56
4	Partick	38	24	5	9	76	44	53
5	Hearts	38	19	6	13	90	63	44
6	Aberdeen	38	17	7	14	79	63	41
7	Cowdenbeath	38	17	7	14	58	65	41
8	Dundee	38	17	5	16	65	63	39
9	Airdrieonians	38	17	5	16	59	66	39
10	Hamilton	38	16	5	17	59	57	37
11	Kilmarnock	38	15	5	18	59	60	35
12	Clyde	38	15	4	19	60	87	34
13	Queen's Park	38	13	7	18	71	72	33
14	Falkirk	38	14	4	20	77	87	32
15	St Mirren	38	11	8	19	49	72	30
16	Morton	38	11	7	20	58	83	29
17	Leith	38	8	11	19	52	85	27
18	Ayr	38	8	11	19	53	92	27
19	Hibernian	38	9	7	22	49	81	25
20	East Fife	38	8	4	26	45	113	20

Scottish Second Division

		P	W	D	L	F	A	Pts
1	Third Lanark	38	27	7	4	107	42	61
2	Dundee United	38	21	8	9	93	54	50
3	Dunfermline	38	20	7	11	83	50	47
4	Raith	38	20	6	12	93	72	46
5	Queen of the S	38	18	6	14	83	66	42
6	St Johnstone	38	18	6	14	76	64	42
7	E Stirlingshire	38	17	7	14	85	74	41
8	Montrose	38	19	3	16	75	90	41
9	Albion	38	14	11	13	80	83	39
10	Dumbarton	38	15	8	15	73	72	38
11	St Bernard's	38	14	9	15	85	66	37
12	Forfar	38	15	6	17	78	83	36
13	Alloa	38	15	5	18	65	87	35
14	King's Park	38	14	6	18	78	70	34
15	Arbroath	38	15	4	19	83	94	34
16	Brechin	38	13	7	18	52	84	33
17	Stenhousemuir	38	13	6	19	78	98	32
18	Armadale	38	13	2	23	74	99	28
19	Clydebank	38	10	2	26	61	108	22
20	Bo'ness	38	9	4	25	54	100	22

FA Cup

Fourth Round

Birmingham v Port Vale	2-0
Watford v Brighton	2-0
Chelsea v Arsenal	2-1
Blackburn Rovers v Bristol Rovers	5-1
Bolton Wanderers v Sunderland	1-1, 1-3
Sheffield United v Notts County	4-1
Bury v Exeter City	1-2
Leeds United v Newcastle United	4-1
Crystal Palace v Everton	0-6
Grimsby Town v Manchester United	1-0
Southport v Blackpool	2-1
Bradford Park Avenue v Burnley	2-0
Brentford v Portsmouth	0-1
West Bromwich Albion v Tottenham Hotspur	1-0

Barnsley v Sheffield Wednesday	2-1
Bradford City v Wolverhampton Wanderers	0-0, 2-4

Fifth Round

Birmingham v Watford	3-0
Chelsea v Blackburn Rovers	3-0
Sunderland v Sheffield United	2-1
Exeter City v Leeds United	3-1
Everton v Grimsby Town	5-3
Southport v Bradford Park Avenue	1-0
Portsmouth v West Bromwich Albion	0-1
Barnsley v Wolverhampton Wanderers	1-3

Sixth Round

Birmingham v Chelsea	2-2, 3-0
Sunderland v Exeter City	1-1, 4-2
Everton v Southport	9-1
West Bromwich Albion v Wolverhampton Wanderers	1-1, 2-1

Semi-Final

Birmingham v Sunderland	2-0
Everton v West Bromwich Albion	0-1

Final

West Bromwich Albion v Birmingham	2-1

Scottish FA Cup

Third Round

Morton v Celtic	1-4
Dundee v Aberdeen	1-1, 0-2
Montrose v Kilmarnock	0-3
Bo'ness v Ayr United	1-0
Hibernian v Motherwell	0-3
Cowdenbeath v St Bernard's	3-0
St Mirren v Falkirk	2-0
Third Lanark v Arbroath	4-2

Fourth Round

Celtic v Aberdeen	4-0
Bo'ness v Kilmarnock	1-1, 0-5
Cowdenbeath v Motherwell	0-1
Third Lanark v St Mirren	1-1, 0-3

Semi-Final

Celtic v Kilmarnock	3-0
Motherwell v St Mirren	1-0

Final

Celtic v Motherwell	2-2, 4-2

1931–32
First Division

		P	W	D	L	F	A	Pts
1	Everton	42	26	4	12	116	64	56
2	Arsenal	42	22	10	10	90	48	54
3	Sheff Wed	42	22	6	14	96	82	50
4	Huddersfield	42	19	10	13	80	63	48
5	Aston Villa	42	19	8	15	104	72	46
6	WBA	42	20	6	16	77	55	46
7	Sheff United	42	20	6	16	80	75	46
8	Portsmouth	42	19	7	16	62	62	45
9	Birmingham	42	18	8	16	78	67	44
10	Liverpool	42	19	6	17	81	93	44
11	Newcastle	42	18	6	18	80	87	42
12	Chelsea	42	16	8	18	69	73	40
13	Sunderland	42	15	10	17	67	73	40
14	Man City	42	13	12	17	83	73	38
15	Derby	42	14	10	18	71	75	38
16	Blackburn	42	16	6	20	89	95	38
17	Bolton	42	17	4	21	72	80	38
18	Middlesbrough	42	15	8	19	64	89	38
19	Leicester	42	15	7	20	74	94	37
20	Blackpool	42	12	9	21	65	102	33
21	Grimsby	42	13	6	23	67	98	32
22	West Ham	42	12	7	23	62	107	31

Second Division

		P	W	D	L	F	A	Pts
1	Wolves	42	24	8	10	115	49	56
2	Leeds	42	22	10	10	78	54	54
3	Stoke	42	19	14	9	69	48	52
4	Plymouth	42	20	9	13	100	66	49
5	Bury	42	21	7	14	70	58	49
6	Bradford PA	42	21	7	14	72	63	49
7	Bradford City	42	16	13	13	80	61	45
8	Tottenham	42	16	11	15	87	78	43
9	Millwall	42	17	9	16	61	61	43
10	Charlton	42	17	9	16	61	66	43
11	Nottm Forest	42	16	10	16	77	72	42
12	Man United	42	17	8	17	71	72	42
13	Preston	42	16	10	16	75	77	42
14	Southampton	42	17	7	18	66	77	41
15	Swansea	42	16	7	19	73	75	39
16	Notts County	42	13	12	17	75	75	38
17	Chesterfield	42	13	11	18	64	86	37
18	Oldham	42	13	10	19	62	84	36
19	Burnley	42	13	9	20	59	87	35
20	Port Vale	42	13	7	22	58	89	33

	P	W	D	L	F	A	Pts
21 Barnsley	42	12	9	21	55	91	33
22 Bristol City	42	6	11	25	39	78	23

Third Division (North)

	P	W	D	L	F	A	Pts
1 Lincoln	40	26	5	9	106	47	57
2 Gateshead	40	25	7	8	94	48	57
3 Chester	40	21	8	11	78	60	50
4 Tranmere	40	19	11	10	107	58	49
5 Barrow	40	24	1	15	86	59	49
6 Crewe	40	21	6	13	95	66	48
7 Southport	40	18	10	12	58	53	46
8 Hull	40	20	5	15	82	53	45
9 York	40	18	7	15	76	81	43
10 Wrexham	40	18	7	15	64	69	43
11 Darlington	40	17	4	19	66	69	38
12 Stockport	40	13	11	16	55	53	37
13 Hartlepools	40	16	5	19	78	100	37
14 Accrington	40	15	6	19	75	80	36
15 Doncaster	40	16	4	20	59	80	36
16 Walsall	40	16	3	21	57	85	35
17 Halifax	40	13	8	19	61	87	34
18 Carlisle	40	11	11	18	64	79	33
19 Rotherham	40	14	4	22	63	72	32
20 New Brighton	40	8	8	24	38	76	24
21 Rochdale	40	4	3	33	48	135	11
22 Wigan Borough	resigned	from	the	League			

Third Division (South)

	P	W	D	L	F	A	Pts
1 Fulham	42	24	9	9	111	62	57
2 Reading	42	23	9	10	97	67	55
3 Southend	42	21	11	10	77	53	53
4 Crystal Palace	42	20	11	11	74	63	51
5 Brentford	42	19	10	13	68	52	48
6 Luton	42	20	7	15	95	70	47
7 Exeter	42	20	7	15	77	62	47
8 Brighton	42	17	12	13	73	58	46
9 Cardiff	42	19	8	15	87	73	46
10 Norwich	42	17	12	13	76	67	46
11 Watford	42	19	8	15	81	79	46
12 Coventry	42	18	8	16	108	97	44
13 QPR	42	15	12	15	79	73	42
14 Northampton	42	16	7	19	69	69	39
15 Bournemouth	42	13	12	17	70	78	38
16 Clapton Orient	42	12	11	19	77	90	35
17 Swindon	42	14	6	22	70	84	34
18 Bristol Rovers	42	13	8	21	65	92	34
19 Torquay	42	12	9	21	72	106	33

	P	W	D	L	F	A	Pts
20 Mansfield	42	11	10	21	75	108	32
21 Gillingham	42	10	8	24	40	82	28
22 Thames	42	7	9	26	53	109	23

Scottish First Division

	P	W	D	L	F	A	Pts
1 Motherwell	38	30	6	2	119	31	66
2 Rangers	38	28	5	5	118	42	61
3 Celtic	38	20	8	10	94	50	48
4 Third Lanark	38	21	4	13	92	81	46
5 St Mirren	38	20	4	14	77	56	44
6 Partick	38	19	4	15	58	59	42
7 Aberdeen	38	16	9	13	57	49	41
8 Hearts	38	17	5	16	63	61	39
9 Kilmarnock	38	16	7	15	68	70	39
10 Hamilton	38	16	6	16	84	65	38
11 Dundee	38	14	10	14	61	72	38
12 Cowdenbeath	38	15	8	15	66	78	38
13 Clyde	38	13	9	16	58	70	35
14 Airdrieonians	38	13	6	19	74	81	32
15 Morton	38	12	7	19	78	87	31
16 Queen's Park	38	13	5	20	59	79	31
17 Ayr	38	11	7	20	70	90	29
18 Falkirk	38	11	5	22	70	76	27
19 Dundee United	38	6	7	25	40	118	19
20 Leith	38	6	4	28	46	137	16

Scottish Second Division

	P	W	D	L	F	A	Pts
1 E Stirlingshire	38	26	3	9	111	55	55
2 St Johnstone	38	24	7	7	102	52	55
3 Raith	38	20	6	12	83	65	46
4 Stenhousemuir	38	19	8	11	88	76	46
5 St Bernard's	38	19	7	12	81	62	45
6 Forfar	38	19	7	12	90	79	45
7 Hibernian	38	18	8	12	73	52	44
8 East Fife	38	18	5	15	107	77	41
9 Queen of the S	38	18	5	15	99	91	41
10 Dunfermline	38	17	6	15	78	73	40
11 Arbroath	38	17	5	16	82	78	39
12 Dumbarton	38	14	10	14	70	68	38
13 Alloa	38	14	7	17	73	74	35
14 Bo'ness	38	15	4	19	70	103	34
15 King's Park	38	14	5	19	97	93	33
16 Albion	38	13	2	23	81	104	28
17 Montrose	38	11	6	21	60	96	28
18 Armadale	38	10	5	23	68	102	25
19 Brechin	38	9	7	22	52	97	25
20 Edinburgh City	38	5	7	26	78	146	17

FA Cup

Fourth Round

Huddersfield Town v Queen's Park Rangers	5-0
Preston North End v Wolverhampton Wanderers	2-0
Portsmouth v Aston Villa	1-1, 1-0
Arsenal v Plymouth Argyle	4-2
Bury v Sheffield United	3-1
Sunderland v Stoke City	1-1, 1-1, 1-2
Manchester City v Brentford	6-1
Derby County v Blackburn Rovers	3-2
Chesterfield v Liverpool	2-4
Grimsby Town v Birmingham	2-1
Sheffield Wednesday v Bournemouth	7-0
Chelsea v West Ham United	3-1
Newcastle United v Southport	1-1, 1-1, 9-0
Port Vale v Leicester City	1-2
Watford v Bristol City	2-1
Bradford Park Avenue v Northampton Town	4-2

Fifth Round

Huddersfield Town v Preston North End	4-0
Portsmouth v Arsenal	0-2
Bury v Stoke City	3-0
Manchester City v Derby County	3-0
Liverpool v Grimsby Town	1-0
Sheffield Wednesday v Chelsea	1-1, 0-2
Newcastle United v Leicester City	3-1
Watford v Bradford Park Avenue	1-0

Sixth Round

Huddersfield Town v Arsenal	1-0
Bury v Manchester City	3-4
Liverpool v Chelsea	0-2
Newcastle United v Watford	5-0

Semi-Final

Arsenal v Manchester City	1-0
Chelsea v Newcastle United	1-2

Final

Newcastle United v Arsenal	2-1

Scottish FA Cup

Third Round

Heart of Midlothian v Rangers	0-1
Motherwell v Celtic	2-0
Clyde v St Bernard's	2-0
Dundee United v Kilmarnock	1-1, 0-3
Hamilton Academicals	bye
Dunfermline Athletic	bye
Airdrieonians	bye
Partick Thistle	bye

Fourth Round

Rangers v Motherwell	2-0
Clyde v Hamilton Academicals	0-2
Dunfermline Athletic v Kilmarnock	1-3
Airdrieonians v Partick Thistle	4-1

Semi-Final

Rangers v Hamilton Academicals	5-2
Kilmarnock v Airdrieonians	3-2

Final

Rangers v Kilmarnock	1-1, 3-0

1932-33
First Division

	P	W	D	L	F	A	Pts
1 Arsenal	42	25	8	9	118	61	58
2 Aston Villa	42	23	8	11	92	67	54
3 Sheff Wed	42	21	9	12	80	68	51
4 WBA	42	20	9	13	83	70	49
5 Newcastle	42	22	5	15	71	63	49
6 Huddersfield	42	18	11	13	66	53	47
7 Derby	42	15	14	13	76	69	44
8 Leeds	42	15	14	13	59	62	44
9 Portsmouth	42	18	7	17	74	76	43
10 Sheff United	42	17	9	16	74	80	43
11 Everton	42	16	9	17	81	74	41
12 Sunderland	42	15	10	17	63	80	40
13 Birmingham	42	14	11	17	57	57	39
14 Liverpool	42	14	11	17	79	84	39
15 Blackburn	42	14	10	18	76	102	38
16 Man City	42	16	5	21	68	71	37
17 Middlesbrough	42	14	9	19	63	73	37
18 Chelsea	42	14	7	21	63	73	35
19 Leicester	42	11	13	18	75	89	35
20 Wolves	42	13	9	20	80	96	35
21 Bolton	42	12	9	21	78	92	33
22 Blackpool	42	14	5	23	69	85	33

Second Division

	P	W	D	L	F	A	Pts
1 Stoke	42	25	6	11	78	39	56
2 Tottenham	42	20	15	7	96	51	55

	P	W	D	L	F	A	Pts
3 Fulham	42	20	10	12	78	65	50
4 Bury	42	20	9	13	84	59	49
5 Nottm Forest	42	17	15	10	67	59	49
6 Man United	42	15	13	14	71	68	43
7 Millwall	42	16	11	15	59	57	43
8 Bradford PA	42	17	8	17	77	71	42
9 Preston	42	16	10	16	74	70	42
10 Swansea	42	19	4	19	50	54	42
11 Bradford City	42	14	13	15	65	61	41
12 Southampton	42	18	5	19	66	66	41
13 Grimsby	42	14	13	15	79	84	41
14 Plymouth	42	16	9	17	63	67	41
15 Notts County	42	15	10	17	67	78	40
16 Oldham	42	15	8	19	67	80	38
17 Port Vale	42	14	10	18	66	79	38
18 Lincoln	42	12	13	17	72	87	37
19 Burnley	42	11	14	17	67	79	36
20 West Ham	42	13	9	20	75	93	35
21 Chesterfield	42	12	10	20	61	84	34
22 Charlton	42	12	7	23	60	91	31

Third Division (North)

	P	W	D	L	F	A	Pts
1 Hull	42	26	7	9	100	45	59
2 Wrexham	42	24	9	9	106	51	57
3 Stockport	42	21	12	9	99	58	54
4 Chester	42	22	8	12	94	66	52
5 Walsall	42	19	10	13	75	58	48
6 Doncaster	42	17	14	11	77	79	48
7 Gateshead	42	19	9	14	78	67	47
8 Barnsley	42	19	8	15	92	80	46
9 Barrow	42	18	7	17	60	60	43
10 Crewe	42	20	3	19	80	84	43
11 Tranmere	42	17	8	17	70	66	42
12 Southport	42	17	7	18	70	67	41
13 Accrington	42	15	10	17	78	76	40
14 Hartlepools	42	16	7	19	87	116	39
15 Halifax	42	15	8	19	71	90	38
16 Mansfield	42	14	7	21	84	100	35
17 Rotherham	42	14	6	22	60	84	34
18 Rochdale	42	13	7	22	58	80	33
19 Carlisle	42	13	7	22	51	75	33
20 York	42	13	6	23	72	92	32
21 New Brighton	42	11	10	21	63	88	32
22 Darlington	42	10	8	24	66	109	28

Third Division (South)

	P	W	D	L	F	A	Pts
1 Brentford	42	26	10	6	90	49	62
2 Exeter	42	24	10	8	88	48	58

	P	W	D	L	F	A	Pts
3 Norwich	42	22	13	7	88	55	57
4 Reading	42	19	13	10	103	71	51
5 Crystal Palace	42	19	8	15	78	64	46
6 Coventry	42	19	6	17	106	77	44
7 Gillingham	42	18	8	16	72	61	44
8 Northampton	42	18	8	16	76	66	44
9 Bristol Rovers	42	15	14	13	61	56	44
10 Torquay	42	16	12	14	72	67	44
11 Watford	42	16	12	14	66	63	44
12 Brighton	42	17	8	17	66	65	42
13 Southend	42	15	11	16	65	82	41
14 Luton	42	13	13	16	78	78	39
15 Bristol City	42	12	13	17	83	90	37
16 QPR	42	13	11	18	72	87	37
17 Aldershot	42	13	10	19	61	72	36
18 Bournemouth	42	12	12	18	60	81	36
19 Cardiff	42	12	7	23	69	99	31
20 Clapton Orient	42	8	13	21	59	93	29
21 Newport	42	11	7	24	61	105	29
22 Swindon	42	9	11	22	60	105	29

Scottish First Division

	P	W	D	L	F	A	Pts
1 Rangers	38	26	10	2	113	43	62
2 Motherwell	38	27	5	6	114	53	59
3 Hearts	38	21	8	9	84	51	50
4 Celtic	38	20	8	10	75	44	48
5 St Johnstone	38	17	10	11	70	57	44
6 Aberdeen	38	18	6	14	85	58	42
7 St Mirren	38	18	6	14	73	60	42
8 Hamilton	38	18	6	14	92	78	42
9 Queen's Park	38	17	7	14	78	79	41
10 Partick	38	17	6	15	75	55	40
11 Falkirk	38	15	6	17	70	70	36
12 Clyde	38	15	5	18	69	75	35
13 Third Lanark	38	14	7	17	70	80	35
14 Kilmarnock	38	13	9	16	72	86	35
15 Dundee	38	12	9	17	58	74	33
16 Ayr	38	13	4	21	62	96	30
17 Cowdenbeath	38	10	5	23	65	111	25
18 Airdrieonians	38	10	3	25	55	102	23
19 Morton	38	6	9	23	49	97	21
20 E Stirlingshire	38	7	3	28	55	115	17

Socttish Second Division

	P	W	D	L	F	A	Pts
1 Hibernian	34	25	4	5	80	29	54
2 Queen of the S	34	20	9	5	93	59	49
3 Dunfermline	34	20	7	7	89	44	47
4 Stenhousemuir	34	18	6	10	67	58	42
5 Albion	34	19	2	13	82	57	40

6 Raith	34	16	4	14	83	67	36
7 East Fife	34	15	4	15	85	71	34
8 King's Park	34	13	8	13	85	80	34
9 Dumbarton	34	14	6	14	69	67	34
10 Arbroath	34	14	5	15	65	62	33
11 Alloa	34	14	5	15	60	58	33
12 St Bernard's	34	13	6	15	67	64	32
13 Dundee United	34	14	4	16	65	67	32
14 Forfar	34	12	4	18	68	87	28
15 Brechin	34	11	4	19	65	95	26
16 Leith	34	10	5	19	43	81	25
17 Montrose	34	8	5	21	63	89	21
18 Edinburgh City	34	4	4	26	39	133	12

FA Cup

Fourth Round

Burnley v Sheffield United	3-1
Darlington v Chesterfield	0-2
Bolton Wanderers v Grimsby Town	2-1
Manchester City v Walsall	2-0
Southend United v Derby County	2-3
Aldershot v Millwall	1-0
Aston Villa v Sunderland	0-3
Blackpool v Huddersfield Town	2-0
Everton v Bury	3-1
Tranmere Rovers v Leeds United	0-0, 0-4
Chester v Halifax Town	0-0, 2-3
Luton Town v Tottenham Hotspur	2-0
Brighton v Bradford Park Avenue	2-1
West Ham United v West Bromwich Albion	2-0
Middlesbrough v Stoke City	4-1
Birmingham v Blackburn Rovers	3-0

Fifth Round

Burnley v Chesterfield	1-0
Bolton Wanderers v Manchester City	2-4
Derby County v Aldershot	2-0
Sunderland v Blackpool	1-0
Everton v Leeds United	2-0
Halifax Town v Luton Town	0-2
Brighton v West Ham United	2-2, 0-1
Middlesbrough v Birmingham	0-0, 0-3

Sixth Round

Burnley v Manchester City	0-1
Derby County v Sunderland	4-4, 1-0
Everton v Luton Town	6-0
West Ham United v Birmingham	4-0

Semi-Final

Manchester City v Derby County	3-2
Everton v West Ham United	2-1

Final

Everton v Manchester City	3-0

Scottish FA Cup

Third Round

Celtic v Partick Thistle	2-1
Heart of Midlothian v St Johnstone	2-0
Motherwell v Dundee	5-0
Kilmarnock v Rangers	1-0
Albion Rovers	bye
Hibernian	bye
Clyde	bye
Stenhousemuir	bye

Fourth Round

Celtic v Albion Rovers	1-1, 3-1
Heart of Midlothian v Hibernian	2-0
Motherwell v Kilmarnock	3-3, 8-3
Clyde v Stenhousemuir	3-2

Semi-Final

Celtic v Heart of Midlothian	0-0, 2-1
Motherwell v Clyde	2-0

Final

Celtic v Motherwell	1-0

1933–34
First Division

	P	W	D	L	F	A	Pts
1 Arsenal	42	25	9	8	75	47	59
2 Huddersfield	42	23	10	9	90	61	56
3 Tottenham	42	21	7	14	79	56	49
4 Derby	42	17	11	14	68	54	45
5 Man City	42	17	11	14	65	72	45
6 Sunderland	42	16	12	14	81	56	44
7 WBA	42	17	10	15	78	70	44
8 Blackburn	42	18	7	17	74	81	43
9 Leeds	42	17	8	17	75	66	42
10 Portsmouth	42	15	12	15	52	55	42
11 Sheff Wed	42	16	9	17	62	67	41
12 Stoke	42	15	11	16	58	71	41
13 Aston Villa	42	14	12	16	78	75	40
14 Everton	42	12	16	14	62	63	40
15 Wolves	42	14	12	16	74	86	40
16 Middlesbrough	42	16	7	19	68	80	39
17 Leicester	42	14	11	17	59	74	39
18 Liverpool	42	14	10	18	79	87	38
19 Chelsea	42	14	8	20	67	69	36
20 Birmingham	42	12	12	18	54	56	36

	P	W	D	L	F	A	Pts
21 Newcastle	42	10	14	18	68	77	34
22 Sheff United	42	12	7	23	58	101	31

Second Division

	P	W	D	L	F	A	Pts
1 Grimsby	42	27	5	10	103	59	59
2 Preston	42	23	6	13	71	52	52
3 Bolton	42	21	9	12	79	55	51
4 Brentford	42	22	7	13	85	60	51
5 Bradford PA	42	23	3	16	86	67	49
6 Bradford City	42	20	6	16	73	67	46
7 West Ham	42	17	11	14	78	70	45
8 Port Vale	42	19	7	16	60	55	45
9 Oldham	42	17	10	15	72	60	44
10 Plymouth	42	15	13	14	69	70	43
11 Blackpool	42	15	13	14	62	64	43
12 Bury	42	17	9	16	70	73	43
13 Burnley	42	18	6	18	60	72	42
14 Southampton	42	15	8	19	54	58	38
15 Hull	42	13	12	17	52	68	38
16 Fulham	42	15	7	20	48	67	37
17 Nottm Forest	42	13	9	20	73	74	35
18 Notts County	42	12	11	19	53	62	35
19 Swansea	42	10	15	17	51	60	35
20 Man United	42	14	6	22	59	85	34
21 Millwall	42	11	11	20	39	68	33
22 Lincoln	42	9	8	25	44	75	26

Third Division (North)

	P	W	D	L	F	A	Pts
1 Barnsley	42	27	8	7	118	61	62
2 Chesterfield	42	27	7	8	86	43	61
3 Stockport	42	24	11	7	115	52	59
4 Walsall	42	23	7	12	97	60	53
5 Doncaster	42	22	9	11	83	61	53
6 Wrexham	42	23	5	14	102	73	51
7 Tranmere	42	20	7	15	84	63	47
8 Barrow	42	19	9	14	116	94	47
9 Halifax	42	20	4	18	80	91	44
10 Chester	42	17	6	19	89	86	40
11 Hartlepools	42	16	7	19	89	93	39
12 York	42	15	8	19	71	74	38
13 Carlisle	42	15	8	19	66	81	38
14 Crewe	42	15	6	21	81	97	36
15 New Brighton	42	14	8	20	62	87	36
16 Darlington	42	13	9	20	70	101	35
17 Mansfield	42	11	12	19	81	88	34
18 Southport	42	8	17	17	63	90	33
19 Gateshead	42	12	9	21	76	110	33
20 Accrington	42	13	7	22	65	101	33

Third Division (South)

	P	W	D	L	F	A	Pts
21 Rotherham	42	10	8	24	53	91	28
22 Rochdale .	42	9	6	27	53	103	24
1 Norwich	42	25	11	6	88	49	61
2 Coventry	42	21	12	9	100	54	54
3 Reading	42	21	12	9	82	50	54
4 QPR	42	24	6	12	70	51	54
5 Charlton	42	22	8	12	83	56	52
6 Luton	42	21	10	11	83	61	52
7 Bristol Rovers	42	20	11	11	77	47	51
8 Swindon	42	17	11	14	64	68	45
9 Exeter	42	16	11	15	68	57	43
10 Brighton	42	15	13	14	68	60	43
11 Clapton Orient	42	16	10	16	75	69	42
12 Crystal Palace	42	16	9	17	71	67	41
13 Northampton	42	14	12	16	71	78	40
14 Aldershot	42	13	12	17	52	71	38
15 Watford	42	15	7	20	71	63	37
16 Southend	42	12	10	20	51	74	34
17 Gillingham	42	11	11	20	75	96	33
18 Newport	42	8	17	17	49	70	33
19 Bristol City	42	10	13	19	58	85	33
20 Torquay	42	13	7	22	53	93	33
21 Bournemouth	42	9	9	24	60	102	27
22 Cardiff	42	9	6	27	57	105	24

Scottish First Division

	P	W	D	L	F	A	Pts
1 Rangers	38	30	6	2	118	41	66
2 Motherwell	38	29	4	5	97	45	62
3 Celtic	38	18	11	9	78	53	47
4 Queen of the S	38	21	3	14	75	78	45
5 Aberdeen	38	18	8	12	90	57	44
6 Hearts	38	17	10	11	86	59	44
7 Kilmarnock	38	17	9	12	73	64	43
8 Ayr	38	16	10	12	87	92	42
9 St Johnstone	38	17	6	15	74	53	40
10 Falkirk	38	16	6	16	73	68	38
11 Hamilton	38	15	8	15	65	79	38
12 Dundee	38	15	6	17	68	64	36
13 Partick	38	14	5	19	73	78	33
14 Clyde	38	10	11	17	56	70	31
15 Queen's Park	38	13	5	20	65	85	31
16 Hibernian	38	12	3	23	51	69	27
17 St Mirren	38	9	9	20	46	75	27
18 Airdrieonians	38	10	6	22	59	103	26
19 Third Lanark	38	8	9	21	62	103	25
20 Cowdenbeath	38	5	5	28	58	118	15

Scottish Second Division

	P	W	D	L	F	A	Pts
1 Albion	34	20	5	9	74	47	45
2 Dunfermline	34	20	4	10	90	52	44
3 Arbroath	34	20	4	10	83	53	44
4 Stenhousemuir	34	18	4	12	70	73	40
5 Morton	34	17	5	12	67	64	39
6 Dumbarton	34	17	3	14	67	68	37
7 King's Park	34	14	8	12	78	70	36
8 Raith	34	15	5	14	71	55	35
9 E Stirlingshire	34	14	7	13	65	74	35
10 St Bernard's	34	15	4	15	75	56	34
11 Forfar	34	13	7	14	77	71	33
12 Leith	34	12	8	14	63	60	32
13 East Fife	34	12	8	14	71	76	32
14 Brechin	34	13	5	16	60	70	31
15 Alloa	34	11	9	14	55	68	31
16 Montrose	34	11	4	19	53	81	26
17 Dundee United	34	10	4	20	81	88	24
18 Edinburgh City	34	4	6	24	37	111	14

FA Cup

Fourth Round

Portsmouth v Grimsby Town	2-0
Bury v Swansea Town	1-1, 0-3
Liverpool v Tranmere Rovers	3-1
Brighton v Bolton Wanderers	1-1, 1-6
Workington v Preston North End	1-2
Huddersfield Town v Northampton Town	0-2
Birmingham v Charlton Athletic	1-0
Millwall v Leicester City	3-6
Aston Villa v Sunderland	7-2
Tottenham Hotspur v West Ham United	4-1
Derby County v Wolverhampton Wanderers	3-0
Arsenal v Crystal Palace	7-0
Stoke City v Blackpool	3-0
Chelsea v Nottingham Forest	1-1, 3-0
Oldham Athletic v Sheffield Wednesday	1-1, 1-6
Hull City v Manchester City	2-2, 1-4

Fifth Round

Swansea Town v Portsmouth	0-1
Liverpool v Bolton Wanderers	0-3
Preston North End v Northampton Town	4-0
Birmingham v Leicester City	1-2
Tottenham Hotspur v Aston Villa	0-1
Arsenal v Derby County	1-0
Stoke City v Chelsea	3-1
Sheffield Wednesday v Manchester City	2-2, 0-2

Sixth Round

Bolton Wanderers v Portsmouth	0-3
Preston North End v Leicester City	0-1
Arsenal v Aston Villa	1-2
Manchester City v Stoke City	1-0

Semi-Final

Portsmouth v Leicester City	4-1
Manchester City v Aston Villa	6-1

Final

Manchester City v Portsmouth	2-1

Scottish FA Cup

Third Round

Rangers v Heart of Midlothian	0-0, 2-1
Hibernian v Aberdeen	0-1
Queen of the South v Cowdenbeath	3-0
Celtic v Falkirk	3-1
Albion Rovers v Ross County	6-1
Motherwell v East Stirlingshire	5-0
St Johnstone	bye
St Mirren	bye

Fourth Round

Rangers v Aberdeen	1-0
St Johnstone v Queen of the South	2-0
St Mirren v Celtic	2-0
Albion Rovers v Motherwell	1-1, 0-6

Semi-Final

Rangers v St Johnstone	1-0
St Mirren v Motherwell	3-1

Final

Rangers v St Mirren	5-0

1934–35
First Division

	P	W	D	L	F	A	Pts
1 Arsenal	42	23	12	7	115	46	58
2 Sunderland	42	19	16	7	90	51	54
3 Sheff Wed	42	18	13	11	70	64	49
4 Man City	42	20	8	14	82	67	48
5 Grimsby	42	17	11	14	78	60	45

	P	W	D	L	F	A	Pts
6 Derby	42	18	9	15	81	66	45
7 Liverpool	42	19	7	16	85	88	45
8 Everton	42	16	12	14	89	88	44
9 WBA	42	17	10	15	83	83	44
10 Stoke	42	18	6	18	71	70	42
11 Preston	42	15	12	15	62	67	42
12 Chelsea	42	16	9	17	73	82	41
13 Aston Villa	42	14	13	15	74	88	41
14 Portsmouth	42	15	10	17	71	72	40
15 Blackburn	42	14	11	17	66	78	39
16 Huddersfield	42	14	10	18	76	71	38
17 Wolves	42	15	8	19	88	94	38
18 Leeds	42	13	12	17	75	92	38
19 Birmingham	42	13	10	19	63	81	36
20 Middlesbrough	42	10	14	18	70	90	34
21 Leicester	42	12	9	21	61	86	33
22 Tottenham	42	10	10	22	54	93	30

Second Division

	P	W	D	L	F	A	Pts
1 Brentford	42	26	9	7	93	48	61
2 Bolton	42	26	4	12	96	48	56
3 West Ham	42	26	4	12	80	63	56
4 Blackpool	42	21	11	10	79	57	53
5 Man United	42	23	4	15	76	55	50
6 Newcastle	42	22	4	16	89	68	48
7 Fulham	42	17	12	13	76	56	46
8 Plymouth	42	19	8	15	75	64	46
9 Nottm Forest	42	17	8	17	76	70	42
10 Bury	42	19	4	19	62	73	42
11 Sheff United	42	16	9	17	79	70	41
12 Burnley	42	16	9	17	63	73	41
13 Hull	42	16	8	18	63	74	40
14 Norwich	42	14	11	17	71	61	39
15 Bradford PA	42	11	16	15	55	63	38
16 Barnsley	42	13	12	17	60	83	38
17 Swansea	42	14	8	20	56	67	36
18 Port Vale	42	11	12	19	55	74	34
19 Southampton	42	11	12	19	46	75	34
20 Bradford City	42	12	8	22	50	68	32
21 Oldham	42	10	6	26	56	95	26
22 Notts County	42	9	7	26	46	97	25

Third Division (North)

	P	W	D	L	F	A	Pts
1 Doncaster	42	26	5	11	87	44	57
2 Halifax	42	25	5	12	76	67	55
3 Chester	42	20	14	8	91	58	54
4 Lincoln	42	22	7	13	87	58	51

	P	W	D	L	F	A	Pts
5 Darlington	42	21	9	12	80	59	51
6 Tranmere	42	20	11	11	74	55	51
7 Stockport	42	22	3	17	90	72	47
8 Mansfield	42	19	9	14	75	62	47
9 Rotherham	42	19	7	16	86	73	45
10 Chesterfield	42	17	10	15	71	52	44
11 Wrexham	42	16	11	15	76	69	43
12 Hartlepools	42	17	7	18	80	78	41
13 Crewe	42	14	11	17	66	86	39
14 Walsall	42	13	10	19	81	72	36
15 York	42	15	6	21	76	82	36
16 New Brighton	42	14	8	20	59	76	36
17 Barrow	42	13	9	20	58	87	35
18 Accrington	42	12	10	20	63	89	34
19 Gateshead	42	13	8	21	58	96	34
20 Rochdale	42	11	11	20	53	71	33
21 Southport	42	10	12	20	55	85	32
22 Carlisle	42	8	7	27	51	102	23

Third Division (South)

	P	W	D	L	F	A	Pts
1 Charlton	42	27	7	8	103	52	61
2 Reading	42	21	11	10	89	65	53
3 Coventry	42	21	9	12	86	50	51
4 Luton	42	19	12	11	92	60	50
5 Crystal Palace	42	19	10	13	86	64	48
6 Watford	42	19	9	14	76	49	47
7 Northampton	42	19	8	15	65	67	46
8 Bristol Rovers	42	17	10	15	73	77	44
9 Brighton	42	17	9	16	69	62	43
10 Torquay	42	18	6	18	81	75	42
11 Exeter	42	16	9	17	70	75	41
12 Millwall	42	17	7	18	57	62	41
13 QPR	42	16	9	17	63	72	41
14 Clapton Orient	42	15	10	17	65	65	40
15 Bristol City	42	15	9	18	52	68	39
16 Swindon	42	13	12	17	67	78	38
17 Bournemouth	42	15	7	20	54	71	37
18 Aldershot	42	13	10	19	50	75	36
19 Cardiff	42	13	9	20	62	82	35
20 Gillingham	42	11	13	18	55	75	35
21 Southend	42	11	9	22	65	78	31
22 Newport	42	10	5	27	54	112	25

Scottish First Division

	P	W	D	L	F	A	Pts
1 Rangers	38	25	5	8	96	46	55
2 Celtic	38	24	4	10	92	45	52
3 Hearts	38	20	10	8	87	51	50

4 Hamilton	38	19	10	9	87	67	48
5 St Johnstone	38	18	10	10	66	46	46
6 Aberdeen	38	17	10	11	68	54	44
7 Motherwell	38	15	10	13	83	64	40
8 Dundee	38	16	8	14	63	63	40
9 Kilmarnock	38	16	6	16	76	68	38
10 Clyde	38	14	10	14	71	69	38
11 Hibernian	38	14	8	16	59	70	36
12 Queen's Park	38	13	10	15	61	80	36
13 Partick	38	15	5	18	61	68	35
14 Airdrieonians	38	13	7	18	64	72	33
15 Dunfermline	38	13	5	20	56	96	31
16 Albion	38	10	9	19	62	77	29
17 Queen of the S	38	11	7	20	52	72	29
18 Ayr	38	12	5	21	61	112	29
19 St Mirren	38	11	5	22	49	70	27
20 Falkirk	38	9	6	23	58	82	24

Scottish Second Division

	P	W	D	L	F	A	Pts
1 Third Lanark	34	23	6	5	94	43	52
2 Arbroath	34	23	4	7	78	42	50
3 St Bernard's	34	20	7	7	103	47	47
4 Dundee United	34	18	6	10	105	65	42
5 Stenhousemuir	34	17	5	12	86	80	39
6 Morton	34	17	4	13	88	64	38
7 King's Park	34	18	2	14	86	71	38
8 Leith	34	16	5	13	69	71	37
9 East Fife	34	16	3	15	79	73	35
10 Alloa	34	12	10	12	68	61	34
11 Forfar	34	13	8	13	77	73	34
12 Cowdenbeath	34	13	6	15	84	75	32
13 Raith	34	13	3	18	68	73	29
14 E Stirlingshire	34	11	7	16	57	76	29
15 Brechin	34	10	6	18	51	98	26
16 Dumbarton	34	9	4	21	60	105	22
17 Montrose	34	7	6	21	58	105	20
18 Edinburgh City	34	3	2	29	45	134	8

FA CUP

Fourth Round

Wolverhampton Wanderers v Sheffield Wednesday	1-2
Norwich City v Leeds United	3-3, 2-1
Reading v Millwall	1-0
Leicester City v Arsenal	0-1
Southampton v Birmingham	0-3
Blackburn Rovers v Liverpool	1-0
Nottingham Forest v Manchester United	0-0, 3-0

Burnley v Luton Town	3-1
Plymouth Argyle v Bolton Wanderers	1-4
Tottenham Hotspur v Newcastle United	2-0
Derby County v Swansea Town	3-0
Sunderland v Everton	1-1, 4-6
Swindon Town v Preston North End	0-2
Portsmouth v Bristol City	0-0, 0-2
Bradford City v Stockport County	0-0, 2-3
West Bromwich Albion v Sheffield United	7-1

Fifth Round

Norwich City v Sheffield Wednesday	0-1
Reading v Arsenal	0-1
Blackburn Rovers v Birmingham	1-2
Nottingham Forest v Burnley	0-0, 0-3
Tottenham Hotspur v Bolton Wanderers	1-1, 1-1, 0-2
Everton v Derby County	3-1
Bristol City v Preston North End	0-0, 0-5
Stockport County v West Bromwich Albion	0-5

Sixth Round

Sheffield Wednesday v Arsenal	2-1
Burnley v Birmingham	3-2
Everton v Bolton Wanderers	1-2
West Bromwich Albion v Preston North End	1-0

Semi-Final

Sheffield Wednesday v Burnley	3-0
Bolton Wanderers v West Bromwich Albion	1-1, 0-2

Final

Sheffield Wednesday v West Bromwich Albion	4-2

Scottish FA Cup

Third Round

Rangers v St Mirren	1-0
Airdrieonians v King's Park	6-2
Heart of Midlothian v Dundee United	2-2, 4-2
Aberdeen v Hibernian	0-0, 1-1, 3-2
Brechin City v Hamilton Academicals	2-4
Buckie Thistle v St Johnstone	0-1
Motherwell	bye
Celtic	bye

Fourth Round

Motherwell v Rangers	1-4
Airdrieonians v Heart of Midlothian	2-3
Aberdeen v Celtic	3-1
Hamilton Academicals v St Johnstone	3-0

Semi-Final

| Rangers v Heart of Midlothian | 1-1, 2-0 |
| Aberdeen v Hamilton Academicals | 1-2 |

Final

| Rangers v Hamilton Academicals | 2-1 |

1935–36
First Division

		P	W	D	L	F	A	Pts
1	Sunderland	42	25	6	11	109	74	56
2	Derby	42	18	12	12	61	52	48
3	Huddersfield	42	18	12	12	59	56	48
4	Stoke	42	20	7	15	57	57	47
5	Brentford	42	17	12	13	81	60	46
6	Arsenal	42	15	15	12	78	48	45
7	Preston	42	18	8	16	67	64	44
8	Chelsea	42	15	13	14	65	72	43
9	Man City	42	17	8	17	68	60	42
10	Portsmouth	42	17	8	17	54	67	42
11	Leeds	42	15	11	16	66	64	41
12	Birmingham	42	15	11	16	61	63	41
13	Bolton	42	14	13	15	67	76	41
14	Middlesbrough	42	15	10	17	84	70	40
15	Wolves	42	15	10	17	77	76	40
16	Everton	42	13	13	16	89	89	39
17	Grimsby	42	17	5	20	65	73	39
18	WBA	42	16	6	20	89	88	38
19	Liverpool	42	13	12	17	60	64	38
20	Sheff Wed	42	13	12	17	63	77	38
21	Aston Villa	42	13	9	20	81	110	35
22	Blackburn	42	12	9	21	55	96	33

Second Division

		P	W	D	L	F	A	Pts
1	Man United	42	22	12	8	85	43	56
2	Charlton	42	22	11	9	85	58	55
3	Sheff United	42	20	12	10	79	50	52
4	West Ham	42	22	8	12	90	68	52
5	Tottenham	42	18	13	11	91	55	49
6	Leicester	42	19	10	13	79	57	48
7	Plymouth	42	20	8	14	71	57	48

		P	W	D	L	F	A	Pts
8	Newcastle	42	20	6	16	88	79	46
9	Fulham	42	15	14	13	76	52	44
10	Blackpool	42	18	7	17	93	72	43
11	Norwich	42	17	9	16	72	65	43
12	Bradford City	42	15	13	14	55	65	43
13	Swansea	42	15	9	18	67	76	39
14	Bury	42	13	12	17	66	84	38
15	Burnley	42	12	13	17	50	59	37
16	Bradford PA	42	14	9	19	62	84	37
17	Southampton	42	14	9	19	47	65	37
18	Doncaster	42	14	9	19	51	71	37
19	Nottm Forest	42	12	11	19	69	76	35
20	Barnsley	42	12	9	21	54	80	33
21	Port Vale	42	12	8	22	56	106	32
22	Hull	42	5	10	27	47	111	20

Third Division (North)

		P	W	D	L	F	A	Pts
1	Chesterfield	42	24	12	6	92	39	60
2	Chester	42	22	11	9	100	45	55
3	Tranmere	42	22	11	9	93	58	55
4	Lincoln	42	22	10	8	91	51	53
5	Stockport	42	20	8	14	65	49	48
6	Crewe	42	19	9	14	80	76	47
7	Oldham	42	18	9	15	86	73	45
8	Hartlepools	42	15	12	15	57	61	42
9	Accrington	42	17	8	17	63	72	42
10	Walsall	42	16	9	17	79	59	41
11	Rotherham	42	16	9	17	69	66	41
12	Darlington	42	17	6	19	74	79	40
13	Carlisle	42	14	12	16	56	62	40
14	Gateshead	42	13	14	15	56	76	40
15	Barrow	42	13	12	17	58	65	38
16	York	42	13	12	17	62	95	38
17	Halifax	42	15	7	20	57	61	37
18	Wrexham	42	15	7	20	66	75	37
19	Mansfield	42	14	9	19	80	91	37
20	Rochdale	42	10	13	19	58	88	33
21	Southport	42	11	9	22	48	90	31
22	New Brighton	42	9	6	27	43	102	24

Third Division (South)

		P	W	D	L	F	A	Pts
1	Coventry	42	24	9	9	102	45	57
2	Luton	42	22	12	8	81	45	56
3	Reading	42	26	2	14	87	62	54
4	QPR	42	22	9	11	84	53	53
5	Watford	42	20	9	13	80	54	49
6	Crystal Palace	52	22	5	15	96	74	49
7	Brighton	42	18	8	16	70	63	44

8 Bournemouth	42	16	11	15	60	56	43
9 Notts County	42	15	12	15	60	57	42
10 Torquay	42	16	9	17	62	62	41
11 Aldershot	42	14	12	16	53	61	40
12 Millwall	42	14	12	16	58	71	40
13 Bristol City	42	15	10	17	48	59	40
14 Clapton Orient	42	16	6	20	55	61	38
15 Northampton	42	15	8	19	62	90	38
16 Gillingham	42	14	9	19	66	77	37
17 Bristol Rovers	42	14	9	19	69	95	37
18 Southend	42	13	10	19	61	62	36
19 Swindon	42	14	8	20	64	73	36
20 Cardiff	42	13	10	19	60	73	36
21 Newport	42	11	9	22	60	111	31
22 Exeter	42	8	11	23	59	93	27

Scottish First Division

	P	W	D	L	F	A	Pts
1 Celtic	38	32	2	4	115	33	66
2 Rangers	38	27	7	4	110	43	61
3 Aberdeen	38	26	9	3	96	50	61
4 Motherwell	38	18	12	8	77	58	48
5 Hearts	38	20	7	11	88	55	47
6 Hamilton	38	15	7	16	77	74	37
7 St Johnstone	38	15	7	16	70	81	37
8 Kilmarnock	38	14	7	17	69	64	35
9 Partick	38	12	10	16	64	72	34
10 Dunfermline	38	13	8	17	73	92	34
11 Third Lanark	38	14	5	19	63	71	33
12 Arbroath	38	11	11	16	46	69	33
13 Dundee	38	11	10	17	67	80	32
14 Queen's Park	38	11	10	17	58	75	32
15 Queen of the S	38	11	9	18	54	72	31
16 Albion	38	13	4	21	69	92	30
17 Hibernian	38	11	7	20	56	82	29
18 Clyde	38	10	8	20	63	84	28
19 Airdrieonians	38	9	9	20	68	91	27
20 Ayr	38	11	3	24	53	98	25

Scottish Second Division

	P	W	D	L	F	A	Pts
1 Falkirk	34	28	3	3	132	34	59
2 St Mirren	34	25	2	7	114	41	52
3 Morton	34	21	6	7	117	60	48
4 Alloa	34	19	6	9	65	51	44
5 St Bernard's	34	18	4	12	106	78	40
6 East Fife	34	16	6	12	86	79	38
7 Dundee United	34	16	5	13	108	81	37
8 E Stirlingshire	34	13	8	13	70	75	34
9 Leith	34	15	3	16	67	77	33
10 Cowdenbeath	34	13	5	16	76	77	31

11 Stenhousemuir	34	13	3	18	59	78	29
12 Montrose	34	13	3	18	58	82	29
13 Forfar	34	10	7	17	60	81	27
14 King's Park	34	11	5	18	55	109	27
15 Edinburgh City	34	8	9	17	57	83	25
16 Brechin	34	8	6	20	57	96	22
17 Raith	34	9	3	22	60	96	21
18 Dumbarton	34	5	6	23	52	121	16

FA CUP

Fourth Round

Liverpool v Arsenal	0-2
Sheffield Wednesday v Newcastle United	1-1, 1-3
Tranmere Rovers v Barnsley	2-4
Stoke City v Manchester United	0-0, 0-2
Port Vale v Grimsby Town	0-4
Manchester City v Luton Town	2-1
Middlesbrough v Clapton Orient	3-0
Leicester City v Watford	6-3
Fulham v Blackpool	5-2
Chelsea v Plymouth Argyle	4-1
Bradford City v Blackburn Rovers	3-1
Derby County v Nottingham Forest	2-0
Preston North End v Sheffield United	0-0, 0-2
Leeds United v Bury	2-1*, 3-2
Tottenham Hotspur v Huddersfield Town	1-0
Bradford Park Avenue v West Bromwich Albion	1-1, 1-1, 2-0

*abandoned

Fifth Round

Newcastle United v Arsenal	3-3, 0-3
Barnsley v Stoke City	2-1
Grimsby Town v Manchester City	3-2
Middlesbrough v Leicester City	2-1
Chelsea v Fulham	0-0, 2-3
Bradford City v Derby County	0-1
Sheffield United v Leeds United	3-1
Bradford Park Avenue v Tottenham Hotspur	0-0, 1-2

Sixth Round

Arsenal v Barnsley	4-1
Grimsby Town v Middlesbrough	3-1
Fulham v Derby County	3-0
Sheffield United v Tottenham Hotspur	3-1

Semi-Final

Arsenal v Grimsby Town	1-0

Fulham v Sheffield United   1-2

Final
Arsenal v Sheffield United   1-0

Scottish FA Cup

Third Round
Aberdeen v St Johnstone   1-1, 1-0
St Mirren v Rangers   1-2
Clyde v Dundee   1-1, 3-0
Cowdenbeath v Motherwell   1-3
Morton v Queen of the South   2-0
Third Lanark v Dumbarton   8-0
Falkirk   bye
Dunfermline Athletic   bye

Fourth Round
Aberdeen v Rangers   0-1
Clyde v Motherwell   3-2
Falkirk v Dunfermline Athletic   5-0
Morton v Third Lanark   3-5

Semi-Final
Rangers v Clyde   3-0
Falkirk v Third Lanark   1-3

Final
Rangers v Third Lanark   1-0

1936–37
First Division

	P	W	D	L	F	A	Pts
1 Man City	42	22	13	7	107	61	57
2 Charlton	42	21	12	9	58	49	54
3 Arsenal	42	18	16	8	80	49	52
4 Derby	42	21	7	14	96	90	49
5 Wolves	42	21	5	16	84	67	47
6 Brentford	42	18	10	14	82	78	46
7 Middlesbrough	42	19	8	15	74	71	46
8 Sunderland	42	19	6	17	89	87	44
9 Portsmouth	42	17	10	15	62	66	44
10 Stoke	42	15	12	15	72	57	42
11 Birmingham	42	13	15	14	64	60	41
12 Grimsby	42	17	7	18	86	81	41
13 Chelsea	42	14	13	15	52	55	41
14 Preston	42	14	13	15	56	67	41
15 Huddersfield	42	12	15	15	62	64	39
16 WBA	42	16	6	20	77	98	38
17 Everton	42	14	9	19	81	78	37
18 Liverpool	42	12	11	19	62	84	35
19 Leeds	42	15	4	23	60	80	34
20 Bolton	42	10	14	18	43	66	34
21 Man United	42	10	12	20	55	78	32
22 Sheff Wed	42	9	12	21	53	69	30

Second Division

	P	W	D	L	F	A	Pts
1 Leicester	42	24	8	10	89	57	56
2 Blackpool	42	24	7	11	88	53	55
3 Bury	42	22	8	12	74	55	52
4 Newcastle	42	22	5	15	80	56	49
5 Plymouth	42	18	13	11	71	53	49
6 West Ham	42	19	11	12	73	55	49
7 Sheff United	42	18	10	14	66	54	46
8 Coventry	42	17	11	14	66	54	45
9 Aston Villa	42	16	12	14	82	70	44
10 Tottenham	42	17	9	16	88	66	43
11 Fulham	42	15	13	14	71	61	43
12 Blackburn	42	16	10	16	70	62	42
13 Burnley	42	16	10	16	57	61	42
14 Barnsley	42	16	9	17	50	64	41
15 Chesterfield	42	16	8	18	84	89	40
16 Swansea	42	15	7	20	50	65	37
17 Norwich	42	14	8	20	63	71	36
18 Nottm Forest	42	12	10	20	68	90	34
19 Southampton	42	11	12	19	53	77	34
20 Bradford PA	42	12	9	21	52	88	33
21 Bradford City	42	9	12	21	54	94	30
22 Doncaster	42	7	10	25	30	84	24

Third Division (North)

	P	W	D	L	F	A	Pts
1 Stockport	42	23	14	5	84	39	60
2 Lincoln	42	25	7	10	103	57	57
3 Chester	42	22	9	11	87	57	53
4 Oldham	42	20	11	11	77	59	51
5 Hull	42	17	12	13	68	69	46
6 Hartlepools	42	19	7	16	75	69	45
7 Halifax	42	18	9	15	68	63	45
8 Wrexham	42	16	12	14	71	57	44
9 Mansfield	42	18	8	16	91	76	44
10 Carlisle	42	18	8	16	65	68	44
11 Port Vale	42	17	10	15	58	64	44
12 York	42	16	11	15	79	70	43
13 Accrington	42	16	9	17	76	69	41
14 Southport	42	12	13	17	73	87	37
15 New Brighton	42	13	11	18	55	70	37
16 Barrow	42	13	10	19	70	86	36
17 Rotherham	42	14	7	21	78	91	35
18 Rochdale	42	13	9	20	69	86	35
19 Tranmere	42	12	9	21	71	88	33

20 Crewe	42	10	12	20	55	83	32
21 Gateshead	42	11	10	21	63	98	32
22 Darlington	42	8	14	20	66	96	30

Third Division (South)

	P	W	D	L	F	A	Pts
1 Luton	42	27	4	11	103	53	58
2 Notts County	42	23	10	9	74	52	56
3 Brighton	42	24	5	13	74	43	53
4 Watford	42	19	11	12	85	60	49
5 Reading	42	19	11	12	76	60	49
6 Bournemouth	42	20	9	13	65	59	49
7 Northampton	42	20	6	16	85	68	46
8 Millwall	42	18	10	14	64	54	46
9 QPR	42	18	9	15	73	52	45
10 Southend	42	17	11	14	78	67	45
11 Gillingham	42	18	8	16	52	66	44
12 Clapton Orient	42	14	15	13	52	52	43
13 Swindon	42	14	11	17	75	73	39
14 Crystal Palace	42	13	12	17	62	61	38
15 Bristol Rovers	42	16	4	22	71	80	36
16 Bristol City	42	15	6	21	58	70	36
17 Walsall	42	13	10	19	62	84	36
18 Cardiff	42	14	7	21	54	87	35
19 Newport	42	12	10	20	67	98	34
20 Torquay	42	11	10	21	57	80	32
21 Exeter	42	10	12	20	59	88	32
22 Aldershot	42	7	9	26	50	89	23

Scottish First Division

	P	W	D	L	F	A	Pts
1 Rangers	38	26	9	3	88	32	61
2 Aberdeen	38	23	8	7	89	44	54
3 Celtic	38	22	8	8	89	58	52
4 Motherwell	38	22	7	9	96	54	51
5 Hearts	38	24	3	11	99	60	51
6 Third Lanark	38	20	6	12	79	61	46
7 Falkirk	38	19	6	13	98	66	44
8 Hamilton	38	18	5	15	91	96	41
9 Dundee	38	12	15	11	58	69	39
10 Clyde	38	16	6	16	59	70	38
11 Kilmarnock	38	14	9	15	60	70	37
12 St Johnstone	38	14	8	16	74	68	36
13 Partick	38	11	12	15	73	68	34
14 Arbroath	38	13	5	20	57	84	31
15 Queen's Park	38	9	12	17	51	77	30
16 St Mirren	38	11	7	20	68	81	29
17 Hibernian	38	6	13	19	54	83	25
18 Queen of the S	38	8	8	22	49	95	24
19 Dunfermline	38	5	11	22	65	98	21
20 Albion	38	5	6	27	53	116	16

Scottish Second Division

	P	W	D	L	F	A	Pts
1 Ayr	34	25	4	5	122	49	54
2 Morton	34	23	5	6	110	42	51
3 St Bernard's	34	22	4	8	102	51	48
4 Airdrieonians	34	18	8	8	85	60	44
5 East Fife	34	15	8	11	76	51	38
6 Cowdenbeath	34	14	10	10	75	59	38
7 E Stirlingshire	34	18	2	14	81	78	38
8 Raith	34	16	4	14	72	66	36
9 Alloa	34	13	7	14	64	65	33
10 Stenhousemuir	34	14	4	16	82	86	32
11 Leith	34	13	5	16	62	65	31
12 Forfar	34	11	8	15	73	89	30
13 Montrose	34	11	6	17	65	100	28
14 Dundee United	34	9	9	16	72	97	27
15 Dumbarton	34	11	5	18	57	83	27
16 Brechin	34	8	9	17	64	98	25
17 King's Park	34	11	3	20	61	106	25
18 Edinburgh City	34	2	3	29	42	120	7

FA CUP

Fourth Round

Luton Town v Sunderland	2-2, 1-3
Swansea Town v York City	0-0, 3-1
Grimsby Town v Walsall	5-1
Wolverhampton Wanderers v Sheffield United	2-2, 2-1
Millwall v Chelsea	3-0
Derby County v Brentford	3-0
Bolton Wanderers v Norwich City	1-1, 2-1
Manchester City v Accrington Stanley	2-0
Tottenham Hotspur v Plymouth Argyle	1-0
Everton v Sheffield Wednesday	3-0
Preston North End v Stoke City	5-1
Exeter City v Leicester City	3-1
Coventry City v Chester	2-0
West Bromwich Albion v Darlington	3-2
Burnley v Bury	4-1
Arsenal v Manchester United	5-0

Fifth Round

Sunderland v Swansea Town	3-0
Grimsby Town v Wolverhampton Wanderers	1-1, 2-6
Millwall v Derby County	2-1
Bolton Wanderers v Manchester City	0-5
Everton v Tottenham Hotspur	1-1, 3-4
Preston North End v Exeter City	5-3

Coventry City v West Bromwich Albion
2-3

Burnley v Arsenal   1-7

Sixth Round

Wolverhampton Wanderers v
   Sunderland   1-1, 2-2, 0-4
Millwall v Manchester City   2-0
Tottenham Hotspur v Preston North
   End   1-3
West Bromwich Albion v Arsenal   3-1

Semi-Final

Sunderland v Millwall   2-1
Preston North End v West Bromwich
   Albion   4-1

Final

Sunderland v Preston North End   3-1

Scottish FA Cup

Third Round

East Fife v Celtic   0-3
Duns v Motherwell   2-5
St Mirren v Cowdenbeath   1-0
Clyde v Dundee   0-0, 1-0
Hamilton Academicals v Heart of
   Midlothian   2-1
Morton v Partick Thistle   1-1, 2-1
Aberdeen   bye
Queen of the South   bye

Fourth Round

Celtic v Motherwell   4-4, 2-1
St Mirren v Clyde   0-3
Hamilton Academicals v Aberdeen   1-2
Morton v Queen of the South   4-1

Semi-Final

Celtic v Clyde   2-0
Aberdeen v Morton   2-0

Final

Celtic v Aberdeen   2-1

1937–38
First Division

	P	W	D	L	F	A	Pts
1 Arsenal	42	21	10	11	77	44	52
2 Wolves	42	20	11	11	72	49	51
3 Preston	42	16	17	9	64	44	49
4 Charlton	42	16	14	12	65	51	46
5 Middlesbrough	42	19	8	15	72	65	46
6 Brentford	42	18	9	15	69	59	45
7 Bolton	42	15	15	12	64	60	45
8 Sunderland	42	14	16	12	55	57	44
9 Leeds	42	14	15	13	64	69	43
10 Chelsea	42	14	13	15	65	65	41
11 Liverpool	42	15	11	16	65	71	41
12 Blackpool	42	16	8	18	61	66	40
13 Derby	42	15	10	17	66	87	40
14 Everton	42	16	7	19	79	75	39
15 Huddersfield	42	17	5	20	55	68	39
16 Leicester	42	14	11	17	54	75	39
17 Stoke	42	13	12	17	58	59	38
18 Birmingham	42	10	18	14	58	62	38
19 Portsmouth	42	13	12	17	62	68	38
20 Grimsby	42	13	12	17	51	68	38
21 Man City	42	14	8	20	80	77	36
22 WBA	42	14	8	20	74	91	36

Second Division

	P	W	D	L	F	A	Pts
1 Aston Villa	42	25	7	10	73	35	57
2 Man United	42	22	9	11	82	50	53
3 Sheff United	42	22	9	11	73	56	53
4 Coventry	42	20	12	10	66	45	52
5 Tottenham	42	19	6	17	76	54	44
6 Burnley	42	17	10	15	54	54	44
7 Bradford PA	42	17	9	16	69	56	43
8 Fulham	42	16	11	15	61	57	43
9 West Ham	42	14	14	14	53	52	42
10 Bury	42	18	5	19	63	60	41
11 Chesterfield	42	16	9	17	63	63	41
12 Luton	42	15	10	17	89	86	40
13 Plymouth	42	14	12	16	57	65	40
14 Norwich	42	14	11	17	56	75	39
15 Southampton	42	15	9	18	55	77	39
16 Blackburn	42	14	10	18	71	80	38
17 Sheff Wed	42	14	10	18	49	56	38
18 Swansea	42	13	12	17	45	73	38
19 Newcastle	42	14	8	20	51	58	36
20 Nottm Forest	42	14	8	20	47	60	36
21 Barnsley	42	11	14	17	50	64	36
22 Stockport	42	11	9	22	43	70	31

Third Division (North)

	P	W	D	L	F	A	Pts
1 Tranmere	42	23	10	9	81	41	56
2 Doncaster	42	21	12	9	74	49	54
3 Hull	42	20	13	9	80	43	53
4 Oldham	42	19	13	10	67	46	51

	P	W	D	L	F	A	Pts
5 Gateshead	42	20	11	11	84	59	51
6 Rotherham	42	20	10	12	68	56	50
7 Lincoln	42	19	8	15	66	50	46
8 Crewe	42	18	9	15	71	53	45
9 Chester	42	16	12	14	77	72	44
10 Wrexham	42	16	11	15	58	63	43
11 York	42	16	10	16	70	68	42
12 Carlisle	42	15	9	18	57	67	39
13 New Brighton	42	15	8	19	60	61	38
14 Bradford City	42	14	10	18	66	69	38
15 Port Vale	42	12	14	16	65	73	38
16 Southport	42	12	14	16	53	82	38
17 Rochdale	42	13	11	18	67	78	37
18 Halifax	42	12	12	18	44	66	36
19 Darlington	42	11	10	21	54	79	32
20 Hartlepools	42	10	12	20	53	80	32
21 Barrow	42	11	10	21	41	71	32
22 Accrington	42	11	7	24	45	75	29

Third Division (South)

	P	W	D	L	F	A	Pts
1 Millwall	42	23	10	9	83	37	56
2 Bristol City	42	21	13	8	68	40	55
3 QPR	42	22	9	11	80	47	53
4 Watford	42	21	11	10	73	43	53
5 Brighton	42	21	9	12	64	44	51
6 Reading	42	20	11	11	71	63	51
7 Crystal Palace	42	18	12	12	67	47	48
8 Swindon	42	17	10	15	49	49	44
9 Northampton	42	17	9	16	51	57	43
10 Cardiff	42	15	12	15	67	54	42
11 Notts County	42	16	9	17	50	50	41
12 Southend	42	15	10	17	70	68	40
13 Bournemouth	42	14	12	16	56	57	40
14 Mansfield	42	15	9	18	62	67	39
15 Bristol Rovers	42	13	13	16	46	61	39
16 Newport	42	11	16	15	43	52	38
17 Exeter	42	13	12	17	57	70	38
18 Aldershot	42	15	5	22	39	59	35
19 Clapton Orient	42	13	7	22	42	61	33
20 Torquay	42	9	12	21	38	73	30
21 Walsall	42	11	7	24	52	88	29
22 Gillingham	42	10	6	26	36	77	26

Scottish First Division

	P	W	D	L	F	A	Pts
1 Celtic	38	27	7	4	114	42	61
2 Hearts	38	26	6	6	90	50	58
3 Rangers	38	18	13	7	75	49	49
4 Falkirk	38	19	9	10	82	52	47

	P	W	D	L	F	A	Pts
5 Motherwell	38	17	10	11	78	69	44
6 Aberdeen	38	15	9	14	74	59	39
7 Partick	38	15	9	14	68	70	39
8 St Johnstone	38	16	7	15	78	81	39
9 Third Lanark	38	11	13	14	68	73	35
10 Hibernian	38	11	13	14	57	65	35
11 Arbroath	38	11	13	14	58	79	35
12 Queen's Park	38	11	12	15	59	74	34
13 Hamilton	38	13	7	18	81	76	33
14 St Mirren	38	14	5	19	58	66	33
15 Clyde	38	10	13	15	68	78	33
16 Queen of the S	38	11	11	16	58	71	33
17 Ayr	38	9	15	14	66	85	33
18 Kilmarnock	38	12	9	17	65	91	33
19 Dundee	38	13	6	19	70	74	32
20 Morton	38	6	3	29	64	127	15

Scottish Second Division

	P	W	D	L	F	A	Pts
1 Raith	34	27	5	2	142	54	59
2 Albion	34	20	8	6	97	50	48
3 Airdrieonians	34	21	5	8	100	53	47
4 St Bernard's	34	20	5	9	75	49	45
5 East Fife	34	19	5	10	104	61	43
6 Cowdenbeath	34	17	9	8	115	71	43
7 Dumbarton	34	17	5	12	85	66	39
8 Stenhousemuir	34	17	5	12	87	78	39
9 Dunfermline	34	17	5	12	82	76	39
10 Leith	34	16	5	13	71	56	37
11 Alloa	34	11	4	19	78	106	26
12 King's Park	34	11	4	19	64	96	26
13 E Stirlingshire	34	9	7	18	55	95	25
14 Dundee United	34	9	5	20	69	104	23
15 Forfar	34	8	6	20	67	100	22
16 Montrose	34	7	8	19	56	88	22
17 Edinburgh City	34	7	3	24	77	135	17
18 Brechin	34	5	2	27	53	139	12

FA Cup

Fourth Round

Preston North End v Leicester City	2-0
Wolverhampton Wanderers v Arsenal	1-2
Barnsley v Manchester United	2-2, 0-1
Brentford v Portsmouth	2-1
Manchester City v Bury	3-1
Luton Town v Swindon Town	2-1
Charlton Athletic v Leeds United	2-1
Aston Villa v Blackpool	4-0
Everton v Sunderland	0-1

Bradford Park Avenue v Stoke City
1-1, 2-1
Chesterfield v Burnley   3-2
New Brighton v Tottenham Hotspur
0-0, 2-5
York City v West Bromwich Albion 3-2
Nottingham Forest v Middlesbrough 1-3
Sheffield United v Liverpool   1-1, 0-1
Huddersfield Town v Notts County   1-0

Fifth Round
Arsenal v Preston North End   0-1
Brentford v Manchester United   2-0
Luton Town v Manchester City   1-3
Charlton Athletic v Aston Villa
1-1, 2-2, 1-4
Sunderland v Bradford Park Avenue   1-0
Chesterfield v Tottenham Hotspur 2-2, 1-2
York City v Middlesbrough   1-0
Liverpool v Huddersfield Town   0-1

Sixth Round
Brentford v Preston North End   0-3
Aston Villa v Manchester City   3-2
Tottenham Hotspur v Sunderland   0-1
York City v Huddersfield Town 0-0, 1-2

Semi-Final
Preston North End v Aston Villa   2-1
Sunderland v Huddersfield Town   1-3

Final
Preston North End v Huddersfield Town
1-0

Scottish FA Cup

Third Round
Falkirk v Albion Rovers   4-0
Morton v Ayr United   1-1, 1-4
Celtic v Kilmarnock   1-2
Motherwell v Hamilton Academicals 2-0
Partick Thistle v Raith Rovers   1-2
East Fife v Aberdeen   1-1, 2-1
Rangers   bye
St Bernard's   bye

Fourth Round
Falkirk v Rangers   1-2
Kilmarnock v Ayr United   1-1, 5-0
St Bernard's v Motherwell   3-1
East Fife v Raith Rovers   2-2, 3-2

Semi-Final
Rangers v Kilmarnock   3-4

St Bernard's v East Fife   1-1, 1-1, 1-2
Final
Kilmarnock v East Fife   1-1, 2-4

1938-39
First Division

	P	W	D	L	F	A	Pts
1 Everton	42	27	5	10	88	52	59
2 Wolves	42	22	11	9	88	39	55
3 Charlton	42	22	6	14	75	59	50
4 Middlesbrough	42	20	9	13	93	74	49
5 Arsenal	42	19	9	14	55	41	47
6 Derby	42	19	8	15	66	55	46
7 Stoke	42	17	12	13	71	68	46
8 Bolton	42	15	15	12	67	58	45
9 Preston	42	16	12	14	63	59	44
10 Grimsby	42	16	11	15	61	69	43
11 Liverpool	42	14	14	14	62	63	42
12 Aston Villa	42	15	11	16	71	60	41
13 Leeds	42	16	9	17	59	67	41
14 Man United	42	11	16	15	57	65	38
15 Blackpool	42	12	14	16	56	68	38
16 Sunderland	42	13	12	17	54	67	38
17 Portsmouth	42	12	13	17	47	70	37
18 Brentford	42	14	8	20	53	74	36
19 Huddersfield	42	12	11	19	58	64	35
20 Chelsea	42	12	9	21	64	80	33
21 Birmingham	42	12	8	22	62	84	32
22 Leicester	42	9	11	22	48	82	29

Second Division

	P	W	D	L	F	A	Pts
1 Blackburn	42	25	5	12	94	60	55
2 Sheff United	42	20	14	8	69	41	54
3 Sheff Wed	42	21	11	10	88	59	53
4 Coventry	42	21	8	13	62	45	50
5 Man City	42	21	7	14	96	72	49
6 Chesterfield	42	20	9	13	69	52	49
7 Luton	42	22	5	15	82	66	49
8 Tottenham	42	19	9	14	67	62	47
9 Newcastle	42	18	10	14	61	48	46
10 WBA	42	18	9	15	89	72	45
11 West Ham	42	17	10	15	70	52	44
12 Fulham	42	17	10	15	61	55	44
13 Millwall	42	14	14	14	64	53	42
14 Burnley	42	15	9	18	50	56	39
15 Plymouth	42	15	8	19	49	55	38

16 Bury	42	12	13	17	65	74	37
17 Bradford PA	42	12	11	19	61	82	35
18 Southampton	42	13	9	20	56	82	35
19 Swansea	42	11	12	19	50	83	34
20 Nottm Forest	42	10	11	21	49	82	31
21 Norwich	42	13	5	24	50	91	31
22 Tranmere	42	6	5	31	39	99	17

Third Division (North)

	P	W	D	L	F	A	Pts
1 Barnsley	42	30	7	5	94	34	67
2 Doncaster	42	21	14	7	87	47	56
3 Bradford City	42	22	8	12	89	56	52
4 Southport	42	20	10	12	75	54	50
5 Oldham	42	22	5	15	76	59	49
6 Chester	42	20	9	13	88	70	49
7 Hull	42	18	10	14	83	74	46
8 Crewe	42	19	6	17	82	70	44
9 Stockport	42	17	9	16	91	77	43
10 Gateshead	42	14	14	14	74	67	42
11 Rotherham	42	17	8	17	64	64	42
12 Halifax	42	13	16	13	52	54	42
13 Barrow	42	16	9	17	66	65	41
14 Wrexham	42	17	7	18	66	79	41
15 Rochdale	42	15	9	18	92	82	39
16 New Brighton	42	15	9	18	68	73	39
17 Lincoln	42	12	9	21	66	92	33
18 Darlington	42	13	7	22	62	92	33
19 Carlisle	42	13	7	22	64	111	33
20 York	42	12	8	22	66	92	32
21 Hartlepools	42	12	7	23	55	94	31
22 Accrington	42	7	6	29	49	103	20

Third Division (South)

	P	W	D	L	F	A	Pts
1 Newport	42	22	11	9	58	45	55
2 Crystal Palace	42	20	12	10	71	52	52
3 Brighton	42	19	11	12	68	49	49
4 Watford	42	17	12	13	62	51	46
5 Reading	42	16	14	12	69	59	46
6 QPR	42	15	14	13	68	49	44
7 Ipswich	42	16	12	14	62	52	44
8 Bristol City	42	16	12	14	61	63	44
9 Swindon	42	18	8	16	72	77	44
10 Aldershot	42	16	12	14	53	66	44
11 Notts County	42	17	9	16	59	54	43
12 Southend	42	16	9	17	61	64	41
13 Cardiff	42	15	11	16	61	65	41
14 Exeter	42	13	14	15	65	82	40
15 Bournemouth	42	13	13	16	52	58	39

16 Mansfield	42	12	15	15	44	62	39
17 Northampton	42	15	8	19	51	58	38
18 Port Vale	42	14	9	19	52	58	37
19 Torquay	42	14	9	19	54	70	37
20 Clapton Orient	42	11	13	18	53	55	35
21 Walsall	42	11	11	20	68	69	33
22 Bristol Rovers	42	10	13	19	55	61	33

Scottish First Division

	P	W	D	L	F	A	Pts
1 Rangers	38	25	9	4	112	55	59
2 Celtic	38	20	8	10	99	53	48
3 Aberdeen	38	20	6	12	91	61	46
4 Hearts	38	20	5	13	98	70	45
5 Falkirk	38	19	7	12	73	63	45
6 Queen of the S	38	17	9	12	69	64	43
7 Hamilton	38	18	5	15	67	71	41
8 St Johnstone	38	17	6	15	85	82	40
9 Clyde	38	17	5	16	78	70	39
10 Kilmarnock	38	15	9	14	73	86	39
11 Partick	38	17	4	17	74	87	38
12 Motherwell	38	16	5	17	82	86	37
13 Hibernian	38	14	7	17	68	69	35
14 Ayr	38	13	9	16	76	83	35
15 Third Lanark	38	12	8	18	80	96	32
16 Albion	38	12	6	20	65	90	30
17 Arbroath	38	11	8	19	54	75	30
18 St Mirren	38	11	7	20	57	80	29
19 Queen's Park	38	11	5	22	57	83	27
20 Raith	38	10	2	26	65	99	22

Scottish Second Division

	P	W	D	L	F	A	Pts
1 Cowdenbeath	34	28	4	2	120	45	60
2 Alloa	34	22	4	8	91	46	48
3 East Fife	34	21	6	7	99	61	48
4 Airdrieonians	34	21	5	8	85	57	47
5 Dunfermline	34	18	5	11	99	78	41
6 Dundee	34	15	7	12	99	63	37
7 St Bernard's	34	15	6	13	79	79	36
8 Stenhousemuir	34	15	5	14	74	69	35
9 Dundee United	34	15	3	16	78	69	33
10 Brechin	34	11	9	14	82	106	31
11 Dumbarton	34	9	12	13	68	76	30
12 Morton	34	11	6	17	74	88	28
13 King's Park	34	12	2	20	87	92	26
14 Montrose	34	10	5	19	82	96	25
15 Forfar	34	11	3	20	74	138	25
16 Leith	34	10	4	20	57	83	24
17 E Stirlingshire	34	9	4	21	89	130	22
18 Edinburgh	34	6	4	24	58	119	16

FA Cup

Fourth Round
Portsmouth v West Bromwich Albion 2-0
West Ham United v Tottenham Hotspur
                                    3-3, 1-1, 2-1
Preston North End v Aston Villa   2-0
Cardiff City v Newcastle United 0-0, 1-4
Leeds United v Huddersfield Town   2-4
Notts County, v Walsall   0-0, 0-4
Middlesbrough v Sunderland   0-2
Blackburn Rovers v Southend United 4-2
Wolverhampton Wanderers v Leicester
        City   5-1
Liverpool v Stockport County   5-1
Everton v Doncaster Rovers   8-0
Birmingham v Chelmsford City   6-0
Chelsea v Fulham   3-0
Sheffield Wednesday v Chester
                         1-1, 1-1, 2-0
Sheffield United v Manchester City   2-0
Millwall v Grimsby Town   2-2, 2-3

Fifth Round
Portsmouth v West Ham United   2-0
Newcastle United v Preston North End
                                     1-2
Huddersfield Town v Walsall   3-0
Sunderland v Blackburn Rovers
                         1-1, 0-0, 0-1
Wolverhampton Wanderers v Liverpool
                                     4-1
Birmingham v Everton   2-2, 1-2
Chelsea v Sheffield Wednesday
                         1-1, 0-0, 3-1
Sheffield United v Grimsby Town 0-0, 0-1

Sixth Round
Portsmouth v Preston North End   1-0
Huddersfield Town v Blackburn Rovers
                                1-1, 2-1
Wolverhampton Wanderers v Everton 2-0
Chelsea v Grimsby Town   0-1

Semi-Final
Portsmouth v Huddersfield Town   2-1
Wolverhampton Wanderers v Grimsby
        Town   5-0

Final
Portsmouth v Wolverhampton Wanderers
                                     4-1

Scottish FA Cup

Third Round
Rangers v Clyde   1-4
Buckie Thistle v Third Lanark   0-6
Dunfermline Athletic v Alloa Athletic
                                1-1, 2-3
Falkirk v Aberdeen   2-3
Heart of Midlothian v Celtic   2-2, 1-2
Motherwell v St Mirren   4-2
Hibernian   bye
Queen of the South   bye

Fourth Round
Clyde v Third Lanark   1-0
Hibernian v Alloa Athletic   3-1
Aberdeen v Queen of the South   2-0
Motherwell v Celtic   3-1

Semi-Final
Clyde v Hibernian   1-0
Aberdeen v Motherwell   1-1, 1-3

Final
Clyde v Motherwell   4-0

1945–46
FA Cup

Fourth Round (two legs)
Stoke City v Sheffield United   2-0, 2-3
Sheffield Wednesday v York City 5-1, 6-1
Bolton Wanderers v Liverpool   5-0, 0-2
Blackpool v Middlesbrough 3-2, 2-3, 0-1
Manchester United v Preston North End
                                1-0, 1-3
Charlton Athletic v Wolverhampton
        Wanderers   5-2, 1-1
Southampton v Queen's Park Rangers
                                0-1, 3-4
Bristol City v Brentford   2-1, 0-5
Chelsea v West Ham United   2-0, 0-1
Millwall v Aston Villa   2-4, 1-9
Brighton v Aldershot   3-0, 4-1
Derby County v West Bromwich
        Albion   1-0, 3-1
Barnsley v Rotherham United   3-0, 1-2
Bradford Park Avenue v Manchester
        City   1-3, 8-2
Sunderland v Bury   3-1, 4-5
Birmingham City v Watford   5-0, 1-1

Fifth Round (two legs)
Stoke City v Sheffield Wednesday 2–0, 0–0
Bolton Wanderers v Middlesbrough
                  1–0, 1–1
Preston North End v Charlton Athletic
                  1–1, 0–6
Queen's Park Rangers v Brentford 1–3, 0–0
Chelsea v Aston Villa   0–1, 0–1
Brighton v Derby County   1–4, 0–6
Barnsley v Bradford Park Avenue 0–1, 1–1
Sunderland v Birmingham City 1–0, 1–3

Sixth Round (two legs)
Stoke City v Bolton Wanderers 0–2, 0–0
Charlton Athletic v Brentford 6–3, 3–1
Aston Villa v Derby County   3–4, 1–1
Bradford Park Avenue v Birmingham
    City   2–2, 0–6

Semi-Final
Bolton Wanderers v Charlton Athletic 0–2
Derby County v Birmingham City
                  1–1, 4–0

Final
Derby County v Charlton Athletic   4–1

1946–47
First Division

	P	W	D	L	F	A	Pts
1 Liverpool	42	25	7	10	84	52	57
2 Man United	42	22	12	8	95	54	56
3 Wolves	42	25	6	11	98	56	56
4 Stoke	42	24	7	11	90	53	55
5 Blackpool	42	22	6	14	71	70	50
6 Sheff United	42	21	7	14	89	75	49
7 Preston	42	18	11	13	76	74	47
8 Aston Villa	42	18	9	15	67	53	45
9 Sunderland	42	18	8	16	65	66	44
10 Everton	42	17	9	16	62	67	43
11 Middlesbrough	42	17	8	17	73	68	42
12 Portsmouth	42	16	9	17	66	60	41
13 Arsenal	42	16	9	17	72	70	41
14 Derby	42	18	5	19	73	79	41
15 Chelsea	42	16	7	19	69	84	39
16 Grimsby	42	13	12	17	61	82	38
17 Blackburn	42	14	8	20	45	53	36
18 Bolton	42	13	8	21	57	69	34
19 Charlton	42	11	12	19	57	71	34
20 Huddersfield	42	13	7	22	53	79	33
21 Brentford	42	9	7	26	45	88	25

	P	W	D	L	F	A	Pts
22 Leeds	42	6	6	30	45	90	18

Second Division

	P	W	D	L	F	A	Pts
1 Man City	42	26	10	6	78	35	62
2 Burnley	42	22	14	6	65	29	58
3 Birmingham	24	25	5	12	74	33	55
4 Chesterfield	42	18	14	10	58	44	50
5 Newcastle	42	19	10	13	95	62	48
6 Tottenham	42	17	14	11	65	53	48
7 WBA	42	20	8	14	88	75	48
8 Coventry	42	16	13	13	66	59	45
9 Leicester	42	18	7	17	69	64	43
10 Barnsley	42	17	8	17	84	86	42
11 Nottm Forest	42	15	10	17	69	74	40
12 West Ham	42	16	8	18	70	76	40
13 Luton	42	16	7	19	71	73	39
14 Southampton	42	15	9	18	69	76	39
15 Fulham	42	15	9	18	63	74	39
16 Bradford PA	42	14	11	17	65	77	39
17 Bury	42	12	12	18	80	78	36
18 Millwall	42	14	8	20	56	79	36
19 Plymouth	42	14	5	23	79	96	33
20 Sheff Wed	42	12	8	22	67	88	32
21 Swansea	42	11	7	24	55	83	29
22 Newport	42	10	3	29	61	133	23

Third Division (North)

	P	W	D	L	F	A	Pts
1 Doncaster	42	33	6	3	123	40	72
2 Rotherham	42	29	6	7	114	53	64
3 Chester	42	25	6	11	95	51	56
4 Stockport	42	24	2	16	78	53	50
5 Bradford City	42	20	10	12	62	47	50
6 Rochdale	42	19	10	13	80	64	48
7 Wrexham	42	17	12	13	65	51	46
8 Crewe	42	17	9	16	70	74	43
9 Barrow	42	17	7	18	54	62	41
10 Tranmere	42	17	7	18	66	77	41
11 Hull	42	16	8	18	49	53	40
12 Lincoln	42	17	5	20	86	87	39
13 Hartlepools	42	15	9	18	64	73	39
14 Gateshead	42	16	6	20	62	72	38
15 York	42	14	9	19	67	81	37
16 Carlisle	42	14	9	19	70	93	37
17 Darlington	42	15	6	21	68	80	36
18 New Brighton	42	14	8	20	57	77	36
19 Oldham	42	12	8	22	55	80	32
20 Accrington	42	14	4	24	56	92	32
21 Southport	42	7	11	24	53	85	25

22 Halifax   42 8 6 28 43 92 22

Third Division (South)

	P	W	D	L	F	A	Pts
1 Cardiff	42	30	6	6	93	30	66
2 QPR	42	23	11	8	74	40	57
3 Bristol City	42	20	11	11	94	56	51
4 Swindon	42	19	11	12	84	73	49
5 Walsall	42	17	12	13	74	59	46
6 Ipswich	42	16	14	12	61	53	46
7 Bournemouth	42	18	8	16	72	54	44
8 Southend	42	17	10	15	71	60	44
9 Reading	42	16	11	15	83	74	43
10 Port Vale	42	17	9	16	68	63	43
11 Torquay	42	15	12	15	52	61	42
12 Notts County	42	15	10	17	63	63	40
13 Northampton	42	15	10	17	72	75	40
14 Bristol Rovers	42	16	8	18	59	69	40
15 Exeter	42	15	9	18	60	69	39
16 Watford	42	17	5	20	61	76	39
17 Brighton	42	13	12	17	54	72	38
18 Crystal Palace	42	13	11	18	49	62	37
19 Leyton Orient	42	12	8	22	54	75	32
20 Aldershot	42	10	12	20	48	78	32
21 Norwich	42	10	8	24	64	100	28
22 Mansfield	42	9	10	23	48	96	28

Scottish Division 'A'

	P	W	D	L	F	A	Pts
1 Rangers	30	21	4	5	76	26	46
2 Hibernian	30	19	6	5	69	33	44
3 Aberdeen	30	16	7	7	58	41	39
4 Hearts	30	16	6	8	52	43	38
5 Partick	30	16	3	11	74	59	35
6 Morton	30	12	10	8	58	45	34
7 Celtic	30	13	6	11	53	55	32
8 Motherwell	30	12	5	13	58	54	29
9 Third Lanark	30	11	6	13	56	64	28
10 Clyde	30	9	9	12	55	65	27
11 Falkirk	30	8	10	12	62	61	26
12 Queen of the S	30	9	8	13	44	69	26
13 Queen's Park	30	8	6	16	47	60	22
14 St Mirren	30	9	4	17	47	65	22
15 Kilmarnock	30	6	9	15	44	66	21
16 Hamilton	30	2	7	21	38	85	11

Scottish Division 'B'

	P	W	D	L	F	A	Pts
1 Dundee	26	21	3	2	113	30	45

2 Airdrieonians	26	19	4	3	78	38	42
3 East Fife	26	12	7	7	58	39	31
4 Albion	26	10	7	9	50	54	27
5 Alloa	26	11	5	10	51	57	27
6 Raith	26	10	6	10	45	52	26
7 Stenhousemuir	26	8	7	11	43	53	23
8 Dunfermline	26	10	3	13	50	72	23
9 St Johnstone	26	9	4	13	45	47	22
10 Dundee United	26	9	4	13	53	60	22
11 Ayr	26	9	·2	15	56	73	20
12 Arbroath	26	7	6	13	42	63	20
13 Dumbarton	26	7	4	15	41	54	18
14 Cowdenbeath	26	6	6	14	44	77	18

FA Cup

Fourth Round

West Bromwich Albion v Charlton Athletic	1-2
Blackburn Rovers v Port Vale	2-0
Preston North End v Barnsley	6-0
Sheffield Wednesday v Everton	2-1
Newcastle United v Southampton	3-1
Brentford v Leicester City	0-0, 0-0, 1-4
Wolverhampton Wanderers v Sheffield United	0-0, 0-2
Chester v Stoke City	0-0, 2-3
Burnley v Coventry City	2-0
Luton Town v Swansea Town	2-0
Middlesbrough v Chesterfield	2-1
Manchester United v Nottingham Forest	0-2
Liverpool v Grimsby Town	2-0
Chelsea v Derby County	2-2, 0-1
Birmingham City v Portsmouth	1-0
Bolton Wanderers v Manchester City	3-3, 0-1

Fifth Round

Charlton Athletic v Blackburn Rovers	1-0
Sheffield Wednesday v Preston North End	0-2
Newcastle United v Leicester City	1-1, 2-1
Stoke City v Sheffield United	0-1
Luton Town v Burnley	0-0, 0-3
Nottingham Forest v Middlesbrough	2-2, 2-6
Liverpool v Derby County	1-0
Birmingham City v Manchester City	5-0

Sixth Round

Charlton Athletic v Preston North End	2-1
Sheffield United v Newcastle United	0-2
Middlesbrough v Burnley	1-1, 0-1

Liverpool v Birmingham City   4-1

Semi-Final
Charlton Athletic v Newcastle United 4-0
Burnley v Liverpool   0-0, 1-0

Final
Charlton Athletic v Burnley   1-0

Scottish FA Cup

Third Round
Morton v Aberdeen	1-1, 1-2
Dundee v Albion Rovers	3-0
Arbroath v Raith Rovers	5-4
Heart of Midlothain v Cowdenbeath	2-0
Rangers v Hibernian	0-0, 0-2
Dumbarton v Third Lanark	2-0
Falkirk v Motherwell	0-0, 0-1
East Fife v Queen's Park	3-1

Fourth Round
Dundee v Aberdeen	1-2
Arbroath v Heart of Midlothian	2-1
Hibernian v Dumbarton	2-0
East Fife v Motherwell	0-2

Semi-Final
Aberdeen v Arbroath	2-0
Hibernian v Motherwell	2-0

Final
Aberdeen v Hibernian	2-1

1947-48
First Division

	P	W	D	L	F	A	Pts
1 Arsenal	42	23	13	6	81	32	59
2 Man United	42	19	14	9	81	48	52
3 Burnley	42	20	12	10	56	43	52
4 Derby	42	19	12	11	77	57	50
5 Wolves	42	19	9	14	83	70	47
6 Aston Villa	42	19	9	14	65	57	47
7 Preston	42	20	7	15	67	68	47
8 Portsmouth	42	19	7	16	68	50	45
9 Blackpool	42	17	10	15	57	41	44
10 Man City	42	15	12	15	52	47	42
11 Liverpool	42	16	10	16	65	61	42
12 Sheff United	42	16	10	16	65	70	42
13 Charlton	24	17	6	19	57	66	40
14 Everton	42	17	6	19	52	66	40

	P	W	D	L	F	A	Pts
15 Stoke	42	14	10	18	41	55	38
16 Middlesbrough	42	14	9	19	71	73	37
17 Bolton	42	16	5	21	46	58	37
18 Chelsea	42	14	9	19	53	71	37
19 Huddersfield	42	12	12	18	51	60	36
20 Sunderland	42	13	10	19	56	67	36
21 Blackburn	42	11	10	21	54	72	32
22 Grimsby	42	8	6	28	45	111	22

Second Division

	P	W	D	L	F	A	Pts
1 Birmingham	42	22	15	5	55	24	59
2 Newcastle	42	24	8	10	72	41	56
3 Southampton	42	21	10	11	71	53	52
4 Sheff Wed	42	20	11	11	66	53	51
5 Cardiff	42	18	11	13	61	58	47
6 West Ham	42	16	14	12	55	53	46
7 WBA	42	18	9	15	63	58	45
8 Tottenham	42	15	14	13	56	43	44
9 Leicester	42	16	11	15	60	57	43
10 Coventry	42	14	13	15	59	52	41
11 Fulham	42	15	10	17	47	46	40
12 Barnsley	42	15	10	17	62	64	40
13 Luton	42	14	12	16	56	59	40
14 Bradford PA	42	16	8	18	68	72	40
15 Brentford	42	13	14	15	44	61	40
16 Chesterfield	42	16	7	19	54	55	39
17 Plymouth	42	9	20	13	40	58	38
18 Leeds	42	14	8	20	62	72	36
19 Nottm Forest	42	12	11	19	54	60	35
20 Bury	42	9	16	17	58	68	34
21 Doncaster	42	9	11	22	40	66	29
22 Millwall	42	9	11	22	44	74	29

Third Division (North)

	P	W	D	L	F	A	Pts
1 Lincoln	42	26	8	8	81	40	60
2 Rotherham	42	25	9	8	95	49	59
3 Wrexham	42	21	8	13	74	54	50
4 Gateshead	42	19	11	12	75	57	49
5 Hull	42	18	11	13	59	48	47
6 Accrington	42	20	6	16	62	59	46
7 Barrow	42	16	13	13	49	40	45
8 Mansfield	42	17	11	14	57	51	45
9 Carlisle	42	18	7	17	88	77	43
10 Crewe	42	18	7	17	61	63	43
11 Oldham	42	14	13	15	63	64	41
12 Rochdale	42	15	11	16	48	72	41
13 York	42	13	14	15	65	60	40
14 Bradford City	42	15	10	17	65	66	40

	P	W	D	L	F	A	Pts
15 Southport	42	14	11	17	60	63	39
16 Darlington	42	13	13	16	54	70	39
17 Stockport	42	13	12	17	63	67	38
18 Tranmere	42	16	4	22	54	72	36
19 Hartlepools	42	14	8	20	51	73	36
20 Chester	42	13	9	20	64	67	35
21 Halifax	42	7	13	22	43	76	27
22 New Brighton	42	8	9	25	38	81	25

Third Division (South)

	P	W	D	L	F	A	Pts
1 QPR	42	26	9	7	74	37	61
2 Bournemouth	42	24	9	9	76	35	57
3 Walsall	42	21	9	12	70	40	51
4 Ipswich	42	23	3	16	67	61	49
5 Swansea	42	18	12	12	70	52	48
6 Notts County	42	19	8	15	68	59	46
7 Bristol City	42	18	7	17	77	65	43
8 Port Vale	42	16	11	15	63	54	43
9 Southend	42	15	13	14	51	58	43
10 Reading	42	15	11	16	56	58	41
11 Exeter	42	15	11	16	55	63	41
12 Newport	42	14	13	15	61	73	41
13 Crystal Palace	42	13	13	16	49	49	39
14 Northampton	42	14	11	17	58	72	39
15 Watford	42	14	10	18	57	79	38
16 Swindon	42	10	16	16	41	46	36
17 Leyton Orient	42	13	10	19	51	73	36
18 Torquay	42	11	13	18	63	62	35
19 Aldershot	42	10	15	17	45	67	35
20 Bristol Rovers	42	13	8	21	71	75	34
21 Norwich	42	13	8	21	61	76	34
22 Brighton	42	11	12	19	43	73	34

Scottish Division 'A'

	P	W	D	L	F	A	Pts
1 Hibernian	30	22	4	4	86	27	48
2 Rangers	30	21	4	5	64	28	46
3 Partick	30	16	4	10	61	42	36
4 Dundee	30	15	3	12	67	51	33
5 St Mirren	30	13	5	12	54	58	31
6 Clyde	30	12	7	11	52	57	31
7 Falkirk	30	10	10	10	55	48	30
8 Motherwell	30	13	3	14	45	47	29
9 Hearts	30	10	8	12	37	42	28
10 Aberdeen	30	10	7	13	45	45	27
11 Third Lanark	30	10	6	14	56	73	26
12 Celtic	30	10	5	15	41	56	25
13 Queen of the S	30	10	5	15	49	74	25
14 Morton	30	9	6	15	47	43	24
15 Airdrieonians	30	7	7	16	39	78	21
16 Queen's Park	30	9	2	19	45	75	20

Scottish Division 'B'

	P	W	D	L	F	A	Pts
1 East Fife	30	25	3	2	103	36	53
2 Albion	30	19	4	7	58	49	42
3 Hamilton	30	17	6	7	75	45	40
4 Raith	30	14	6	10	83	66	34
5 Cowdenbeath	30	12	8	10	56	53	32
6 Kilmarnock	30	13	4	13	72	62	30
7 Dunfermline	30	13	3	14	72	71	29
8 Stirling	30	11	6	13	85	66	28
9 St Johnstone	30	11	5	14	69	63	27
10 Ayr	30	9	9	12	59	61	27
11 Dumbarton	30	9	7	14	66	79	25
12 Alloa*	30	10	6	14	53	77	24
13 Arbroath	30	10	3	17	55	62	23
14 Stenhousemuir	30	6	11	13	53	83	23
15 Dundee United	30	10	2	18	58	88	22
16 Leith	30	6	7	17	45	84	19

*Two points deducted for fielding unregistered players

FA Cup

Fourth Round

Queen's Park Rangers v Stoke City	3–0
Luton Town v Coventry City	3–2
Brentford v Middlesbrough	1–2
Crewe Alexander v Derby County	0–3
Manchester United v Liverpool	3–0
Charlton Athletic v Stockport County	3–0
Manchester City v Chelsea	2–0
Portsmouth v Preston North End	1–3
Fulham v Bristol Rovers	5–2
Wolverhampton Wanderers v Everton	1–1, 2–3
Blackpool v Chester	4–0
Colchester United v Bradford Park Avenue	3–2
Southampton v Blackburn Rovers	3–2
Swindon Town v Notts County	1–0
Tottenham Hotspur v West Bromwich Albion	3–1
Leicester City v Sheffield Wednesday	2–1

Fifth Round

Queen's Park Rangers v Luton Town	3–1
Middlesbrough v Derby County	1–2
Manchester United v Charlton Athletic	2–0

Manchester City v Preston North End

        0-1

Fulham v Everton   1-1, 1-0

Blackpool v Colchester United 5-0

Southampton v Swindon Town 3-0

Tottenham Hotspur v Leicester City 5-2

Sixth Round

Queen's Park Rangers v Derby County

        1-1, 0-5

Manchester United v Preston North End

        4-1

Fulham v Blackpool 0-2

Southampton v Tottenham Hotspur 0-1

Semi-Final

Derby County v Manchester United 1-3

Blackpool v Tottenham Hotspur 3-1

Final

Manchester United v Blackpool 4-2

Scottish FA Cup

Third Round

Rangers v Partick Thistle	3-0
Dumbarton v East Fife	0-1
Hibernian v Aberdeen	4-2
St Mirren v Clyde	2-1
Morton v Queen's Park	3-0
Airdrieonians v Raith Rovers	3-0
Celtic v Motherwell	1-0
Montrose v Queen of the South	2-1

Fourth Round

Rangers v East Fife	1-0
Hibernian v St Mirren	3-1
Airdrieonians v Morton	0-3
Celtic v Montrose	4-0

Semi-Final

Rangers v Hibernian	1-0
Morton v Celtic	1-0

Final

Rangers v Morton	1-1, 1-0

1948–49
First Division

	P	W	D	L	F	A	Pts
1 Portsmouth	42	25	8	9	84	42	58
2 Man United	42	21	11	10	77	44	53
3 Derby	42	22	9	11	74	55	53
4 Newcastle	42	20	12	10	70	56	52
5 Arsenal	42	18	13	11	74	44	49
6 Wolves	42	17	12	13	79	66	46
7 Man City	42	15	15	12	47	51	45
8 Sunderland	42	13	17	12	49	58	43
9 Charlton	42	15	12	15	63	67	42
10 Aston Villa	42	16	10	16	60	76	42
11 Stoke	42	16	9	17	66	68	41
12 Liverpool	42	13	14	15	53	43	40
13 Chelsea	42	12	14	16	69	68	38
14 Bolton	42	14	10	18	59	68	38
15 Burnley	42	12	14	16	43	50	38
16 Blackpool	42	11	16	15	54	67	38
17 Birmingham	42	11	15	16	36	38	37
18 Everton	42	13	11	18	41	63	37
19 Middlesbrough	42	11	12	19	46	57	34
20 Huddersfield	42	12	10	20	40	69	34
21 Preston	42	11	11	20	62	75	33
22 Sheff United	42	11	11	20	57	78	33

Second Division

	P	W	D	L	F	A	Pts
1 Fulham	42	24	9	9	77	37	57
2 WBA	42	24	8	10	69	39	56
3 Southampton	42	23	9	10	69	36	55
4 Cardiff	42	19	13	10	62	47	51
5 Tottenham	42	17	16	9	72	44	50
6 Chesterfield	42	15	17	10	51	45	47
7 West Ham	42	18	10	14	56	58	46
8 Sheff Wed	42	15	13	14	63	56	43
9 Barnsley	42	14	12	16	62	61	40
10 Luton	42	14	12	16	55	57	40
11 Grimsby	42	15	10	17	72	76	40
12 Bury	42	17	6	19	67	76	40
13 QPR	42	14	11	17	44	62	39
14 Blackburn	42	15	8	19	53	63	38
15 Leeds	42	12	13	17	55	63	37
16 Coventry	42	15	7	20	55	64	37
17 Bradford PA	42	13	11	18	65	78	37
18 Brentford	42	11	14	17	42	53	36
19 Leicester	42	10	16	16	62	79	36
20 Plymouth	42	12	12	18	49	64	36
21 Nottm Forest	42	14	7	21	50	54	35
22 Lincoln	42	8	12	22	53	91	28

Third Division (North)

	P	W	D	L	F	A	Pts
1 Hull	42	27	11	4	93	28	65

	P	W	D	L	F	A	Pts
2 Rotherham	42	28	6	8	90	46	62
3 Doncaster	42	20	10	12	53	40	50
4 Darlington	42	20	6	16	83	74	46
5 Gateshead	42	16	13	13	69	58	45
6 Oldham	42	18	9	15	75	67	45
7 Rochdale	42	18	9	15	55	53	45
8 Stockport	42	16	11	15	61	56	43
9 Wrexham	42	17	9	16	56	62	43
10 Mansfield	42	14	14	14	52	48	42
11 Tranmere	42	13	15	14	46	57	41
12 Crewe	42	16	9	17	52	74	41
13 Barrow	42	14	12	16	41	48	40
14 York	42	15	9	18	74	74	39
15 Carlisle	42	14	11	17	60	77	39
16 Hartlepools	42	14	10	18	45	58	38
17 New Brighton	42	14	8	20	46	58	36
18 Chester	42	11	13	18	57	56	35
19 Halifax	42	12	11	19	45	62	35
20 Accrington	42	12	10	20	55	64	34
21 Southport	42	11	9	22	45	64	31
22 Bradford City	42	10	9	23	48	77	29

Third Division (South)

	P	W	D	L	F	A	Pts
1 Swansea	42	27	8	7	87	34	62
2 Reading	42	25	5	12	77	50	55
3 Bournemouth	42	22	8	12	69	48	52
4 Swindon	42	18	15	9	64	56	51
5 Bristol Rovers	42	19	10	13	61	51	48
6 Brighton	42	15	18	9	55	55	48
7 Ipswich	42	18	9	15	78	77	45
8 Millwall	42	17	11	14	63	64	45
9 Torquay	42	17	11	14	65	70	45
10 Norwich	42	16	12	14	67	49	44
11 Notts County	42	19	5	18	102	68	43
12 Exeter	42	15	10	17	63	76	40
13 Port Vale	42	14	11	17	51	54	39
14 Walsall	42	15	8	19	56	64	38
15 Newport	42	14	9	19	68	92	37
16 Bristol City	42	11	14	17	44	62	36
17 Watford	42	10	15	17	41	54	35
18 Southend	42	9	16	17	41	46	34
19 Leyton Orient	42	11	12	19	58	80	34
20 Northampton	42	12	9	21	51	62	33
21 Aldershot	42	11	11	20	48	59	33
22 Crystal Palace	42	8	11	23	38	76	27

Scottish Division 'A'

	P	W	D	L	F	A	Pts
1 Rangers	30	20	6	4	63	32	46
2 Dundee	30	20	5	5	71	48	45
3 Hibernian	30	17	5	8	75	52	39
4 East Fife	30	16	3	11	64	46	35
5 Falkirk	30	12	8	10	70	54	32
6 Celtic	30	12	7	11	48	40	31
7 Third Lanark	30	13	5	12	56	52	31
8 Hearts	30	12	6	12	64	54	30
9 St Mirren	30	13	4	13	51	47	30
10 Queen of the S	30	11	8	11	47	53	30
11 Partick	30	9	9	12	50	63	27
12 Motherwell	30	10	5	15	44	49	25
13 Aberdeen	30	7	11	12	39	48	25
14 Clyde	30	9	6	15	50	67	24
15 Morton	30	7	8	15	39	51	22
16 Albion	30	3	2	25	30	105	8

Scottish Division 'B'

	P	W	D	L	F	A	Pts
1 Raith	30	20	2	8	80	44	42
2 Stirling	30	20	2	8	71	47	42
3 Airdrieonians	30	16	9	5	76	42	41
4 Dunfermline	30	16	9	5	80	58	41
5 Queen's Park	30	14	7	9	66	49	35
6 St Johnstone	30	14	4	12	58	51	32
7 Arbroath	30	12	8	10	62	56	32
8 Dundee United	30	10	7	13	60	67	27
9 Ayr	30	10	7	13	51	70	27
10 Hamilton	30	9	8	13	48	57	26
11 Kilmarnock	30	9	7	14	58	61	25
12 Stenhousemuir	30	8	8	14	50	54	24
13 Cowdenbeath	30	9	5	16	53	58	23
14 Alloa	30	10	3	17	42	85	23
15 Dumbarton	30	8	6	16	52	79	22
16 E Stirlingshire	30	6	6	18	38	67	18

FA Cup

Fourth Round

Manchester United v Bradford Park Avenue	1-1, 1-1, 5-0
Yeovil Town v Sunderland	2-1
Hull City v Grimsby Town	3-2
Stoke City v Blackpool	1-1, 1-0
Wolverhampton Wanderers v Sheffield United	3-0
Liverpool v Notts County	1-0
West Bromwich Albion v Gateshead	3-1
Chelsea v Everton	2-0
Leicester City v Preston North End	2-0
Luton Town v Walsall	4-0
Brentford v Torquay United	1-0
Burnley v Rotherham United	1-0

Portsmouth v Sheffield Wednesday   2-1
Newport County v Huddersfield Town
                                    3-3, 3-1
Derby County v Arsenal   1-0
Cardiff City v Aston Villa   2-1

Fifth Round

Manchester United v Yeovil Town   8-0
Hull City v Stoke City   2-0
Wolverhampton Wanderers v Liverpool
                                    3-1
West Bromwich Albion v Chelsea   3-0
Leicester City v Luton Town   5-5, 5-3
Brentford v Burnley   4-2
Portsmouth v Newport County   3-2
Derby County v Cardiff City   2-1

Sixth Round

Hull City v Manchester United   0-1
Wolverhampton Wanderers v West
        Bromwich Albion   1-0
Leicester City v Brentford   2-0
Portsmouth v Derby County   2-1

Semi-Final

Manchester United v Wolverhampton
        Wanderers   1-1, 0-1
Leicester City v Portsmouth   3-1

Final

Wolverhampton Wanderers v Leicester
        City   3-1

Scottish FA Cup

Third Round

Clyde v Morton   2-0
Heart of Midlothian v Dumbarton   3-0
Rangers   bye
Partick Thistle   bye
East Fife   bye
Hibernian   bye
Stenhousemuir   bye
Dundee   bye

Fourth Round

Rangers v Partick Thistle   4-0
Hibernian v East Fife   0-2
Stenhousemuir v Clyde   0-1
Heart of Midlothian v Dundee   2-4

Semi-Final

Rangers v East Fife   3-0
Clyde v Dundee   2-2, 2-1

Final

Rangers v Clyde   4-1

1949–50
First Division

		P	W	D	L	F	A	Pts
1	Portsmouth	42	22	9	11	74	38	53
2	Wolves	42	20	13	9	76	49	53
3	Sunderland	42	21	10	11	83	62	52
4	Man United	42	18	14	10	69	44	50
5	Newcastle	42	19	12	11	77	55	50
6	Arsenal	42	19	11	12	79	55	49
7	Blackpool	42	17	15	10	46	35	49
8	Liverpool	42	17	14	11	64	54	48
9	Middlesbrough	42	20	7	15	59	48	47
10	Burnley	42	16	13	13	40	40	45
11	Derby	42	17	10	15	69	61	44
12	Aston Villa	42	15	12	15	61	61	42
13	Chelsea	42	12	16	14	58	65	40
14	WBA	42	14	12	16	47	53	40
15	Huddersfield	42	14	9	19	52	73	34
16	Bolton	42	10	14	18	45	59	34
17	Fulham	42	10	14	18	41	54	34
18	Everton	42	10	14	18	42	66	34
19	Stoke	42	11	12	19	45	75	34
20	Charlton	42	13	6	23	53	65	32
21	Man City	42	8	13	21	36	68	29
22	Birmingham	42	7	14	21	31	67	28

Second Division

		P	W	D	L	F	A	Pts
1	Tottenham	42	27	7	8	81	35	61
2	Sheff Wed	42	18	16	8	67	48	52
3	Sheff United	42	19	14	9	68	49	52
4	Southampton	42	19	14	9	64	48	52
5	Leeds	42	17	13	12	54	45	47
6	Preston	42	18	9	15	60	49	45
7	Hull	42	17	11	14	64	72	45
8	Swansea	42	17	9	16	53	49	43
9	Brentford	42	15	13	14	44	49	43
10	Cardiff	42	16	10	16	41	44	42
11	Grimsby	42	16	8	18	74	73	40
12	Coventry	42	13	13	16	55	55	39
13	Barnsley	42	13	13	16	64	67	39
14	Chesterfield	42	15	9	18	43	47	39
15	Leicester	42	12	15	15	55	65	39
16	Blackburn	42	14	10	18	55	60	38
17	Luton	42	10	18	14	41	51	38

	P	W	D	L	F	A	Pts
18 Bury	42	14	9	19	60	65	37
19 West Ham	42	12	12	18	53	61	36
20 QPR	42	11	12	19	40	57	34
21 Plymouth	42	8	16	18	44	65	32
22 Bradford PA	42	10	11	21	51	77	31

Third Division (North)

	P	W	D	L	F	A	Pts
1 Doncaster	42	19	17	6	66	38	55
2 Gateshead	42	23	7	12	87	54	53
3 Rochdale	42	21	9	12	68	41	51
4 Lincoln	42	21	9	12	60	39	51
5 Tranmere	42	19	11	12	51	48	49
6 Rotherham	42	19	10	13	80	59	48
7 Crewe	42	17	14	11	68	55	48
8 Mansfield	42	18	12	12	66	54	48
9 Carlisle	42	16	15	11	68	51	47
10 Stockport	42	19	7	16	55	52	45
11 Oldham	42	16	11	15	58	63	43
12 Chester	42	17	6	19	70	79	40
13 Accrington	42	16	7	19	57	62	39
14 New Brighton	42	14	10	18	45	63	38
15 Barrow	42	14	9	19	47	53	37
16 Southport	42	12	13	17	51	71	37
17 Darlington	42	11	13	18	56	69	35
18 Hartlepools	42	14	5	23	52	79	33
19 Bradford City	42	12	8	22	61	76	32
20 Wrexham	42	10	12	20	39	54	32
21 Halifax	42	12	8	22	58	85	32
22 York	42	9	13	20	52	70	31

Third Division (South)

	P	W	D	L	F	A	Pts
1 Notts County	42	25	8	9	95	50	58
2 Northampton	42	20	11	11	72	50	51
3 Southend	42	19	13	10	66	48	51
4 Nottm Forest	42	20	9	13	67	39	49
5 Torquay	42	19	10	13	66	63	48
6 Watford	42	16	13	13	45	35	45
7 Crystal Palace	42	15	14	13	55	54	44
8 Brighton	42	16	12	14	57	69	44
9 Bristol Rovers	42	19	5	18	51	51	43
10 Reading	42	17	8	17	70	64	42
11 Norwich	42	16	10	16	65	63	42
12 Bournemouth	42	16	10	16	57	56	42
13 Port Vale	42	15	11	16	47	42	41
14 Swindon	42	15	11	16	59	62	41
15 Bristol City	42	15	10	17	60	61	40
16 Exeter	42	14	11	17	63	75	39
17 Ipswich	42	12	11	19	57	86	35

	P	W	D	L	F	A	Pts
18 Leyton Orient	42	12	11	19	53	85	35
19 Walsall	42	9	16	17	61	62	34
20 Aldershot	42	13	8	21	48	60	34
21 Newport	42	13	8	21	67	98	34
22 Millwall	42	14	4	24	55	63	32

Scottish Division 'A'

	P	W	D	L	F	A	Pts
1 Rangers	30	22	6	2	58	26	50
2 Hibernian	30	22	5	3	86	34	49
3 Hearts	30	20	3	7	86	40	43
4 East Fife	30	15	7	8	58	43	37
5 Celtic	30	14	7	9	51	50	35
6 Dundee	30	12	7	11	49	46	31
7 Partick	30	13	3	14	55	45	29
8 Aberdeen	30	11	4	15	48	56	26
9 Raith	30	9	8	13	45	54	26
10 Motherwell	30	10	5	15	53	58	25
11 St Mirren	30	8	9	13	42	49	25
12 Third Lanark	30	11	3	16	44	62	25
13 Clyde	30	10	4	16	56	73	24
14 Falkirk	30	7	10	13	48	72	24
15 Queen of the S	30	5	6	19	31	63	16
16 Stirling	30	6	3	21	38	77	15

Scottish Division 'B'

	P	W	D	L	F	A	Pts
1 Morton	30	20	7	3	77	33	47
2 Airdrieonians	30	19	6	5	79	40	44
3 Dunfermline	30	16	4	10	71	57	36
4 St Johnstone	30	15	6	9	64	56	36
5 Cowdenbeath	30	16	3	11	63	56	35
6 Hamilton	30	14	6	10	57	44	34
7 Kilmarnock	30	14	5	11	50	43	33
8 Dundee United	30	14	5	11	74	56	33
9 Queen's Park	30	12	7	11	63	59	31
10 Forfar	30	11	8	11	53	56	30
11 Albion	30	10	7	13	49	61	27
12 Stenhousemuir	30	8	8	14	54	72	24
13 Ayr	30	8	6	16	53	80	22
14 Arbroath	30	5	9	16	47	69	19
15 Dumbarton	30	6	4	20	39	62	16
16 Alloa	30	5	3	22	47	96	13

FA Cup

Fourth Round

Arsenal v Swansea Town	2-1
Burnley v Port Vale	2-1

Leeds United v Bolton Wanderers
                                         1-1, 3-2
Charlton Athletic v Cardiff City 1-1, 0-2
Chelsea v Newcastle United   3-0
Chesterfield v Middlesbrough   3-2
Watford v Manchester United   0-1
Portsmouth v Grimsby Town   5-0
Liverpool v Exeter City   3-1
Stockport County v Hull City   0-0, 2-0
Blackpool v Doncaster Rovers   2-1
Wolverhampton Wanderers v Sheffield
    United   0-0, 4-3
West Ham United v Everton   1-2
Tottenham Hotspur v Sunderland   5-1
Bury v Derby County   2-2, 2-5
Bournemouth v Northampton Town
                                       1-1, 1-2

Fifth Round
Arsenal v Burnley   2-0
Leeds United v Cardiff City   3-1
Chesterfield v Chelsea   1-1, 0-3
Manchester United v Portsmouth 3-3, 3-1
Stockport County v Liverpool   1-2
Wolverhampton Wanderers v Blackpool
                                       0-0, 0-1
Everton v Tottenham Hotspur   1-0
Derby County v Northampton Town 4-2

Sixth Round
Arsenal v Leeds United   1-0
Chelsea v Manchester United   2-0
Liverpool v Blackpool   2-1
Derby County v Everton   1-2

Semi-Final
Arsenal v Chelsea   2-2, 1-0
Liverpool v Everton   2-0

Final
Arsenal v Liverpool   2-0

Scottish FA Cup

Third Round
Celtic v Aberdeen   0-1
Dunfermline Athletic v Stenhousemuir
                                       1-4
Rangers   bye
Raith Rovers   bye
Queen of the South   bye
Partick Thistle   bye
Stirling Albion   bye
East Fife   bye

Fourth Round
Rangers v Raith Rovers   1-1, 1-1, 2-0
Queen of the South v Aberdeen   3-3, 2-1
Partick Thistle v Stirling Albion   5-1
Stenhousemuir v East Fife   0-3

Semi-Final
Rangers v Queen of the South   1-1, 3-0
Partick Thistle v East Fife   1-2

Final
Rangers v East Fife   3-0

1950-51
First Division

	P	W	D	L	F	A	Pts
1 Tottenham	42	25	10	7	82	44	60
2 Man United	42	24	8	10	74	40	56
3 Blackpool	42	20	10	12	79	53	50
4 Newcastle	42	18	13	11	62	53	49
5 Arsenal	42	19	9	14	73	56	47
6 Middlesbrough	42	18	11	13	76	65	47
7 Portsmouth	42	16	15	11	71	68	47
8 Bolton	42	19	7	16	64	61	45
9 Liverpool	42	16	11	15	53	59	43
10 Burnley	42	14	14	14	48	43	42
11 Derby	42	16	8	18	81	75	40
12 Sunderland	42	12	16	14	63	73	40
13 Stoke	42	13	14	15	50	59	40
14 Wolves	42	15	8	19	74	61	38
15 Aston Villa	42	12	13	17	66	68	37
16 WBA	42	13	11	18	53	61	37
17 Charlton	42	14	9	19	63	80	37
18 Fulham	42	13	11	18	52	68	37
19 Huddersfield	42	15	6	21	64	92	36
20 Chelsea	42	12	8	22	53	65	32
21 Sheff Wed	42	12	8	22	64	83	32
22 Everton	42	12	8	22	48	86	32

Second Division

	P	W	D	L	F	A	Pts
1 Preston	42	26	5	11	91	49	57
2 Man City	42	19	14	9	89	61	52
3 Cardiff	42	17	16	9	53	45	50
4 Birmingham	42	20	9	13	64	53	49
5 Leeds	42	20	8	14	63	55	48
6 Blackburn	42	19	8	15	65	66	46
7 Coventry	42	19	7	16	75	59	45

8 Sheff United	42 16 12 14 72 62 44
9 Brentford	42 18 8 16 75 74 44
10 Hull	42 16 11 15 74 70 43
11 Doncaster	42 15 13 14 64 68 43
12 Southampton	42 15 13 14 66 73 43
13 West Ham	42 16 10 16 68 69 42
14 Leicester	42 15 11 16 68 58 41
15 Barnsley	42 15 10 17 74 68 40
16 QPR	42 15 10 17 71 82 40
17 Notts County	42 13 13 16 61 60 39
18 Swansea	42 16 4 22 54 77 36
19 Luton	42 9 14 19 57 70 32
20 Bury	42 12 8 22 60 86 32
21 Chesterfield	42 9 12 21 44 69 30
22 Grimsby	42 8 12 22 61 95 28

Third Division (North)

	P WD L F A Pts
1 Rotherham	46 31 9 6 103 41 71
2 Mansfield	46 26 12 8 78 48 64
3 Carlisle	46 25 12 9 79 50 62
4 Tranmere	46 24 11 11 83 62 59
5 Lincoln	46 25 8 13 89 58 58
6 Bradford PA	46 23 8 15 90 72 54
7 Bradford City	46 21 10 15 90 63 52
8 Gateshead	46 21 8 17 84 62 50
9 Crewe	46 19 10 17 61 60 48
10 Stockport	46 20 8 18 63 63 48
11 Rochdale	46 17 11 18 69 62 45
12 Scunthorpe	46 13 18 15 58 57 44
13 Chester	46 17 9 20 62 64 43
14 Wrexham	46 15 12 19 55 71 42
15 Oldham	46 16 8 22 73 73 40
16 Hartlepools	46 16 7 23 64 66 39
17 York	46 12 15 19 66 77 39
18 Darlington	46 13 13 20 59 77 39
19 Barrow	46 15 6 24 51 76 38
20 Shrewsbury	46 15 7 24 43 74 37
21 Southport	46 13 10 23 56 72 36
22 Halifax	46 11 12 23 50 69 34
23 Accrington	46 11 10 25 42 101 32
24 New Brighton	46 11 8 27 40 90 30

Third Division (South)

	P WD L F A Pts
1 Nottm Forest	46 30 10 6 110 40 70
2 Norwich	46 25 14 7 82 45 64
3 Reading	46 21 15 10 88 53 57
4 Plymouth	46 24 9 13 85 55 57
5 Millwall	46 23 10 13 80 57 56

6 Bristol Rovers	46 20 15 11 64 42 55
7 Southend	46 21 10 15 92 69 52
8 Ipswich	46 23 6 17 69 58 52
9 Bournemouth	46 22 7 17 65 57 51
10 Bristol City	46 20 11 15 64 59 51
11 Newport	46 19 9 18 77 70 47
12 Port Vale	46 16 13 17 60 65 45
13 Brighton	46 13 17 16 71 79 43
14 Exeter	46 18 6 22 62 85 42
15 Walsall	46 15 10 21 52 62 40
16 Colchester	46 14 12 20 63 76 40
17 Swindon	46 18 4 24 55 67 40
18 Aldershot	46 15 10 21 56 88 40
19 Leyton Orient	46 15 8 23 53 75 38
20 Torquay	46 14 9 23 64 81 37
21 Northampton	46 10 16 20 55 67 36
22 Gillingham	46 13 9 24 69 101 35
23 Watford	46 9 11 26 54 88 29
24 Crystal Palace	46 8 11 27 33 84 27

Scottish Division 'A'

	P WD L F A Pts
1 Hibernian	30 22 4 4 78 26 48
2 Rangers	30 17 4 9 64 37 38
3 Dundee	30 15 8 7 47 30 38
4 Hearts	30 16 5 9 72 45 37
5 Aberdeen	30 15 5 10 61 50 35
6 Partick	30 13 7 10 57 48 33
7 Celtic	30 12 5 13 48 46 29
8 Raith	30 13 2 15 52 52 28
9 Motherwell	30 11 6 13 58 65 28
10 East Fife	30 10 8 12 48 66 28
11 St Mirren	30 9 7 14 35 51 25
12 Morton	30 10 4 16 47 59 24
13 Third Lanark	30 11 2 17 40 51 24
14 Airdrieonians	30 10 4 16 52 67 24
15 Clyde	30 8 7 15 37 57 23
16 Falkirk	30 7 4 19 35 81 18

Scottish Division 'B'

	P WD L F A Pts
1 Queen of the S	30 21 3 6 69 35 45
2 Stirling	30 21 3 6 78 44 45
3 Ayr	30 15 6 9 64 40 36
4 Dundee United	30 16 4 10 78 58 36
5 St Johnstone	30 14 5 11 68 53 33
6 Queen's Park	30 13 7 10 56 53 33
7 Hamilton	30 12 8 10 65 49 32
8 Albion	30 14 4 12 56 51 32
9 Dumbarton	30 12 5 13 52 53 29

10 Dunfermline	30	12	4	14	58	73	28
11 Cowdenbeath	30	12	3	15	61	57	27
12 Kilmarnock	30	8	8	14	44	49	24
13 Arbroath	30	8	5	17	46	78	21
14 Forfar	30	9	3	18	43	76	21
15 Stenhousemuir	30	9	2	19	51	80	20
16 Alloa	30	7	4	19	58	98	18

FA Cup

Fourth Round

Newcastle United v Bolton Wanderers	3-2
Stoke City v West Ham United	1-0
Luton Town v Bristol Rovers	1-2
Hull City v Rotherham United	2-0
Wolverhampton Wanderers v Aston Villa	3-1
Preston North End v Huddersfield Town	0-2
Sunderland v Southampton	2-0
Newport County v Norwich City	0-2
Blackpool v Stockport County	2-1
Sheffield United v Mansfield Town	0-0, 1-2
Exeter City v Chelsea	1-1, 0-2
Millwall v Fulham	0-1
Derby County v Birmingham City	1-3
Bristol City v Brighton	1-0
Manchester United v Leeds United	4-0
Arsenal v Northampton Town	3-2

Fifth Round

Stoke City v Newcastle United	2-4
Bristol Rovers v Hull City	3-0
Wolverhampton Wanderers v Huddersfield Town	2-0
Sunderland v Norwich City	3-1
Blackpool v Mansfield Town	2-0
Chelsea v Fulham	1-1, 0-3
Birmingham City v Bristol City	2-0
Manchester United v Arsenal	1-0

Sixth Round

Newcastle United v Bristol Rovers	0-0, 3-1
Sunderland v Wolverhampton Wanderers	1-1, 1-3
Blackpool v Fulham	1-0
Birmingham City v Manchester United	1-0

Semi-Final

Newcastle United v Wolverhampton Wanderers	0-0, 2-1

Blackpool v Birmingham City	0-0, 2-1

Final

Blackpool v Newcastle United	0-2

Scottish FA Cup

Third Round

Heart of Midlothian v Celtic	1-2
Airdrieonians v Clyde	4-0
Aberdeen	bye
Dundee	bye
Raith Rovers	bye
Hibernian	bye
Ayr United	bye
Motherwell	bye

Fourth Round

Celtic v Aberdeen	3-0
Dundee v Raith Rovers	1-2
Airdrieonians v Hibernian	0-3
Ayr United v Motherwell	2-2, 1-2

Semi-Final

Celtic v Raith Rovers	3-2
Hibernian v Motherwell	2-3

Final

Celtic v Motherwell	1-0

1951–52
First Division

	P	W	D	L	F	A	Pts
1 Man United	42	23	11	8	95	52	57
2 Tottenham	42	22	9	11	76	51	53
3 Arsenal	42	21	11	10	80	61	53
4 Portsmouth	42	20	8	14	68	58	48
5 Bolton	42	19	10	13	65	61	48
6 Aston Villa	42	19	9	14	79	70	47
7 Preston	42	17	12	13	74	54	46
8 Newcastle	42	18	9	15	98	73	45
9 Blackpool	42	18	9	15	64	64	45
10 Charlton	42	17	10	15	68	63	44
11 Liverpool	42	12	19	11	57	61	43
12 Sunderland	42	15	12	15	70	61	42
13 WBA	42	14	13	15	74	77	41
14 Burnley	42	15	10	17	56	63	40
15 Man City	42	13	13	16	58	61	39
16 Wolves	42	12	14	16	73	73	38
17 Derby	42	15	7	20	63	80	37

	P	W	D	L	F	A	Pts
18 Middlesbrough	42	15	6	21	64	88	36
19 Chelsea	42	14	8	20	52	72	36
20 Stoke	42	12	7	23	49	88	31
21 Huddersfield	42	10	8	24	49	82	28
22 Fulham	42	8	11	23	58	77	27

Second Division

	P	W	D	L	F	A	Pts
1 Sheff Wed	42	21	11	10	100	66	53
2 Cardiff	42	20	11	11	72	54	51
3 Birmingham	42	21	9	12	67	56	51
4 Nottm Forest	42	18	13	11	77	62	49
5 Leicester	42	19	9	14	78	64	47
6 Leeds	42	18	11	13	59	57	47
7 Everton	42	17	10	15	64	58	44
8 Luton	42	16	12	14	77	78	44
9 Rotherham	42	17	8	17	73	71	42
10 Brentford	42	15	12	15	54	55	42
11 Sheff United	42	18	5	19	90	76	41
12 West Ham	42	15	11	16	67	77	41
13 Southampton	42	15	11	16	61	73	41
14 Blackburn	42	17	6	19	54	63	40
15 Notts County	42	16	7	19	71	68	39
16 Doncaster	42	13	12	17	55	60	38
17 Bury	42	15	7	20	67	69	37
18 Hull	42	13	11	18	60	70	37
19 Swansea	42	12	12	18	72	76	36
20 Barnsley	42	11	14	17	59	72	36
21 Coventry	42	14	6	22	59	82	34
22 QPR	42	11	12	19	52	81	34

Third Division (North)

	P	W	D	L	F	A	Pts
1 Lincoln	46	30	9	7	121	52	69
2 Grimsby	46	29	8	9	96	45	66
3 Stockport	46	23	13	10	74	40	59
4 Oldham	46	24	9	13	90	61	57
5 Gateshead	46	21	11	14	66	49	53
6 Mansfield	46	22	8	16	73	60	52
7 Carlisle	46	19	13	14	62	57	51
8 Bradford PA	46	19	12	15	74	64	50
9 Hartlepools	46	21	8	17	71	65	50
10 York	46	18	13	15	73	52	49
11 Tranmere	46	21	6	19	76	71	48
12 Barrow	46	17	12	17	57	61	46
13 Chesterfield	46	17	11	18	65	66	45
14 Scunthorpe	46	14	16	16	65	74	44
15 Bradford City	46	16	10	20	61	68	42
16 Crewe	46	17	8	21	63	82	42
17 Southport	46	15	11	20	53	71	41

	P	W	D	L	F	A	Pts
18 Wrexham	46	15	9	22	63	73	39
19 Chester	46	15	9	22	72	85	39
20 Halifax	46	14	7	25	61	97	35
21 Rochdale	46	11	13	22	47	79	35
22 Accrington	46	10	12	24	61	92	32
23 Darlington	46	11	9	26	64	103	31
24 Workington	46	11	7	28	50	91	29

Third Division (South)

	P	W	D	L	F	A	Pts
1 Plymouth	46	29	8	9	107	53	66
2 Reading	46	29	3	14	112	60	61
3 Norwich	46	26	9	11	89	50	61
4 Millwall	46	23	12	11	74	53	58
5 Brighton	46	24	10	12	87	63	58
6 Newport	46	21	12	13	77	76	54
7 Bristol Rovers	46	20	12	14	89	53	52
8 Northampton	46	22	5	19	93	74	49
9 Southend	46	19	10	17	75	66	48
10 Colchester	46	17	12	17	56	77	46
11 Torquay	46	17	10	19	86	98	44
12 Aldershot	46	18	8	20	78	89	44
13 Port Vale	46	14	15	17	50	66	43
14 Bournemouth	46	16	10	20	69	75	42
15 Bristol City	46	15	12	19	58	69	42
16 Swindon	46	14	14	18	51	68	42
17 Ipswich	46	16	9	21	63	74	41
18 Leyton Orient	46	16	9	21	55	68	41
19 Crystal Palace	46	15	9	22	61	80	39
20 Shrewsbury	46	13	10	23	62	86	36
21 Watford	46	13	10	23	57	81	36
22 Gillingham	46	11	13	22	71	81	35
23 Exeter	46	13	9	24	65	86	35
24 Walsall	46	13	5	28	55	94	31

Scottish Division 'A'

	P	W	D	L	F	A	Pts
1 Hibernian	30	20	5	5	92	36	45
2 Rangers	30	16	9	5	61	31	41
3 East Fife	30	17	3	10	71	49	37
4 Hearts	30	14	7	9	69	53	35
5 Raith	30	14	5	11	43	42	33
6 Partick	30	12	7	11	48	51	31
7 Motherwell	30	12	7	11	51	57	31
8 Dundee	30	11	6	13	53	52	28
9 Celtic	30	10	8	12	52	55	28
10 Queen of the S	30	10	8	12	50	60	28
11 Aberdeen	30	10	7	13	65	58	27
12 Third Lanark	30	9	8	13	51	62	26
13 Airdrieonians	30	11	4	15	54	69	26

14 St Mirren	30	10	5	15	43 58	25
15 Morton	30	9	6	15	49 56	24
16 Stirling	30	5	5	20	36 99	15

Scottish Division 'B'

	P	W	D	L	F	A	Pts
1 Clyde	30	19	6	5	100	45	44
2 Falkirk	30	18	7	5	80	34	43
3 Ayr	30	17	5	8	55	45	39
4 Dundee United	30	16	5	9	75	60	37
5 Kilmarnock	30	16	2	12	62	48	34
6 Dunfermline	30	15	2	13	74	65	32
7 Alloa	30	13	6	11	55	49	32
8 Cowdenbeath	30	12	8	10	66	67	32
9 Hamilton	30	12	6	12	47	51	30
10 Dumbarton	30	10	8	12	51	57	28
11 St Johnstone	30	9	7	14	62	68	25
12 Forfar	30	10	4	16	59	97	24
13 Stenhousemuir	30	8	6	16	57	74	22
14 Albion	30	6	10	14	39	57	22
15 Queen's Park	30	8	4	18	40	62	20
16 Arbroath	30	6	4	20	40	83	16

FA Cup

Fourth Round

Tottenham Hotspur v Newcastle United	0–3
Swansea Town v Rotherham United	3–0
Notts County v Portsmouth	1–3
Middlesbrough v Doncaster Rovers	1–4
Blackburn Rovers v Hull City	2–0
Gateshead v West Bromwich Albion	0–2
Burnley v Coventry City	2–0
Liverpool v Wolverhampton Wanderers	2–1
Arsenal v Barnsley	4–0
Birmingham City v Leyton Orient	0–1
Luton Town v Brentford	2–2, 0–0, 3–2
Swindon Town v Stoke City	1–1, 1–0
Chelsea v Tranmere Rovers	4–0
Leeds United v Bradford Park Avenue	2–0
West Ham United v Sheffield United	0–0, 2–4
Southend United v Bristol Rovers	2–1

Fifth Round

Swansea Town v Newcastle United	0–1
Portsmouth v Doncaster Rovers	4–0
Blackburn Rovers v West Bromwich Albion	1–0
Burnley v Liverpool	2–0
Leyton Orient v Arsenal	0–3
Luton Town v Swindon Town	3–1
Leeds United v Chelsea	1–1, 1–1, 1–5
Southend United v Sheffield United	1–2

Sixth Round

Portsmouth v Newcastle United	2–4
Blackburn Rovers v Burnley	3–1
Luton Town v Arsenal	2–3
Sheffield United v Chelsea	0–1

Semi-Final

Newcastle United v Blackburn Rovers	0–0, 2–1
Arsenal v Chelsea	1–1, 3–0

Final

Newcastle United v Arsenal	1–0

Scottish FA Cup

Third Round

Dunfermline Athletic v Motherwell	1–1, 0–4
Arbroath v Rangers	0–2
Queen of the South v Heart of Midlothian	1–3
Airdrieonians v Morton	4–0
Dundee v Berwick Rangers	1–0
Dundee United v Aberdeen	2–2, 2–3
Albion Rovers v Third Lanark	1–3
Dumbarton v Falkirk	1–3

Fourth Round

Rangers v Motherwell	1–1, 1–2
Airdrieonians v Heart of Midlothian	2–2, 4–6
Dundee v Aberdeen	4–0
Third Lanark v Falkirk	1–0

Semi-Final

Motherwell v Heart of Midlothian	1–1, 1–1, 3–1
Dundee v Third Lanark	2–0

Final

Motherwell v Dundee	4–0

1952–53
First Division

	P	W	D	L	F	A	Pts
1 Arsenal	42	21	12	9	97	64	54
2 Preston	42	21	12	9	85	60	54

	P	W	D	L	F	A	Pts
3 Wolves	42	19	13	10	86	63	51
4 WBA	42	21	8	13	66	60	50
5 Charlton	42	19	11	12	77	63	49
6 Burnley	42	18	12	12	67	52	48
7 Blackpool	42	19	9	14	71	70	47
8 Man United	42	18	10	14	69	72	46
9 Sunderland	42	15	13	14	68	82	43
10 Tottenham	42	15	11	16	78	69	41
11 Aston Villa	42	14	13	15	63	61	41
12 Cardiff	42	14	12	16	54	46	40
13 Middlesbrough	42	14	11	17	70	77	39
14 Bolton	42	15	9	18	61	69	39
15 Portsmouth	42	14	10	18	74	83	38
16 Newcastle	42	14	9	19	59	70	37
17 Liverpool	42	14	8	20	61	82	36
18 Sheff Wed	42	12	11	19	62	72	35
19 Chelsea	42	12	11	19	56	66	35
20 Man City	42	14	7	21	72	87	35
21 Stoke	42	12	10	20	53	66	34
22 Derby	42	11	10	21	59	74	32

Second Division

	P	W	D	L	F	A	Pts
1 Sheff United	42	25	10	7	97	55	60
2 Huddersfield	42	24	10	8	84	33	58
3 Luton	42	22	8	12	84	49	52
4 Plymouth	42	20	9	13	65	60	49
5 Leicester	42	18	12	12	89	74	48
6 Birmingham	42	19	10	13	71	66	48
7 Nottm Forest	42	18	8	16	77	67	44
8 Fulham	42	17	10	15	81	71	44
9 Blackburn	42	18	8	16	68	65	44
10 Leeds	42	14	15	13	71	63	43
11 Swansea	42	15	12	15	78	81	42
12 Rotherham	42	16	9	17	75	74	41
13 Doncaster	42	12	16	14	58	64	40
14 West Ham	42	13	13	16	58	60	39
15 Lincoln	42	11	17	14	64	71	39
16 Everton	42	12	14	16	71	75	38
17 Brentford	42	13	11	18	59	76	37
18 Hull	42	14	8	20	57	69	36
19 Notts County	42	14	8	20	60	88	36
20 Bury	42	13	9	20	53	81	35
21 Southampton	42	10	13	19	68	85	33
22 Barnsley	42	5	8	29	47	108	18

Third Division (North)

	P	W	D	L	F	A	Pts
1 Oldham	46	22	15	9	77	45	59
2 Port Vale	46	20	18	8	67	35	58
3 Wrexham	46	24	8	14	86	66	56

	P	W	D	L	F	A	Pts
4 York	46	20	13	13	60	45	53
5 Grimsby	46	21	10	15	75	59	52
6 Southport	46	20	11	15	63	60	51
7 Bradford PA	46	19	12	15	75	61	50
8 Gateshead	46	17	15	14	76	60	49
9 Carlisle	46	18	13	15	82	68	49
10 Crewe	46	20	8	18	70	68	48
11 Stockport	46	17	13	16	82	69	47
12 Chesterfield	46	18	11	17	65	63	47
12 Tranmere	46	21	5	20	65	63	47
14 Halifax	46	16	15	15	68	68	47
15 Scunthorpe	46	16	14	16	62	56	46
16 Bradford City	46	14	18	14	75	80	46
17 Hartlepools	46	16	14	16	57	61	46
18 Mansfield	46	16	14	16	55	62	46
19 Barrow	46	16	12	18	66	71	44
20 Chester	46	11	15	20	64	85	37
21 Darlington	46	14	6	26	58	96	34
22 Rochdale	46	14	5	27	62	83	33
23 Workington	46	11	10	25	55	91	32
24 Accrington	46	8	11	27	39	89	27

Third Division (South)

	P	W	D	L	F	A	Pts
1 Bristol Rovers	46	26	12	8	92	46	64
2 Millwall	46	24	14	8	82	44	62
3 Northampton	46	26	10	10	109	70	62
4 Norwich	46	25	10	11	99	55	60
5 Bristol City	46	22	15	9	95	61	59
6 Coventry	46	19	12	15	77	62	50
7 Brighton	46	19	12	15	81	75	50
8 Southend	46	18	13	15	69	74	49
9 Bournemouth	46	19	9	18	74	69	47
10 Watford	46	15	17	14	62	63	47
11 Reading	46	19	8	19	69	64	46
12 Torquay	46	18	9	19	87	88	45
13 Crystal Palace	46	15	13	18	66	82	43
14 Leyton Orient	46	16	10	20	68	73	42
15 Newport	46	16	10	20	70	82	42
16 Ipswich	46	13	15	18	60	69	41
17 Exeter	46	13	14	19	61	71	40
18 Swindon	46	14	12	20	64	79	40
19 Aldershot	46	12	15	19	61	77	39
20 Gillingham	46	12	15	19	55	74	39
21 QPR	46	12	15	19	61	82	39
22 Colchester	46	12	14	20	59	76	38
23 Shrewsbury	46	12	12	22	68	91	36
24 Walsall	46	7	10	29	56	118	24

Scottish Division 'A'

	P	W	D	L	F	A	Pts
1 Rangers	30	18	7	5	80	39	43
2 Hibernian	30	19	5	6	93	51	43
3 East Fife	30	16	7	7	72	48	39
4 Hearts	30	12	6	12	59	50	30
5 Clyde	30	13	4	13	78	78	30
6 St Mirren	30	11	8	11	52	58	30
7 Dundee	30	9	11	10	44	37	29
8 Celtic	30	11	7	12	51	54	29
9 Partick	30	10	9	11	55	63	29
10 Queen of the S	30	10	8	12	43	61	28
11 Aberdeen	30	11	5	14	64	68	27
12 Raith	30	9	8	13	47	53	26
13 Falkirk	30	11	4	15	53	63	26
14 Airdrieonians	30	10	6	14	53	75	26
15 Motherwell	30	10	5	15	57	80	25
16 Third Lanark	30	8	4	18	52	75	20

Scottish Division 'B'

	P	W	D	L	F	A	Pts
1 Stirling	30	20	4	6	64	43	44
2 Hamilton	30	20	3	7	72	40	43
3 Queen's Park	30	15	7	8	70	46	37
4 Kilmarnock	30	17	2	11	74	48	36
5 Ayr	30	17	2	11	76	56	36
6 Morton	30	15	3	12	79	57	33
7 Arbroath	30	13	7	10	52	57	33
8 Dundee United	30	12	5	13	52	56	29
9 Alloa	30	12	5	13	63	68	29
10 Dumbarton	30	11	6	13	58	67	28
11 Dunfermline	30	9	9	12	51	58	27
12 Stenhousemuir	30	10	6	14	56	65	26
13 Cowdenbeath	30	8	7	15	37	54	23
14 St Johnstone	30	8	6	16	41	63	22
15 Forfar	30	8	4	18	54	88	20
16 Albion	30	5	4	21	44	77	14

FA Cup

Fourth Round

Blackpool v Huddersfield Town	1-0
Shrewsbury Town v Southampton	1-4
Arsenal v Bury	6-2
Burnley v Sunderland	2-0
Preston North End v Tottenham Hotspur	2-2, 0-1
Halifax Town v Stoke City	1-0
Sheffield United v Birmingham City	1-1, 1-3

Chelsea v West Bromwich Albion
1-1, 0-0, 1-1, 4-0
Bolton Wanderers v Notts County
1-1, 2-2, 1-0
Manchester City v Luton Town   1-1, 1-5
Hull City v Gateshead   1-2
Plymouth Argyle v Barnsley   1-0
Everton v Nottingham Forest   4-1
Manchester United v Walthamstow
Avenue   1-1, 5-2
Aston Villa v Brentford   0-0, 2-1
Newcastle United v Rotherham United
1-3

Fifth Round

Blackpool v Southampton	1-1, 2-1
Burnley v Arsenal	0-2
Halifax Town v Tottenham Hotspur	0-3
Chelsea v Birmingham City	0-4
Luton Town v Bolton Wanderers	0-1
Plymouth Argyle v Gateshead	0-1
Everton v Manchester United	2-1
Rotherham United v Aston Villa	1-3

Sixth Round

Arsenal v Blackpool	1-2
Birmingham City v Tottenham Hotspur	1-1, 2-2, 0-1
Gateshead v Bolton Wanderers	0-1
Aston Villa v Everton	0-1

Semi-Final

Blackpool v Tottenham Hotspur	2-1
Bolton Wanderers v Everton	4-3

Final

Blackpool v Bolton Wanderers	4-3

Scottish FA Cup

Third Round

Morton v Rangers	1-4
Falkirk v Celtic	2-3
Heart of Midlothian v Montrose	3-1
Queen of the South v Albion Rovers	2-0
Clyde v Ayr United	8-3
Third Lanark v Hamilton Academicals	1-0
Airdrieonians v Hibernian	0-4
Aberdeen v Motherwell	5-5, 6-1

Fourth Round

Rangers v Celtic	2-0
Heart of Midlothian v Queen of the South	2-1

Clyde v Third Lanark   1-2
Hibernian v Aberdeen   1-1, 0-2

Semi-Final

Rangers v Heart of Midlothian   2-1
Third Lanark v Aberdeen   1-1, 1-2

Final

Aberdeen v Rangers   1-1, 0-1

1953–54
First Division

	P	W	D	L	F	A	Pts
1 Wolves	42	25	7	10	96	56	57
2 WBA	42	22	9	11	86	63	53
3 Huddersfield	42	20	11	11	78	61	51
4 Man United	42	18	12	12	73	58	48
5 Bolton	42	18	12	12	75	60	48
6 Blackpool	42	19	10	13	80	69	48
7 Burnley	42	21	4	17	78	67	46
8 Chelsea	42	16	12	14	74	68	44
9 Charlton	42	19	6	17	75	77	44
10 Cardiff	42	18	8	16	51	71	44
11 Preston	42	19	5	18	87	58	43
12 Arsenal	42	15	13	14	75	73	43
13 Aston Villa	42	16	9	17	70	68	41
14 Portsmouth	42	14	11	17	81	89	39
15 Newcastle	42	14	10	18	72	77	38
16 Tottenham	42	16	5	21	65	76	37
17 Man City	42	14	9	19	62	77	37
18 Sunderland	42	14	8	20	81	89	36
19 Sheff Wed	42	15	6	21	70	91	36
20 Sheff United	42	11	11	20	69	90	33
21 Middlesbrough	42	10	10	22	60	91	30
22 Liverpool	42	9	10	23	68	97	28

Second Division

	P	W	D	L	F	A	Pts
1 Leicester	42	23	10	9	97	60	56
2 Everton	42	20	16	6	92	58	56
3 Blackburn	42	23	9	10	86	50	55
4 Nottm Forest	42	20	12	10	86	59	52
5 Rotherham	42	21	7	14	80	67	49
6 Luton	42	18	12	12	64	59	48
7 Birmingham	42	18	11	13	78	58	47
8 Fulham	42	17	10	15	98	85	44
9 Bristol Rovers	42	14	16	12	64	58	44
10 Leeds	42	15	13	14	89	81	43
11 Stoke	42	12	17	13	71	60	41

12 Doncaster	42	16	9	17	59	63	41
13 West Ham	42	15	9	18	67	69	39
14 Notts County	42	13	13	16	54	74	39
15 Hull	42	16	6	20	64	66	38
16 Lincoln	42	14	9	19	65	83	37
17 Bury	42	11	14	17	54	72	36
18 Derby	42	12	11	19	64	82	35
19 Plymouth	42	9	16	17	65	82	34
20 Swansea	42	13	8	21	58	82	34
21 Brentford	42	10	11	21	40	78	31
22 Oldham	42	8	9	25	40	89	25

Third Division (North)

	P	W	D	L	F	A	Pts
1 Port Vale	46	26	17	3	74	21	69
2 Barnsley	46	24	10	12	77	57	58
3 Scunthorpe	46	21	15	10	77	56	57
4 Gateshead	46	21	13	12	74	55	55
5 Bradford City	46	22	9	15	60	55	53
6 Chesterfield	46	19	14	13	76	64	52
7 Mansfield	46	20	11	15	88	67	51
8 Wrexham	46	21	9	16	81	68	51
9 Bradford PA	46	18	14	14	77	68	50
10 Stockport	46	18	11	17	77	67	47
11 Southport	46	17	12	17	63	60	46
12 Barrow	46	16	12	18	72	71	44
13 Carlisle	46	14	15	17	83	71	43
14 Tranmere	46	18	7	21	59	70	43
15 Accrington	46	16	10	20	66	74	42
16 Crewe	46	14	13	19	49	67	41
17 Grimsby	46	16	9	21	51	77	41
18 Hartlepools	46	13	14	19	59	65	40
19 Rochdale	46	15	10	21	59	77	40
20 Workington	46	13	14	19	59	80	40
21 Darlington	46	12	14	20	50	71	38
22 York	46	12	13	21	64	86	37
23 Halifax	46	12	10	24	44	73	34
24 Chester	46	11	10	25	48	67	32

Third Division (South)

	P	W	D	L	F	A	Pts
1 Ipswich	46	27	10	9	82	51	64
2 Brighton	46	26	9	11	86	61	61
3 Bristol City	46	25	6	15	88	66	56
4 Watford	46	21	10	15	85	69	52
5 Northampton	46	20	11	15	82	55	51
6 Southampton	46	22	7	17	76	63	51
7 Norwich	46	20	11	15	73	66	51
8 Reading	46	20	9	17	86	73	49
9 Exeter	46	20	8	18	68	58	48

10 Gillingham	46	19	10	17	61	66	48
11 Leyton Orient	46	18	11	17	79	73	47
12 Millwall	46	19	9	18	74	77	47
13 Torquay	46	17	12	17	81	88	46
14 Coventry	46	18	9	19	61	56	45
15 Newport	46	19	6	21	61	81	44
16 Southend	46	18	7	21	69	71	43
17 Aldershot	46	17	9	20	74	86	43
18 QPR	46	16	10	20	60	68	42
19 Bournemouth	46	16	8	22	67	70	40
20 Swindon	46	15	10	21	67	70	40
21 Shrewsbury	46	14	12	20	65	76	40
22 Crystal Palace	46	14	12	20	60	86	40
23 Colchester	46	10	10	26	50	78	30
24 Walsall	46	9	8	29	40	87	26

Scottish Division 'A'

	P	W	D	L	F	A	Pts
1 Celtic	30	20	3	7	72	29	43
2 Hearts	30	16	6	8	70	45	38
3 Partick	30	17	1	12	76	54	35
4 Rangers	30	13	8	9	56	35	34
5 Hibernian	30	15	4	11	72	51	34
6 East Fife	30	13	8	9	55	45	34
7 Dundee	30	14	6	10	46	47	34
8 Clyde	30	15	4	11	64	67	34
9 Aberdeen	30	15	3	12	66	51	33
10 Queen of the S	30	14	4	12	72	58	32
11 St Mirren	30	12	4	14	44	54	28
12 Raith	30	10	6	14	56	60	26
13 Falkirk	30	9	7	14	47	61	25
14 Stirling	30	10	4	16	39	62	24
15 Airdrieonians	30	5	5	20	41	92	15
16 Hamilton	30	4	3	23	29	94	11

Scottish Division 'B'

	P	W	D	L	F	A	Pts
1 Motherwell	30	21	3	6	109	43	45
2 Kilmarnock	30	19	4	7	71	39	42
3 Third Lanark	30	13	10	7	78	48	36
4 Stenhousemuir	30	14	8	8	66	58	36
5 Morton	30	15	3	12	85	65	33
6 St Johnstone	30	14	3	13	80	71	31
7 Albion	30	12	7	11	55	63	31
8 Dunfermline	30	11	9	10	48	57	31
9 Ayr	30	11	8	11	50	56	30
10 Queen's Park	30	9	9	12	56	51	27
11 Alloa	30	7	10	13	50	72	24
12 Forfar	30	10	4	16	38	69	24
13 Cowdenbeath	30	9	5	16	67	81	23

14 Arbroath	30	8	7	15	53	67	23
15 Dundee United	30	8	6	16	54	79	22
16 Dumbarton	30	7	8	15	51	92	22

FA Cup

Fourth Round

West Bromwich Albion v Rotherham United	4-0
Burnley v Newcastle United	1-1, 0-1
Blackburn Rovers v Hull City	2-2, 1-2
Manchester City v Tottenham Hotspur	0-1
Leyton Orient v Fulham	2-1
Plymouth Argyle v Doncaster Rovers	0-2
Cardiff City v Port Vale	0-2
West Ham United v Blackpool	1-1, 1-3
Sheffield Wednesday v Chesterfield	0-0, 4-2
Everton v Swansea Town	3-0
Headington United v Bolton Wanderers	2-4
Scunthorpe United v Portsmouth	1-1, 2-2, 0-4
Arsenal v Norwich City	1-2
Stoke City v Leicester City	0-0, 1-3
Lincoln City v Preston North End	0-2
Ipswich Town v Birmingham City	1-0

Fifth Round

West Bromwich Albion v Newcastle United	3-2
Hull City v Tottenham Hotspur	1-1, 0-2
Leyton Orient v Doncaster Rovers	3-1
Port Vale v Blackpool	2-0
Sheffield Wednesday v Everton	3-1
Bolton Wanderers v Portsmouth	0-0, 2-1
Norwich City v Leicester City	1-2
Preston North End v Ipswich Town	6-1

Sixth Round

West Bromwich Albion v Tottenham Hotspur	3-0
Leyton Orient v Port Vale	0-1
Sheffield Wednesday v Bolton Wanderers	1-1, 2-0
Leicester City v Preston North End	1-1, 2-2, 1-3

Semi-Final

West Bromwich Albion v Port Vale	2-1
Sheffield Wednesday v Preston North End	0-2

Final
West Bromwich Albion v Preston North
 End   3–2

Scottish FA Cup

Third Round
Stirling Albion v Celtic	3–4
Hamilton Academicals v Morton	2–0
Partick Thistle v Buckie Thistle	5–3
Motherwell v Raith Rovers	4–1
Third Lanark v Rangers	0–0, 4–4, 2–3
Berwick Rangers v Dundee	3–0
Queen of the South v Heart of Midlothian	1–2
Hibernian v Aberdeen	1–3

Fourth Round
Hamilton Academicals v Celtic	1–2
Partick Thistle v Motherwell	1–1, 1–2
Rangers v Berwick Rangers	4–0
Aberdeen v Heart of Midlothian	3–0

Semi-Final
Celtic v Motherwell	2–2, 3–1
Rangers v Aberdeen	0–6

Final
Aberdeen v Celtic	1–2

1954–55
First Division

		P	W	D	L	F	A	Pts
1	Chelsea	42	20	12	10	81	57	52
2	Wolves	42	19	10	13	89	70	48
3	Portsmouth	42	18	12	12	74	62	48
4	Sunderland	41	15	18	9	64	54	48
5	Man United	42	20	7	15	84	74	47
6	Aston Villa	42	20	7	15	72	73	47
7	Man City	42	18	10	14	76	69	46
8	Newcastle	42	17	9	16	89	77	43
9	Arsenal	42	17	9	16	69	63	43
10	Burnley	42	17	9	16	51	48	43
11	Everton	42	16	10	16	62	68	42
12	Huddersfield	42	14	13	15	63	68	41
13	Sheff United	42	17	7	18	70	86	41
14	Preston	42	16	8	18	83	64	40
15	Charlton	42	15	10	17	76	75	40
16	Tottenham	42	16	8	18	72	73	40
17	WBA	42	16	8	18	76	96	40
18	Bolton	42	13	13	16	62	69	39
19	Blackpool	42	14	10	18	60	64	38
20	Cardiff	42	13	11	18	62	76	37
21	Leicester	42	12	11	19	74	86	35
22	Sheff Wed	42	8	10	24	63	100	26

Second Division

		P	W	D	L	F	A	Pts
1	Birmingham	42	22	10	10	92	47	54
2	Luton	42	23	8	11	88	53	54
3	Rotherham	42	25	4	13	94	64	54
4	Leeds	42	23	7	12	70	53	53
5	Stoke	42	21	10	11	69	46	52
6	Blackburn	42	22	6	14	114	79	50
7	Notts County	42	21	6	15	74	71	48
8	West Ham	42	18	10	14	74	70	46
9	Bristol Rovers	42	19	7	16	75	70	45
10	Swansea	42	17	9	16	86	83	43
11	Liverpool	42	16	10	16	92	96	42
12	Middlesbrough	42	18	6	18	73	82	42
13	Bury	42	15	11	16	77	72	41
14	Fulham	42	14	11	17	76	79	39
15	Nottm Forest	42	16	7	19	58	62	39
16	Lincoln	42	13	10	19	68	79	36
17	Port Vale	42	12	11	19	48	71	35
18	Doncaster	42	14	7	21	58	95	35
19	Hull	42	12	10	20	44	69	34
10	Plymouth	42	12	7	23	57	82	31
21	Ipswich	42	11	6	25	57	92	28
22	Derby	42	7	9	26	53	82	23

Third Division (North)

		P	W	D	L	F	A	Pts
1	Barnsley	46	30	5	11	86	46	65
2	Accrington	46	25	11	10	96	67	61
3	Scunthorpe	46	23	12	11	81	53	58
4	York	46	24	10	12	92	63	58
5	Hartlepools	46	25	5	16	64	49	55
6	Chesterfield	46	24	6	16	81	70	54
7	Gateshead	46	20	12	14	65	69	52
8	Workington	46	18	14	14	68	55	50
9	Stockport	46	18	12	16	84	70	48
10	Oldham	46	19	10	17	74	68	48
11	Southport	46	16	16	14	47	44	48
12	Rochdale	46	17	14	15	69	66	48
13	Mansfield	46	18	9	19	65	71	45
14	Halifax	46	15	13	18	63	67	43
15	Darlington	46	14	14	18	62	73	42
16	Bradford PA	46	15	11	20	56	70	41
17	Barrow	46	17	6	23	70	89	40
18	Wrexham	46	13	12	21	65	77	38

	P	W	D	L	F	A	Pts
19 Tranmere	46	13	11	22	55	70	37
20 Carlisle	46	15	6	25	78	89	36
21 Bradford City	46	13	10	23	47	55	36
22 Crewe	46	10	14	22	68	91	34
23 Grimsby	46	13	8	25	47	78	34
24 Chester	46	12	9	25	44	77	33

Third Division (South)

	P	W	D	L	F	A	Pts
1 Bristol City	46	30	10	6	101	47	70
2 Leyton Orient	46	26	9	11	89	47	61
3 Southampton	46	24	11	11	75	51	59
4 Gillingham	46	20	15	11	77	66	55
5 Millwall	46	20	11	15	72	68	51
6 Brighton	46	20	10	16	76	63	50
7 Watford	46	18	14	14	71	62	50
8 Torquay	46	18	12	16	82	82	48
9 Coventry	46	18	11	17	67	59	47
10 Southend	46	17	12	17	83	80	46
11 Brentford	46	16	14	16	82	82	46
12 Norwich	46	18	10	18	60	60	46
13 Northampton	46	19	8	19	73	81	46
14 Aldershot	46	16	13	17	75	71	45
15 QPR	46	15	14	17	69	75	44
16 Shrewsbury	46	16	10	20	70	78	42
17 Bournemouth	46	12	18	16	57	65	42
18 Reading	46	13	15	18	65	73	41
19 Newport	46	11	16	19	60	73	38
20 Crystal Palace	46	11	16	19	52	80	38
21 Swindon	46	11	15	20	46	64	37
22 Exeter	46	11	15	20	47	73	37
23 Walsall	46	10	14	22	75	86	34
24 Colchester	46	9	13	24	53	91	31

Scottish Division 'A'

	P	W	D	L	F	A	Pts
1 Aberdeen	30	24	1	5	73	26	49
2 Celtic	30	19	8	3	76	37	46
3 Rangers	30	19	3	8	67	33	41
4 Hearts	30	16	7	7	74	45	39
5 Hibernian	30	15	4	11	64	54	34
6 St Mirren	30	12	8	10	55	54	32
7 Clyde	30	11	9	10	59	50	31
8 Dundee	30	13	4	13	48	48	30
9 Partick	30	11	7	12	49	61	29
10 Kilmarnock	30	10	6	14	46	58	26
11 East Fife	30	9	6	15	51	62	24
12 Falkirk	30	8	8	14	42	54	24
13 Queen of the S	30	9	6	15	38	56	24
14 Raith	30	10	3	17	49	57	23
15 Motherwell	30	9	4	17	42	62	22
16 Stirling	30	2	2	26	29	105	6

Scottish Division 'B'

	P	W	D	L	F	A	Pts
1 Airdrieonians	30	18	10	2	103	61	46
2 Dunfermline	30	19	4	7	72	40	42
3 Hamilton	30	17	5	8	74	51	39
4 Queen's Park	30	15	5	10	65	36	35
5 Third Lanark	30	13	7	10	63	49	33
6 Stenhousemuir	30	12	8	10	70	51	32
7 St Johnstone	30	15	2	13	60	51	32
8 Ayr	30	14	4	12	61	73	32
9 Morton	30	12	5	13	58	69	29
10 Forfar	30	11	6	13	63	80	28
11 Albion	30	8	10	12	50	69	26
12 Arbroath	30	8	8	14	55	72	24
13 Dundee United	30	8	6	16	55	70	22
14 Cowdenbeath	30	8	5	17	55	72	21
15 Alloa	30	7	6	17	51	75	20
16 Brechin	30	8	3	19	53	89	19

FA Cup

Fourth Round

Everton v Liverpool	0–4
Torquay United v Huddersfield Town	0–1
Hartlepools United v Nottingham Forest	1–1, 1–2
Newcastle United v Brentford	3–2
Sheffield Wednesday v Notts County	1–1, 0–1
Bristol Rovers v Chelsea	1–3
Bishop Auckland v York City	1–3
Tottenham Hotspur v Port Vale	4–2
Swansea Town v Stoke City	3–1
Preston North End v Sunderland	3–3, 0–2
Wolverhampton Wanderers v Arsenal	1–0
West Bromwich Albion v Charlton Athletic	2–4
Birmingham City v Bolton Wanderers	2–1
Doncaster Rovers v Aston Villa	0–0, 2–2, 1–1, 0–0, 3–1
Rotherham United v Luton Town	1–5
Manchester City v Manchester United	2–0

Fifth Round

Liverpool v Huddersfield Town	0–2
Nottingham Forest v Newcastle United	1–1, 2–2, 1–2
Notts County v Chelsea	1–0
York City v Tottenham Hotspur	3–1

Swansea Town v Sunderland   2-2, 0-1
Wolverhampton Wanderers v Charlton
Athletic   4-1
Birmingham City v Doncaster Rovers 2-1
Luton Town v Manchester City   0-2

Sixth Round

Huddersfield Town v Newcastle United
1-1, 0-2
Notts County v York City   0-1
Sunderland v Wolverhampton Wanderers
2-0
Birmingham City v Manchester City 0-1

Semi-Final

Newcastle United v York City   1-1, 2-0
Sunderland v Manchester City   0-1

Final

Newcastle United v Manchester City 3-1

Scottish FA Cup

Fifth Round

Clyde v Albion Rovers   3-0
Morton v Raith Rovers   1-3
Ayr United v Inverness Caledonian
1-1, 2-4
Heart of Midlothian v Hibernian   5-0
Stirling Albion v Aberdeen   0-6
Dundee v Rangers   0-0, 0-1
Airdrieonians v Forfar Athletic   4-3
Dunfermline Athletic v Partick Thistle 4-2
Third Lanark v Queen of the South   2-1
Forres Mechanics v Motherwell   3-4
East Fife v Kilmarnock   1-2
Alloa Athletic v Celtic   2-4
Arbroath v St Johnstone   0-4
Hamilton Academicals v St Mirren   2-1
Falkirk v Stenhousemuir   4-0
Buckie Thistle v Inverness Thistle   2-0

Sixth Round

Clyde v Raith Rovers   3-1
Inverness Caledonian v Falkirk   0-7
Buckie Thistle v Heart of Midlothian 0-6
Aberdeen v Rangers   2-1
Airdrieonians v Dunfermline Athletic 7-0
Third Lanark v Motherwell   1-3
Celtic v Kilmarnock   1-1, 1-0
St Johnstone v Hamilton Academicals 0-1

Seventh Round

Clyde v Falkirk   5-0

Aberdeen v Heart of Midlothian 1-1, 2-0
Airdrieonians v Motherwell   4-1
Celtic v Hamilton Academicals   2-1

Semi-Final

Aberdeen v Clyde   2-2, 0-1
Airdrieonians v Celtic   2-2, 0-0

Final

Celtic v Clyde   1-1, 0-1

1955–56
First Division

	P	W	D	L	F	A	Pts
1 Man United	42	25	10	7	83	51	60
2 Blackpool	42	20	9	13	86	62	49
3 Wolves	42	20	9	13	89	65	49
4 Man City	42	18	10	14	82	69	46
5 Arsenal	42	18	10	14	60	61	46
6 Birmingham	42	18	9	15	75	57	45
7 Burnley	42	18	8	16	64	54	44
8 Bolton	42	18	7	17	71	58	43
9 Sunderland	42	17	9	16	80	95	43
10 Luton	42	17	8	17	66	64	42
11 Newcastle	42	17	7	18	85	70	41
12 Portsmouth	42	16	9	17	78	85	41
13 WBA	42	18	5	19	58	70	41
14 Charlton	42	17	6	19	75	81	40
15 Everton	42	15	10	17	55	69	40
16 Chelsea	42	14	11	17	64	77	39
17 Cardiff	42	15	9	18	55	69	39
18 Tottenham	42	15	7	20	61	71	37
19 Preston	42	14	8	20	73	72	36
20 Aston Villa	42	11	13	18	52	69	35
21 Huddersfield	42	14	7	21	54	83	35
22 Sheff United	42	12	9	21	63	77	33

Second Division

	P	W	D	L	F	A	Pts
1 Sheff Wed	42	21	13	8	101	62	55
2 Leeds	42	23	6	13	80	60	52
3 Liverpool	42	21	6	15	85	63	48
4 Blackburn	42	21	6	15	84	65	48
5 Leicester	42	21	6	15	94	78	48
6 Bristol Rovers	42	21	6	15	84	70	48
7 Nottm Forest	42	19	9	14	68	63	47
8 Lincoln	42	18	10	14	79	65	46
9 Fulham	42	20	6	16	89	79	46

	P	W	D	L	F	A	Pts
10 Swansea	42	20	6	16	83	81	46
11 Bristol City	42	19	7	16	80	64	45
12 Port Vale	42	16	13	13	60	58	45
13 Stoke	42	20	4	18	71	62	44
14 Middlesbrough	42	16	8	18	76	78	40
15 Bury	42	16	8	18	86	90	40
16 West Ham	42	14	11	17	74	69	39
17 Doncaster	42	12	11	19	69	96	35
18 Barnsley	42	11	12	19	47	84	34
19 Rotherham	42	12	9	21	56	75	33
20 Notts County	42	11	9	22	55	82	31
21 Plymouth	42	10	8	24	54	87	28
22 Hull	42	10	6	26	53	97	26

Third Division (North)

	P	W	D	L	F	A	Pts
1 Grimsby	46	31	6	9	76	29	68
2 Derby	46	28	7	11	110	55	63
3 Accrington	46	25	9	12	92	57	59
4 Hartlepools	46	26	5	15	81	60	57
5 Southport	46	23	11	12	66	53	57
6 Chesterfield	46	25	4	17	94	66	54
7 Stockport	46	21	9	16	90	61	51
8 Bradford City	46	18	13	15	78	64	49
9 Scunthorpe	46	20	8	18	75	63	48
10 Workington	46	19	9	18	75	63	47
11 York	46	19	9	18	85	72	47
12 Rochdale	46	17	13	16	66	84	47
13 Gateshead	46	17	11	18	77	84	45
14 Wrexham	46	16	10	20	66	73	42
15 Darlington	46	16	9	21	60	73	41
16 Tranmere	46	16	9	21	59	84	41
17 Chester	46	13	14	19	52	82	40
18 Mansfield	46	14	11	21	84	81	39
19 Halifax	46	14	11	21	66	76	39
20 Oldham	46	10	18	18	76	86	38
21 Carlisle	46	15	8	23	71	95	38
22 Barrow	46	12	9	25	61	83	33
23 Bradford PA	46	13	7	26	61	122	33
24 Crewe	46	9	10	27	50	105	28

Third Division (South)

	P	W	D	L	F	A	Pts
1 Leyton Orient	46	29	8	9	106	49	66
2 Brighton	46	29	7	10	112	50	65
3 Ipswich	46	25	14	7	106	60	64
4 Southend	46	21	11	14	88	80	53
5 Torquay	46	20	12	14	86	63	52
6 Brentford	46	19	14	13	69	66	52
7 Norwich	46	19	13	14	86	82	51

	P	W	D	L	F	A	Pts
8 Coventry	46	20	9	17	73	60	49
9 Bournemouth	46	19	10	17	63	51	48
10 Gillingham	46	19	10	17	69	71	48
11 Northampton	46	20	7	19	67	71	47
12 Colchester	46	18	11	17	76	81	47
13 Shrewsbury	46	17	12	17	69	66	46
14 Southampton	46	18	8	20	91	81	44
15 Aldershot	46	12	16	18	70	90	40
16 Exeter	46	15	10	21	58	77	40
17 Reading	46	15	9	22	70	79	39
18 QPR	46	14	11	21	64	86	39
19 Newport	46	15	9	22	58	79	39
20 Walsall	46	15	8	23	68	84	38
21 Watford	46	13	11	22	52	85	37
22 Millwall	46	15	6	25	83	100	36
23 Crystal Palace	46	12	10	24	54	83	34
24 Swindon	46	8	14	24	34	78	30

Scottish League 'A'

	P	W	D	L	F	A	Pts
1 Rangers	34	22	8	4	85	27	52
2 Aberdeen	34	18	10	6	87	50	46
3 Hearts	34	19	7	8	99	47	45
4 Hibernian	34	19	7	8	86	50	45
5 Celtic	34	16	9	9	55	39	41
6 Queen of the S	34	16	5	13	69	73	37
7 Airdrieonians	34	14	8	12	85	96	36
8 Kilmarnock	34	12	10	12	52	45	34
9 Partick	34	13	7	14	62	60	33
10 Motherwell	34	11	11	12	53	59	33
11 Raith	34	12	9	13	58	75	33
12 East Fife	34	13	5	16	61	69	31
13 Dundee	34	12	6	16	56	65	30
14 Falkirk	34	11	6	17	58	75	28
15 St Mirren	34	10	7	17	57	70	27
16 Dunfermline	34	10	6	18	42	82	26
17 Clyde	34	8	6	20	50	74	22
18 Stirling	34	4	5	25	23	82	13

Scottish League 'B'

	P	W	D	L	F	A	Pts
1 Queen's Park	36	23	8	5	78	28	54
2 Ayr	36	24	3	9	103	55	51
3 St Johnstone	36	21	7	8	86	45	49
4 Dumbarton	36	21	5	10	83	62	47
5 Stenhousemuir	36	20	4	12	82	54	44
6 Brechin	36	18	6	12	60	56	42
7 Cowdenbeath	36	16	7	13	80	85	39
8 Dundee United	36	12	14	10	78	65	38
9 Morton	36	15	6	15	71	69	36

10 Third Lanark	36	16	3 17	80	64	35
11 Hamilton	36	13	7 16	86	84	33
12 Stranraer	36	14	5 17	77	92	33
13 Alloa	36	12	7 17	67	73	31
14 Berwick	36	11	9 16	52	77	31
15 Forfar	36	10	9 17	62	75	29
16 E Stirlingshire	36	9	10 17	66	94	28
17 Albion	36	8	11 17	58	82	27
18 Arbroath	36	10	6 20	47	67	26
19 Montrose	36	4	3 29	44	133	11

FA Cup

Fourth Round

Leyton Orient v Birmingham City	0-4
West Bromwich Albion v Portsmouth	2-0
Charlton Athletic v Swindon Town	2-1
Arsenal v Aston Villa	4-1
Fulham v Newcastle United	4-5
Leicester City v Stoke City	3-3, 1-2
Bolton Wanderers v Sheffield United	1-2
York City v Sunderland	0-0, 1-2
Bristol Rovers v Doncaster Rovers	1-1, 0-1
Tottenham Hotspur v Middlesbrough	3-1
West Ham United v Cardiff City	2-1
Barnsley v Blackburn Rovers	0-1
Port Vale v Everton	2-3
Burnley v Chelsea 1-1, 1-1, 2-2, 0-0, 0-2
Liverpool v Scunthorpe United	3-3, 2-1
Southend United v Manchester City	0-1

Fifth Round

West Bromwich Albion v Birmingham City	0-1
Charlton Athletic v Arsenal	0-2
Newcastle United v Stoke City	2-1
Sheffield United v Sunderland	0-0, 0-1
Doncaster Rovers v Tottenham Hotspur	0-2
West Ham United v Blackburn Rovers	0-0, 3-2
Everton v Chelsea	1-0
Manchester City v Liverpool	0-0, 2-1

Sixth Round

Arsenal v Birmingham City	1-3
Newcastle United v Sunderland	0-2
Tottenham Hotspur v West Ham United	3-3, 2-1
Manchester City v Everton	2-1

Semi-Final

Birmingham City v Sunderland	3-0

Tottenham Hotspur v Manchester City	0-1

Final

Manchester City v Birmingham City	3-1

Scottish FA Cup

Fifth Round

Heart of Midlothian v Forfar Athletic	3-0
Stirling Albion v St Johnstone	2-1
Rangers v Aberdeen	2-1
Dundee v Dundee United	2-2, 3-0
Hibernian v Raith Rovers	1-1, 1-3
Motherwell v Queen's Park	0-2
Partick Thistle v Alloa Athletic	2-0
Brechin City v Arbroath	1-1, 3-2
Falkirk v Kilmarnock	0-3
Queen of the South v Cowdenbeath	3-1
East Fife v Stenhousemuir	1-3
Clyde v Dunfermline Athletic	5-0
St Mirren v Third Lanark	6-0
Airdrieonians v Hamilton Academicals	7-1
Ayr United v Berwick Rangers	5-2
Morton v Celtic	0-2

Sixth Round

Heart of Midlothian v Stirling Albion	5-0
Dundee v Rangers	0-1
Raith Rovers v Queen's Park	2-2, 2-1
Partick Thistle v Brechin City	3-1
Kilmarnock v Queen of the South	2-2, 0-2
Stenhousemuir v Clyde	0-1
St Mirren v Airdrieonians	4-4, 1-3
Ayr United v Celtic	0-3

Seventh Round

Heart of Midlothian v Rangers	4-0
Raith Rovers v Partick Thistle	2-1
Queen of the South v Clyde	2-4
Celtic v Airdrieonians	2-1

Semi-Final

Heart of Midlothian v Raith Rovers	0-0, 3-0
Celtic v Clyde	2-0

Final

Heart of Midlothian v Celtic	3-1

1956–57
First Division

	P	W	D	L	F	A	Pts
1 Man United	42	28	8	6	103	54	64
2 Tottenham	42	22	12	8	104	56	56
3 Preston	42	23	10	9	84	56	56
4 Blackpool	42	22	9	11	93	65	53
5 Arsenal	42	21	8	13	85	69	50
6 Wolves	42	20	8	14	94	70	48
7 Burnley	42	18	10	14	56	50	46
8 Leeds	42	15	14	13	72	63	44
9 Bolton	42	16	12	14	65	65	44
10 Aston Villa	42	14	15	13	65	55	43
11 WBA	42	14	14	14	59	61	42
12 Birmingham	42	15	9	18	69	69	39
12 Chelsea	42	13	13	16	73	73	39
14 Sheff Wed	42	16	6	20	82	88	38
15 Everton	42	14	10	18	61	79	38
16 Luton	42	14	9	19	58	76	37
17 Newcastle	42	14	8	20	67	87	36
18 Man City	42	13	9	20	78	88	35
19 Portsmouth	42	10	13	19	62	92	33
20 Sunderland	42	12	8	22	67	88	32
21 Cardiff	42	10	9	23	53	88	29
22 Charlton	42	9	4	29	62	120	22

Second Division

	P	W	D	L	F	A	Pts
1 Leicester	42	25	11	6	109	67	61
2 Nottm Forest	42	22	10	10	94	55	54
3 Liverpool	42	21	11	10	82	54	53
4 Blackburn	42	21	10	11	83	75	52
5 Stoke	42	20	8	14	83	58	48
6 Middlesbrough	42	19	10	13	84	60	48
7 Sheff United	42	19	8	15	87	76	46
8 West Ham	42	19	8	15	59	63	46
9 Bristol Rovers	42	18	9	15	81	67	45
10 Swansea	42	19	7	16	90	90	45
11 Fulham	42	19	4	19	84	76	42
12 Huddersfield	42	18	6	18	68	74	42
13 Bristol City	42	16	9	17	74	79	41
14 Doncaster	42	15	10	17	77	77	40
15 Leyton Orient	42	15	10	17	66	84	40
16 Grimsby	42	17	5	20	61	62	39
17 Rotherham	42	13	11	18	74	75	37
18 Lincoln	42	14	6	22	54	80	34
19 Barnsley	42	12	10	20	59	89	34
20 Notts County	42	9	12	21	58	86	30

| 21 Bury | 42 | 8 | 9 | 25 | 60 | 96 | 25 |
| 22 Port Vale | 42 | 8 | 6 | 28 | 57 | 101 | 22 |

Third Division (North)

	P	W	D	L	F	A	Pts
1 Derby	46	26	11	9	111	53	63
2 Hartlepools	46	25	9	12	90	63	59
3 Accrington	46	25	8	13	95	64	58
4 Workington	46	24	10	12	93	63	58
5 Stockport	46	23	8	15	91	75	54
6 Chesterfield	46	22	9	15	96	79	53
7 York	46	21	10	15	75	61	52
8 Hull	46	21	10	15	84	69	52
9 Bradford City	46	22	8	16	78	68	52
10 Barrow	46	21	9	16	76	62	51
11 Halifax	46	21	7	18	65	70	49
12 Wrexham	46	19	10	17	97	74	48
13 Rochdale	46	18	12	16	65	65	48
14 Scunthorpe	46	15	15	16	71	69	45
15 Carlisle	46	16	13	17	76	85	45
16 Mansfield	46	17	10	19	91	90	44
17 Gateshead	46	17	10	19	72	90	44
18 Darlington	46	17	8	21	82	95	42
19 Oldham	46	12	15	19	66	74	39
20 Bradford PA	46	16	3	27	66	93	35
21 Chester	46	10	13	23	55	84	33
22 Southport	46	10	12	24	52	94	32
23 Tranmere	46	7	13	26	51	91	27
24 Crewe	46	6	9	31	43	110	21

Third Division (South)

	P	W	D	L	F	A	Pts
1 Ipswich	46	25	9	12	101	54	59
2 Torquay	46	24	11	11	89	64	59
3 Colchester	46	22	14	10	84	56	58
4 Southampton	46	22	10	14	76	52	54
5 Bournemouth	46	19	14	13	88	62	52
6 Brighton	46	19	14	13	86	65	52
7 Southend	46	18	12	16	73	65	48
8 Brentford	46	16	16	14	78	76	48
9 Shrewsbury	46	15	18	13	72	79	48
10 QPR	46	18	11	17	61	60	47
11 Watford	46	18	10	18	72	75	46
12 Newport	46	16	13	17	65	62	45
13 Reading	46	18	9	19	80	81	45
14 Northampton	46	18	9	19	66	73	45
15 Walsall	46	16	12	18	80	74	44
16 Coventry	46	16	12	18	74	84	44
17 Millwall	46	16	12	18	64	84	44
18 Plymouth	46	16	11	19	68	73	43

	P	W	D	L	F	A	Pts
19 Aldershot	46	15	12	19	79	92	42
20 Crystal Palace	46	11	18	17	62	75	40
21 Exeter	46	12	13	21	61	79	37
22 Gillingham	46	12	13	21	54	85	37
23 Swindon	46	15	6	25	66	96	36
24 Norwich	46	8	15	23	61	94	31

Scottish First Division

	P	W	D	L	F	A	Pts
1 Rangers	34	26	3	5	96	48	55
2 Hearts	34	24	5	5	81	48	53
3 Kilmarnock	34	16	10	8	57	39	42
4 Raith	34	16	7	11	84	58	39
5 Celtic	34	15	8	11	58	43	38
6 Aberdeen	34	18	2	14	79	59	38
7 Motherwell	34	16	5	13	72	66	37
8 Partick	34	13	8	13	53	51	34
9 Hibernian	34	12	9	13	69	56	33
10 Dundee	34	13	6	15	55	61	32
11 Airdrieonians	34	13	4	17	77	89	30
12 St Mirren	34	12	6	16	58	72	30
13 Queen's Park	34	11	7	16	55	59	29
14 Falkirk	34	10	8	16	51	70	28
15 East Fife	34	10	6	18	59	82	26
16 Queen of the S	34	10	5	19	54	96	25
17 Dunfermline	34	9	6	19	54	74	24
18 Ayr	34	7	5	22	48	89	19

Scottish Second Division

	P	W	D	L	F	A	Pts
1 Clyde	36	29	6	1	122	39	64
2 Third Lanark	36	24	3	9	105	51	51
3 Cowdenbeath	36	20	5	11	87	65	45
4 Morton	36	18	7	11	81	70	43
5 Albion	36	18	6	12	98	80	42
6 Brechin	36	15	10	11	72	68	40
7 Stranraer	36	15	10	11	79	77	40
8 Stirling	36	17	5	14	81	64	39
9 Dumbarton	36	17	4	15	101	70	38
10 Arbroath	36	17	4	15	79	57	38
11 Hamilton	36	14	8	14	69	68	36
12 St Johnstone	36	14	6	16	79	80	34
13 Dundee United	36	14	6	16	75	80	34
14 Stenhousemuir	36	13	6	17	71	81	32
15 Alloa	36	11	5	20	66	99	27
16 Forfar	36	9	5	22	75	100	23
17 Montrose	36	7	7	22	54	124	21
18 Berwick	36	7	6	23	58	114	20
19 E Stirlingshire	36	5	7	24	56	121	17

FA Cup

Fourth Round

Middlesbrough v Aston Villa	2-3
Bristol City v Rhyl	3-0
Burnley v New Brighton	9-0
Huddersfield Town v Peterborough United	3-1
Newport County v Arsenal	0-2
Bristol Rovers v Preston North End	1-4
Blackpool v Fulham	6-2
West Bromwich Albion v Sunderland	4-2
Wrexham v Manchester United	0-5
Everton v West Ham United	2-1
Wolverhampton Wanderers v Bournemouth	0-1
Tottenham Hotspur v Chelsea	4-0
Southend United v Birmingham City	1-6
Millwall v Newcastle United	2-1
Cardiff City v Barnsley	0-1
Portsmouth v Nottingham Forest	1-3

Fifth Round

Aston Villa v Bristol City	2-1
Huddersfield Town v Burnley	1-2
Preston North End v Arsenal	3-3, 1-2
Blackpool v West Bromwich Albion	0-0, 1-2
Manchester United v Everton	1-0
Bournemouth v Tottenham Hotspur	3-1
Millwall v Birmingham City	1-4
Barnsley v Nottingham Forest	1-2

Sixth Round

Burnley v Aston Villa	1-1, 0-2
West Bromwich Albion v Arsenal	2-2, 2-1
Bournemouth v Manchester United	1-2
Birmingham City v Nottingham Forest	0-0, 1-0

Semi-Final

Aston Villa v West Bromwich Albion	2-2, 1-0
Manchester United v Birmingham City	2-0

Final

Aston Villa v Manchester United	2-1

Scottish FA Cup

Fifth Round

Berwick Rangers v Falkirk	1-2
Hibernian v Aberdeen	3-4

Dundee v Clyde   0–0, 1–2
Queen's Park v Brechin City   3–0
Inverness Caledonian v Raith Rovers   2–4
Stenhousemuir v Dundee United 1–1, 0–4
Queen of the South v Dumbarton 2–2, 2–4
Stirling Albion v Motherwell   1–2
Dunfermline Athletic v Morton   3–0
St Mirren v Partick Thistle   1–1, 2–2, 5–1
Heart of Midlothian v Rangers   0–4
Forres Mechanics v Celtic   0–5
Hamilton Academicals v Alloa Athletic
                                                   2–2, 5–3
Stranraer v Airdrieonians   1–2
East Fife v St Johnstone   4–0
Kilmarnock v Ayr United   1–0

Sixth Round

Falkirk v Aberdeen   3–1
Queen's Park v Clyde   1–1, 0–2
Raith Rovers v Dundee United   7–0
Motherwell v Dumbarton   1–3
St Mirren v Dunfermline Athletic   1–0
Celtic v Rangers   4–4, 2–0
Hamilton Academicals v Airdrieonians 1–2
East Fife v Kilmarnock   0–0, 0–2

Seventh Round

Falkirk v Clyde   2–1
Dumbarton v Raith Rovers   0–4
Celtic v St Mirren   2–1
Kilmarnock v Airdrieonians   3–1

Semi-Final

Falkirk v Raith Rovers   2–2, 2–0
Celtic v Kilmarnock   1–1, 1–3

Final

Falkirk v Kilmarnock   1–1, 2–1

1957–58
First Division

	P	W	D	L	F	A	Pts
1 Wolves	42	28	8	6	103	47	64
2 Preston	42	26	7	9	100	51	59
3 Tottenham	42	21	9	12	93	77	51
4 WBA	42	18	14	10	92	70	50
5 Man City	42	22	5	15	104	100	49
6 Burnley	42	21	5	16	80	74	47
7 Blackpool	42	19	6	17	80	67	44
8 Luton	42	19	6	17	69	63	44

9 Man United	42	16	11	15	85	75	43
10 Nottm Forest	42	16	10	16	69	63	42
11 Chelsea	42	15	12	15	83	79	42
12 Arsenal	42	16	7	19	73	85	39
13 Birmingham	42	14	11	17	76	89	39
14 Aston Villa	42	16	7	19	73	86	39
15 Bolton	42	14	10	18	65	87	38
16 Everton	42	13	11	18	65	75	37
17 Leeds	42	14	9	19	51	63	37
18 Leicester	42	14	5	23	91	112	33
19 Newcastle	42	12	8	22	73	81	32
20 Portsmouth	42	12	8	22	73	88	32
21 Sunderland	42	10	12	20	54	97	32
22 Sheff Wed	42	12	7	23	69	92	31

Second Division

	P	W	D	L	F	A	Pts
1 West Ham	42	23	11	8	101	54	57
2 Blackburn	42	22	12	8	93	57	56
3 Charlton	42	24	7	11	107	69	55
4 Liverpool	42	22	10	10	79	54	54
5 Fulham	42	20	12	10	97	59	52
6 Sheff United	42	21	10	11	75	50	52
7 Middlesbrough	42	19	7	16	83	74	45
8 Ipswich	42	16	12	14	68	69	44
9 Huddersfield	42	14	16	12	63	66	44
10 Bristol Rovers	42	17	8	17	85	80	42
11 Stoke	42	18	6	18	75	73	42
12 Leyton Orient	42	18	5	19	77	79	41
13 Grimsby	42	17	6	19	86	83	40
14 Barnsley	42	14	12	16	70	74	40
15 Cardiff	42	14	9	19	63	77	37
16 Derby	42	14	8	20	60	81	36
17 Bristol City	42	13	9	20	63	88	35
18 Rotherham	42	14	5	23	65	101	33
19 Swansea	42	11	9	22	72	99	31
20 Lincoln	42	11	9	22	55	82	31
21 Notts County	42	12	6	24	44	80	30
22 Doncaster	42	8	11	23	56	88	27

Third Division (North)

	P	W	D	L	F	A	Pts
1 Scunthorpe	46	29	8	9	88	50	66
2 Accrington	46	25	9	12	83	61	59
3 Bradford City	46	21	15	10	73	49	57
4 Bury	46	23	10	13	94	62	56
5 Hull	46	19	15	12	78	67	53
6 Mansfield	46	22	8	16	100	92	52
7 Halifax	46	20	11	15	83	69	51
8 Chesterfield	46	18	15	13	71	69	51

9 Stockport	46	18	11	17	74 67	47
10 Rochdale	46	19	8	19	79 67	46
11 Tranmere	46	18	10	18	82 76	46
12 Wrexham	46	17	12	17	61 63	46
13 York	46	17	12	17	68 76	46
14 Gateshead	46	15	15	16	68 76	45
15 Oldham	46	14	17	15	72 84	45
16 Carlisle	46	19	6	21	80 78	44
17 Hartlepools	46	16	12	18	73 76	44
18 Barrow	46	13	15	18	66 74	41
19 Workington	46	14	13	19	72 81	41
20 Darlington	46	17	7	22	78 89	41
21 Chester	46	13	13	20	73 81	39
22 Bradford PA	46	13	11	22	68 95	37
23 Southport	46	11	6	29	52 88	28
24 Crewe	46	8	7	31	47 93	23

Third Division (South)

	P	W	D	L	F	A	Pts
1 Brighton	46	24	12	10	88	64	60
2 Brentford	46	24	10	12	82	56	58
3 Plymouth	46	25	8	13	67	48	58
4 Swindon	46	21	15	10	79	50	57
5 Reading	46	21	13	12	79	51	55
6 Southampton	46	22	10	14	112	72	54
7 Southend	46	21	12	13	90	58	54
8 Norwich	46	19	15	12	75	70	53
9 Bournemouth	46	21	9	16	81	74	51
10 QPR	46	18	14	14	64	65	50
11 Newport	46	17	14	15	73	67	48
12 Colchester	46	17	13	16	77	79	47
13 Northampton	46	19	6	21	87	79	44
14 Crystal Palace	46	15	13	18	70	72	43
15 Port Vale	46	16	10	20	67	58	42
16 Watford	46	13	16	17	59	77	42
17 Shrewsbury	46	15	10	21	49	71	40
18 Aldershot	46	12	16	18	59	89	40
19 Coventry	46	13	13	20	61	81	39
20 Walsall	46	14	9	23	61	75	37
21 Torquay	46	11	13	22	49	74	35
22 Gillingham	46	13	9	24	52	81	35
23 Millwall	46	11	9	26	63	91	31
24 Exeter	46	11	9	26	57	99	31

Scottish First Division

	P	W	D	L	F	A	Pts
1 Hearts	34	29	4	1	132	29	62
2 Rangers	34	22	5	7	89	49	49
3 Celtic	34	19	8	7	84	47	46
4 Clyde	34	18	6	10	84	61	42

5 Kilmarnock	34	14	9	11	60 55	37
6 Partick	34	17	3	14	69 71	37
7 Raith	34	14	7	13	66 56	35
8 Motherwell	34	12	8	14	68 67	32
9 Hibernian	34	13	5	16	59 60	31
10 Falkirk	34	11	9	14	64 82	31
11 Dundee	34	13	5	16	49 65	31
12 Aberdeen	34	14	2	18	68 76	30
13 St Mirren	34	11	8	15	59 66	30
14 Third Lanark	34	13	4	17	69 88	30
15 Queen of the S	34	12	5	17	61 72	29
16 Airdrieonians	34	13	2	19	71 92	28
17 East Fife	34	10	3	21	45 88	23
18 Queen's Park	34	4	1	29	41 114	9

Scottish Second Division

	P	W	D	L	F	A	Pts
1 Stirling	36	25	5	6	105	48	55
2 Dunfermline	36	24	5	7	120	42	53
3 Arbroath	36	21	5	10	89	72	47
4 Dumbarton	36	20	4	12	92	57	44
5 Ayr	36	18	6	12	98	81	42
6 Cowdenbeath	36	17	8	11	100	85	42
7 Brechin	36	16	8	12	80	81	40
8 Alloa	36	15	9	12	88	78	39
9 Dundee United	36	12	9	15	81	77	33
10 Hamilton	36	12	9	15	70	79	33
11 St Johnstone	36	12	9	15	67	85	33
12 Forfar	36	13	6	17	70	71	32
13 Morton	36	12	8	16	77	83	32
14 Montrose	36	13	6	17	55	72	32
15 E Stirlingshire	36	12	5	19	55	79	29
16 Stenhousemuir	36	12	5	19	68	98	29
17 Albion	36	12	5	19	53	79	29
18 Stranraer	36	9	7	20	54	83	25
19 Berwick	36	5	5	26	37	109	15

FA Cup

Fourth Round

Everton v Blackburn Rovers	1-2
Cardiff City v Leyton Orient	4-1
Liverpool v Northampton Town	3-1
Newcastle United v Scunthorpe United	1-3
Wolverhampton Wanderers v Portsmouth	5-1
Chelsea v Darlington	3-3, 1-4
Stoke City v Middlesbrough	3-1
York City v Bolton Wanderers	0-0, 0-3
Manchester United v Ipswich Town	2-0

Sheffield Wednesday v Hull City   4-3
West Bromwich Albion v Nottingham
       Forest   3-3, 5-1
Tottenham Hotspur v Sheffield United
                                    0-3
Bristol Rovers v Burnley   2-2, 3-2
Notts County v Bristol City   1-2
West Ham United v Stockport County
                                    3-2
Fulham v Charlton Athletic   1-1, 2-0

Fifth Round

Cardiff City v Blackburn Rovers 0-0, 1-2
Scunthorpe United v Liverpool   0-1
Wolverhampton Wanderers v Darlington
                                    6-1
Bolton Wanderers v Stoke City   3-1
Manchester United v Sheffield Wednesday
                                    3-0
Sheffield United v West Bromwich Albion
                                    1-1, 1-4
Bristol City v Bristol Rovers   3-4
West Ham United v Fulham   2-3

Sixth Round

Blackburn Rovers v Liverpool   2-1
Bolton Wnaderers v Wolverhampton
       Wanderers   2-1
West Bromwich Albion v Manchester
       United   2-2, 0-1
Fulham v Bristol Rovers   3-1

Semi-Final

Blackburn Rovers v Bolton Wanderers
                                    1-2
Manchester United v Fulham   2-2, 5-3

Final

Bolton Wanderers v Manchester United
                                    2-0

Scottish FA Cup

Third Round

Clyde v Celtic   2-0
Buckie Thistle v Falkirk   1-2
Inverness Caledonian v Motherwell   0-7
Dundee v Aberdeen   1-3
Dunfermline Athletic v Rangers   1-2
Kilmarnock v Queen of the South 2-2, 0-3
Heart of Midlothian v Hibernian   3-4
Third Lanark v Queen's Park   5-3

Fourth Round

Clyde v Falkirk   2-1

Motherwell v Aberdeen   2-1
Queen of the South v Rangers   3-4
Hibernian v Third Lanark   3-2

Semi-Final

Clyde v Motherwell   3-2
Rangers v Hibernian   2-2, 1-2

Final

Clyde v Hibernian   1-0

1958–59
First Division

	P	W	D	L	F	A	Pts
1 Wolves	42	28	5	9	110	49	61
2 Man United	42	24	7	11	103	66	55
3 Arsenal	42	21	8	13	88	68	50
4 Bolton	42	20	10	12	79	66	50
5 WBA	42	18	13	11	88	68	49
6 West Ham	42	21	6	15	85	70	48
7 Burnley	42	19	10	13	81	70	48
8 Blackpool	42	18	11	13	66	49	47
9 Birmingham	42	20	6	16	84	68	46
10 Blackburn	42	17	10	15	76	70	44
11 Newcastle	42	17	7	18	80	80	41
12 Preston	42	17	7	18	70	77	41
13 Nottm Forest	42	17	6	19	71	74	40
14 Chelsea	42	18	4	20	77	98	40
15 Leeds	42	15	9	18	57	74	39
16 Everton	42	17	4	21	71	87	38
17 Luton	42	12	13	17	68	71	37
18 Tottenham	42	13	10	19	85	95	36
19 Leicester	42	11	10	21	67	98	32
20 Man City	42	11	9	22	64	95	31
21 Aston Villa	42	11	8	23	58	87	30
22 Portsmouth	42	6	9	27	64	112	21

Second Division

	P	W	D	L	F	A	Pts
1 Sheff Wed	42	28	6	8	106	48	62
2 Fulham	42	27	6	9	96	61	60
3 Sheff United	42	23	7	12	82	48	53
4 Liverpool	42	24	5	13	87	62	53
5 Stoke	42	21	7	14	72	58	49
6 Bristol Rovers	42	18	12	12	80	64	48
7 Derby	42	20	8	14	74	71	48
8 Charlton	42	18	7	17	92	90	43
9 Cardiff	42	18	7	17	65	65	43

	P W D L F A Pts
10 Bristol City	42 17 7 18 74 70 41
11 Swansea	42 16 9 17 79 81 41
12 Brighton	42 15 11 16 74 90 41
13 Middlesbrough	42 15 10 17 87 71 40
14 Huddersfield	42 16 8 18 62 55 40
15 Sunderland	42 16 8 18 64 75 40
16 Ipswich	42 17 6 19 62 77 40
17 Leyton Orient	42 14 8 20 71 78 36
18 Scunthorpe	42 12 9 21 55 84 33
19 Lincoln	42 11 7 24 63 93 29
20 Rotherham	42 10 9 23 42 82 29
21 Grimsby	42 9 10 23 62 90 28
22 Barnsley	42 10 7 25 55 91 27

Third Division

	P W D L F A Pts
1 Plymouth	46 23 16 7 89 59 62
2 Hull	46 26 9 11 90 55 61
3 Brentford	46 21 15 10 76 49 57
4 Norwich	46 22 13 11 89 62 57
5 Colchester	46 21 10 15 71 67 52
6 Reading	46 21 8 17 78 63 50
7 Tranmere	46 21 8 17 82 67 50
8 Southend	46 21 8 17 85 80 50
9 Halifax	46 21 8 17 80 77 50
10 Bury	46 17 14 15 69 58 48
11 Bradford City	46 18 11 17 84 76 47
12 Bournemouth	46 17 12 17 69 69 46
13 QPR	46 19 8 19 74 77 46
14 Southampton	46 17 11 18 88 80 45
15 Swindon	46 16 13 17 59 57 45
16 Chesterfield	46 17 10 19 67 64 44
17 Newport	46 17 9 20 69 68 43
18 Wrexham	46 14 14 18 63 77 42
19 Accrington	46 15 12 19 71 87 42
20 Mansfield	46 14 13 19 73 98 41
21 Stockport	46 13 10 23 65 78 36
22 Doncaster	46 14 5 27 50 90 33
23 Notts County	46 8 13 25 55 96 29
24 Rochdale	46 8 12 26 37 79 28

Fourth Division

	P W D L F A Pts
1 Port Vale	46 26 12 8 110 58 64
2 Coventry	46 24 12 10 84 47 60
3 York	46 21 18 7 73 52 60
4 Shrewsbury	46 24 10 12 101 63 58
5 Exeter	46 23 11 12 87 61 57
6 Walsall	46 21 10 15 95 64 52
7 Crystal Palace	46 20 12 14 90 71 52

	P W D L F A Pts
8 Northampton	46 21 9 16 85 78 51
9 Millwall	46 20 10 16 76 69 50
10 Carlisle	46 19 12 15 62 65 50
11 Gillingham	46 20 9 17 82 77 49
12 Torquay	46 16 12 18 78 77 44
13 Chester	46 16 12 18 72 84 44
14 Bradford PA	46 18 7 21 75 77 43
15 Watford	46 16 10 20 81 79 42
16 Darlington	46 13 16 17 66 68 42
17 Workington	46 12 17 17 63 78 41
18 Crewe	46 15 10 21 70 82 40
19 Hartlepools	46 15 10 21 74 88 40
20 Gateshead	46 16 8 22 56 85 40
21 Oldham	46 16 4 26 59 84 36
22 Aldershot	46 14 7 25 63 97 35
23 Barrow	46 9 10 27 51 104 28
24 Southport	46 7 12 27 41 86 26

Scottish First Division

	P W D L F A Pts
1 Rangers	34 21 8 5 92 51 50
2 Hearts	34 21 6 7 92 51 48
3 Motherwell	34 18 8 8 83 50 44
4 Dundee	34 16 9 9 61 51 41
5 Airdrieonians	34 15 7 12 64 62 37
6 Celtic	34 14 8 12 70 53 36
7 St Mirren	34 14 7 13 71 74 35
8 Kilmarnock	34 13 8 13 58 51 34
9 Partick	34 14 6 14 59 66 34
10 Hibernian	34 13 6 15 68 70 32
11 Third Lanark	34 11 10 13 74 83 32
12 Stirling	34 11 8 15 54 64 30
13 Aberdeen	34 12 5 17 63 66 29
14 Raith	34 10 9 15 60 70 29
15 Clyde	34 12 4 18 62 66 28
16 Dunfermline	34 10 8 16 68 87 28
17 Falkirk	34 10 7 17 58 79 27
18 Queen of the S	34 6 6 22 38 101 18

Scottish Second Division

	P W D L F A Pts
1 Ayr	36 28 4 4 115 48 60
2 Arbroath	36 23 5 8 86 59 51
3 Stenhousemuir	36 20 6 10 87 68 46
4 Dumbarton	36 19 7 10 94 61 45
5 Brechin	36 16 10 10 79 65 42
6 St Johnstone	36 15 10 11 54 44 40
7 Hamilton	36 15 8 13 76 62 38
8 East Fife	36 15 8 13 83 81 38
9 Berwick	36 16 6 14 63 66 38

10 Albion	36 14 7 15 84 79 35
11 Morton	36 13 8 15 68 85 34
12 Forfar	36 12 9 15 73 87 33
13 Alloa	36 12 7 17 76 81 31
14 Cowdenbeath	36 13 5 18 67 79 31
15 E Stirlingshire	36 10 8 18 50 79 28
16 Stranraer	36 8 11 17 63 76 27
17 Dundee United	36 9 7 20 62 86 25
18 Queen's Park	36 9 6 21 53 80 24
19 Montrose	36 6 6 24 49 96 18

FA Cup

Fourth Round

Nottingham Forest v Grimsby Town	4-1
Birmingham City v Fulham	1-1, 3-2
Wolverhampton W v Bolton W	1-2
Preston North End v Bradford City	3-2
Charlton Athletic v Everton	2-2, 1-4
Chelsea v Aston Villa	1-2
Blackburn Rovers v Burnley	1-2
Accrington Stanley v Portsmouth	0-0, 1-4
Colchester United v Arsenal	2-2, 0-4
Worcester City v Sheffield United	0-2
Tottenham Hotspur v Newport County	4-1
Norwich City v Cardiff City	3-2
Bristol City v Blackpool	1-1, 0-1
West Bromwich Albion v Brentford	2-0
Stoke City v Ipswich Town	0-1
Leicester City v Luton Town	1-1, 1-4

Fifth Round

Birmingham City v Nottingham Forest	1-1, 1-1, 0-5
Bolton Wanderers v Preston North End	2-2, 1-1, 1-0
Everton v Aston Villa	1-4
Burnley v Portsmouth	1-0
Arsenal v Sheffield United	2-2, 0-3
Tottenham Hotspur v Norwich City	1-1, 0-1
Blackpool v West Bromwich Albion	3-1
Ipswich Town v Luton Town	2-5

Sixth Round

Nottingham Forest v Bolton Wanderers	2-1
Aston Villa v Burnley	0-0, 2-0
Sheffield United v Norwich City	1-1, 2-3
Blackpool v Luton Town	1-1, 0-1

Semi-Final

Nottingham Forest v Aston Villa	1-0

Norwich City v Luton Town	1-1, 0-1

Final

Nottingham Forest v Luton Town	2-1

Scottish FA Cup

Third Round

St Mirren v Motherwell	3-2
Dunfermline Athletic v Ayr United	2-1
Stirling Albion v Morton	3-1
Celtic v Rangers	2-1
Third Lanark v Alloa Athletic	3-2
Hibernian v Partick Thistle	4-1
St Johnstone v Aberdeen	1-2
Hamilton Academicals v Kilmarnock	0-5

Fourth Round

St Mirren v Dunfermline Athletic	2-1
Stirling Albion v Celtic	1-3
Third Lanark v Hibernian	2-1
Aberdeen v Kilmarnock	3-1

Semi-Final

St Mirren v Celtic	4-0
Third Lanark v Aberdeen	1-1, 0-1

Final

St Mirren v Aberdeen	3-1

1959–60
First Division

	P W D L F A Pts
1 Burnley	42 24 7 11 85 61 55
2 Wolves	42 24 6 12 106 67 54
3 Tottenham	42 21 11 10 86 50 53
4 WBA	42 19 11 12 83 57 49
5 Sheff Wed	42 19 11 12 80 59 49
6 Bolton	42 20 8 14 59 51 48
7 Man United	42 19 7 16 102 80 45
8 Newcastle	42 18 8 16 82 78 44
9 Preston	42 16 12 14 79 76 44
10 Fulham	42 17 10 15 73 80 44
11 Blackpool	42 15 10 17 59 71 40
12 Leicester	42 13 13 16 66 75 39
13 Arsenal	42 15 9 18 68 80 39
14 West Ham	42 16 6 20 75 91 38
15 Man City	42 17 3 22 78 84 37
16 Everton	42 13 11 18 73 78 37
17 Blackburn	42 16 5 21 60 70 37
18 Chelsea	42 14 9 19 76 91 37

	P	W	D	L	F	A	Pts
19 Birmingham	42	13	10	19	63	80	36
20 Nottm Forest	42	13	9	20	50	74	35
21 Leeds	42	12	10	20	65	92	34
22 Luton	42	9	12	21	50	73	30

Second Division

	P	W	D	L	F	A	Pts
1 Aston Villa	42	25	9	8	89	43	59
2 Cardiff	42	23	12	7	90	62	58
3 Liverpool	42	20	10	12	90	66	50
4 Sheff United	42	19	12	11	68	51	50
5 Middlesbrough	42	19	10	13	90	64	48
6 Huddersfield	42	19	9	14	73	52	47
7 Charlton	42	17	13	12	90	87	47
8 Rotherham	42	17	13	12	61	60	47
9 Bristol Rovers	42	18	11	13	72	78	47
10 Leyton Orient	42	15	14	13	76	61	44
11 Ipswich	42	19	6	17	78	68	44
12 Swansea	42	15	10	17	82	84	40
13 Lincoln	42	16	7	19	75	78	39
14 Brighton	42	13	12	17	67	76	38
15 Scunthorpe	42	13	10	19	57	71	36
16 Sunderland	42	12	12	18	52	65	36
17 Stoke	42	14	7	21	66	83	35
18 Derby	42	14	7	21	61	77	35
19 Plymouth	42	13	9	20	61	89	35
20 Portsmouth	42	10	12	20	59	77	32
21 Hull	42	10	10	22	48	76	30
22 Bristol City	42	11	5	26	60	97	27

Third Division

	P	W	D	L	F	A	Pts
1 Southampton	46	26	9	11	106	75	61
2 Norwich	46	24	11	11	82	54	59
3 Shrewsbury	46	18	16	12	97	75	52
4 Coventry	46	21	10	15	78	63	52
5 Grimsby	46	18	16	12	87	70	52
6 Brentford	46	21	9	16	78	61	51
7 Bury	46	21	9	16	64	51	51
8 QPR	46	18	13	15	73	54	49
9 Colchester	46	18	11	17	83	74	47
10 Bournemouth	46	17	13	16	72	72	47
11 Reading	46	18	10	18	84	77	46
12 Southend	46	19	8	19	76	74	46
13 Newport	46	20	6	20	80	79	46
14 Port Vale	46	19	8	19	80	79	46
15 Halifax	46	18	10	18	70	72	46
16 Swindon	46	19	8	19	69	78	46
17 Barnsley	46	15	14	17	65	66	44
18 Chesterfield	46	18	7	21	71	84	43
19 Bradford City	46	15	12	19	66	74	42

	P	W	D	L	F	A	Pts
20 Tranmere	46	14	13	19	72	75	41
21 York	46	13	12	21	57	73	38
22 Mansfield	46	15	6	25	81	112	36
23 Wrexham	46	14	8	24	68	101	36
24 Accrington	46	11	5	30	57	123	27

Fourth Division

	P	W	D	L	F	A	Pts
1 Walsall	46	28	9	9	102	60	65
2 Notts County	46	26	8	12	107	69	60
3 Torquay	46	26	8	12	84	58	60
4 Watford	46	24	9	13	92	67	57
5 Millwall	46	18	17	11	84	61	53
6 Northampton	46	22	9	15	85	63	53
7 Gillingham	46	21	10	15	74	69	52
8 Crystal Palace	46	19	12	15	84	64	50
9 Exeter	46	19	11	16	80	70	49
10 Stockport	46	19	11	16	58	54	49
11 Bradford PA	46	17	15	14	70	68	49
12 Rochdale	46	18	10	18	65	60	46
13 Aldershot	46	18	9	19	77	74	45
14 Crewe	46	18	9	19	79	88	45
15 Darlington	46	17	9	20	63	73	43
16 Workington	46	14	14	18	68	60	42
17 Doncaster	46	16	10	20	69	76	42
18 Barrow	46	15	11	20	77	87	41
19 Carlisle	46	15	11	20	51	66	41
20 Chester	46	14	12	20	59	77	40
21 Southport	46	10	14	22	48	92	34
22 Gateshead	46	12	9	25	58	86	33
23 Oldham	46	8	12	26	41	83	28
24 Hartlepools	46	10	7	29	59	109	27

Scottish First Division

	P	W	D	L	F	A	Pts
1 Hearts	34	23	8	3	102	51	54
2 Kilmarnock	34	24	2	8	67	45	50
3 Rangers	34	17	8	9	72	38	42
4 Dundee	34	16	10	8	70	49	42
5 Motherwell	34	16	8	10	71	61	40
6 Clyde	34	15	9	10	77	69	39
7 Hibernian	34	14	7	13	106	85	35
8 Ayr	34	14	6	14	65	73	34
9 Celtic	34	12	9	13	73	59	33
10 Partick	34	14	4	16	54	78	32
11 Raith	34	14	3	17	64	62	31
12 Third Lanark	34	13	4	17	75	83	30
13 Dunfermline	34	10	9	15	72	80	29
14 St Mirren	34	11	6	17	78	86	28
15 Aberdeen	34	11	6	17	54	72	28
16 Airdrieonians	34	11	6	17	56	80	28

	P	W	D	L	F	A	Pts
17 Stirling	34	7	8	19	55	72	22
18 Arbroath	34	4	7	23	38	106	15

Scottish Second Division

	P	W	D	L	F	A	Pts
1 St Johnstone	36	24	5	7	87	47	53
2 Dundee United	36	22	6	8	90	45	50
3 Queen of the S	36	21	7	8	94	52	49
4 Hamilton	36	21	6	9	91	62	48
5 Stenhousemuir	36	20	4	12	86	67	44
6 Dumbarton	36	18	7	11	67	53	43
7 Montrose	36	19	5	12	60	52	43
8 Falkirk	36	15	9	12	77	43	39
9 Berwick	36	16	5	15	62	55	37
10 Albion	36	14	8	14	71	78	36
11 Queen's Park	36	17	2	17	65	79	36
12 Brechin	36	14	6	16	66	66	34
13 Alloa	36	13	5	18	70	85	31
14 Morton	36	10	8	18	67	79	28
15 E Stirlingshire	36	10	8	18	68	82	28
16 Forfar	36	10	8	18	53	84	28
17 Stranraer	36	10	3	23	53	79	23
18 East Fife	36	7	6	23	50	87	20
19 Cowdenbeath	36	6	2	28	42	124	14

FA Cup

Fourth Round

Wolverhampton v Charlton Athletic	2-1
Huddersfield Town v Luton Town	0-1
Leicester City v Fulham	2-1
West Bromwich Albion v Bolton Wanderers	2-0
Bristol Rovers v Preston North End	3-3, 1-5
Rotherham United v Brighton	1-1, 1-1, 0-6
Scunthorpe United v Port Vale	0-1
Chelsea v Aston Villa	1-2
Sheffield United v Nottingham Forest	3-0
Southampton v Watford	2-2, 0-1
Liverpool v Manchester United	1-3
Sheffield Wednesday v Peterborough United	2-0
Bradford City v Bournemouth	3-1
Swansea Town v Burnley	0-0, 1-2
Crewe Alexandra v Tottenham Hotspur	2-2, 2-13
Blackburn Rovers v Blackpool	1-1, 3-0

Fifth Round

Luton Town v Wolverhampton	1-4
Leicester City v West Bromwich Albion	2-1
Preston North End v Brighton	2-1
Port Vale v Aston Villa	1-2
Sheffield United v Watford	3-2
Manchester United v Sheffield Wednesday	0-1
Bradford City v Burnley	2-2, 0-5
Tottenham Hotspur v Blackburn Rovers	1-3

Sixth Round

Leicester City v Wolverhampton Wanderers	1-2
Aston Villa v Preston North End	2-0
Sheffield United v Sheffield Wednesday	0-2
Burnley v Blackburn Rovers	3-3, 0-2

Semi-Final

Wolverhampton Wanderers v Aston Villa	1-0
Sheffield Wednesday v Blackburn Rovers	1-2

Final

Wolverhampton Wanderers v Blackburn Rovers	3-0

Scottish FA Cup

Third Round

Stenhousemuir v Rangers	0-3
East Stirlingshire v Hibernian	0-3
Elgin City v Celtic	1-2
Partick Thistle v Queen of the South	3-2
Ayr United v Airdrieonians	4-2
Clyde v Queen's Park	6-0
Eyemouth United v Cowdenbeath	3-0
Kilmarnock v Motherwell	2-0

Fourth Round

Rangers v Hibernian	3-2
Celtic v Partick Thistle	2-0
Ayr United v Clyde	0-2
Eyemouth United v Kilmarnock	1-2

Semi-Final

Rangers v Celtic	1-1, 4-1
Clyde v Kilmarnock	0-2

Final

Rangers v Kilmarnock	2-0

1960-61
First Division

	P	W	D	L	F	A	Pts
1 Tottenham	42	31	4	7	115	55	66
2 Sheff Wed	42	23	12	7	78	47	58
3 Wolves	42	25	7	10	103	75	57
4 Burnley	42	22	7	13	102	77	51
5 Everton	42	22	6	14	87	69	50
6 Leicester	42	18	9	15	87	70	45
7 Man United	42	18	9	15	88	76	45
8 Blackburn	42	15	13	14	77	76	43
9 Aston Villa	42	17	9	16	78	77	43
10 WBA	42	18	5	19	67	71	41
11 Arsenal	42	15	11	16	77	85	41
12 Chelsea	42	15	7	20	98	100	37
13 Man City	42	13	11	18	79	90	37
14 Nottm Forest	42	14	9	19	62	78	37
15 Cardiff	42	13	11	18	60	85	37
16 West Ham	42	13	10	19	77	88	36
17 Fulham	42	14	8	20	72	95	36
18 Bolton	42	12	11	19	58	73	35
19 Birmingham	42	14	6	22	62	84	34
20 Blackpool	42	12	9	21	68	73	33
21 Newcastle	42	11	10	21	86	109	32
22 Preston	42	10	10	22	43	71	30

Second Division

	P	W	D	L	F	A	Pts
1 Ipswich	42	26	7	9	100	55	59
2 Sheff United	42	26	6	10	81	51	58
3 Liverpool	42	21	10	11	87	58	52
4 Norwich	42	20	9	13	70	53	49
5 Middlesbrough	42	18	12	12	83	74	48
6 Sunderland	42	17	13	12	75	60	47
7 Swansea	42	18	11	13	77	73	47
8 Southampton	42	18	8	16	84	81	44
9 Scunthorpe	42	14	15	13	69	64	43
10 Charlton	42	16	11	15	97	91	43
11 Plymouth	42	17	8	17	81	82	42
12 Derby	42	15	10	17	80	80	40
13 Luton	42	15	9	18	71	79	39
14 Leeds	42	14	10	18	75	83	38
15 Rotherham	42	12	13	17	65	64	37
16 Brighton	42	14	9	19	61	75	37
17 Bristol Rovers	42	15	7	20	73	92	37
18 Stoke	42	12	12	18	51	59	36
19 Leyton Orient	42	14	8	20	55	78	36
20 Huddersfield	42	13	9	20	62	71	35
21 Portsmouth	42	11	11	20	64	91	33
22 Lincoln	42	8	8	26	48	95	24

Third Division

	P	W	D	L	F	A	Pts
1 Bury	46	30	8	8	108	45	68
2 Walsall	46	28	6	12	98	60	62
3 QPR	46	25	10	11	93	60	60
4 Watford	46	20	12	14	85	72	52
5 Notts County	46	21	9	16	82	77	51
6 Grimsby	46	20	10	16	77	69	50
7 Port Vale	46	17	15	14	96	79	49
8 Barnsley	46	21	7	18	83	80	49
9 Halifax	46	16	17	13	71	78	49
10 Shrewsbury	46	15	16	15	83	75	46
11 Hull	46	17	12	17	73	73	46
12 Torquay	46	14	17	15	75	83	45
13 Newport	46	17	11	18	81	90	45
14 Bristol City	46	17	10	19	70	68	44
15 Coventry	46	16	12	18	80	83	44
16 Swindon	46	14	15	17	62	55	43
17 Brentford	46	13	17	16	56	70	43
18 Reading	46	14	12	20	72	83	40
19 Bournemouth	46	15	10	21	58	76	40
20 Southend	46	14	11	21	60	76	39
21 Tranmere	46	15	8	23	79	115	38
22 Bradford City	46	11	14	21	65	87	36
23 Colchester	46	11	11	24	68	101	33
24 Chesterfield	46	10	12	24	67	87	32

Fourth Division

	P	W	D	L	F	A	Pts
1 Peterborough	46	28	10	8	134	65	66
2 Crystal Palace	46	29	6	11	110	69	64
3 Northampton	46	25	10	11	90	62	60
4 Bradford PA	46	26	8	12	84	74	60
5 York	46	21	9	16	80	60	51
6 Millwall	46	21	8	17	97	86	50
7 Darlington	46	18	13	15	78	70	49
8 Workington	46	21	7	18	74	76	49
9 Crewe	46	20	9	17	61	67	49
10 Aldershot	46	18	9	19	79	69	45
11 Doncaster	46	19	7	20	76	78	45
12 Oldham	46	19	7	20	79	88	45
13 Stockport	46	18	9	19	57	66	45
14 Southport	46	19	6	21	69	67	44
15 Gillingham	46	15	13	18	64	66	43
16 Wrexham	46	17	8	21	62	56	42
17 Rochdale	46	17	8	21	60	66	42
18 Accrington	46	16	8	22	74	88	40

19 Carlisle	46	13	13	20	61	79	39
20 Mansfield	46	16	6	24	71	78	38
21 Exeter	46	14	10	22	66	94	38
22 Barrow	46	13	11	22	52	79	37
23 Hartlepools	46	12	8	26	71	103	32
24 Chester	46	11	9	26	61	104	31

Scottish First Division

	P	W	D	L	F	A	Pts
1 Rangers	34	23	5	6	88	46	51
2 Kilmarnock	34	21	8	5	77	45	50
3 Third Lanark	34	20	2	12	100	80	42
4 Celtic	34	15	9	10	64	46	39
5 Motherwell	34	15	8	11	70	57	38
6 Aberdeen	34	14	8	12	72	72	36
7 Hibernian	34	15	4	15	66	69	34
8 Hearts	34	13	8	13	51	53	34
9 Dundee United	34	13	7	14	60	58	33
10 Dundee	34	13	6	15	61	53	32
11 Partick	34	13	6	15	59	69	32
12 Dunfermline	34	12	7	15	65	81	31
13 Airdrieonians	34	10	10	14	61	71	30
14 St Mirren	34	11	7	16	53	58	29
15 St Johnstone	34	10	9	15	47	63	29
16 Raith	34	10	7	17	46	67	27
17 Clyde	34	6	11	17	55	77	23
18 Ayr	34	5	12	17	51	81	22

Scottish Second Division

	P	W	D	L	F	A	Pts
1 Stirling	36	24	7	5	89	37	55
2 Falkirk	36	24	6	6	100	40	54
3 Stenhousemuir	36	24	2	10	99	69	50
4 Stranraer	36	19	6	11	83	55	44
5 Queen of the S	36	20	3	13	77	52	43
6 Hamilton	36	17	7	12	84	80	41
7 Montrose	36	19	2	15	75	65	40
8 Cowdenbeath	36	17	6	13	71	65	40
9 Berwick	36	14	9	13	62	69	37
10 Dumbarton	36	15	5	16	78	82	35
11 Alloa	36	13	7	16	78	68	33
12 Arbroath	36	13	7	16	56	76	33
13 East Fife	36	14	4	18	70	80	32
14 Brechin	36	9	9	18	60	78	27
15 Queen's Park	36	10	6	20	61	87	26
16 E Stirlingshire	36	9	7	20	59	100	25
17 Albion	36	9	6	21	60	89	24
18 Forfar	36	10	4	22	65	98	24
19 Morton	36	5	11	20	56	93	21

FA Cup

Fourth Round
Leicester City v Bristol City   5-1
Birmingham City v Rotherham United
                                            4-0
Huddersfield Town v Barnsley   1-1, 0-1
Luton Town v Manchester City   3-1
Newcastle United v Stockport County 4-0
Stoke City v Aldershot   0-0, 0-0, 3-0
Sheffield United v Lincoln City   3-1
Bolton Wanderers v Blackburn Rovers
                                       3-3, 0-4
Southampton v Leyton Orient   0-1
Sheffield Wednesday v Manchester
     United   1-1, 7-2
Brighton v Burnley   3-3, 0-2
Swansea Town v Preston North End 2-1
Scunthorpe United v Norwich City   1-4
Liverpool v Sunderland   0-2
Peterborough United v Aston Villa
                                   1-1, 1-2
Tottenham Hotspur v Crewe Alexandra
                                       5-1

Fifth Round
Birmingham City v Leicester City 1-1, 1-2
Barnsley v Luton Town   1-0
Newcastle United v Stoke City   3-1
Sheffield United v Blackburn Rovers   2-1
Leyton Orient v Sheffield Wednesday 0-2
Burnley v Swansea Town   4-0
Norwich City v Sunderland   0-1
Aston Villa v Tottenham Hotspur   0-2

Sixth Round
Leicester City v Barnsley   0-0, 2-1
Newcastle United v Sheffield United 1-3
Sheffield Wednesday v Burnley 0-0, 0-2
Sunderland v Tottenham Hotspur 1-1, 0-5

Semi-Final
Leicester City v Sheffield United
                              0-0, 0-0, 2-0
Burnley v Tottenham Hotspur   0-3

Final
Leicester City v Tottenham Hotspur   0-2

Scottish FA Cup

Third Round
Raith Rovers v Celtic   1-4
Hamilton Academicals v Hibernian   0-4

Brechin City v Airdrieonians	0-3
Motherwell v Rangers	2-2, 5-2
Partick Thistle v Heart of Midlothian	1-2
St Mirren v Third Lanark	3-3, 8-0
Aberdeen v Dunfermline Athletic	3-6
Alloa Athletic v Forfar Athletic	2-1

Fourth Round

Celtic v Hibernian	1-1, 1-0
Motherwell v Airdrieonians	0-1
Heart of Midlothian v St Mirren	0-1
Dunfermline Athletic v Alloa Athletic	4-0

Semi-Final

Celtic v Airdrieonians	4-0
Dunfermline Athletic v St Mirren	0-0, 1-0

Final

Celtic v Dunfermline Athletic	0-0, 0-2

1961-62
First Division

	P	W	D	L	F	A	Pts
1 Ipswich	42	24	8	10	93	67	56
2 Burnley	42	21	11	10	101	67	53
3 Tottenham	42	21	10	11	88	69	52
4 Everton	42	20	11	11	88	54	51
5 Sheff United	42	19	9	14	61	69	47
6 Sheff Wed	42	20	6	16	72	58	46
7 Aston Villa	42	18	8	16	65	56	44
8 West Ham	42	17	10	15	76	82	44
9 WBA	42	15	13	14	83	67	43
10 Arsenal	42	16	11	15	71	72	43
11 Bolton	42	16	10	16	62	66	42
12 Man City	42	17	7	18	78	81	41
13 Blackpool	42	15	11	16	70	75	41
14 Leicester	42	17	6	19	72	71	40
15 Man United	42	15	9	18	72	75	39
16 Blackburn	42	14	11	17	50	58	39
17 Birmingham	42	14	10	18	65	81	38
18 Wolves	42	13	10	19	73	86	36
19 Nottm Forest	42	13	10	19	63	79	36
20 Fulham	42	13	7	22	66	74	33
21 Cardiff	42	9	14	19	50	81	32
22 Chelsea	42	9	10	23	63	94	28

Second Division

	P	W	D	L	F	A	Pts
1 Liverpool	42	27	8	7	99	43	62
2 Leyton Orient	42	22	10	10	69	40	54
3 Sunderland	42	22	9	11	85	50	53
4 Scunthorpe	42	21	7	14	86	71	49
5 Plymouth	42	19	8	15	75	75	46
6 Southampton	42	18	9	15	77	62	45
7 Huddersfield	42	16	12	14	67	59	44
8 Stoke	42	17	8	17	55	57	42
9 Rotherham	42	16	9	17	70	76	41
10 Preston	42	15	10	17	55	57	40
11 Newcastle	42	15	9	18	64	58	39
12 Middlesbrough	42	16	7	19	76	72	39
13 Luton	42	17	5	20	69	71	39
14 Walsall	42	14	11	17	70	75	39
15 Charlton	42	15	9	18	69	75	39
16 Derby	42	14	11	17	68	75	39
17 Norwich	42	14	11	17	61	70	39
18 Bury	42	17	5	20	52	76	39
19 Leeds	42	12	12	18	50	61	36
20 Swansea	42	12	12	18	61	83	36
21 Bristol Rovers	42	13	7	22	53	81	33
22 Brighton	42	10	11	21	42	86	31

Third Division

	P	W	D	L	F	A	Pts
1 Portsmouth	46	27	11	8	87	47	65
2 Grimsby	46	28	6	12	80	56	62
3 Bournemouth	46	21	17	8	69	45	59
4 QPR	46	24	11	11	111	73	59
5 Peterborough	46	26	6	14	107	82	58
6 Bristol City	46	23	8	15	94	72	54
7 Reading	46	22	9	15	77	66	53
8 Northampton	46	20	11	15	85	57	51
9 Swindon	46	17	15	14	78	71	49
10 Hull	46	20	8	18	67	54	48
11 Bradford PA	46	20	7	19	80	78	47
12 Port Vale	46	17	11	18	65	58	45
13 Notts County	46	17	9	20	67	74	43
14 Coventry	46	16	11	19	64	71	43
15 Crystal Palace	46	14	14	18	83	80	42
16 Southend	46	13	16	17	57	69	42
17 Watford	46	14	13	19	63	74	41
18 Halifax	46	15	10	21	62	84	40
19 Shrewsbury	46	13	12	21	73	84	38
20 Barnsley	46	13	12	21	71	95	38
21 Torquay	46	15	6	25	76	100	36
22 Lincoln	46	9	17	20	57	87	35
23 Brentford	46	13	8	25	53	93	34
24 Newport	46	7	8	31	46	102	22

Fourth Division

	P	W	D	L	F	A	Pts
1 Millwall	44	23	10	11	87	62	56
2 Colchester	44	23	9	12	104	71	55
3 Wrexham	44	22	9	13	96	56	53
4 Carlisle	44	22	8	14	64	63	52
5 Bradford City	44	21	9	14	94	86	51
6 York	44	20	10	14	84	53	50
7 Aldershot	44	22	5	17	81	60	49
8 Workington	44	19	11	14	69	70	49
9 Barrow	44	17	14	13	74	58	48
10 Crewe	44	20	6	18	79	70	46
11 Oldham	44	17	12	15	77	70	46
12 Rochdale	44	19	7	18	71	71	45
13 Darlington	44	18	9	17	61	73	45
14 Mansfield	44	19	6	19	77	66	44
15 Tranmere	44	20	4	20	70	81	44
16 Stockport	44	17	9	18	70	69	43
17 Southport	44	17	9	18	61	71	43
18 Exeter	44	13	11	20	62	77	37
19 Chesterfield	44	14	9	21	70	87	37
20 Gillingham	44	13	11	20	73	94	37
21 Doncaster	44	11	7	26	60	85	29
22 Hartlepools	44	8	11	25	52	101	27
23 Chester	44	7	12	25	54	96	26

24 Accrington Stanley resigned from the League

Scottish First Division

	P	W	D	L	F	A	Pts
1 Dundee	34	25	4	5	80	46	54
2 Rangers	34	22	7	5	84	31	51
3 Celtic	34	19	8	7	81	37	46
4 Dunfermline	34	19	5	10	77	46	43
5 Kilmarnock	34	16	10	8	74	58	42
6 Hearts	34	16	6	12	54	49	38
7 Partick	34	16	3	15	60	55	35
8 Hibernian	34	14	5	15	58	72	33
9 Motherwell	34	13	6	15	65	62	32
10 Dundee United	34	13	6	15	70	71	32
11 Third Lanark	34	13	5	16	59	60	31
12 Aberdeen	34	10	9	15	60	73	29
13 Raith	34	10	7	17	51	73	27
14 Falkirk	34	11	4	19	45	68	26
15 Airdrieonians	34	9	7	18	57	78	25
16 St Mirren	34	10	5	19	52	80	25
17 St Johnstone	34	9	7	18	35	61	25
18 Stirling	34	6	6	22	34	76	18

Scottish Second Division

	P	W	D	L	F	A	Pts
1 Clyde	36	15	4	7	108	47	54
2 Queen of the S	36	24	5	7	78	33	53
3 Morton	36	19	6	11	78	64	44
4 Alloa	36	17	8	11	92	78	42
5 Montrose	36	15	11	10	63	50	41
6 Arbroath	36	17	7	12	66	59	41
7 Stranraer	36	14	11	11	61	62	39
8 Berwick	36	16	6	14	83	70	38
9 Ayr	36	15	8	13	71	63	38
10 East Fife	36	15	7	14	60	59	37
11 E Stirlingshire	36	15	4	17	70	81	34
12 Queen's Park	36	12	9	15	64	62	33
13 Hamilton	36	14	5	17	78	79	33
14 Cowdenbeath	36	11	9	16	65	77	31
15 Stenhousemuir	36	13	5	18	69	86	31
16 Forfar	36	11	8	17	68	76	30
17 Dumbarton	36	9	10	17	49	66	28
18 Albion	36	10	5	21	42	74	25
19 Brechin	36	5	2	29	44	123	12

FA Cup

Fourth Round

Burnley v Leyton Orient	1-1, 1-0
Everton v Manchester City	2-0
Peterborough United v Sheffield United	1-3
Norwich City v Ipswich Town	1-1, 2-1
Fulham v Walsall	2-2, 2-0
Sunderland v Port Vale	0-0, 1-3
Stoke City v Blackburn Rovers	0-1
Shrewsbury Town v Middlesbrough	2-2, 1-5
Oldham Athletic v Liverpool	1-2
Preston North End v Weymouth	2-0
Manchester United v Arsenal	1-0
Nottingham Forest v Sheffield Wednesday	0-2
Aston Villa v Huddersfield Town	2-1
Charlton Athletic v Derby County	2-1
Wolverhampton Wanderers v West Bromwich Albion	1-2
Plymouth Argyle v Tottenham Hotspur	1-5

Fifth Round

Burnley v Everton	3-1
Sheffield United v Norwich City	3-1
Fulham v Port Vale	1-0
Blackburn Rovers v Middlesbrough	2-1

Liverpool v Preston North End

0–0, 0–0, 0–1

Manchester United v Sheffield Wednesday

0–0, 2–0

Aston Villa v Charlton Athletic   2–1

West Bromwich Albion v Tottenham

Hotspur   2–4

Sixth Round

Sheffield United v Burnley	0–1
Fulham v Blackburn Rovers	2–2, 1–0
Preston North End v Manchester United	
	0–0, 1–2
Tottenham Hotspur v Aston Villa	2–0

Semi-Final

Burnley v Fulham	1–1, 2–1
Manchester United v Tottenham Hotspur	
	1–3

Final

Burnley v Tottenham Hotspur	1–3

Scottish FA Cup

Third Round

Aberdeen v Rangers	2–2, 1–5
Kilmarnock v Ross County	7–0
Stirling Albion v East Fife	4–1
Stranraer v Motherwell	1–3
Heart of Midlothian v Celtic	3–4
Third Lanark v Inverness Caledonian	6–1
Dunfermline Athletic v Stenhousemuir	
	0–0, 3–0
Raith Rovers v St Mirren	1–1, 0–4

Fourth Round

Kilmarnock v Rangers	2–4
Stirling Albion v Motherwell	0–6
Celtic v Third Lanark	4–4, 4–0
Dunfermline Athletic v St Mirren	0–1

Semi-Final

Rangers v Motherwell	3–1
Celtic v St Mirren	1–3

Final

Rangers v St Mirren	2–0

1962–63
First Division

	P	W	D	L	F	A	Pts
1 Everton	42	25	11	6	84	42	61
2 Tottenham	42	23	9	10	111	62	55
3 Burnley	42	22	10	10	78	57	54
4 Leicester	42	20	12	10	79	53	52
5 Wolves	42	20	10	12	93	65	50
6 Sheff Wed	42	19	10	13	77	63	48
7 Arsenal	42	18	10	14	86	77	46
8 Liverpool	42	17	10	15	71	59	44
9 Nottm Forest	42	17	10	15	67	69	44
10 Sheff United	42	16	12	14	58	60	44
11 Blackburn	42	15	12	15	79	71	42
12 West Ham	42	14	12	16	73	69	40
13 Blackpool	42	13	14	15	58	64	40
14 WBA	42	16	7	19	71	79	39
15 Aston Villa	42	15	8	19	62	68	38
16 Fulham	42	14	10	18	50	71	38
17 Ipswich	42	12	11	19	59	78	35
18 Bolton	42	15	5	22	55	75	35
19 Man United	42	12	10	20	67	81	34
20 Birmingham	42	10	13	19	63	90	33
21 Man City	42	10	11	21	58	102	31
22 Leyton Orient	42	6	9	27	37	81	21

Second Division

	P	W	D	L	F	S	Pts
1 Stoke	42	20	13	9	73	50	53
2 Chelsea	42	24	4	14	81	42	52
3 Sunderland	42	20	12	10	84	55	52
4 Middlesbrough	42	20	9	13	86	85	49
5 Leeds	42	19	10	13	79	53	48
6 Huddersfield	42	17	14	11	63	50	48
7 Newcastle	42	18	11	13	79	59	47
8 Bury	42	18	11	13	51	47	47
9 Scunthorpe	42	16	12	14	57	59	44
10 Cardiff	42	18	7	17	83	73	43
11 Southampton	42	17	8	17	72	67	42
12 Plymouth	42	15	12	15	76	73	42
13 Norwich	42	17	8	17	80	79	42
14 Rotherham	42	17	6	19	67	74	40
15 Swansea	42	15	9	18	51	72	39
16 Portsmouth	42	13	11	18	63	79	37
17 Preston	42	13	11	18	59	74	37
18 Derby	42	12	12	18	61	72	36
19 Grimsby	42	11	13	18	55	66	35
20 Charlton	42	13	5	24	62	94	31

	P	W	D	L	F	A	Pts
21 Walsall	42	11	9	22	53	89	31
22 Luton	42	11	7	24	61	84	29

Third Division

	P	W	D	L	F	A	Pts
1 Northampton	46	26	10	10	109	60	62
2 Swindon	46	22	14	10	87	56	58
3 Port Vale	46	23	8	15	72	58	54
4 Coventry	46	18	17	11	83	69	53
5 Bournemouth	46	18	16	12	63	46	52
6 Peterborough	46	20	11	15	93	75	51
7 Notts County	46	19	13	14	73	74	51
8 Southend	46	19	12	15	75	77	50
9 Wrexham	46	20	9	17	84	83	49
10 Hull	46	19	10	17	74	69	48
11 Crystal Palace	46	17	13	16	68	58	47
12 Colchester	46	18	11	17	73	93	47
13 QPR	46	17	11	18	85	76	45
14 Bristol City	46	16	13	17	100	92	45
15 Shrewsbury	46	16	12	18	83	81	44
16 Millwall	46	15	13	18	82	87	43
17 Watford	46	17	8	21	82	85	42
18 Barnsley	46	15	11	20	63	74	41
19 Bristol Rovers	46	15	11	20	70	88	41
20 Reading	46	16	8	22	74	78	40
21 Bradford PA	46	14	12	20	79	97	40
22 Brighton	46	12	12	22	58	84	36
23 Carlisle	46	13	9	24	61	89	35
24 Halifax	46	9	12	25	64	106	30

Fourth Division

	P	W	D	L	F	A	Pts
1 Brentford	46	27	8	11	98	64	62
2 Oldham	46	24	11	11	95	60	59
3 Crewe	46	24	11	11	86	58	59
4 Mansfield	46	24	9	13	108	69	57
5 Gillingham	46	22	13	11	71	49	57
6 Torquay	46	20	16	10	75	56	56
7 Rochdale	46	20	11	15	67	59	51
8 Tranmere	46	20	10	16	81	67	50
9 Barrow	46	19	12	15	82	80	50
10 Workington	46	17	13	16	76	68	47
11 Aldershot	46	15	17	14	73	69	47
12 Darlington	46	19	6	21	72	87	44
13 Southport	46	15	14	17	72	106	44
14 York	46	16	11	19	67	62	43
15 Chesterfield	46	13	16	17	70	64	42
16 Doncaster	46	14	14	18	64	77	42
17 Exeter	46	16	10	20	57	77	42
18 Oxford	46	13	15	18	70	71	41

	P	W	D	L	F	A	Pts
19 Stockport	46	15	11	20	56	70	41
20 Newport	46	14	11	21	76	90	39
21 Chester	46	15	9	22	51	66	39
22 Lincoln	46	13	9	24	68	89	35
23 Bradford City	46	11	10	25	64	93	32
24 Hartlepools	46	7	11	28	56	104	25

Scottish First Division

	P	W	D	L	F	A	Pts
1 Rangers	34	25	7	2	94	28	57
2 Kilmarnock	34	20	8	6	92	40	48
3 Partick	34	20	6	8	66	44	46
4 Celtic	34	19	6	9	76	44	44
5 Hearts	34	17	9	8	85	59	43
6 Aberdeen	34	17	7	10	70	47	41
7 Dundee United	34	15	11	8	67	52	41
8 Dunfermline	34	13	8	13	50	47	34
9 Dundee	34	12	9	13	60	49	33
10 Motherwell	34	10	11	13	60	63	31
11 Airdrieonians	34	14	2	18	52	76	30
12 St Mirren	34	10	8	16	52	72	28
13 Falkirk	34	12	3	19	54	69	27
14 Third Lanark	34	9	8	17	56	68	26
15 Queen of the S	34	10	6	18	36	75	26
16 Hibernian	34	8	9	17	47	67	25
17 Clyde	34	9	5	20	49	83	23
18 Raith	34	2	5	27	35	118	9

Scottish Second Division

	P	W	D	L	F	A	Pts
1 St Johnstone	36	25	5	6	83	37	55
2 E Stirlingshire	36	20	9	7	80	50	49
3 Morton	36	23	2	11	100	49	48
4 Hamilton	36	18	8	10	69	56	44
5 Stranraer	36	16	10	10	81	70	42
6 Arbroath	36	18	4	14	74	51	40
7 Albion	36	18	2	16	72	79	38
8 Cowdenbeath	36	15	7	14	72	61	37
9 Alloa	36	15	6	15	57	56	36
10 Stirling	36	16	4	16	74	75	36
11 East Fife	36	15	6	15	60	69	36
12 Dumbarton	36	15	4	17	64	64	34
13 Ayr	36	13	8	15	68	77	34
14 Queen's Park	36	13	6	17	66	72	32
15 Montrose	36	13	5	18	57	70	31
16 Stenhousemuir	36	13	5	18	54	75	31
17 Berwick	36	11	7	18	57	77	29
18 Forfar	36	9	5	22	73	99	23
19 Brechin	36	3	3	30	39	113	9

FA Cup

Fourth Round

Leicester City v Ipswich Town	3-1
Leyton Orient v Derby County	3-0
Manchester City v Bury	1-0
Norwich City v Newcastle United	5-0
Arsenal v Sheffield Wednesday	2-0
Burnley v Liverpool	1-1, 1-2
West Ham United v Swansea Town	1-0
Swindon Town v Everton	1-5
West Bromwich Albion v Nottingham Forest	0-0, 1-2
Middlesbrough v Leeds United	0-2
Southampton v Watford	3-1
Port Vale v Sheffield United	1-2
Portsmouth v Coventry City	1-1, 2-2, 1-2
Gravesend v Sunderland	1-1, 2-5
Charlton Athletic v Chelsea	0-3
Manchester United v Aston Villa	1-0

Fifth Round

Leicester City v Leyton Orient	1-0
Manchester City v Norwich City	1-2
Arsenal v Liverpool	1-2
West Ham United v Everton	1-0
Nottingham Forest v Leeds United	3-0
Southampton v Sheffield United	1-0
Coventry City v Sunderland	2-1
Manchester United v Chelsea	2-1

Sixth Round

Norwich City v Leicester City	0-2
Liverpool v West Ham United	1-0
Nottingham Forest v Southampton	1-1, 3-3, 0-5
Coventry City v Manchester United	1-3

Semi-Final

Leicester City v Liverpool	1-0
Southampton v Manchester United	0-1

Final

Leicester City v Manchester United	1-3

Scottish FA Cup

Third Round

Rangers v East Stirlingshire	7-2
Dundee v Hibernian	1-0
Queen's Park v Dundee United	1-1, 1-3
Queen of the South v Hamilton Academicals	3-0
Third Lanark v Raith Rovers	0-1
Aberdeen v Dunfermline Athletic	4-0
St Mirren v Partick Thistle	1-1, 1-0
Celtic v Gala Fairydean	6-0

Fourth Round

Dundee v Rangers	1-1, 2-3
Dundee United v Queen of the South	1-1, 1-1, 4-0
Raith Rovers v Aberdeen	2-1
St Mirren v Celtic	0-1

Semi-Final

Rangers v Dundee United	5-2
Raith Rovers v Celtic	2-5

Final

Rangers v Celtic	1-1, 3-0

1963–64
First Division

		P	W	D	L	F	A	Pts
1	Liverpool	42	26	5	11	92	45	57
2	Man United	42	23	7	12	90	62	53
3	Everton	42	21	10	11	84	64	52
4	Tottenham	42	22	7	13	97	81	51
5	Chelsea	42	20	10	12	72	56	50
6	Sheff Wed	42	19	11	12	84	67	49
7	Blackburn	42	18	10	14	89	65	46
8	Arsenal	42	17	11	14	90	82	45
9	Burnley	42	17	10	15	71	64	44
10	WBA	42	16	11	15	70	61	43
11	Leicester	42	16	11	15	61	58	43
12	Sheff United	42	16	11	15	61	64	43
13	Nottm Forest	42	16	9	17	64	68	41
14	West Ham	42	14	12	16	69	74	40
15	Fulham	42	13	13	16	58	65	39
16	Wolves	42	12	15	15	70	80	39
17	Stoke	42	14	10	18	77	78	38
18	Blackpool	42	13	9	20	52	73	35
19	Aston Villa	42	11	12	19	62	71	34
20	Birmingham	42	11	7	24	54	92	29
21	Bolton	42	10	8	24	48	80	28
22	Ipswich	42	9	7	26	56	121	25

Second Division

		P	W	D	L	F	A	Pts
1	Leeds	42	24	15	3	71	34	63
2	Sunderland	42	25	11	6	81	37	61

	P	W	D	L	F	A	Pts
3 Preston	42	23	10	9	79	54	56
4 Charlton	42	19	10	13	76	70	48
5 Southampton	42	19	9	14	100	73	47
6 Man City	42	18	10	14	84	66	46
7 Rotherham	42	19	7	16	90	78	45
8 Newcastle	42	20	5	17	74	69	45
9 Portsmouth	42	16	11	15	79	70	43
10 Middlesbrough	42	15	11	16	67	52	41
11 Northampton	42	16	9	17	58	60	41
12 Huddersfield	42	15	10	17	57	64	40
13 Derby	42	14	11	17	56	67	39
14 Swindon	42	14	10	18	57	69	38
15 Cardiff	42	14	10	18	56	81	38
16 Leyton Orient	42	13	10	19	54	72	36
17 Norwich	42	11	13	18	64	80	35
18 Bury	42	13	9	20	57	73	35
19 Swansea	42	12	9	21	63	74	33
20 Plymouth	42	8	16	18	45	67	32
21 Grimsby	42	9	14	19	47	75	32
22 Scunthorpe	42	10	10	22	52	82	30

Third Division

	P	W	D	L	F	A	Pts
1 Coventry	46	22	16	8	98	61	60
2 Crystal Palace	46	23	14	9	73	51	60
3 Watford	46	23	12	11	79	59	58
4 Bournemouth	46	24	8	14	79	58	56
5 Bristol City	46	20	15	11	84	64	55
6 Reading	46	21	10	15	79	62	52
7 Mansfield	46	20	11	15	76	62	51
8 Hull	46	16	17	13	73	68	49
9 Oldham	46	20	8	18	73	70	48
10 Peterborough	46	18	11	17	75	70	47
11 Shrewsbury	46	18	11	17	73	80	47
12 Bristol Rovers	46	19	8	19	91	79	46
13 Port Vale	46	16	14	16	53	49	46
14 Southend	46	15	15	16	77	78	45
15 QPR	46	18	9	19	76	78	45
16 Brentford	46	15	14	17	87	80	44
17 Colchester	46	12	19	15	70	68	43
18 Luton	46	16	10	20	64	80	42
19 Walsall	46	13	14	19	59	76	40
20 Barnsley	46	12	15	19	68	94	39
21 Millwall	46	14	10	22	53	67	38
22 Crewe	46	11	12	23	50	77	34
23 Wrexham	46	13	6	27	75	107	32
24 Notts County	46	9	9	28	45	92	27

Fourth Division

	P	W	D	L	F	A	Pts
1 Gillingham	46	23	14	9	59	30	60

	P	W	D	L	F	A	Pts
2 Carlisle	46	25	10	11	113	58	60
3 Workington	46	24	11	11	76	52	59
4 Exeter	46	20	18	8	62	37	58
5 Bradford City	46	25	6	15	76	62	56
6 Torquay	46	20	11	15	80	54	51
7 Tranmere	46	20	11	15	85	73	51
8 Brighton	46	19	12	15	71	52	50
9 Aldershot	46	19	10	17	83	78	48
10 Halifax	46	17	14	15	77	77	48
11 Lincoln	46	19	9	18	67	75	47
12 Chester	46	19	8	19	65	60	46
13 Bradford PA	46	18	9	19	75	81	45
14 Doncaster	46	15	12	19	70	75	42
15 Newport	46	17	8	21	64	73	42
16 Chesterfield	46	15	12	19	57	71	42
17 Stockport	46	15	12	19	50	68	42
18 Oxford	46	14	13	19	59	63	41
19 Darlington	46	14	12	20	66	93	40
20 Rochdale	46	12	15	19	56	59	39
21 Southport	46	15	9	22	63	88	39
22 York	46	14	7	25	52	66	35
23 Hartlepools	46	12	9	25	54	93	33
24 Barrow	46	6	18	22	51	93	30

Scottish First Division

	P	W	D	L	F	A	Pts
1 Rangers	34	25	5	4	85	31	55
2 Kilmarnock	34	22	5	7	77	40	49
3 Celtic	34	19	9	6	89	34	47
4 Hearts	34	19	9	6	74	40	47
5 Dunfermline	34	18	9	7	64	33	45
6 Dundee	34	20	5	9	94	50	45
7 Partick	34	15	5	14	55	54	35
8 Dundee United	34	13	8	13	65	49	34
9 Aberdeen	34	12	8	14	53	53	32
10 Hibernian	34	12	6	16	59	66	30
11 Motherwell	34	9	11	14	51	62	29
12 St Mirren	34	12	5	17	44	74	29
13 St Johnstone	34	11	6	17	54	70	28
14 Falkirk	34	11	6	17	54	84	28
15 Airdrieonians	34	11	4	19	52	97	26
16 Third Lanark	34	9	7	18	47	74	25
17 Queen of the S	34	5	6	23	40	92	16
18 E Stirlingshire	34	5	2	27	37	91	12

Scottish Second Division

	P	W	D	L	F	A	Pts
1 Morton	36	32	3	1	135	37	67
2 Clyde	36	22	9	5	81	44	53
3 Arbroath	36	20	6	10	79	46	46
4 East Fife	36	16	13	7	92	57	45

5 Montrose	36 19 6 11 79 57 44
6 Dumbarton	36 16 6 14 67 59 38
7 Queen's Park	36 17 4 15 57 54 38
8 Stranraer	36 16 6 14 71 73 38
9 Albion	36 12 12 12 67 71 36
10 Raith	36 15 5 16 70 61 35
11 Stenhousemuir	36 15 5 16 83 75 35
12 Berwick	36 10 10 16 68 84 30
13 Hamilton	36 12 6 18 65 81 30
14 Ayr	36 12 5 19 58 83 29
15 Brechin	36 10 8 18 61 98 28
16 Alloa	36 11 5 20 64 92 27
17 Cowdenbeath	36 7 11 18 46 72 25
18 Forfar	36 6 8 22 57 104 20
19 Stirling	36 6 8 22 47 99 20

FA Cup

Fourth Round

West Ham United v Leyton Orient
	1-1, 3-0
Aldershot v Swindon Town	1-2
Burnley v Newport County	2-1
Chelsea v Huddersfield Town	1-2
Sunderland v Bristol City	6-1
Leeds United v Everton	1-1, 0-2
Barnsley v Bury	2-1
Manchester United v Bristol Rovers	4-1
Ipswich Town v Stoke City	1-1, 0-1
Sheffield United v Swansea Town	1-1, 0-4

West Bromwich Albion v Arsenal
	3-3, 0-2
Liverpool v Port Vale	0-0, 2-1
Oxford United v Brentford	2-2, 2-1
Blackburn Rovers v Fulham	2-0
Bedford Town v Carlisle United	0-3

Bolton Wanderers v Preston North End
	2-2, 1-2

Fifth Round

West Ham United v Swindon Town	3-1
Burnley v Huddersfield Town	3-0
Sunderland v Everton	3-1
Barnsley v Manchester United	0-4
Stoke City v Swansea Town	2-2, 0-2
Arsenal v Liverpool	0-1
Oxford United v Blackburn Rovers	3-1
Carlisle United v Preston North End	0-1

Sixth Round

West Ham United v Burnley	3-2

Manchester United v Sunderland
	3-3, 2-2, 5-1
Liverpool v Swansea Town	1-2

Oxford United v Preston North End   1-2

Semi-Final

West Ham United v Manchester United
	3-1
Swansea Town v Preston North End	1-2

Final

West Ham United v Preston North End
	3-2

Scottish FA Cup

Third Round

Rangers v Partick Thistle	3-0
Celtic v Airdrieonians	4-1

East Stirlingshire v Dunfermline Athletic
	1-6
Aberdeen v Ayr United	1-2
Kilmarnock v Albion Rovers	2-0
St Mirren v Falkirk	0-1

Motherwell v Heart of Midlothian
	3-3, 2-1
Dundee v Forfar Athletic	6-1

Fourth Round

Rangers v Celtic	2-0
Dunfermline Athletic v Ayr United	7-0
Kilmarnock v Falkirk	2-1
Dundee v Motherwell	1-1, 4-2

Semi-Final

Rangers v Dunfermline Athletic	1-0
Kilmarnock v Dundee	0-4

Final

Rangers v Dundee	3-1

1964–65
First Division

		P	W	D	L	F	A	Pts
1	Man United	42	26	9	7	89	39	61
2	Leeds	42	26	9	7	83	52	61
3	Chelsea	42	24	8	10	89	54	56
4	Everton	42	17	15	10	69	60	49
5	Notttm Forest	42	17	13	12	71	67	47
6	Tottenham	42	19	7	16	87	71	45
7	Liverpool	42	17	10	15	67	73	44
8	Sheff Wed	42	16	11	15	57	55	43
9	West Ham	42	19	4	19	82	71	42
10	Blackburn	42	16	10	16	83	79	42
11	Stoke	42	16	10	16	67	66	42

	P	W	D	L	F	A	Pts
12 Burnley	42	16	10	16	70	70	42
13 Arsenal	42	17	7	18	69	75	41
14 WBA	42	13	13	16	70	65	39
15 Sunderland	42	14	9	19	64	74	37
16 Aston Villa	42	16	5	21	57	82	37
17 Blackpool	42	12	11	19	67	78	35
18 Leicester	42	11	13	18	69	85	35
19 Sheff United	42	12	11	19	50	64	35
20 Fulham	42	11	12	19	60	78	34
21 Wolves	42	13	4	25	59	89	30
22 Birmingham	42	8	11	23	64	96	27

Second Division

	P	W	D	L	F	A	Pts
1 Newcastle	42	24	9	9	81	45	57
2 Northampton	42	20	16	6	66	50	56
3 Bolton	42	20	10	12	80	58	50
4 Southampton	42	17	14	11	83	63	48
5 Ipswich	42	15	17	10	74	67	47
6 Norwich	42	20	7	15	61	57	47
7 Crystal Palace	42	16	13	13	55	51	45
8 Huddersfield	42	17	10	15	53	51	44
9 Derby	42	16	11	15	84	79	43
10 Coventry	42	17	9	16	72	70	43
11 Man City	42	16	9	17	63	62	41
12 Preston	42	14	13	15	76	81	41
13 Cardiff	42	13	14	15	64	57	40
14 Rotherham	24	14	12	16	70	69	40
15 Plymouth	42	16	8	18	63	79	40
16 Bury	42	14	10	18	60	66	38
17 Middlesbrough	42	13	9	20	70	76	35
18 Charlton	42	13	9	20	64	75	35
19 Leyton Orient	42	12	11	19	50	72	35
20 Portsmouth	42	12	10	20	56	77	34
21 Swindon	42	14	5	23	63	81	33
22 Swansea	42	11	10	21	62	84	32

Third Division

	P	W	D	L	F	A	Pts
1 Carlisle	46	25	10	11	76	53	60
2 Bristol City	46	24	11	11	92	55	59
3 Mansfield	46	24	11	11	95	61	59
4 Hull	46	23	12	11	91	57	58
5 Brentford	46	24	9	13	83	55	57
6 Bristol Rovers	46	20	15	11	82	58	55
7 Gillingham	46	23	9	14	70	50	55
8 Peterborough	46	22	7	17	85	74	51
9 Watford	46	17	16	13	71	64	50
10 Grimsby	46	16	17	13	68	67	49
11 Bournemouth	46	18	11	17	72	63	47
12 Southend	46	19	8	19	78	71	46

	P	W	D	L	F	A	Pts
13 Reading	46	16	14	16	70	70	46
14 QPR	46	17	12	17	72	80	46
15 Workington	46	17	12	17	58	69	46
16 Shrewsbury	46	15	12	19	76	84	42
17 Exeter	46	12	17	17	51	52	41
18 Scunthorpe	46	14	12	20	65	72	40
19 Walsall	46	15	7	24	55	80	37
20 Oldham	46	13	10	23	61	83	36
21 Luton	46	11	11	24	51	94	33
22 Port Vale	46	9	14	23	41	76	32
23 Colchester	46	10	10	26	50	89	30
24 Barnsley	46	9	11	26	54	90	29

Fourth Division

	P	W	D	L	F	A	Pts
1 Brighton	46	26	11	9	102	57	63
2 Millwall	46	23	16	7	78	45	62
3 York	46	28	6	12	91	56	62
4 Oxford	46	23	15	8	87	44	61
5 Tranmere	46	27	6	13	99	56	60
6 Rochdale	46	22	14	10	74	53	58
7 Bradford PA	46	20	17	9	86	62	57
8 Chester	46	25	6	15	119	81	56
9 Doncaster	46	20	11	15	84	72	51
10 Crewe	46	18	13	15	90	81	49
11 Torquay	46	21	7	18	70	70	49
12 Chesterfield	46	20	8	18	58	70	48
13 Notts County	46	15	14	17	61	73	44
14 Wrexham	46	17	9	20	84	92	43
15 Hartlepools	46	15	13	18	61	85	43
16 Newport	46	17	8	21	85	81	42
17 Darlington	46	18	6	22	84	87	42
18 Aldershot	46	15	7	24	64	84	37
19 Bradford City	46	12	8	26	70	88	32
20 Southport	46	8	16	22	58	89	32
21 Barrow	46	12	6	28	59	105	30
22 Lincoln	46	11	6	29	58	99	28
23 Halifax	46	11	6	29	54	103	28
24 Stockport	46	10	7	29	44	87	27

Scottish First Division

	P	W	D	L	F	A	Pts
1 Kilmarnock	34	22	6	6	62	33	50
2 Hearts	34	22	6	6	90	49	50
3 Dunfermline	34	22	5	7	83	36	49
4 Hibernian	34	21	4	9	75	47	46
5 Rangers	34	18	8	8	78	35	44
6 Dundee	34	15	10	9	86	63	40
7 Clyde	34	17	6	11	64	58	40
8 Celtic	34	16	5	13	76	57	37
9 Dundee United	34	15	6	13	59	51	36

	P	W	D	L	F	A	Pts
10 Morton	34	13	7	14	54	54	33
11 Partick	34	11	10	13	57	58	32
12 Aberdeen	34	12	8	14	59	75	32
13 St Johnstone	34	9	11	14	57	62	29
14 Motherwell	34	10	8	16	45	54	28
15 St Mirren	34	9	6	19	38	70	24
16 Falkirk	34	7	7	20	43	85	21
17 Airdrieonians	34	5	4	25	48	110	14
18 Third Lanark	34	3	1	30	22	99	7

Scottish Second Division

	P	W	D	L	F	A	Pts
1 Stirling	36	26	7	3	84	31	59
2 Hamilton	36	21	8	7	86	53	50
3 Queen of the S	36	16	13	7	84	50	45
4 Queen's Park	36	17	9	10	57	41	43
5 ES Clydebank	36	15	10	11	64	50	40
6 Stranraer	36	17	6	13	74	64	40
7 Arbroath	36	13	13	10	56	51	39
8 Berwick	36	15	9	12	73	70	39
9 East Fife	36	15	7	14	78	77	37
10 Alloa	36	14	8	14	71	81	36
11 Albion	36	14	5	17	56	60	33
12 Cowdenbeath	36	11	10	15	55	62	32
13 Raith	36	9	14	13	54	61	32
14 Dumbarton	36	13	6	17	55	67	32
15 Stenhousemuir	36	11	8	17	49	74	30
16 Montrose	36	10	9	17	80	91	29
17 Forfar	36	9	7	20	63	89	25
18 Ayr	36	9	6	21	49	67	24
19 Brechin	36	6	7	23	53	102	19

FA Cup

Fourth Round

Liverpool v Stockport County	1-1, 2-0
Preston North End v Bolton Wanderers	1-2
Leicester City v Plymouth Argyle	5-0
Charlton Athletic v Middlesbrough	1-1, 1-2
West Ham United v Chelsea	0-1
Tottenham Hotspur v Ipswich Town	5-0
Peterborough United v Arsenal	2-1
Swansea Town v Huddersfield Town	1-0
Wolverhampton Wanderers v Rotherham United	2-2, 3-0
Sheffield United v Aston Villa	0-2
Stoke City v Manchester United	0-0, 0-1
Reading v Burnley	1-1, 0-1
Southampton v Crystal Palace	1-2

Sunderland v Nottingham Forest	1-3
Millwall v Shrewsbury Town	1-2
Leeds United v Everton	1-1, 2-1

Fifth Round

Bolton Wanderers v Liverpool	0-1
Middlesbrough v Leicester City	0-3
Chelsea v Tottenham Hotspur	1-0
Peterborough United v Swansea Town	0-0, 2-0
Aston Villa v Wolverhampton Wanderers	1-1, 0-0, 1-3
Manchester United v Burnley	2-1
Crystal Palace v Nottingham Forest	3-1
Leeds United v Shrewsbury Town	2-0

Sixth Round

Leicester City v Liverpool	0-0, 0-1
Chelsea v Peterborough United	5-1
Wolverhampton Wanderers v Manchester United	3-5
Crystal Palace v Leeds United	0-3

Semi-Final

Liverpool v Chelsea	2-0
Manchester United v Leeds United	0-0, 0-1

Final

Leeds United v Liverpool	1-2

Scottish FA Cup

Third Round

Celtic v Kilmarnock	3-2
Motherwell v Heart of Midlothian	1-0
Hibernian v Rangers	2-1
Dunfermline Athletic v Stirling Albion	2-0

Semi-Final

Celtic v Motherwell	2-2, 3-0
Hibernian v Dunfermline Athletic	0-2

Final

Celtic v Dunfermline Athletic	3-2

1965–66
First Division

	P	W	D	L	F	A	Pts
1 Liverpool	42	26	9	7	79	34	61
2 Leeds	42	23	9	10	79	38	55

	P	W	D	L	F	A	Pts
3 Burnley	42	24	7	11	79	47	55
4 Man United	42	18	15	9	84	59	51
5 Chelsea	42	22	7	13	65	53	51
6 WBA	42	19	12	11	91	69	50
7 Leicester	42	21	7	14	80	65	49
8 Tottenham	42	16	12	14	75	66	44
9 Sheff United	42	16	11	15	56	59	43
10 Stoke	42	15	12	15	65	64	42
11 Everton	42	15	11	16	56	62	41
12 West Ham	42	15	9	18	70	83	39
13 Blackpool	42	14	9	19	55	65	37
14 Arsenal	42	12	13	17	62	75	37
15 Newcastle	42	14	9	19	50	63	37
16 Aston Villa	42	15	6	21	69	80	36
17 Sheff Wed	42	14	8	20	56	66	36
18 Nottm Forest	42	14	8	20	56	72	36
19 Sunderland	42	14	8	20	51	72	36
20 Fulham	42	14	7	21	67	85	35
21 Northampton	42	10	13	19	55	92	33
22 Blackburn	42	8	4	30	57	88	20

Second Division

	P	W	D	L	F	A	Pts
1 Man City	42	22	15	5	76	44	59
2 Southampton	42	22	10	10	85	56	54
3 Coventry	42	20	13	9	73	53	53
4 Huddersfield	42	19	13	10	62	36	51
5 Bristol City	42	17	17	8	63	48	51
6 Wolves	42	20	10	12	87	61	50
7 Rotherham	42	16	14	12	75	74	46
8 Derby	42	16	11	15	71	68	43
9 Bolton	42	16	9	17	62	59	41
10 Birmingham	42	16	9	17	70	75	41
11 Crystal Palace	42	14	13	15	47	52	41
12 Portsmouth	42	16	8	18	74	78	40
13 Norwich	42	12	15	15	52	52	39
14 Carlisle	42	17	5	20	60	63	39
15 Ipswich	42	15	9	18	58	66	39
16 Charlton	42	12	14	16	61	70	38
17 Preston	42	11	15	16	62	70	37
18 Plymouth	42	12	13	17	54	63	37
19 Bury	42	14	7	21	62	76	35
20 Cardiff	42	12	10	20	71	91	34
21 Middlesbrough	42	10	13	19	58	86	33
22 Leyton Orient	42	5	13	24	38	80	23

Third Division

	P	W	D	L	F	A	Pts
1 Hull	46	31	7	8	109	62	69
2 Millwall	46	27	11	8	76	43	65
3 QPR	46	24	9	13	95	65	57
4 Scunthorpe	46	21	11	14	80	67	53
5 Workington	46	19	14	13	67	57	52
6 Gillingham	46	22	8	16	62	54	52
7 Swindon	46	19	13	14	74	48	51
8 Reading	46	19	13	14	70	63	51
9 Walsall	46	20	10	16	77	64	50
10 Shrewsbury	46	19	11	16	73	64	49
11 Grimsby	46	17	13	16	68	62	47
12 Watford	46	17	13	16	55	51	47
13 Peterborough	46	17	12	17	80	66	46
14 Oxford	46	19	8	19	70	74	46
15 Brighton	46	16	11	19	67	65	43
16 Bristol Rovers	46	14	14	18	64	64	42
17 Swansea	46	15	11	20	81	96	41
18 Bournemouth	46	13	12	21	38	56	38
19 Mansfield	46	15	8	23	59	89	38
20 Oldham	46	12	13	21	55	81	37
21 Southend	46	16	4	26	54	83	36
22 Exeter	46	12	11	23	53	79	35
23 Brentford	46	10	12	24	48	69	32
24 York	46	9	9	28	53	106	27

Fourth Division

	P	W	D	L	F	A	Pt
1 Doncaster	46	24	11	11	85	54	59
2 Darlington	46	25	9	12	72	53	59
3 Torquay	46	24	10	12	72	49	58
4 Colchester	46	23	10	13	70	47	56
5 Tranmere	46	24	8	14	93	66	56
6 Luton	46	24	8	14	90	70	56
7 Chester	46	20	12	14	79	70	52
8 Notts County	46	19	12	15	61	53	50
9 Newport	46	18	12	16	75	75	48
10 Southport	46	18	12	16	68	69	48
11 Bradford PA	46	21	5	20	102	92	47
12 Barrow	46	16	15	15	72	76	47
13 Stockport	46	18	6	22	71	70	42
14 Crewe	46	16	9	21	61	63	41
15 Halifax	46	15	11	20	67	75	41
16 Barnsley	46	15	10	21	74	78	40
17 Aldershot	46	15	10	21	75	84	40
18 Hartlepools	46	16	8	22	63	75	40
19 Port Vale	46	15	9	22	48	59	39
20 Chesterfield	46	13	13	20	62	78	39
21 Rochdale	46	16	5	25	71	87	37
22 Lincoln	46	13	11	22	57	82	37
23 Bradford City	46	12	13	21	63	94	37
24 Wrexham	46	13	9	24	72	104	35

Scottish First Division

	P	W	D	L	F	A	Pts
1 Celtic	34	27	3	4	106	30	57
2 Rangers	34	25	5	4	91	29	55
3 Kilmarnock	34	20	5	9	73	46	45
4 Dunfermline	34	19	6	9	94	55	44
5 Dundee United	34	19	5	10	79	51	43
6 Hibernian	34	16	6	12	81	55	38
7 Hearts	34	13	12	9	56	48	38
8 Aberdeen	34	15	6	13	61	54	36
9 Dundee	34	14	6	14	61	61	34
10 Falkirk	34	15	1	18	48	72	31
11 Clyde	34	13	4	17	62	64	30
12 Partick	34	10	10	14	55	64	30
13 Motherwell	34	12	4	18	52	69	28
14 St Johnstone	34	9	8	17	58	81	26
15 Stirling	34	9	8	17	40	68	26
16 St Mirren	34	9	4	21	44	82	22
17 Morton	34	8	5	21	42	84	21
18 Hamilton	34	3	2	29	27	117	8

Scottish Second Division

	P	W	D	L	F	A	Pts
1 Ayr	36	22	9	5	78	37	53
2 Airdrieonians	36	22	6	8	107	56	50
3 Queen of the S	36	18	11	7	83	53	47
4 East Fife	36	20	4	12	72	55	44
5 Raith	36	16	11	9	71	43	43
6 Arbroath	36	15	13	8	72	52	43
7 Albion	36	18	7	11	58	54	43
8 Alloa	36	14	10	12	65	65	38
9 Montrose	36	15	7	14	67	63	37
10 Cowdenbeath	36	15	7	14	69	68	37
11 Berwick	36	12	11	13	69	58	35
12 Dumbarton	36	14	7	15	63	61	35
13 Queen's Park	36	13	7	16	62	65	33
14 Third Lanark	36	12	8	16	55	65	32
15 Stranraer	36	9	10	17	64	83	28
16 Brechin	36	10	7	19	52	92	27
17 E Stirlingshire	36	9	5	22	59	91	23
18 Stenhousemuir	36	6	7	23	47	93	19
19 Forfar	36	7	3	26	61	120	17

FA Cup

Fourth Round
Bedford Town v Everton	0–3
Crewe Alexandra v Coventry City	1–1, 1–4
Manchester City v Grimsby Town	2–0

Birmingham City v Leicester City	1–2
Manchester United v Rotherham United	0–0, 1–0
Wolverhampton Wanderers v Sheffield United	3–0
Bolton Wanderers v Preston North End	1–1, 2–3
Tottenham Hotspur v Burnley	4–3
Chelsea v Leeds United	1–0
Shrewsbury Town v Carlisle United	0–0, 1–1, 4–3
Hull City v Nottingham Forest	2–0
Southport v Cardiff City	2–0
Norwich City v Walsall	3–2
West Ham United v Blackburn Rovers	3–3, 1–4
Plymouth Argyle v Huddersfield Town	0–2
Newcastle United v Sheffield Wednesday	1–2

Fifth Round
Everton v Coventry City	3–0
Manchester City v Leicester City	2–2, 1–0
Wolverhampton Wanderers v Manchester United	2–4
Preston North End v Tottenham Hotspur	2–1
Chelsea v Shrewsbury Town	3–2
Hull City v Southport	2–0
Norwich City v Blackburn Rovers	2–2, 2–3
Huddersfield Town v Sheffield Wednesday	1–2

Sixth Round
Manchester City v Everton	0–0, 0–0, 0–2
Preston North End v Manchester United	1–1, 1–3
Chelsea v Hull City	2–2, 3–1
Blackburn Rovers v Sheffield Wednesday	1–2

Semi-Final
Everton v Manchester United	1–0
Chelsea v Sheffield Wednesday	0–2

Final
Everton v Sheffield Wednesday	3–2

Scottish FA Cup

Third Round
Celtic v Heart of Midlothian	3–3, 3–1
Dunfermline Athletic v Kilmarnock	2–1

| Dumbarton v Aberdeen | 0–3 |
| Rangers v St Johnstone | 2–0 |

Semi-Final

| Celtic v Dunfermline Athletic | 2–0 |
| Aberdeen v Rangers | 0–0, 1–2 |

Final

| Celtic v Rangers | 0–0, 0–1 |

1966–67
First Division

		P	W	D	L	F	A	Pts
1	Man United	42	24	12	6	84	45	60
2	Nottm Forest	42	23	10	9	64	41	56
3	Tottenham	42	24	8	10	71	48	56
4	Leeds	42	22	11	9	62	42	55
5	Liverpool	42	19	13	10	64	47	51
6	Everton	42	19	10	13	65	46	48
7	Arsenal	42	16	14	12	58	47	46
8	Leicester	42	18	8	16	78	71	44
9	Chelsea	42	15	14	13	67	62	44
10	Sheff United	42	16	10	16	52	59	42
11	Sheff Wed	42	14	13	15	56	47	41
12	Stoke	42	17	7	18	63	58	41
13	WBA	42	16	7	19	77	73	39
14	Burnley	42	15	9	18	66	76	39
15	Man City	42	12	15	15	43	52	39
16	West Ham	42	14	8	20	80	84	36
17	Sunderland	42	14	8	20	58	72	36
18	Fulham	42	11	12	19	71	83	34
19	Southampton	42	14	6	22	74	92	34
20	Newcastle	42	12	9	21	39	81	33
21	Aston Villa	42	11	7	24	54	85	29
22	Blackpool	42	6	9	27	41	76	21

Second Division

		P	W	D	L	F	A	Pts
1	Coventry	42	23	13	6	74	43	59
2	Wolves	42	25	8	9	88	48	58
3	Carlisle	42	23	6	13	71	54	52
4	Blackburn	42	19	13	10	56	46	51
5	Ipswich	42	17	16	9	70	54	50
6	Huddersfield	42	20	9	13	58	46	49
7	Crystal Palace	42	19	10	13	61	55	48
8	Millwall	42	18	9	15	49	58	45
9	Bolton	42	14	14	14	64	58	42
10	Birmingham	42	16	8	18	70	66	40

11	Norwich	42	13	14	15	49	55	40
12	Hull	42	16	7	19	77	72	39
13	Preston	42	16	7	19	65	67	39
14	Portsmouth	42	13	13	16	59	70	39
15	Bristol City	42	12	14	16	56	62	38
16	Plymouth	42	14	9	19	59	58	37
17	Derby	42	12	12	18	68	72	36
18	Rotherham	42	13	10	19	61	70	36
19	Charlton	42	13	9	20	49	53	35
20	Cardiff	42	12	9	21	61	87	33
21	Northampton	42	12	6	24	47	84	30
22	Bury	42	11	6	25	49	83	28

Third Division

		P	W	D	L	F	A	Pts
1	QPR	46	26	15	5	103	38	67
2	Middlesbrough	46	23	9	14	87	64	55
3	Watford	46	20	14	12	61	46	54
4	Reading	46	22	9	15	76	57	53
5	Bristol Rovers	46	20	13	13	76	67	53
6	Shrewsbury	46	20	12	14	77	62	52
7	Torquay	46	21	9	16	73	54	51
8	Swindon	46	20	10	16	81	59	50
9	Mansfield	46	20	9	17	84	79	49
10	Oldham	46	19	10	17	80	63	48
11	Gillingham	46	15	16	15	58	62	46
12	Walsall	46	18	10	18	65	72	46
13	Colchester	46	17	10	19	76	73	44
14	Leyton Orient	46	13	18	15	58	68	44
14	Peterborough	46	14	15	17	66	71	43
16	Oxford	46	15	13	18	61	66	43
17	Grimsby	46	17	9	20	61	68	43
18	Scunthorpe	46	17	8	21	58	73	42
19	Brighton	46	13	15	18	61	71	41
20	Bournemouth	46	12	17	17	39	57	41
21	Swansea	46	12	15	19	85	89	39
22	Darlington	46	13	11	22	47	81	37
23	Doncaster	46	12	8	26	58	117	32
24	Workington	46	12	7	27	55	89	31

Fourth Division

		P	W	D	L	F	A	Pts
1	Stockport	46	26	12	8	69	42	64
2	Southport	46	23	13	10	69	42	59
3	Barrow	46	24	11	11	76	54	59
4	Tranmere	46	22	14	10	66	43	58
5	Crewe	46	21	12	13	70	55	54
6	Southend	46	22	9	15	70	49	53
7	Wrexham	46	16	20	10	76	62	52
8	Hartlepools	46	22	7	17	66	64	51

	P	W	D	L	F	A	Pts
9 Brentford	46	18	13	15	58	56	49
10 Aldershot	46	18	12	16	72	57	48
11 Bradford City	46	19	10	17	74	62	48
12 Halifax	46	15	14	17	59	68	44
13 Port Vale	46	14	15	17	55	58	43
14 Exeter	46	14	15	17	50	60	43
15 Chesterfield	46	17	8	21	60	63	42
16 Barnsley	46	13	15	18	60	64	41
17 Luton	46	16	9	21	59	73	41
18 Newport	46	12	16	18	56	63	40
19 Chester	46	15	10	21	54	78	40
20 Notts County	46	13	11	22	53	72	37
21 Rochdale	46	13	11	22	53	75	37
22 York	46	12	11	23	65	79	35
23 Bradford PA	46	11	13	22	52	79	35
24 Lincoln	46	9	13	24	58	82	31

Scottish First Division

	P	W	D	L	F	A	Pts
1 Celtic	34	26	6	2	111	33	58
2 Rangers	34	24	7	3	92	31	55
3 Clyde	34	20	6	8	64	48	46
4 Aberdeen	34	17	8	9	72	38	42
5 Hibernian	34	19	4	11	72	49	42
6 Dundee	34	16	9	9	74	51	41
7 Kilmarnock	34	16	8	10	59	46	40
8 Dunfermline	34	14	10	10	72	52	38
9 Dundee United	34	14	9	11	68	62	37
10 Motherwell	34	10	11	13	59	60	31
11 Hearts	34	11	8	15	39	48	30
12 Partick	34	9	12	13	49	68	30
13 Airdrieonians	34	11	6	17	41	53	28
14 Falkirk	34	11	4	19	33	70	26
15 St Johnstone	34	10	5	19	53	73	25
16 Stirling	34	5	9	20	31	85	19
17 St Mirren	34	4	7	23	25	81	15
18 Ayr	34	1	7	26	20	86	9

Scottish Second Division

	P	W	D	L	F	A	Pts
1 Morton	38	33	3	2	113	20	69
2 Raith	38	27	4	7	95	44	58
3 Arbroath	38	25	7	6	75	32	57
4 Hamilton	38	18	8	12	74	60	44
5 East Fife	38	19	4	15	70	63	42
6 Cowdenbeath	38	16	8	14	70	55	40
7 Queen's Park	38	15	10	13	78	68	40
8 Albion	38	17	6	15	66	62	40
9 Queen of the S	38	15	9	14	84	76	39
10 Berwick	38	16	6	16	63	55	38

	P	W	D	L	F	A	Pts
11 Third Lanark*	38	13	8	17	67	78	34
12 Montrose	38	13	8	17	63	77	34
13 Alloa	38	15	4	19	55	74	34
14 Dumbarton	38	12	9	17	56	64	33
15 Stranraer	38	13	7	18	57	73	33
16 Forfar	38	12	3	23	74	106	27
17 Stenhousemuir	38	9	9	20	62	104	27
18 Clydebank	38	8	8	22	59	92	24
19 E Stirlingshire	38	7	10	21	44	87	24
20 Brechin	38	8	7	23	58	93	23

*Third Lanark resigned from League at end of the season

FA Cup

Fourth Round

Brighton & Hove Albion v Chelsea	1-1 0-4
Fulham v Sheffield United	1-1, 1-3
Manchester United v Norwich City	1-2
Sheffield Wednesday v Mansfield Town	4-0
Sunderland v Peterborough United	7-1
Leeds United v West Bromwich Albion	5-0
Cardiff City v Manchester City	1-1, 1-3
Ipswich Town v Carlisle United	2-0
Rotherham United v Birmingham City	0-0, 1-2
Bolton Wanderers v Arsenal	0-0, 0-3
Tottenham Hotspur v Portsmouth	3-1
Bristol City v Southampton	1-0
Nottingham Forest v Newcastle United	3-0
Swindon Town v Bury	2-1
Wolverhampton Wanderers v Everton	1-1, 1-3
Liverpool v Aston Villa	1-0

Fifth Round

Chelsea v Sheffield United	2-0
Norwich City v Sheffield Wednesday	1-3
Sunderland v Leeds United	1-1, 1-1, 1-2
Manchester City v Ipswich Town	1-1, 3-0
Birmingham City v Arsenal	1-0
Tottenham Hotspur v Bristol City	2-0
Nottingham Forest v Swindon Town	0-0, 1-1, 3-0
Everton v Liverpool	1-0

Sixth Round

Chelsea v Sheffield Wednesday	1-0
Leeds United v Manchester City	1-0

Birmingham City v Tottenham Hotspur
                                0-0, 0-6
Nottingham Forest v Everton   3-2

Semi-Final
Chelsea v Leeds United   1-0
Tottenham Hotspur v Nottingham Forest
                                 2-1
Final
Chelsea v Tottenham Hotspur   1-2

Scottish FA Cup

Third Round
Celtic v Queen's Park   5-3
Clyde v Hamilton Academicals   0-0, 5-1
Dundee United v Dunfermline Athletic
                                 1-0
Hibernian v Aberdeen   1-1, 0-3

Semi-Final
Celtic v Clyde   0-0, 2-0
Dundee United v Aberdeen   0-1

Final
Celtic v Aberdeen   2-0

1967-68
First Division

	P	W	D	L	F	A	Pts
1 Man City	42	26	6	10	86	43	58
2 Man United	42	24	8	10	89	55	56
3 Liverpool	42	22	11	9	71	40	55
4 Leeds	42	22	9	11	71	41	53
5 Everton	42	23	6	13	67	40	52
6 Chelsea	42	18	12	12	62	68	48
7 Tottenham	42	19	9	14	70	59	47
8 WBA	42	17	12	13	75	62	46
9 Arsenal	42	17	10	15	60	56	44
10 Newcastle	42	13	15	14	54	67	41
11 Nottm Forest	42	14	11	17	52	64	39
12 West Ham	42	14	10	18	73	69	38
13 Leicester	42	13	12	17	64	69	38
14 Burnley	42	14	10	18	64	71	38
15 Sunderland	42	13	11	18	51	61	37
16 Southampton	42	13	11	18	66	83	37
17 Wolves	42	14	8	20	66	75	36
18 Stoke	42	14	7	21	50	73	35
19 Sheff Wed	42	11	12	19	51	63	34
20 Coventry	42	9	15	18	51	71	33

| 21 Sheff United | 42 | 11 | 10 | 21 | 49 | 70 | 32 |
| 22 Fulham | 42 | 10 | 7 | 25 | 56 | 98 | 27 |

Second Division

	P	W	D	L	F	A	Pts
1 Ipswich	42	22	15	5	79	44	59
2 QPR	42	25	8	9	67	36	58
3 Blackpool	42	24	10	8	71	43	58
4 Birmingham	42	19	14	9	83	51	52
5 Portsmouth	42	18	13	11	68	55	49
6 Middlesbrough	42	17	12	13	60	54	46
7 Millwall	42	14	17	11	62	50	45
8 Blackburn	42	16	11	15	56	49	43
9 Norwich	42	16	11	15	60	65	43
10 Carlisle	42	14	13	15	58	52	41
11 Crystal Palace	42	14	11	17	56	56	39
12 Bolton	42	13	13	16	60	63	39
13 Cardiff	42	13	12	17	60	66	38
14 Huddersfield	42	13	12	17	46	61	38
15 Charlton	42	12	13	17	63	68	37
16 Aston Villa	42	15	7	20	54	64	37
17 Hull	42	12	13	17	58	73	37
18 Derby	42	13	10	19	71	78	36
19 Bristol City	42	13	10	19	48	62	36
20 Preston	42	12	11	19	43	65	35
21 Rotherham	42	10	11	21	42	76	31
22 Plymouth	42	9	9	24	38	72	27

Third Division

	P	W	D	L	F	A	Pts
1 Oxford	46	22	13	11	69	47	57
2 Bury	46	24	8	14	91	66	56
3 Shrewsbury	46	20	15	11	61	49	55
4 Torquay	46	21	11	14	60	56	53
5 Reading	46	21	9	16	70	60	51
6 Watford	46	21	8	17	74	50	50
7 Walsall	46	19	12	15	74	61	50
8 Barrow	46	21	8	17	65	54	50
9 Swindon	46	16	17	13	74	51	49
10 Brighton	46	16	16	14	57	55	48
11 Gillingham	46	18	12	16	59	63	48
12 Bournemouth	46	16	15	15	56	51	47
13 Stockport	46	19	9	18	70	75	47
14 Southport	46	17	12	17	65	65	46
15 Bristol Rovers	46	17	9	20	72	78	43
16 Oldham	46	18	7	21	60	65	43
17 Northampton	46	14	13	19	58	72	41
18 Leyton Orient	46	12	17	17	46	62	41
19 Tranmere	46	14	12	20	62	74	40
20 Mansfield	46	12	13	21	51	67	37

	P	W	D	L	F	A	Pts
21 Grimsby	46	14	9	23	52	69	37
22 Colchester	46	9	15	22	50	87	33
23 Scunthorpe	46	10	12	24	56	87	32
24 Peterborough*	46	20	10	16	79	67	31

*Peterborough had 19 points deducted for offering bonuses to their players. They were automatically demoted to the Fourth Division.

Fourth Division

	P	W	D	L	F	A	Pts
1 Luton	46	27	12	7	87	44	66
2 Barnsley	46	24	13	9	68	46	61
3 Hartlepools	46	25	10	11	60	46	60
4 Crewe	46	20	18	8	74	49	58
5 Bradford City	46	23	11	12	72	51	57
6 Southend	46	20	14	12	77	58	54
7 Chesterfield	46	21	11	14	71	50	53
8 Wrexham	46	20	13	13	72	53	53
9 Aldershot	46	18	17	11	70	55	53
10 Doncaster	46	18	15	13	66	56	51
11 Halifax	46	15	16	15	52	49	46
12 Newport	46	16	13	17	58	63	45
13 Lincoln	46	17	9	20	71	68	43
14 Brentford	46	18	7	21	61	64	43
15 Swansea	46	16	10	20	63	77	42
16 Darlington	46	12	17	17	47	53	41
17 Notts County	46	15	11	20	53	79	41
18 Port Vale	46	12	15	19	61	72	39
19 Rochdale	46	12	14	20	51	72	38
20 Exeter	46	11	16	19	45	65	38
21 York	46	11	14	21	65	68	36
22 Chester	46	9	14	23	57	78	32
23 Workington	46	10	11	25	54	87	31
24 Bradford PA	46	4	15	27	30	82	23

Scottish First Division

	P	W	D	L	F	A	Pts
1 Celtic	34	30	3	1	106	24	63
2 Rangers	34	28	5	1	93	34	61
3 Hibernian	34	20	5	9	67	49	45
4 Dunfermline	34	17	5	12	64	41	39
5 Aberdeen	34	16	5	13	63	48	37
6 Morton	34	15	6	13	57	53	36
7 Kilmarnock	34	13	8	13	59	57	34
8 Clyde	34	15	4	15	55	55	34
9 Dundee	34	13	7	14	62	59	33
10 Partick	34	12	7	15	51	67	31
11 Dundee United	34	10	11	13	53	72	31
12 Hearts	34	13	4	17	56	61	30
13 Airdrieonians	34	10	9	15	45	58	29

	P	W	D	L	F	A	Pts
14 St Johnstone	34	10	7	17	43	52	27
15 Falkirk	34	7	12	15	36	50	26
16 Raith	34	9	7	18	58	86	25
17 Motherwell	34	6	7	21	40	66	19
18 Stirling	34	4	4	26	29	105	12

Scottish Second Division

	P	W	D	L	F	A	Pts
1 St Mirren	36	27	8	1	100	23	62
2 Arbroath	36	24	5	7	87	34	53
3 East Fife	36	21	7	8	71	47	49
4 Queen's Park	36	20	8	8	76	47	48
5 Ayr	36	18	6	12	69	48	42
6 Queen of the S	36	16	6	14	73	57	38
7 Forfar	36	14	10	12	57	63	38
8 Albion	36	14	9	13	62	55	37
9 Clydebank	36	13	8	15	62	73	34
10 Dumbarton	36	11	11	14	63	74	33
11 Hamilton	36	13	7	16	49	58	33
12 Cowdenbeath	36	12	8	16	57	62	32
13 Montrose	36	10	11	15	54	64	31
14 Berwick	36	13	4	19	34	54	30
15 E Stirlingshire	36	9	10	17	61	74	28
16 Brechin	36	8	12	16	45	62	28
17 Alloa	36	11	6	19	42	69	28
18 Stenhousemuir	36	7	6	23	34	93	20
19 Stranraer	36	8	4	24	41	80	20

FA Cup

Fourth Round

Carlisle United v Everton	0-2
Coventry City v Tranmere Rovers	1-1, 0-2
Aston Villa v Rotherham United	0-1
Manchester City v Leicester City	0-0, 3-4
Leeds United v Nottingham Forest	2-1
Middlesbrough v Bristol City	1-1, 1-2
Stoke City v West Ham United	0-3
Sheffield United v Blackpool	2-1
Swansea Town v Arsenal	0-1
Birmingham City v Leyton Orient	3-0
Sheffield Wednesday v Swindon Town	2-1
Chelsea v Norwich City	1-0
Fulham v Portsmouth	0-0, 0-1
West Bromwich Albion v Southampton	1-1, 3-2
Tottenham Hotspur v Preston North End	3-1
Walsall v Liverpool	0-0, 2-5

Fifth Round

Everton v Tranmere Rovers	2-0
Rotherham United v Leicester City	1-1, 0-2
Leeds United v Bristol City	2-0
West Ham United v Sheffield United	1-2
Arsenal v Birmingham City	1-1, 1-2
Sheffield Wednesday v Chelsea	2-2, 0-2
Portsmouth v West Bromwich Albion	1-2
Tottenham Hotspur v Liverpool	1-1, 1-2

Sixth Round

Everton v Leicester City	3-1
Leeds United v Sheffield United	1-0
Birmingham City v Chelsea	1-0
West Bromwich Albion v Liverpool	0-0, 1-1, 2-1

Semi-Final

Everton v Leeds United	1-0
West Bromwich Albion v Birmingham City	2-0

Final

Everton v West Bromwich Albion	0-1

Scottish FA Cup

Third Round

Rangers v Heart of Midlothian	1-1, 0-1
Morton v Elgin City	2-1
Dunfermline Athletic v Partick Thistle	1-0
St Johnstone v Airdrieonians	2-1

Semi-Final

Heart of Midlothian v Morton	1-1, 2-1
Dunfermline Athletic v St Johnstone	1-1, 2-1

Final

Dunfermline Athletic v Heart of Midlothian	3-1

1968–69
First Division

	P	W	D	L	F	A	Pts
1 Leeds	42	27	13	2	66	26	67
2 Liverpool	42	25	11	6	63	24	61
3 Everton	42	21	15	6	77	36	57
4 Arsenal	42	22	12	8	56	27	56
5 Chelsea	42	20	10	12	73	53	50
6 Tottenham	42	14	17	11	61	51	45
7 Southampton	42	16	13	13	57	48	45
8 West Ham	42	13	18	11	66	50	44
9 Newcastle	42	15	14	13	61	55	44
10 WBA	42	16	11	15	64	67	43
11 Man United	42	15	12	15	57	53	42
12 Ipswich	42	15	11	16	59	60	41
13 Man City	42	15	10	17	64	55	40
14 Burnley	42	15	9	18	55	82	39
15 Sheff Wed	42	10	16	16	41	54	36
16 Wolves	42	10	15	17	41	58	35
17 Sunderland	42	11	12	19	43	67	34
18 Nottm Forest	42	10	13	19	45	57	33
19 Stoke	42	9	15	18	40	63	33
20 Coventry	42	10	11	21	46	64	31
21 Leicester	42	9	12	21	39	68	30
22 QPR	42	4	10	28	39	95	18

Second Division

	P	W	D	L	F	A	Pts
1 Derby	42	26	11	5	65	32	63
2 Crystal Palace	42	22	12	8	70	47	56
3 Charlton	42	18	14	10	61	52	50
4 Middlesbrough	42	19	11	12	58	49	49
5 Cardiff	42	20	7	15	67	54	47
6 Huddersfield	42	17	12	13	53	46	46
7 Birmingham	42	18	8	16	73	59	44
8 Blackpool	42	14	15	13	51	41	43
9 Sheff United	42	16	11	15	61	50	43
10 Millwall	42	17	9	16	57	49	43
11 Hull	42	13	16	13	59	52	42
12 Carlisle	42	16	10	16	46	49	42
13 Norwich	42	15	10	17	53	56	40
14 Preston	42	12	15	15	38	44	39
15 Portsmouth	42	12	14	16	58	58	38
16 Bristol City	42	11	16	15	46	53	38
17 Bolton	42	12	14	16	55	67	38
18 Aston Villa	42	12	14	16	37	48	38
19 Blackburn	42	13	11	18	52	63	37
20 Oxford	42	12	9	21	34	55	33
21 Bury	42	11	8	23	51	80	30
22 Fulham	42	7	11	24	40	81	25

Third Division

	P	W	D	L	F	A	Pts
1 Watford	46	27	10	9	74	34	64
2 Swindon	46	27	10	9	71	35	64
3 Luton	46	25	11	10	74	38	61
4 Bournemouth	46	21	9	16	60	45	51
5 Plymouth	46	17	15	14	53	49	49

	P	W	D	L	F	A	Pts
6 Torquay	46	18	12	16	54	46	48
7 Tranmere	46	19	10	17	70	68	48
8 Southport	46	17	13	16	71	64	47
9 Stockport	46	16	14	16	67	68	46
10 Barnsley	46	16	14	16	58	63	46
11 Rotherham	46	16	13	17	56	50	45
12 Brighton	46	16	13	17	72	65	45
13 Walsall	46	14	16	16	50	49	44
14 Reading	46	15	13	18	67	66	43
15 Mansfield	46	16	11	19	58	62	43
16 Bristol Rovers	46	16	11	19	63	71	43
17 Shrewsbury	46	16	11	19	51	67	43
18 Orient	46	14	14	18	51	58	42
19 Barrow	46	17	8	21	56	75	42
20 Gillingham	46	13	15	18	54	63	41
21 Northampton	46	14	12	20	54	61	40
22 Hartlepool	46	10	19	17	40	70	39
23 Crewe	46	13	9	24	52	76	35
24 Oldham	46	13	9	24	50	83	35

Fourth Division

	P	W	D	L	F	A	Pts
1 Doncaster	46	21	17	8	65	38	59
2 Halifax	46	20	17	9	53	37	57
3 Rochdale	46	18	20	8	68	35	56
4 Bradford City	46	18	20	8	65	46	56
5 Darlington	46	17	18	11	62	45	52
6 Colchester	46	20	12	14	57	53	52
7 Southend	46	19	13	14	78	61	51
8 Lincoln	46	17	17	12	54	52	51
9 Wrexham	46	18	14	14	61	52	50
10 Swansea	46	19	11	16	58	54	49
11 Brentford	46	18	12	16	64	65	48
12 Workington	46	15	17	14	40	43	47
13 Port Vale	46	16	14	16	46	46	46
14 Chester	46	16	13	17	76	66	45
15 Aldershot	46	19	7	20	66	66	45
16 Scunthorpe	46	18	8	20	61	60	44
17 Exeter	46	16	11	19	66	65	43
18 Peterborough	46	13	16	17	60	57	42
19 Notts County	46	12	18	16	48	57	42
20 Chesterfield	46	13	15	18	43	50	41
21 York	46	14	11	21	53	75	39
22 Newport	46	11	14	21	49	74	36
23 Grimsby	46	9	15	22	47	69	33
24 Bradford PA	46	5	10	31	32	106	20

Scottish First Division

	P	W	D	L	F	A	Pts
1 Celtic	34	23	8	3	89	32	54
2 Rangers	34	21	7	6	81	32	49
3 Dunfermline	34	19	7	8	63	45	45
4 Kilmarnock	34	15	14	5	50	32	44
5 Dundee United	34	17	9	8	61	49	43
6 St Johnstone	34	16	5	13	66	59	37
7 Airdrieonians	34	13	11	10	46	44	37
8 Hearts	43	14	8	12	52	54	36
9 Dundee	34	10	12	12	47	48	32
10 Morton	34	12	8	14	58	68	32
11 St Mirren	34	11	10	13	40	54	32
12 Hibernian	34	12	7	15	60	59	31
13 Clyde	34	9	13	12	35	50	31
14 Partick	34	9	10	15	39	53	28
15 Aberdeen	34	9	8	17	50	59	26
16 Raith	34	8	5	21	45	67	21
17 Falkirk	34	5	8	21	33	69	18
18 Arbroath	34	5	6	23	41	82	16

Scottish Second Division

	P	W	D	L	F	A	Pts
1 Motherwell	36	30	4	2	112	23	64
2 Ayr	36	23	7	6	82	31	53
3 East Fife	36	21	6	9	82	45	48
4 Stirling	36	21	6	9	67	40	48
5 Queen of the S	36	20	7	9	75	41	47
6 Forfar	36	18	7	11	71	56	43
7 Albion	36	19	5	12	60	56	43
8 Stranraer	36	17	7	12	57	45	41
9 E Stirlingshire	36	17	5	14	70	62	39
10 Montrose	36	15	4	17	59	71	34
11 Queen's Park	36	13	7	16	50	59	33
12 Cowdenbeath	36	12	5	19	54	67	29
13 Clydebank	36	6	15	15	52	67	27
14 Dumbarton	36	11	5	20	46	69	27
15 Hamilton	36	8	8	20	37	72	24
16 Berwick	36	7	9	20	42	70	23
17 Brechin	36	8	6	22	40	78	22
18 Alloa	36	7	7	22	45	79	21
19 Stenhousemuir	36	6	6	24	55	125	18

FA Cup

Fourth Round

Newcastle United v Manchester City 0-0, 0-2

Blackburn Rovers v Portsmouth 4-0

Tottenham Hotspur v Wolverhampton Wanderers 2-1

Southampton v Aston Villa 2-2, 1-2

Sheffield Wednesday v Birmingham City 2-2, 1-2

Manchester United v Watford   1-1, 2-0
Bolton Wanderers v Bristol Rovers   1-2
Coventry City v Everton   0-2
West Bromwich Albion v Fulham   2-1
Arsenal v Charlton Athletic   2-0
Preston North End v Chelsea   0-0, 1-2
Stoke City v Halifax Town   1-1, 3-0
Mansfield Town v Southend United   2-1
Huddersfield v West Ham United   0-2
Liverpool v Burnley   2-1
Millwall v Leicester City   0-1

Fifth Round

Manchester City v Blackburn Rovers   4-1
Tottenham Hotspur v Aston Villa   3-2
Birmingham City v Manchester United
2-2, 2-6
Bristol Rovers v Everton   0-1
West Bromwich Albion v Arsenal   1-0
Chelsea v Stoke City   3-2
Mansfield Town v West Ham United   3-0
Liverpool v Leicester City   0-0, 0-1

Sixth Round

Manchester City v Tottenham Hotspur
1-0
Manchester United v Everton   0-1
Chelsea v West Bromwich Albion   1-2
Mansfield Town v Leicester City   0-1

Semi-Final

Manchester City v Everton   1-0
West Bromwich Albion v Leicester City
0-1

Final

Leicester City v Manchester City   0-1

Scottish FA Cup

Third Round

Rangers v Airdrieonians   1-0
Aberdeen v Kilmarnock   0-0, 3-0
Dundee United v Morton   2-3
Celtic v St Johnstone   3-2

Semi-Final

Rangers v Aberdeen   6-1
Morton v Celtic   1-4

Final

Celtic v Rangers   4-0

1969-70
First Division

	P	W	D	L	F	A	Pts
1 Everton	42	29	8	5	72	34	66
2 Leeds	42	21	15	6	84	49	57
3 Chelsea	42	21	13	8	70	50	55
4 Derby	42	22	9	11	64	37	53
5 Liverpool	42	20	11	11	65	42	51
6 Coventry	42	19	11	12	58	48	49
7 Newcastle	42	17	13	12	57	35	47
8 Man United	42	14	17	11	66	61	45
9 Stoke	42	15	15	12	56	52	45
10 Man City	42	16	11	15	55	48	43
11 Tottenham	42	17	9	16	54	55	43
12 Arsenal	42	12	18	12	51	49	42
13 Wolves	42	12	16	14	55	57	40
14 Burnley	42	12	15	15	56	61	39
15 Nottm Forest	42	10	18	14	50	71	38
16 WBA	42	14	9	19	58	66	37
17 West Ham	42	12	12	18	51	60	36
18 Ipswich	42	10	11	21	40	63	31
19 Southampton	42	6	17	19	46	67	29
20 Crystal Palace	42	6	15	21	34	68	27
21 Sunderland	42	6	14	22	30	68	26
22 Sheff Wed	42	8	9	25	40	71	25

Second Division

	P	W	D	L	F	A	Pts
1 Huddersfield	42	24	12	6	68	37	60
2 Blackpool	42	20	13	9	56	45	53
3 Leicester	42	19	13	10	64	50	51
4 Middlesbrough	42	20	10	12	55	45	50
5 Swindon	42	17	16	9	57	47	50
6 Sheff United	42	22	5	15	73	38	49
7 Cardiff	42	18	13	11	61	41	49
8 Blackburn	42	20	7	15	54	50	47
9 QPR	42	17	11	14	66	57	45
10 Millwall	42	15	14	13	56	56	44
11 Norwich	42	16	11	15	49	46	43
12 Carlisle	42	14	13	15	58	56	41
13 Hull	42	15	11	16	72	70	41
14 Bristol City	42	13	13	16	54	50	39
15 Oxford	42	12	15	15	35	42	39
16 Bolton	42	12	12	18	54	61	36
17 Portsmouth	42	13	9	20	66	80	35
18 Birmingham	42	11	11	20	51	78	33
19 Watford	42	9	13	20	44	57	31
20 Charlton	42	7	17	18	35	76	31

		P	W	D	L	F	A	Pts
21	Aston Villa	42	8	13	21	36	62	29
22	Preston	42	8	12	22	43	63	28

Third Division

		P	W	D	L	F	A	Pts
1	Orient	46	25	12	9	67	36	62
2	Luton	46	23	14	9	77	43	60
3	Bristol Rovers	46	20	16	10	80	59	56
4	Fulham	46	20	15	11	81	55	55
5	Brighton	46	23	9	14	57	43	55
6	Mansfield	46	21	11	14	70	49	53
7	Barnsley	46	19	15	12	68	59	53
8	Reading	46	21	11	14	87	77	53
9	Rochdale	46	18	10	18	69	60	46
10	Bradford City	46	17	12	17	57	50	46
11	Doncaster	46	17	12	17	52	54	46
12	Walsall	46	17	12	17	54	67	46
13	Torquay	46	14	17	15	62	59	45
14	Rotherham	46	15	14	17	62	54	44
15	Shrewsbury	46	13	18	15	62	63	44
16	Tranmere	46	14	16	16	56	72	44
17	Plymouth	46	16	11	19	56	64	43
18	Halifax	46	14	15	17	47	63	43
19	Bury	46	15	11	20	75	80	41
20	Gillingham	46	13	13	20	52	64	39
21	Bournemouth	46	12	15	19	48	71	39
22	Southport	46	14	10	22	48	66	38
23	Barrow	46	8	14	24	46	81	30
24	Stockport	46	6	11	29	27	71	23

Fourth Division

		P	W	D	L	F	A	Pts
1	Chesterfield	46	27	10	9	77	32	64
2	Wrexham	46	26	9	11	84	49	61
3	Swansea	46	21	18	7	66	45	60
4	Port Vale	46	20	19	7	61	33	59
5	Brentford	46	20	16	10	58	39	56
6	Aldershot	46	20	13	13	78	65	53
7	Notts County	46	22	8	16	73	62	52
8	Lincoln	46	17	16	13	66	52	50
9	Peterborough	46	17	14	15	77	69	48
10	Colchester	46	17	14	15	64	63	48
11	Chester	46	21	6	19	58	66	48
12	Scunthorpe	46	18	10	18	67	65	46
13	York	46	16	14	16	55	62	46
14	Northampton	46	16	12	18	64	55	44
15	Crewe	46	16	12	18	51	51	44
16	Grimsby	46	14	15	17	54	58	43
17	Southend	46	15	10	21	59	85	40
18	Exeter	46	14	11	21	57	59	39

		P	W	D	L	F	A	Pts
19	Oldham	46	13	13	20	60	65	39
20	Workington	46	12	14	20	46	64	38
21	Newport	46	13	11	22	53	74	37
22	Darlington	46	13	10	23	53	73	36
23	Hartlepool	46	10	10	26	42	82	30
24	Bradford PA	46	6	11	29	41	96	23

Scottish First Division

		P	W	D	L	F	A	Pts
1	Celtic	34	27	3	4	96	33	57
2	Rangers	34	19	7	8	67	40	45
3	Hibernian	34	19	6	9	65	40	44
4	Hearts	34	13	12	9	50	36	38
5	Dundee United	34	16	6	12	62	64	38
6	Dundee	34	15	6	13	49	44	36
7	Kilmarnock	34	13	10	11	62	57	36
8	Aberdeen	34	14	7	13	55	45	35
9	Dunfermline	34	15	5	14	45	45	35
10	Morton	34	13	9	12	52	52	35
11	Motherwell	34	11	10	13	49	51	32
12	Airdrieonians	34	12	8	14	59	64	32
13	St Johnstone	34	11	9	14	50	62	31
14	Ayr	34	12	6	16	37	52	30
15	St Mirren	34	8	9	17	39	54	25
16	Clyde	34	9	7	18	34	56	25
17	Raith	34	5	11	18	32	67	21
18	Partick	34	5	7	22	41	82	17

Scottish Second Division

		P	W	D	L	F	A	Pts
1	Falkirk	36	25	6	5	94	34	56
2	Cowdenbeath	36	24	7	5	81	35	55
3	Queen of the S	36	22	6	8	72	49	50
4	Stirling	36	18	10	8	70	40	46
5	Arbroath	36	20	4	12	76	39	44
6	Alloa	36	19	5	12	62	41	43
7	Dumbarton	36	17	6	13	55	46	40
8	Montrose	36	15	7	14	57	55	37
9	Berwick	36	15	5	16	67	55	35
10	East Fife	36	15	4	17	59	63	34
11	Albion	36	14	5	17	53	64	33
12	E Stirlingshire	36	14	5	17	58	75	33
13	Clydebank	36	10	10	16	47	65	30
14	Brechin	36	11	6	19	47	74	28
15	Queen's Park	36	10	6	20	38	62	26
16	Stenhousemuir	36	10	6	20	47	89	26
17	Stranraer	36	9	7	20	56	75	25
18	Forfar	36	11	1	24	55	83	23
19	Hamilton	36	8	4	24	42	92	20

FA Cup

Fourth Round

Chelsea v Burnley	2-2, 3-1
Tottenham Hotspur v Crystal Palace	
	0-0, 0-1
Charlton Athletic v Queen's Park Rangers	
	2-3
Derby County v Sheffield United	3-0
Watford v Stoke City	1-0
Gillingham v Peterborough United	5-1
Liverpool v Wrexham	3-1
Southampton v Leicester City	1-1, 2-4
Tranmere Rovers v Northampton Town	
	0-0, 1-2
Manchester United v Manchester City	3-0
Carlisle United v Aldershot	2-2, 4-1
Middlesbrough v York City	4-1
Swindon Town v Chester	4-2
Sheffield Wednesday v Scunthorpe United	
	1-2
Blackpool v Mansfield Town	0-2
Sutton United v Leeds United	0-6

Fifth Round

Chelsea v Crystal Palace	4-1
Queen's Park Rangers v Derby County	1-0
Watford v Gillingham	2-1
Liverpool v Leicester City	0-0, 2-0
Northampton Town v Manchester United	
	2-8
Carlisle United v Middlesbrough	1-2
Swindon Town v Scunthorpe United	3-1
Mansfield Town v Leeds United	0-2

Sixth Round

Queen's Park Rangers v Chelsea	2-4
Watford v Liverpool	1-0
Manchester United v Middlesbrough	
	1-1, 2-1
Swindon Town v Leeds United	0-2

Semi-Final

Chelsea v Watford	5-1
Manchester United v Leeds United	
	0-0, 0-0, 0-1

Third Place Play-off

Manchester United v Watford	2-0

Final

Chelsea v Leeds United	2-2, 2-1

Scottish FA Cup

Third Round

Celtic v Rangers	3-1
East Fife v Dundee	0-1
Motherwell v Kilmarnock	0-1
Falkirk v Aberdeen	0-1

Semi-Final

Celtic v Dundee	2-1
Kilmarnock v Aberdeen	0-1

Final

Celtic v Aberdeen	1-3

1970-71
First Division

	P	W	D	L	F	A	Pts
1 Arsenal	42	29	7	6	71	29	65
2 Leeds	42	27	10	5	72	30	64
3 Tottenham	42	19	14	9	54	33	52
4 Wolves	42	22	8	12	64	54	52
5 Liverpool	42	17	17	8	42	24	51
6 Chelsea	42	18	15	9	52	42	51
7 Southampton	42	17	12	13	56	44	46
8 Man United	42	16	11	15	65	66	43
9 Derby	42	16	10	16	56	54	42
10 Coventry	42	16	10	16	37	38	42
11 Man City	42	12	17	13	47	42	41
12 Newcastle	42	14	13	15	44	46	41
13 Stoke	42	12	13	17	44	48	37
14 Everton	42	12	13	17	54	60	37
15 Huddersfield	42	11	14	17	40	49	36
16 Nottm Forest	42	14	8	20	42	61	36
17 WBA	42	10	15	17	58	75	35
18 Crystal Palace	42	12	11	19	39	57	35
19 Ipswich	42	12	10	20	42	48	34
20 West Ham	42	10	14	18	47	60	34
21 Burnley	42	7	13	22	29	63	27
22 Blackpool	42	4	15	23	34	66	23

Second Division

	P	W	D	L	F	A	Pts
1 Leicester	42	23	13	6	57	30	59
2 Sheff United	42	21	14	7	73	39	56
3 Cardiff	42	20	13	9	64	41	53
4 Carlisle	42	20	13	9	65	43	53
5 Hull	42	19	13	10	54	41	51

	P	W	D	L	F	A	Pts
6 Luton	42	18	13	11	62	43	49
7 Middlesbrough	42	17	14	11	60	43	48
8 Millwall	42	19	9	14	59	42	47
9 Birmingham	42	17	12	13	58	48	46
10 Norwich	42	15	14	13	54	52	44
11 QPR	42	16	11	15	58	53	43
12 Swindon	42	15	12	15	61	51	42
13 Sunderland	42	15	12	15	52	54	42
14 Oxford	42	14	14	14	41	48	42
15 Sheff Wed	42	12	12	18	51	69	36
16 Portsmouth	42	10	14	18	46	61	34
17 Orient	42	9	16	17	29	51	34
18 Watford	42	10	13	19	38	60	33
19 Bristol City	42	10	11	21	46	64	31
20 Charlton	42	8	14	20	41	65	30
21 Blackburn	42	6	15	21	37	69	27
22 Bolton	42	7	10	25	35	74	24

Third Division

	P	W	D	L	F	A	Pts
1 Preston	46	22	17	7	63	39	61
2 Fulham	46	24	12	10	68	41	60
3 Halifax	46	22	12	12	74	55	56
4 Aston Villa	46	19	15	12	54	46	53
5 Chesterfield	46	17	17	12	66	38	51
6 Bristol Rovers	46	19	13	14	69	50	51
7 Mansfield	46	18	15	13	64	62	51
8 Rotherham	46	17	16	13	64	60	50
9 Wrexham	46	18	13	15	72	65	49
10 Torquay	46	19	11	16	54	57	49
11 Swansea	46	15	16	15	59	56	46
12 Barnsley	46	17	11	18	49	52	45
13 Shrewsbury	46	16	13	17	58	62	45
14 Brighton	46	14	16	16	50	47	44
15 Plymouth	46	12	19	15	63	63	43
16 Rochdale	46	14	15	17	61	68	43
17 Port Vale	46	15	12	19	52	59	42
18 Tranmere	46	10	22	14	45	55	42
19 Bradford City	46	13	14	19	49	62	40
20 Walsall	46	14	11	21	51	57	39
21 Reading	46	14	11	21	48	85	39
22 Bury	46	12	13	21	52	60	37
23 Doncaster	46	13	9	24	45	66	35
24 Gillingham	46	10	13	23	42	67	33

Fourth Division

	P	W	D	L	F	A	Pts
1 Notts County	46	30	9	7	89	36	69
2 Bournemouth	46	24	12	10	81	46	60
3 Oldham	46	24	11	11	88	63	59

	P	W	D	L	F	A	Pts
4 York	46	23	10	13	78	54	56
5 Chester	46	24	7	15	69	55	55
6 Colchester	46	21	12	13	70	54	54
7 Northampton	46	19	13	14	63	59	51
8 Southport	46	21	6	19	63	57	48
9 Exeter	46	17	14	15	67	68	48
10 Workington	46	18	12	16	48	49	48
11 Stockport	46	16	14	16	49	65	46
12 Darlington	46	17	11	18	58	57	45
13 Aldershot	46	14	17	15	66	71	45
14 Brentford	46	18	8	20	66	62	44
15 Crewe	46	18	8	20	75	76	44
16 Peterborough	46	18	7	21	70	71	43
17 Scunthorpe	46	15	13	18	56	61	43
18 Southend	46	14	15	17	53	66	43
19 Grimsby	46	18	7	21	57	71	43
20 Cambridge	46	15	13	18	51	66	43
21 Lincoln	46	13	13	20	70	71	39
22 Newport	46	10	8	28	55	85	28
23 Hartlepool	46	8	12	26	34	74	28
24 Barrow	46	7	8	31	51	90	22

Scottish First Division

	P	W	D	L	F	A	Pts
1 Celtic	34	25	6	3	89	23	56
2 Aberdeen	34	24	6	4	68	18	54
3 St Johnstone	34	19	6	9	59	44	44
4 Rangers	34	16	9	9	58	34	41
5 Dundee	34	14	10	10	53	45	38
6 Dundee United	34	14	8	12	53	54	36
7 Falkirk	34	13	9	12	46	53	35
8 Morton	34	13	8	13	44	44	34
9 Motherwell	34	13	8	13	43	47	34
10 Airdrieonians	34	13	8	13	60	65	34
11 Hearts	34	13	7	14	41	40	33
12 Hibernian	34	10	10	14	47	53	30
13 Kilmarnock	34	10	8	16	43	67	28
14 Ayr	34	9	8	17	37	54	26
15 Clyde	34	8	10	16	33	59	26
16 Dunfermline	34	6	11	17	44	56	23
17 St Mirren	43	7	9	18	38	56	23
18 Cowdenbeath	34	7	3	24	33	77	17

Scottish Second Division

	P	W	D	L	F	A	Pts
1 Partick	36	23	10	3	78	26	56
2 East Fife	36	22	7	7	86	44	51
3 Arbroath	36	19	8	9	80	52	46
4 Dumbarton	36	19	6	11	87	46	44
5 Clydebank	36	17	8	11	57	43	42

6 Montrose	36	17	7	12	78	64	41
7 Albion	36	15	9	12	53	52	39
8 Raith	36	15	9	12	62	62	39
9 Stranraer	36	14	8	14	54	52	36
10 Stenhousemuir	36	14	8	14	64	70	36
11 Queen of the S	36	13	9	14	50	56	35
12 Stirling	36	12	8	16	61	61	32
13 Berwick	36	10	10	16	42	60	30
14 Queen's Park	36	13	4	19	51	72	30
15 Forfar	36	9	11	16	63	75	29
16 Alloa	36	9	11	16	56	86	29
17 E Stirlingshire	36	9	9	18	57	86	27
18 Hamilton	36	8	7	21	50	79	23
19 Brechin	36	6	7	23	30	73	19

FA Cup

Fourth Round

Liverpool v Swansea City	3-0
York City v Southampton	3-3, 2-3
Carlisle United v Tottenham Hotspur	
	2-3
Nottingham Forest v Orient	1-1, 1-0
Everton v Middlesbrough	3-0
Derby County v Wolverhampton	
Wanderers	2-1
Rochdale v Colchester United	3-3, 0-5
Leeds United v Swindon Town	4-0
Hull City v Blackpool	2-0
Cardiff City v Brentford	0-2
Stoke City v Huddersfield Town	
	3-3, 0-0, 1-0
West Bromwich Albion v Ipswich Town	
	1-1, 0-3
Leicester City v Torquay United	3-0
Oxford United v Watford	1-1, 2-1
Chelsea v Manchester City	0-3
Portsmouth v Arsenal	1-1, 2-3

Fifth Round

Liverpool v Southampton	0-1
Tottenham Hotspur v Nottingham Forest	
	2-1
Everton v Derby County	1-0
Colchester United v Leeds United	3-2
Hull City v Brentford	2-1
Stoke City v Ipswich Town	0-0, 1-0
Leicester City v Oxford United	1-1, 3-1
Manchester City v Arsenal	1-2

Sixth Round

Liverpool v Tottenham Hotspur	0-0, 1-0
Everton v Colchester United	5-0

Hull City v Stoke City	2-3
Leicester City v Arsenal	0-0, 0-1

Semi-Final

Liverpool v Everton	2-1
Stoke City v Arsenal	2-2, 0-2

Third Place Play-off

Stoke City v Everton	3-2

Final

Liverpool v Arsenal	1-2

Scottish FA Cup

Third Round

Celtic v Queen of the South	5-1
Hibernian v Forfar Athletic	8-1
East Fife v St Mirren	1-1, 1-1, 1-3
St Johnstone v Raith Rovers	2-2, 3-4
Clyde v Brechin City	2-0
Airdrieonians v Alloa Athletic	1-1, 2-0
Rangers v Falkirk	3-0
Aberdeen v Elgin City	5-0
Dundee v Partick Thistle	1-0
Clachnacuddin v Cowdenbeath	0-3
Clydebank v Dundee United	0-0, 1-5
Stirling Albion v Motherwell	3-1
Dunfermline v Arbroath	3-1
Morton v Ayr United	2-0
Queen's Park v Kilmarnock	0-1
Heart of Midlothian v Stranraer	3-0

Fourth Round

Dundee United v Aberdeen	1-1, 0-2
Raith Rovers v Clyde	1-1, 2-0
Morton v Kilmarnock	1-2
Cowdenbeath v Airdrieonians	0-4
St Mirren v Rangers	1-3
Dundee v Stirling Albion	2-0
Celtic v Dunfermline	1-1, 1-0
Heart of Midlothian v Hibernian	1-2

Fifth Round

Rangers v Aberdeen	1-0
Hibernian v Dundee	1-0
Celtic v Raith Rovers	7-1
Kilmarnock v Airdrieonians	2-3

Semi-Final

Hibernian v Rangers	0-0, 1-2
Celtic v Airdrieonians	3-3, 2-0

Final

Rangers v Celtic	1-1, 1-2

1971–72
First Division

	P	W	D	L	F	A	Pts
1 Derby	42	24	10	8	69	33	58
2 Leeds	42	24	9	9	73	31	57
3 Liverpool	42	24	9	9	64	30	57
4 Man City	42	23	11	8	77	45	57
5 Arsenal	42	22	8	12	58	40	52
6 Tottenham	42	19	13	10	63	42	51
7 Chelsea	42	18	12	12	58	49	48
8 Man United	42	19	10	13	69	61	48
9 Wolves	42	18	11	13	65	57	47
10 Sheff United	42	17	12	13	61	60	46
11 Newcastle	42	15	11	16	49	52	41
12 Leicester	42	13	13	16	41	46	39
13 Ipswich	42	11	16	15	39	53	38
14 West Ham	42	12	12	18	47	51	36
15 Everton	42	9	18	15	37	48	36
16 WBA	42	12	11	19	42	54	35
17 Stoke	42	10	15	17	39	56	35
18 Coventry	42	9	15	18	44	67	33
19 Southampton	42	12	7	23	52	80	31
20 Crystal Palace	42	8	13	21	39	65	29
21 Nottm Forest	42	8	9	25	47	81	25
22 Huddersfield	42	6	13	23	27	59	25

Second Division

	P	W	D	L	F	A	Pts
1 Norwich	42	21	15	6	60	36	57
2 Birmingham	42	19	18	5	60	31	56
3 Millwall	42	19	17	6	64	46	55
4 QPR	42	20	14	8	57	28	54
5 Sunderland	42	17	16	9	67	57	50
6 Blackpool	42	20	7	15	70	50	47
7 Burnley	42	20	6	16	70	55	46
8 Bristol City	42	18	10	14	61	49	46
9 Middlesbrough	42	19	8	15	50	48	46
10 Carlisle	42	17	9	16	61	57	43
11 Swindon	42	15	12	15	47	47	42
12 Hull	42	14	10	18	49	53	38
13 Luton	42	10	18	14	43	48	38
14 Sheff Wed	42	13	12	17	51	58	38
15 Oxford	42	12	14	16	43	55	38
16 Portsmouth	42	12	13	17	59	68	37
17 Orient	42	14	9	19	50	61	37
18 Preston	42	12	12	18	52	58	36
19 Cardiff	42	10	14	18	56	69	34
20 Fulham	42	12	10	20	45	68	34
21 Charlton	42	12	9	21	55	77	33
22 Watford	42	5	9	28	24	75	19

Third Division

	P	W	D	L	F	A	Pts
1 Aston Villa	46	32	6	8	85	32	70
2 Brighton	46	27	11	8	82	47	65
3 Bournemouth	46	23	16	7	73	37	62
4 Notts County	46	25	12	9	74	44	62
5 Rotherham	46	20	15	11	69	52	55
6 Bristol Rovers	46	21	12	13	75	56	54
7 Bolton	46	17	16	13	51	41	50
8 Plymouth	46	20	10	16	74	64	50
9 Walsall	46	15	18	13	62	57	48
10 Blackburn	46	19	9	18	54	57	47
11 Oldham	46	17	11	18	59	63	45
12 Shrewsbury	46	17	10	19	73	65	44
13 Chesterfield	46	18	8	20	57	57	44
14 Swansea	46	17	10	19	46	59	44
15 Port Vale	46	13	15	18	43	59	41
16 Wrexham	46	16	8	22	59	63	40
17 Halifax	46	13	12	21	48	61	38
18 Rochdale	46	12	13	21	57	83	37
19 York	46	12	12	22	57	66	36
20 Tranmere	46	10	16	20	50	71	36
21 Mansfield	46	8	20	18	41	63	36
22 Barnsley	46	9	18	19	32	64	36
23 Torquay	46	10	12	24	41	69	32
24 Bradford City	46	11	10	25	45	77	32

Fourth Division

	P	W	D	L	F	A	Pts
1 Grimsby	46	28	7	11	88	56	63
2 Southend	46	24	12	10	81	55	60
3 Brentford	46	24	11	11	76	44	59
4 Scunthorpe	46	22	13	11	56	37	57
5 Lincoln	46	21	14	11	77	59	56
6 Workington	46	16	19	11	50	34	51
7 Southport	46	18	14	14	66	46	50
8 Peterborough	46	17	16	13	82	64	50
9 Bury	46	19	12	15	73	59	50
10 Cambridge	46	17	14	15	62	60	48
11 Colchester	46	19	10	17	70	69	48
12 Doncaster	46	16	14	16	56	63	46
13 Gillingham	46	16	13	17	61	67	45
14 Newport	46	18	8	20	60	72	44
15 Exeter	46	16	11	19	61	68	43
16 Reading	46	17	8	21	56	76	42
17 Aldershot	46	9	22	15	48	54	40
18 Hartlepool	46	17	6	23	58	69	40

19 Darlington	46	14	11	21	64	82	39
20 Chester	46	10	18	18	47	56	38
21 Northampton	46	12	13	21	66	79	37
22 Barrow	46	13	11	22	40	71	37
23 Stockport	46	9	14	23	55	87	32
24 Crewe	46	10	9	27	43	69	29

Scottish First Division

	P	W	D	L	F	A	Pts
1 Celtic	34	28	4	2	96	28	60
2 Aberdeen	34	21	8	5	80	26	50
3 Rangers	34	21	2	11	71	38	44
4 Hibernian	34	19	6	9	62	34	44
5 Dundee	34	14	13	7	59	38	41
6 Hearts	34	13	13	8	53	49	39
7 Partick	34	12	10	12	53	54	34
8 St Johnstone	34	12	8	14	52	58	32
9 Dundee United	34	12	7	15	55	70	31
10 Motherwell	34	11	7	16	49	69	29
11 Kilmarnock	34	11	6	17	49	64	28
12 Ayr	34	9	10	15	40	58	28
13 Morton	34	10	7	17	46	52	27
14 Falkirk	34	10	7	17	44	60	27
15 Airdrieonians	34	7	12	15	44	76	26
16 East Fife	34	5	15	14	34	61	25
17 Clyde	34	7	10	17	33	66	24
18 Dunfermline	34	7	9	18	31	50	23

Scottish Second Division

	P	W	D	L	F	A	Pts
1 Dumbarton	36	24	4	8	89	51	52
2 Arbroath	36	22	8	6	71	41	52
3 Stirling	36	21	8	7	75	37	50
4 St Mirren	36	24	2	10	84	47	50
5 Cowdenbeath	36	19	10	7	69	28	48
6 Stranraer	36	18	8	10	70	62	44
7 Queen of the S	36	17	9	10	56	38	43
8 E Stirlingshire	36	17	7	12	60	58	41
9 Clydebank	36	14	11	11	60	52	39
10 Montrose	36	15	6	15	73	54	36
11 Raith	36	13	8	15	56	56	34
12 Queen's Park	36	12	9	15	47	61	33
13 Berwick	36	14	4	18	53	50	32
14 Stenhousemuir	36	10	8	18	41	58	28
15 Brechin	36	8	7	21	41	79	23
16 Alloa	36	9	4	23	41	75	22
17 Forfar	36	6	9	21	32	84	21
18 Albion	36	7	6	23	36	61	20
19 Hamilton	36	4	8	24	31	93	16

FA Cup

Fourth Round

Liverpool v Leeds United	0-0, 0-2
Cardiff City v Sunderland	1-1, 1-1, 3-1
Everton v Walsall	2-1
Tottenham Hotspur v Rotherham United	2-0
Birmingham City v Ipswich Town	1-0
Portsmouth v Swansea City	2-0
Huddersfield Town v Fulham	3-0
Hereford United v West Ham United	0-0, 1-3
Preston North End v Manchester United	0-2
Millwall v Middlesbrough	2-2, 1-2
Tranmere Rovers v Stoke City	2-2, 0-2
Coventry City v Hull City	0-1
Leicester City v Orient	0-2
Chelsea v Bolton Wanderers	3-0
Derby County v Notts County	6-0
Reading v Arsenal	1-2

Fifth Round

Cardiff City v Leeds United	0-2
Everton v Tottenham Hotspur	0-2
Birmingham City v Portsmouth	3-1
Huddersfield Town v West Ham United	4-2
Manchester United v Middlesbrough	0-0, 3-0
Stoke City v Hull City	4-1
Orient v Chelsea	3-2
Derby County v Arsenal	2-2, 0-0, 0-1

Sixth Round

Leeds United v Tottenham Hotspur	2-1
Birmingham City v Huddersfield Town	3-1
Manchester United v Stoke City	1-1, 1-2
Orient v Arsenal	0-1

Semi-Final

Leeds United v Birmingham City	3-0
Arsenal v Stoke City	1-1, 2-1

Final

Leeds United v Arsenal	1-0

Scottish FA Cup

Third Round

Celtic v Albion Rovers	5-0
Dundee v Queen of the South	3-0

Heart of Midlothian v St Johnstone	2-0
Clydebank v East Fife	1-1, 1-0
Dumbarton v Hamilton Academicals	3-1
Raith Rovers v Dunfermline Athletic	2-0
Elgin City v Inverness Caledonian	3-1
Kilmarnock v Alloa Athletic	5-1
Clyde v Ayr United	0-1
Motherwell v Montrose	2-0
Forfar Athletic v St Mirren	0-1
Falkirk v Rangers	2-2, 0-2
Dundee United v Aberdeen	0-4
Morton v Cowdenbeath	1-0
Arbroath v Airdrieonians	1-3
Partick Thistle v Hibernian	0-2

Fourth Round

Celtic v Dundee	4-0
Heart of Midlothian v Clydebank	4-0
Dumbarton v Raith Rovers	0-3
Elgin City v Kilmarnock	1-4
Ayr United v Motherwell	0-0, 1-2
St Mirren v Rangers	1-4
Aberdeen v Morton	1-0
Hibernian v Airdrieonians	2-0

Fifth Round

Celtic v Heart of Midlothian	1-1, 1-0
Raith Rovers v Kilmarnock	1-3
Motherwell v Rangers	2-2, 2-4
Hibernian v Aberdeen	2-0

Semi-Final

Celtic v Kilmarnock	3-1
Rangers v Hibernian	1-1, 0-2

Final

Celtic v Hibernian	6-1

1972–73
First Division

	P	W	D	L	F	A	Pts
1 Liverpool	42	25	10	6	72	42	60
2 Arsenal	42	23	11	8	57	43	57
3 Leeds	42	21	11	10	71	45	53
4 Ipswich	42	17	14	11	55	45	48
5 Wolves	42	18	11	13	66	54	47
6 West Ham	42	17	12	13	67	53	46
7 Derby	42	19	8	15	56	54	46
8 Tottenham	42	16	13	13	58	48	45
9 Newcastle	42	16	13	13	60	51	45
10 Birmingham	42	15	12	15	53	54	42
11 Man City	42	15	11	16	57	60	41
12 Chelsea	42	13	14	15	49	51	40
13 Southampton	42	11	18	13	47	52	40
14 Sheff United	42	15	10	17	51	59	40
15 Stoke	42	14	10	18	61	56	38
16 Leicester	42	10	17	15	40	46	37
17 Everton	42	13	11	18	41	49	37
18 Man United	42	12	13	17	44	60	37
19 Coventry	42	13	9	20	40	55	35
20 Norwich	42	11	10	21	36	63	32
21 Crystal Palace	42	9	12	21	41	58	30
22 WBA	42	9	10	23	38	62	28

Second Division

	P	W	D	L	F	A	Pts
1 Burnley	42	24	14	4	72	35	62
2 QPR	42	24	13	5	81	37	61
3 Aston Villa	42	18	14	10	51	47	50
4 Middlesbrough	42	17	13	12	46	43	47
5 Bristol City	42	17	12	13	63	51	46
6 Sunderland	42	17	12	13	59	49	46
7 Blackpool	42	18	10	14	56	51	46
8 Oxford	42	19	7	16	52	43	45
9 Fulham	42	16	12	14	58	49	44
10 Sheff Wed	42	17	10	15	59	55	44
11 Millwall	42	16	10	16	55	47	42
12 Luton	42	15	11	16	44	53	41
13 Hull	42	14	12	16	64	59	40
14 Nottm Forest	42	14	12	16	47	52	40
15 Orient	42	12	12	18	49	53	36
16 Swindon	42	10	16	16	46	60	36
17 Portsmouth	42	12	11	19	42	59	35
18 Carlisle	42	11	12	19	50	52	34
19 Preston	42	11	12	19	37	64	34
20 Cardiff	42	11	11	20	43	58	33
21 Huddersfield	42	8	17	17	36	56	33
22 Brighton	42	8	13	21	46	83	29

Third Division

	P	W	D	L	F	A	Pts
1 Bolton	46	25	11	10	73	39	61
2 Notts County	46	23	11	12	67	47	57
3 Blackburn	46	20	15	11	57	47	55
4 Oldham	46	19	16	11	72	54	54
5 Bristol Rovers	46	20	13	13	77	56	53
6 Port Vale	46	21	11	14	56	69	53
7 Bournemouth	46	17	16	13	66	44	50
8 Plymouth	46	20	10	16	74	66	50
9 Grimsby	46	20	8	18	67	61	48
10 Tranmere	46	15	16	15	56	52	46

11 Charlton	46 17 11 18 69 67 45
12 Wrexham	46 14 17 15 55 54 45
13 Rochdale	46 14 17 15 48 54 45
14 Southend	46 17 10 19 61 54 44
15 Shrewsbury	46 15 14 17 46 54 44
16 Chesterfield	46 17 9 20 57 61 43
17 Walsall	46 18 7 21 56 66 43
18 York	46 13 15 18 42 46 41
19 Watford	46 12 17 17 43 48 41
20 Halifax	46 13 15 18 43 53 41
21 Rotherham	46 17 7 22 51 65 41
22 Brentford	46 15 7 24 51 69 37
23 Swansea	46 14 9 23 51 73 37
24 Scunthorpe	46 10 10 26 33 72 30

Fourth Division

	P	W	D	L	F	A	Pts
1 Southport	46	26	10	10	71	48	62
2 Hereford	46	23	12	11	56	38	58
3 Cambridge	46	20	17	9	67	57	57
4 Aldershot	46	22	12	12	60	38	56
5 Newport	46	22	12	12	64	44	56
6 Mansfield	46	20	14	12	78	51	54
7 Reading	46	17	18	11	51	38	52
8 Exeter	46	18	14	14	57	51	50
9 Gillingham	46	19	11	16	63	58	49
10 Lincoln	46	16	16	14	64	57	48
11 Stockport	46	18	12	16	53	53	48
12 Bury	46	14	18	14	58	51	46
13 Workington	46	17	12	17	59	61	46
14 Barnsley	46	14	16	16	58	60	44
15 Chester	46	14	15	17	61	52	43
16 Bradford City	46	16	11	19	61	65	43
17 Doncaster	46	15	12	19	49	58	42
18 Torquay	46	12	17	17	44	47	41
19 Peterborough	46	14	13	19	71	76	41
20 Hartlepool	46	12	17	17	34	49	41
21 Crewe	46	9	18	19	38	61	36
22 Colchester	46	10	11	25	48	76	31
23 Northampton	46	10	11	25	40	73	31
24 Darlington	46	7	15	24	42	85	29

Scottish First Division

	P	W	D	L	F	A	Pts
1 Celtic	34	26	5	3	93	28	57
2 Rangers	34	26	4	4	74	30	56
3 Hibernian	34	19	7	8	74	33	45
4 Aberdeen	34	16	11	7	61	34	43
5 Dundee	34	17	9	8	68	43	43
6 Ayr	34	16	8	10	50	51	40
7 Dundee United	34	17	5	12	56	51	39
8 Motherwell	34	11	9	14	38	48	31
9 East Fife	34	11	8	15	46	54	30
10 Hearts	34	12	6	16	39	50	30
11 St Johnstone	34	10	9	15	52	67	29
12 Morton	34	10	8	16	47	53	28
13 Partick	34	10	8	16	40	53	28
14 Falkirk	34	7	12	15	38	56	26
15 Arbroath	34	9	8	17	39	63	26
16 Dumbarton	34	6	11	17	43	72	23
17 Kilmarnock	34	7	8	19	40	71	22
18 Airdrieonians	34	4	8	22	34	75	16

Scottish Second Division

	P	W	D	L	F	A	Pts
1 Clyde	36	23	10	3	68	28	56
2 Dunfermline	36	23	6	7	95	32	52
3 Raith	36	19	9	8	73	42	47
4 Stirling	36	19	9	8	70	39	47
5 St Mirren	36	19	7	10	79	50	45
6 Montrose	36	18	8	10	82	58	44
7 Cowdenbeath	36	14	10	12	57	53	38
8 Hamilton	36	16	6	14	67	63	38
9 Berwick	36	16	5	15	45	54	37
10 Stenhousemuir	36	14	8	14	44	41	36
11 Queen of the S	36	13	8	15	45	52	34
12 Alloa	36	11	11	14	45	49	33
13 E Stirlingshire	36	12	8	16	52	69	32
14 Queen's Park	36	9	12	15	44	61	30
15 Stranraer	36	13	4	19	56	78	30
16 Forfar	36	10	9	17	38	66	29
17 Clydebank	36	9	6	21	48	72	24
18 Albion	36	5	8	23	35	83	18
19 Brechin	36	5	4	27	46	99	14

FA Cup

Fourth Round

Arsenal v Bradford City	2-0
Bolton Wanderers v Cardiff City	2-2, 1-1, 1-0
Carlisle United v Sheffield United	2-1
Chelsea v Ipswich Town	2-0
Coventry City v Grimsby Town	1-0
Derby County v Tottenham Hotspur	1-1, 5-3
Everton v Millwall	0-2
Hull City v West Ham United	1-0
Leeds United v Plymouth Argyle	2-1
Liverpool v Manchester City	0-0, 0-2
Newcastle United v Luton Town	0-2

Oxford United v Queen's Park Rangers
0-2
Sheffield Wednesday v Crystal Palace
1-1, 1-1, 3-2
Sunderland v Reading   1-1, 3-1
West Bromwich Albion v Swindon
Town   2-0
Wolverhampton Wanderers v Bristol City
1-0

Fifth Round

Bolton Wanderers v Luton Town   0-1
Carlisle United v Arsenal   1-2
Coventry City v Hull City   3-0
Derby County v Queen's Park Rangers 4-2
Leeds United v West Bromwich Albion
2-0
Manchester City v Sunderland   2-2, 1-3
Sheffield Wednesday v Chelsea   1-2
Wolverhampton Wanderers v Millwall
1-0

Sixth Round

Chelsea v Arsenal   2-2, 1-2
Derby County v Leeds United   0-1
Sunderland v Luton Town   2-0
Wolverhampton Wanderers v Coventry
City   2-0

Semi-Final

Arsenal v Sunderland   1-2
Leeds United v Wolverhampton
Wanderers   1-0

Final

Leeds United v Sunderland   0-1

Scottish FA Cup

Third Round

Ayr United v Inverness Thistle   3-0
Berwick Rovers v Falkirk   1-3
Brechin City v Aberdeen   2-4
Celtic v East Fife   4-1
Clyde v Montrose   1-1, 2-4
Dumbarton v Cowdenbeath   4-1
Dunfermline Athletic v Dundee   0-3
Elgin City v Hamilton Academicals 0-1
Heart of Midlothian v Airdrieonians
0-0, 1-3
Hibernian v Morton   2-0
Kilmarnock v Queen of the South 2-1
Motherwell v Raith Rovers   2-1

Rangers v Dundee United   1-0
St Mirren v Partick Thistle   0-1
Stirling Albion v Arbroath   3-3, 1-0
Stranraer v St Johnstone   1-1, 2-1

Fourth Round

Ayr United v Stirling Albion   2-1
Dumbarton v Partick Thistle   2-2, 1-3
Kilmarnock v Airdrieonians   0-1
Montrose v Hamilton Academicals
2-2, 1-0
Motherwell v Celtic   0-4
Rangers v Hibernian   1-1, 2-1
Stranraer v Dundee   2-9
Aberdeen v Falkirk   3-1

Fifth Round

Celtic v Aberdeen   0-0, 1-0
Montrose v Dundee   1-4
Partick Thistle v Ayr United   1-5
Rangers v Airdrieonians   2-0

Semi-Final

Ayr United v Rangers   0-2
Celtic v Dundee   0-0, 3-0

Final

Celtic v Rangers   2-3

1973–74
First Division

	P	W	D	L	F	A	Pts
1 Leeds	42	24	14	4	66	31	62
2 Liverpool	42	22	13	7	52	31	57
3 Derby	42	17	14	11	52	42	48
4 Ipswich	42	18	11	13	67	58	47
5 Stoke	42	15	16	11	54	42	46
6 Burnley	42	16	14	12	56	53	46
7 Everton	42	16	12	14	50	48	44
8 QPR	42	13	17	12	56	52	43
9 Leicester	42	13	16	13	51	41	42
10 Arsenal	42	14	14	14	49	51	42
11 Tottenham	42	14	14	14	45	50	42
12 Wolves	42	13	15	14	49	49	41
13 Sheff United	42	14	12	16	44	49	40
14 Man City	42	14	12	16	39	46	40
15 Newcastle	42	13	12	17	49	48	38
16 Coventry	42	14	10	18	43	54	38
17 Chelsea	42	12	13	17	56	60	37
18 West Ham	42	11	15	16	55	60	37

	P	W	D	L	F	A	Pts
19 Birmingham	42	12	13	17	52	64	37
20 Southampton	42	11	14	17	47	68	36
21 Man United	42	10	12	20	38	48	32
22 Norwich	42	7	15	20	37	62	29

Second Division

	P	W	D	L	F	A	Pts
1 Middlesbrough	42	27	11	4	77	30	65
2 Luton	42	19	12	11	64	51	50
3 Carlisle	42	20	9	13	61	48	49
4 Orient	42	15	18	9	55	42	48
5 Blackpool	42	17	13	12	57	40	47
6 Sunderland	42	19	9	14	58	44	47
7 Nottm Forest	42	15	15	12	57	43	45
8 WBA	42	14	16	12	48	45	44
9 Hull	42	13	17	12	46	47	43
10 Notts County	42	15	13	14	55	60	43
11 Bolton	42	15	12	15	44	40	42
12 Millwall	42	14	14	14	51	51	42
13 Fulham	42	16	10	16	39	43	42
14 Aston Villa	42	13	15	14	48	45	41
15 Portsmouth	42	14	12	16	45	62	40
16 Bristol City	42	14	10	18	47	54	38
17 Cardiff	42	10	16	16	49	62	36
18 Oxford	42	10	16	16	35	46	36
19 Sheff Wed	42	12	11	19	51	63	35
20 Crystal Palace	42	11	12	19	43	56	34
21 Preston*	42	9	14	19	40	62	31
22 Swindon	42	7	11	24	36	72	25

*Preston had one point deducted for fielding an ineligible player

Third Division

	P	W	D	L	F	A	Pts
1 Oldham	46	25	12	9	83	47	62
2 Bristol Rovers	46	22	17	7	65	33	61
3 York	46	21	19	6	67	38	61
4 Wrexham	46	22	12	12	63	43	56
5 Chesterfield	46	21	14	11	55	42	56
6 Grimsby	46	18	15	13	67	50	51
7 Watford	46	19	12	15	64	56	50
8 Aldershot	46	19	11	16	65	52	49
9 Halifax	46	14	21	11	48	51	49
10 Huddersfield	46	17	13	16	56	55	47
11 Bournemouth	46	16	15	15	54	58	47
12 Southend	46	16	14	16	62	62	46
13 Blackburn	46	18	10	18	62	64	46
14 Charlton	46	19	8	19	66	73	46
15 Walsall	46	16	13	17	57	48	45
16 Tranmere	46	15	15	16	50	44	45

	P	W	D	L	F	A	Pts
17 Plymouth	46	17	10	19	59	54	44
18 Hereford	46	14	15	17	53	57	43
19 Brighton	46	16	11	19	52	58	43
20 Port Vale	46	14	14	18	52	58	42
21 Cambridge	46	13	9	24	48	81	35
22 Shrewsbury	46	10	11	25	41	62	31
23 Southport	46	6	16	24	35	82	28
24 Rochdale	46	2	17	27	38	94	21

Fourth Division

	P	W	D	L	F	A	Pts
1 Peterborough	46	27	11	8	75	38	65
2 Gillingham	46	25	12	9	90	49	62
3 Colchester	46	24	12	10	73	36	60
4 Bury	46	24	11	11	81	49	59
5 Northampton	46	20	13	13	63	48	53
6 Reading	46	16	19	11	58	37	51
7 Chester	46	17	15	14	54	55	49
8 Bradford City	46	17	14	15	58	52	48
9 Newport*	46	16	14	16	56	65	45
10 Exeter	45	18	8	19	58	55	44
11 Hartlepool	46	16	12	18	48	47	44
12 Lincoln	46	16	12	18	63	67	44
13 Barnsley	46	17	10	19	58	64	44
14 Swansea	46	16	11	19	45	46	43
15 Rotherham	46	15	13	18	56	58	43
16 Torquay	46	13	17	16	52	57	43
17 Mansfield	46	13	17	16	62	69	43
18 Scunthorpe	45	14	12	19	47	64	42
19 Brentford	46	12	16	18	48	50	40
20 Darlington	46	13	13	20	40	62	39
21 Crewe	46	14	10	22	43	71	38
22 Doncaster	46	12	11	23	47	80	35
23 Workington	46	11	13	22	43	74	35
24 Stockport	46	7	20	19	44	69	34

*Newport had one point deducted for fielding an ineligible player

Scottish First Division

	P	W	D	L	F	A	Pts
1 Celtic	34	23	7	4	82	27	53
2 Hibernian	34	20	9	5	75	42	49
3 Rangers	34	21	6	7	67	34	48
4 Aberdeen	34	13	16	5	46	26	42
5 Dundee	34	16	7	11	67	48	39
6 Hearts	34	14	10	10	54	43	38
7 Ayr	34	15	8	11	44	40	38
8 Dundee United	34	15	7	12	55	51	37
9 Motherwell	34	14	7	13	45	40	35
10 Dumbarton	34	11	7	16	43	58	29

11 Partick	34	9	10	15	33	46	28
12 St Johnstone	34	9	10	15	41	60	28
13 Arbroath	34	10	7	17	52	69	27
14 Morton	34	8	10	16	37	49	26
15 Clyde	34	8	9	17	29	65	25
16 Dunfermline	34	8	8	18	43	65	24
17 East Fife	34	9	6	19	26	51	24
18 Falkirk	34	4	14	16	33	58	22

Scottish Second Division

	P	W	D	L	F	A	Pts
1 Airdrieonians	36	28	4	4	102	25	60
2 Kilmarnock	36	26	6	4	96	44	58
3 Hamilton	36	24	7	5	68	38	55
4 Queen of the S	36	20	7	9	73	41	47
5 Raith	36	18	9	9	69	48	45
6 Berwick	36	16	13	7	53	35	45
7 Stirling	36	17	6	13	76	50	40
8 Montrose	36	15	7	14	71	64	37
9 Stranraer	36	14	8	14	64	70	36
10 Clydebank	36	13	8	15	47	48	34
11 St Mirren	36	12	10	14	62	66	34
12 Alloa	36	15	4	17	47	58	34
13 Cowdenbeath	36	11	9	16	59	85	31
14 Queen's Park	36	12	4	20	42	64	28
15 Stenhousemuir	36	11	5	20	44	59	27
16 E Stirlingshire	36	9	5	22	47	73	23
17 Albion	36	7	6	23	38	72	20
18 Forfar	36	5	6	25	42	94	16
19 Brechin	36	5	4	27	33	99	14

FA Cup

Fourth Round

Arsenal v Aston Villa	1-1, 0-2
Coventry City v Derby County	0-0, 1-0
Everton v West Bromwich Albion	
	0-0, 0-1
Fulham v Leicester City	1-1, 1-2
Hereford United v Bristol City	0-1
Liverpool v Carlisle United	0-0, 2-0
Luton Town v Bradford City	3-0
Manchester United v Ipswich Town	0-1
Newcastle United v Scunthorpe United	
	1-1, 3-0
Nottingham Forest v Manchester City	4-1
Oldham Athletic v Burnley	1-4
Peterborough United v Leeds United	1-4
Portsmouth v Orient	0-0, 1-1, 2-0
Queen's Park Rangers v Birmingham City	
	2-0

Southampton v Bolton Wanderers	
	3-3, 2-0
Wrexham v Middlesbrough	1-0

Fifth Round

Bristol City v Leeds United	1-1, 1-0
Burnley v Aston Villa	1-0
Coventry City v Queen's Park Rangers	
	0-0, 2-3
Liverpool v Ipswich Town	2-0
Luton Town v Leicester City	0-4
Nottingham Forest v Portsmouth	1-0
Southampton v Wrexham	0-1
West Bromwich Albion v Newcastle United	
	0-3

Sixth Round

Bristol City v Liverpool	0-1
Burnley v Wrexham	1-0
Newcastle United v Nottingham Forest	
	4-3*, 0-0, 1-0
Queen's Park Rangers v Leicester City	0-2

*FA ordered replay because of crowd invasion. Second and third games both played at Goodison Park

Semi-Final

Burnley v Newcastle United	0-2
Leicester City v Liverpool	0-0, 1-3

Final

Liverpool v Newcastle United	3-0

Scottish FA Cup

Third Round

Aberdeen v Dundee	0-2
Arbroath v Dumbarton	1-0
Celtic v Clydebank	6-1
Cowdenbeath v Ayr United	0-5
Dundee United v Airdrieonians	4-1
Falkirk v Dunfermline Athletic	2-2, 0-1
Forfar Athletic v St Johnstone	1-6
Heart of Midlothian v Clyde	3-1
Hibernian v Kilmarnock	5-2
Montrose v Stirling Albion	1-1, 1-3
Motherwell v Brechin City	2-0
Partick Thistle v Ferranti Thistle	6-1
Queen of the South v East Fife	1-0
Raith Rovers v Morton	2-2, 0-0, 0-1
Rangers v Queen's Park	8-0
Stranraer v St Mirren	1-1, 1-1, 3-2

Fourth Round

Arbroath v Motherwell	1-3

Celtic v Stirling Albion   6-1
Dundee United v Morton   1-0
Dunfermline Athletic v Queen of the
    South   1-0
Heart of Midlothian v Partick Thistle
                                        1-1, 4-1
Rangers v Dundee   0-3
St Johnstone v Hibernian   1-3
Stranraer v Ayr United   1-7

Fifth Round

Celtic v Motherwell   2-2, 1-0
Dunfermline Athletic v Dundee United
                                        1-1, 0-4
Heart of Midlothian v Ayr United
                                        1-1, 2-1
Hibernian v Dundee   3-3, 0-3

Semi-Final

Celtic v Dundee   1-0
Heart of Midlothian v Dundee United
                                        1-1, 2-4

Final

Celtic v Dundee United   3-0

1974–75
First Division

	P	W	D	L	F	A	Pts
1 Derby	42	21	11	10	67	49	53
2 Liverpool	42	20	11	11	60	39	51
3 Ipswich	42	23	5	14	66	44	51
4 Everton	42	16	18	8	56	42	50
5 Stoke	42	17	15	10	64	48	49
6 Sheff United	42	18	13	11	58	51	49
7 Middlesbrough	42	18	12	12	54	40	48
8 Man City	42	18	10	14	54	54	46
9 Leeds	42	16	13	13	57	49	45
10 Burnley	42	17	11	14	68	67	45
11 QPR	42	16	10	16	54	54	42
12 Wolves	42	14	11	17	57	54	39
13 West Ham	42	13	13	16	58	59	39
14 Coventry	42	12	15	15	51	62	39
15 Newcastle	42	15	9	18	59	72	39
16 Arsenal	42	13	11	18	47	49	37
17 Birmingham	42	14	9	19	53	61	37
18 Leicester	42	12	12	18	46	60	36
19 Tottenham	42	13	8	21	52	63	34
20 Luton	42	11	11	20	47	65	33
21 Chelsea	42	9	15	18	42	72	33

22 Carlisle	42	12	5	25	43	59	29

Second Division

	P	W	D	L	F	A	Pts
1 Man United	42	26	9	7	66	30	61
2 Aston Villa	42	25	8	9	69	32	58
3 Norwich	42	20	13	9	58	37	53
4 Sunderland	42	19	13	10	65	35	51
5 Bristol City	42	21	8	13	47	33	50
6 WBA	42	18	9	15	54	42	45
7 Blackpool	42	14	17	11	38	33	45
8 Hull	42	15	14	13	40	53	44
9 Fulham	42	13	16	13	44	39	42
10 Bolton	42	15	12	15	45	41	42
11 Oxford	42	15	12	15	41	51	42
12 Orient	42	11	20	11	28	39	42
13 Southampton	42	15	11	16	53	54	41
14 Notts County	42	12	16	14	49	59	40
15 York	42	14	10	18	51	55	38
16 Nottm Forest	42	12	14	16	43	55	38
17 Portsmouth	42	12	13	17	44	54	37
18 Oldham	42	10	15	17	40	48	35
19 Bristol Rovers	42	12	11	19	42	64	35
20 Millwall	42	10	12	20	44	56	32
21 Cardiff	42	9	14	19	36	62	32
22 Sheff Wed	42	5	11	26	29	64	21

Third Division

	P	W	D	L	F	A	Pts
1 Blackburn	46	22	16	8	68	45	60
2 Plymouth	46	24	11	11	79	58	59
3 Charlton	46	22	11	13	76	61	55
4 Swindon	46	21	11	14	64	58	53
5 Crystal Palace	46	18	15	13	66	57	51
6 Port Vale	46	18	15	13	61	54	51
7 Peterborough	46	19	12	15	47	53	50
8 Walsall	46	18	13	15	67	52	49
9 Preston	46	19	11	16	63	56	49
10 Gillingham	46	17	14	15	65	60	48
11 Colchester	46	17	13	16	70	63	47
12 Hereford	46	16	14	16	64	66	46
13 Wrexham	46	15	15	16	65	55	45
14 Bury	46	16	12	18	53	50	44
15 Chesterfield	46	16	12	18	62	66	44
16 Grimsby	46	15	13	18	55	64	43
17 Halifax	46	13	17	16	49	65	43
18 Southend	46	13	16	17	46	51	42
19 Brighton	46	16	10	20	56	64	42
20 Aldershot	46	14	11	21	53	63	38
21 Bournemouth	46	13	12	21	44	58	38
22 Tranmere	46	14	9	23	55	57	37

	P	W	D	L	F	A	Pts
23 Watford	46	10	17	19	52	75	37
24 Huddersfield	46	11	10	25	47	76	32

Fourth Division

	P	W	D	L	F	A	Pts
1 Mansfield	46	26	12	6	90	40	68
2 Shrewsbury	46	28	10	10	80	43	62
3 Rotherham	46	22	15	9	71	41	59
4 Chester	46	23	11	12	64	38	57
5 Lincoln	46	21	15	10	79	48	57
6 Cambridge	46	20	14	12	62	42	54
7 Reading	46	21	10	15	63	47	52
8 Brentford	46	18	13	15	53	45	49
9 Exeter	46	19	11	16	60	63	49
10 Bradford City	46	17	13	16	56	51	47
11 Southport	46	15	17	14	56	56	47
12 Newport	46	19	9	18	68	75	47
13 Hartlepool	46	16	11	19	52	62	43
14 Torquay	46	14	14	18	46	61	42
15 Barnsley	46	15	11	20	62	65	41
16 Northampton	46	15	11	20	67	73	41
17 Doncaster	46	14	12	20	65	79	40
18 Crewe	46	11	18	17	34	47	40
19 Rochdale	46	13	13	20	59	75	39
20 Stockport	46	12	14	20	43	70	38
21 Darlington	46	13	10	23	54	67	36
22 Swansea	46	15	6	25	46	73	36
23 Workington	46	10	11	25	36	66	31
24 Scunthorpe	46	7	15	24	41	78	29

Scottish First Division

	P	W	D	L	F	A	Pts
1 Rangers	34	25	6	3	86	33	56
2 Hibernian	34	20	9	5	69	37	49
3 Celtic	34	20	5	9	81	41	45
4 Dundee United	34	19	7	8	72	43	45
5 Aberdeen	34	16	9	9	66	43	41
6 Dundee	34	16	6	12	48	42	38
7 Ayr	34	14	8	11	50	61	36
8 Hearts	34	11	13	10	47	52	35
9 St Johnstone	34	11	12	11	41	44	34
10 Motherwell	34	14	5	15	52	57	33
11 Airdrieonians	34	11	9	14	43	55	31
12 Kilmarnock	34	8	15	11	52	68	31
13 Partick	34	10	10	14	48	62	30
14 Dumbarton	34	7	10	17	44	55	24
15 Dunfermline	34	7	9	18	46	66	23
16 Clyde	34	6	10	18	40	63	22
17 Morton	34	6	10	18	31	62	22
18 Arbroath	34	5	7	22	34	66	17

Scottish Second Division

	P	W	D	L	F	A	Pts
1 Falkirk	38	26	2	10	76	29	54
2 Queen of the S	38	23	7	8	77	33	53
3 Montrose	38	23	7	8	70	37	53
4 Hamilton	38	21	7	10	69	30	49
5 East Fife	38	20	7	11	57	42	47
6 St Mirren	38	19	8	11	74	52	46
7 Clydebank	38	18	8	12	50	40	44
8 Stirling	38	17	9	12	67	55	43
9 E Stirlingshire	38	16	8	14	56	52	40
10 Berwick	38	17	6	15	53	49	40
11 Stenhousemuir	38	14	11	13	52	42	39
12 Albion	38	16	7	15	72	64	39
13 Raith	38	14	9	15	48	44	37
14 Stranraer	38	12	11	15	47	65	35
15 Alloa	38	11	11	16	49	56	33
16 Queen's Park	38	10	10	18	41	54	30
17 Brechin	38	9	7	22	44	85	25
18 Meadowbank	38	9	5	24	26	89	23
19 Cowdenbeath	38	5	11	22	39	76	21
20 Forfar	38	1	7	30	27	102	9

FA Cup

Fourth Round

Aston Villa v Sheffield United	4-1
Bury v Mansfield Town	1-2
Carlisle United v West Bromwich Albion	3-2
Chelsea v Birmingham City	0-1
Coventry City v Arsenal	1-1, 0-3
Derby County v Bristol City	2-0
Fulham v Nottingham Forest	0-0, 1-1, 1-1, 2-1
Ipswich Town v Liverpool	1-0
Leatherhead v Leicester City	2-3
Leeds United v Wimbledon	0-0, 1-0
Middlesbrough v Sunderland	3-1
Plymouth Argyle v Everton	1-3
Queen's Park Rangers v Nottingham County	3-0
Stafford v Peterborough United	1-2
Walsall v Newcastle United	1-0
West Ham United v Swindon Town	1-1, 2-1

Fifth Round

Arsenal v Leicester City	0-0, 1-1, 1-0
Birmingham City v Walsall	2-1
Derby County v Leeds United	0-1
Everton v Fulham	1-2

Ispwich Town v Aston Villa   3-2
Mansfield Town v Carlisle United   0-1
Peterborough United v Middlesbrough
                              1-1, 0-2
West Ham United v Queen's Park Rangers
                                   2-1

Sixth Round
Arsenal v West Ham United   0-2
Birmingham City v Middlesbrough   1-0
Carlisle United v Fulham   0-1
Ipswich Town v Leeds United
                   0-0, 1-1, 0-0, 3-2

Semi-Final
Fulham v Birmingham City   1-1, 1-0
West Ham United v Ipswich Town
                              0-0, 2-1

Final
West Ham United v Fulham   2-0

Scottish FA Cup

Third Round
Aberdeen v Rangers   1-1, 2-1
Arbroath v East Stirlingshire   1-0
Ayr United v Queen's Park   1-2
Clyde v Dundee   0-1
Hibernian v Celtic   0-2
Inverness Caledonian v Albion Rovers 0-1
Motherwell v Partick   0-0, 1-0
Queen of the South v Raith Rovers   2-0
Montrose v Hamilton Academicals
                              0-0, 0-3
Airdrieonians v Morton   0-0, 3-0
Clydebank v Dunfermline Athletic   2-1
Dumbarton v Clachnacuddin   2-1
Hearts v Kilmarnock   2-0
St Johnstone v East Fife   1-0
Ross County v Falkirk   1-5
Dundee United v Berwick Rovers
                              1-1, 1-0

Fourth Round
Airdrieonians v Falkirk   2-0
Arbroath v Albion Rovers   2-0
Celtic v Clydebank   4-1
Hamilton Academicals v Dumbarton   0-1
Motherwell v Queen's Park   4-0
Queen of the South v Hearts   0-2
St Johnstone v Dundee   0-1
Dundee United v Aberdeen   0-1

Fifth Round
Aberdeen v Motherwell   0-1
Arbroath v Airdrieonians   2-2, 0-3
Dumbarton v Celtic   1-2
Hearts v Dundee   1-1, 2-3

Semi-Final
Celtic v Dundee   1-0
Airdrieonians v Motherwell   1-1, 1-0

Final
Airdrieonians v Celtic   1-3

1975–76
First Division

	P	W	D	L	F	A	Pts
1 Liverpool	42	23	14	5	66	31	60
2 QPR	42	24	11	7	67	33	59
3 Man United	42	23	10	9	68	42	56
4 Derby	42	21	11	10	75	58	53
5 Leeds	42	21	9	12	65	46	51
6 Ipswich	42	16	14	12	54	48	46
7 Leicester	42	13	19	10	48	41	45
8 Man City	42	16	11	15	64	46	43
9 Tottenham	42	14	15	13	63	63	43
10 Norwich	42	16	10	16	58	58	42
11 Everton	42	15	12	15	60	66	42
12 Stoke	42	15	11	16	48	50	41
13 Middlesbrough	42	15	10	17	46	45	40
14 Coventry	42	13	14	15	47	57	40
15 Newcastle	42	15	9	18	71	62	39
16 Aston Villa	42	11	17	14	51	59	39
17 Arsenal	42	13	10	19	47	53	36
18 West Ham	42	13	10	19	48	71	36
19 Birmingham	42	13	7	22	57	75	33
20 Wolves	42	10	10	22	51	68	30
21 Burnley	42	9	10	23	43	66	28
22 Sheff United	42	6	10	26	33	82	22

Second Division

	P	W	D	L	F	A	Pts
1 Sunderland	42	24	8	10	67	36	56
2 Bristol City	42	19	15	8	60	35	53
3 WBA	42	20	13	9	50	33	53
4 Bolton	42	20	12	10	64	38	52
5 Notts County	42	19	11	12	60	41	49
6 Southampton	42	21	7	14	66	50	49
7 Luton	42	10	10	13	61	51	48

	P	W	D	L	F	A	Pts
8 Nottm Forest	42	17	12	13	55	40	46
9 Charlton	42	15	8	15	61	72	42
10 Blackpool	42	14	14	14	40	49	42
11 Chelsea	42	12	16	14	53	54	40
12 Fulham	42	13	14	15	45	47	40
13 Orient	42	13	14	15	37	39	40
14 Hull	42	14	11	17	45	49	39
15 Blackburn	42	12	14	16	45	50	38
16 Plymouth	42	13	12	17	48	54	38
17 Oldham	42	13	12	17	57	68	38
18 Bristol Rovers	42	11	16	15	38	50	38
19 Carlisle	42	12	13	17	45	59	37
20 Oxford	42	11	11	20	39	59	33
21 York	42	10	8	24	39	71	28
22 Portsmouth	42	9	7	26	33	61	25

Third Division

	P	W	D	L	F	A	Pts
1 Hereford	46	26	11	9	86	55	63
2 Cardiff	46	22	13	11	69	48	57
3 Millwall	46	20	16	10	54	43	56
4 Brighton	46	22	9	15	78	53	53
5 Crystal Palace	46	18	17	11	61	46	53
6 Wrexham	46	20	12	14	66	55	52
7 Walsall	46	18	14	14	74	61	50
8 Preston	46	19	10	17	62	57	48
9 Shrewsbury	46	19	10	17	61	59	48
10 Peterborough	46	15	18	13	63	63	48
11 Mansfield	46	16	15	15	58	52	47
12 Port Vale	46	15	16	15	55	54	46
13 Bury	46	14	16	16	51	46	44
14 Gillingham	46	12	19	15	58	68	43
15 Chesterfield	46	17	9	20	69	69	43
16 Rotherham	46	15	12	19	54	65	42
17 Chester	46	15	12	19	43	62	42
18 Grimsby	46	15	10	21	62	74	40
19 Swindon	46	16	8	22	62	75	40
20 Sheff Wed	46	12	16	18	48	59	40
21 Aldershot	46	13	13	20	59	75	39
22 Colchester	46	12	14	20	41	65	38
23 Southend	46	15	13	21	65	75	37
24 Halifax	46	11	13	22	41	61	35

Fourth Division

	P	W	D	L	F	A	Pts
1 Lincoln	46	33	10	3	111	39	74
2 Northampton	46	29	10	7	87	40	68
3 Reading	46	24	12	10	70	51	60
4 Tranmere	46	24	10	12	89	55	58
5 Huddersfield	46	21	14	11	56	41	56
6 Bournemouth	46	20	12	14	57	48	52
7 Exeter	46	18	14	14	56	47	50
8 Watford	46	22	6	18	62	62	50
9 Torquay	46	18	14	14	55	63	50
10 Doncaster	46	19	11	16	75	69	49
11 Swansea	46	16	15	15	66	57	47
12 Barnsley	46	14	16	16	52	48	44
13 Cambridge	46	14	15	17	58	62	43
14 Hartlepool	46	16	10	20	62	78	42
15 Rochdale	46	12	18	16	40	54	42
16 Crewe	46	13	15	18	58	57	41
17 Bradford City	46	12	17	17	63	65	41
18 Brentford	46	14	15	19	56	60	41
19 Scunthorpe	46	14	10	22	50	59	38
20 Darlington	46	14	10	22	48	57	38
21 Stockport	46	13	12	21	43	76	38
22 Newport	46	13	9	24	57	90	35
23 Southport	46	8	10	28	41	77	26
24 Workington	46	7	7	32	30	87	21

Scottish Premier Division

	P	W	D	L	F	A	Pts
1 Rangers	36	23	8	5	59	24	54
2 Celtic	36	21	6	9	71	42	48
3 Hibernian	36	20	7	9	58	40	43
4 Motherwell	36	16	8	12	57	49	40
5 Hearts	36	13	9	14	39	44	35
6 Ayr	36	14	5	17	46	59	33
7 Aberdeen	36	11	10	15	49	50	32
8 Dundee United	36	12	8	16	46	48	32
9 Dundee	36	11	10	15	49	62	32
10 St Johnstone	36	3	5	28	29	79	11

Scottish First Division

	P	W	D	L	F	A	Pts
1 Partick	26	17	7	2	47	19	41
2 Kilmarnock	26	16	3	7	44	29	35
3 Montrose	26	12	6	8	53	43	30
4 Dumbarton	26	12	4	10	53	46	28
5 Arbroath	26	11	4	11	41	39	26
6 St Mirren	26	9	8	9	37	37	26
7 Airdrieonians	26	7	11	8	44	41	25
8 Falkirk	26	10	5	11	38	35	25
9 Hamilton	26	7	10	9	37	37	24
10 Queen of the S	36	9	6	11	41	47	24
11 Morton	26	7	9	10	31	40	23
12 East Fife	26	8	7	11	39	53	23
13 Dunfermline	26	5	10	11	30	51	20
14 Clyde	26	5	4	17	34	52	14

Scottish Second Division

	P	W	D	L	F	A	Pts
1 Clydebank	26	17	6	3	44	13	40
2 Raith	26	15	10	1	45	22	40
3 Alloa	26	14	7	5	44	28	35
4 Queen's Park	26	10	9	7	41	33	29
5 Cowdenbeath	26	11	7	8	44	43	29
6 Stirling	26	9	7	10	39	32	25
7 Stranraer	26	11	3	12	49	43	25
8 E Stirlingshire	26	8	8	10	33	33	24
9 Albion	26	7	10	9	35	38	24
10 Stenhousemuir	26	9	5	12	39	44	23
11 Berwick	26	7	5	14	32	44	19
12 Forfar	26	4	10	12	28	38	18
13 Brechin	26	6	5	15	28	51	17
14 Meadowbank	26	5	6	15	24	53	16

FA Cup

Fourth Round

Bradford City v Tooting & Mitcham United	3-1
Charlton Athletic v Portsmouth	1-1, 3-0
Coventry City v Newcastle United	1-1, 0-5
Derby County v Liverpool	1-0
Huddersfield Town v Bolton Wanderers	0-1
Ispwich Town v Wolverhampton Wanderers	0-0, 0-1
Leeds United v Crystal Palace	0-1
Leicester City v Bury	1-0
Manchester United v Peterborough United	3-1
Norwich City v Luton Town	2-0
Southampton v Blackpool	3-1
Southend United v Cardiff City	2-1
Stoke City v Manchester City	1-0
Sunderland v Hull City	1-0
West Bromwich Albion v Lincoln City	3-2
York City v Chelsea	0-2

Fifth Round

Bolton Wanderers v Newcastle United	3-3, 0-0, 1-2
Chelsea v Crystal Palace	2-3
Derby County v Southend United	1-0
Leicester City v Manchester United	1-2
Norwich City v Bradford City	1-2
Stoke City v Sunderland	0-0, 1-2

West Bromwich Albion v Southampton	1-1, 0-4
Wolverhampton Wanderers v Charlton Athletic	3-0

Sixth Round

Bradford City v Southampton	0-1
Derby County v Newcastle United	4-2
Manchester United v Wolverhampton Wanderers	1-1, 3-2
Sunderland v Crystal Palace	0-1

Semi-Final

Manchester United v Derby County	2-0
Southampton v Crystal Palace	2-0

Final

Southampton v Manchester United	1-0

Scottish FA Cup

Third Round

Albion Rovers v Partick Thistle	1-2
Alloa v Aberdeen	0-4
Ayr United v Airdrieonians	4-2
Cowdenbeath v St Mirren	3-0
Dumbarton v Keith	2-0
Dundee v Falkirk	1-2
Dundee United v Hamilton Academicals	4-0
Hearts v Clyde	2-2, 1-0
Hibernian v Dunfermline Athletic	3-2
Motherwell v Celtic	3-2
Morton v Montrose	1-3
Queen of the South v St Johnstone	3-2
Raith Rovers v Arbroath	1-0
Rangers v East Fife	3-0
Stenhousemuir v Kilmarnock	1-1, 0-1
Stirling Albion v Forfar Athletic	2-1

Fourth Round

Ayr United v Queen of the South	2-2, 4-5
Cowdenbeath v Motherwell	0-2
Hearts v Stirling Albion	3-0
Hibernian v Dundee United	1-1, 2-0
Kilmarnock v Falkirk	3-1
Montrose v Raith Rovers	2-1
Partick Thistle v Dumbarton	0-0, 0-1
Rangers v Aberdeen	4-1

Fifth Round

Dumbarton v Kilmarnock	2-1
Montrose v Hearts	2-2, 2-2, 1-2

Motherwell v Hibernian   2-2, 1-1, 2-1
Queen of the South v Rangers   0-1

Semi-Final
Motherwell v Rangers   2-3
Dumbarton v Hearts   0-0, 0-3

Final
Hearts v Rangers   1-3

1976–77
First Division

	P	W	D	L	F	A	Pts
1 Liverpool	42	23	11	8	62	33	57
2 Man City	42	21	14	7	60	34	56
3 Ipswich	42	22	8	12	66	39	52
4 Aston Villa	42	22	7	13	76	50	51
5 Newcastle	42	18	13	11	64	49	49
6 Man United	42	18	11	13	71	62	47
7 WBA	42	16	13	13	62	56	45
8 Arsenal	42	16	11	15	64	59	43
9 Everton	42	14	14	14	62	64	42
10 Leeds	42	15	12	15	48	51	42
11 Leicester	42	12	18	12	47	60	42
12 Middlesbrough	42	14	13	15	40	45	41
13 Birmingham	42	13	12	17	63	61	38
14 QPR	42	13	12	17	47	52	38
15 Derby	42	9	19	14	50	55	37
16 Norwich	42	14	9	19	47	64	37
17 West Ham	42	11	14	17	46	65	36
18 Bristol	42	11	13	18	38	48	35
19 Coventry	42	10	15	17	48	59	35
20 Sunderland	42	11	12	19	46	54	34
21 Stoke	42	10	14	18	28	51	34
22 Tottenham	42	12	9	21	48	72	33

Second Division

	P	W	D	L	F	A	Pts
1 Wolves	42	22	13	7	84	45	57
2 Chelsea	42	21	14	7	73	53	55
3 Notts Forest	42	21	10	11	77	43	52
4 Bolton	42	20	11	11	75	54	51
5 Blackpool	42	17	17	8	58	42	51
6 Luton	42	21	6	15	67	48	48
7 Charlton	42	16	16	10	71	58	48
8 Notts County	42	19	10	13	65	60	48
9 Southampton	42	17	10	15	72	67	44

	P	W	D	L	F	A	Pts
10 Millwall	42	15	13	14	57	53	43
11 Sheff United	42	14	12	16	54	63	40
12 Blackburn	42	15	9	18	42	54	39
13 Oldham	42	14	10	18	52	64	38
14 Hull	42	10	17	15	45	53	37
15 Bristol Rovers	42	12	13	17	53	68	37
16 Burnley	42	11	14	17	46	64	36
17 Fulham	42	11	13	18	54	61	35
18 Cardiff	42	12	10	20	56	67	34
19 Carlisle	42	11	12	19	49	75	34
20 Orient	42	9	16	17	37	55	34
21 Plymouth	42	8	16	18	46	65	32
22 Hereford	42	8	15	19	57	78	31

Third Division

	P	W	D	L	F	A	Pts
1 Mansfield	46	28	8	10	78	42	64
2 Brighton	46	25	11	10	83	40	61
3 Crystal Palace	46	23	13	10	68	40	59
4 Rotherham	46	22	15	9	69	44	59
5 Wrexham	46	24	10	12	80	54	58
6 Preston	46	21	12	13	64	43	54
7 Bury	46	23	8	15	64	59	54
8 Sheff Wed	46	22	9	15	65	55	53
9 Lincoln	46	19	14	13	77	70	52
10 Shrewsbury	46	18	11	17	65	59	47
11 Swindon	46	15	15	16	68	75	45
12 Gillingham	46	16	12	18	55	64	44
13 Chester	46	18	8	20	48	58	44
14 Tranmere	46	13	17	16	51	53	43
15 Walsall	46	13	15	18	57	65	41
16 Peterborough	46	13	15	18	55	65	41
17 Oxford	46	12	15	19	55	65	39
18 Chesterfield	46	14	10	22	56	64	38
19 Port Vale	46	11	16	19	47	71	38
20 Portsmouth	46	11	14	21	53	70	36
21 Reading	46	13	9	24	49	73	35
22 Northampton	46	13	8	25	60	75	34
23 Grimsby	46	12	9	25	45	69	33
24 York	46	10	12	24	50	89	32

Fourth Division

	P	W	D	L	F	A	Pts
1 Cambridge	46	26	13	7	87	40	65
2 Exeter	46	25	12	9	70	46	62
3 Colchester	46	25	9	12	77	43	59
4 Bradford	46	23	13	10	78	51	59
5 Swansea	46	25	8	13	92	68	58
6 Barnsley	46	23	9	14	62	39	55
7 Watford	46	18	15	13	67	50	51

	P	W	D	L	F	A	Pts
8 Doncaster	46	21	9	16	71	65	51
9 Huddersfield	46	19	12	15	60	49	50
10 Southend	46	15	19	12	52	45	49
11 Darlington	46	18	13	15	59	64	49
12 Crewe	46	19	11	16	47	60	49
13 Bournemouth	46	15	18	13	54	44	48
14 Stockport	46	13	19	14	53	57	45
15 Brentford	46	18	7	21	77	76	43
16 Torquay	46	17	9	20	59	67	43
17 Aldershot	46	16	11	19	49	59	43
18 Rochdale	46	13	12	21	50	59	38
19 Newport	46	14	10	22	42	58	38
20 Scunthorpe	46	13	11	22	49	73	37
21 Halifax	46	11	14	21	47	58	36
22 Hartlepool	46	10	12	24	47	73	32
23 Southport	46	3	19	24	33	77	25
24 Workington	46	4	11	31	41	102	19

Scottish Premier Division

	P	W	D	L	F	A	Pts
1 Celtic	36	23	9	4	79	39	55
2 Rangers	36	18	10	8	62	37	46
3 Aberdeen	36	16	11	9	56	42	43
4 Dundee United	36	16	9	11	54	45	41
5 Partick	36	11	13	12	40	44	35
6 Hibernian	36	8	18	10	34	35	34
7 Motherwell	36	10	12	14	57	60	32
8 Ayr United	36	11	8	17	44	68	30
9 Hearts	36	7	13	16	49	66	27
10 Kilmarnock	36	4	9	23	32	71	17

Scottish First Division

	P	W	D	L	F	A	Pts
1 St Mirren	39	25	12	2	91	38	62
2 Clydebank	39	24	10	5	89	38	58
3 Dundee	39	21	9	9	90	55	51
4 Morton	39	20	10	9	77	52	50
5 Montrose	39	16	9	14	61	62	41
6 Airdrieonians	39	13	12	14	63	58	38
7 Dumbarton	39	14	9	16	63	68	37
8 Arbroath	39	17	3	19	46	62	37
9 Queen of the S	39	11	13	15	58	65	35
10 Hamilton	39	11	10	18	44	59	32
11 St Johnstone	39	8	13	18	42	64	29
12 East Fife	39	8	13	18	40	71	29
13 Raith	39	8	11	20	45	68	27
14 Falkirk	39	6	8	25	36	85	20

Scottish Second Division

	P	W	D	L	F	A	Pts
1 Stirling	39	22	11	6	59	29	55
2 Alloa	39	19	13	7	73	45	51
3 Dunfermline	39	20	10	9	52	36	50
4 Stranraer	39	20	6	13	74	53	46
5 Queen's Park	39	17	11	11	65	51	45
6 Albion	39	15	12	12	74	61	42
7 Clyde	39	15	11	13	68	64	41
8 Berwick	39	13	10	16	37	51	36
9 Stenhousemuir	39	15	5	19	38	49	35
10 East Stirling	39	12	8	19	47	63	32
11 Meadowbank	39	8	16	15	41	57	32
12 Cowdenbeath	39	13	5	21	46	64	31
13 Brechin	39	7	12	20	51	77	26
14 Forfar	39	7	10	22	43	68	24

FA Cup

Fourth Round

Arsenal v Coventry City	3–1
Aston Villa v West Ham United	3–0
Birmingham City v Leeds United	1–2
Blackburn Rovers v Orient	3–0
Cardiff City v Wrexham	3–2
Chester v Luton Town	1–0
Colchester United v Derby County	1–1, 0–1
Ipswich Town v Wolverhampton Wanderers	2–2, 0–1
Liverpool v Carlisle United	3–0
Manchester United v Queen's Park Rangers	1–0
Middlesbrough v Hereford United	4–0
Northwich Victoria v Oldham Athletic	1–3
Port Vale v Burnley	2–1
Swindon Town v Everton	2–2, 1–2
Nottingham Forest v Southampton	3–3, 1–2
Newcastle United v Manchester City	1–3

Fifth Round

Aston Villa v Port Vale	3–0
Cardiff City v Everton	1–2
Derby County v Blackburn Rovers	3–1
Leeds United v Manchester City	1–0
Liverpool v Oldham Athletic	3–1
Middlesbrough v Arsenal	4–1

Southampton v
    Manchester United   2-2, 1-2
Wolverhampton Wanderers v Chester 1-0

Sixth Round

Everton v Derby County   2-0
Liverpool v Middlesbrough   2-0
Manchester United v Aston Villa   2-1
Wolverhampton Wanderers v
    Leeds United   0-1

Semi-Final

Everton v Liverpool   2-2, 0-3
Leeds United v Manchester United   1-2

Final

Manchester United v Liverpool   2-1

Scottish FA Cup

Third Round

Airdrieonians v Celtic   1-1, 0-5
Arbroath v Brechin   1-0
Clydebank v
    Hamilton Academicals   0-0, 3-0
Dunfermline Athletic v Aberdeen   0-1
East Fife v Clyde   2-1
East Stirling v Albion Rovers   0-3
Hearts v Dumbarton   1-1, 1-0
Hibernian v Partick Thistle   3-0

Morton v Ayr United   0-1
Motherwell v Kilmarnock   3-0
Queen's Park v Alloa   0-0, 0-1
Queen of the South v Montrose   3-2
Rangers v Falkirk   3-1
St Johnstone v Dundee   1-1, 2-4
St Mirren v Dundee United   4-1
Stirling Albion v Elgin City   1-1, 2-3

Fourth Round

Arbroath v Hibernian   1-1, 2-1
Celtic v Ayr United   1-1, 3-1
Dundee v Aberdeen   0-0, 2-1
East Fife v Albion Rovers   2-1
Hearts v Clydebank   1-0
Motherwell v St Mirren   2-1
Queen of the South v Alloa   2-1
Rangers v Elgin City   3-0

Fifth Round

Arbroath v Dundee   1-3
Celtic v Queen of the South   5-1
Hearts v East Fife   0-0, 3-2
Rangers v Motherwell   2-0

Semi-Final

Celtic v Dundee   2-0
Rangers v Hearts   2-0

Final

Celtic v Rangers   1-0

Leading Goalscorers
from 1919

English League
Divisions 1 and 2

Division 1	Goals	Year	Division 2	Goals
F. Morris, WBA	37	1919–20	S. J. Taylor, Huddersfield	35
J. Smith, Bolton	38	1920–21	S. Puddefoot, Huddersfield	29
A. Wilson, Middlesbrough	31	1921–22	J. Broad, Stoke	25
C. Buchan, Sunderland	30	1922–23	H. Bedford, Blackpool	32
W. Chadwick, Everton	28	1923–24	H. Bedford, Blackpool	34
F. Roberts, Man City	31	1924–25	A. Chandler, Leicester	33
E. Harper, Blackburn	43	1925–26	R. Turnbull, Chelsea	39
J. Trotter, Sheff Wed	37	1926–27	G. Camsell, Middlesbrough	59
W. Dean, Everton	60	1927–28	J. Cookson, WBA	38
D. Halliday, Sunderland	43	1928–29	J. Hampson, Blackpool	40
V. Watson, West Ham	41	1929–30	J. Hampson, Blackpool	45
T. Waring, Aston Villa	49	1930–31	W. Dean, Everton	39
W. Dean, Everton	44	1931–32	C. Pearce, Swansea	35
J. Bowers, Derby	35	1932–33	E. Harper, Preston	37
J. Bowers, Derby	35	1933–34	P. Glover, Grimsby	42
T. Drake, Arsenal	42	1934–35	J. Milsom, Bolton	31
R. Carter, Sunderland	31 ⎫	1935–36	J. Dodds, Sheff United	34
P. Glover, Grimsby	31 ⎬		R. Finan, Blackpool	34
R. Gurney, Sunderland	31 ⎭			
F. Steele, Stoke	33	1936–37	J. Bowers, Leicester	33
T. Lawton, Everton	35	1937–38	G. Henson, Bradford	27
T. Lawton, Everton	35	1938–39	H. Billington, Luton	28
No competition		1939–46	No competition	
D. Westcott, Wolves	37	1946–47	C. Wayman, Newcastle	30
R. Rooke, Arsenal	33	1947–48	E. Quigley, Sheff Wed	23
W. Moir, Bolton	25	1948–49	C. Wayman, Southampton	32
R. Davis, Sunderland	25	1949–50	T. Briggs, Grimsby	35
S. Mortensen, Blackpool	30	1950–51	C. McCormack, Barnsley	33
G. Robledo, Newcastle	33	1951–52	D. Dooley, Sheff Wed	46
C. Wayman, Preston	24	1952–53	A. Rowley, Leicester	39
J. Glazzard, Huddersfield	29	1953–54	J. Charles, Leeds	42
R. Allen, WBA	27	1954–55	T. Briggs, Blackburn	33
N. Lofthouse, Bolton	33	1955–56	W. Gardiner, Leicester	34
J. Charles, Leeds	38	1956–57	A. Rowley, Leicester	44
R. Smith, Tottenham	36	1957–58	B. Clough, Middlesbrough	40
J. Greaves, Chelsea	32	1958–59	B. Clough, Middlesbrough	42
D. Viollet, Man United	32	1959–60	B. Clough, Middlesbrough	39
J. Greaves, Chelsea	41	1960–61	R. Crawford, Ipswich	39
R. Crawford, Ipswich	33	1961–62	R. Hunt, Liverpool	41
J. Greaves, Tottenham	37	1962–63	R. Tambling, Chelsea	35
J. Greaves, Tottenham	35	1963–64	R. Saunders, Portsmouth	33
A. McEvoy, Blackburn	29 ⎫	1964–65	G. O'Brien, Southampton	32
J. Greaves, Tottenham	29 ⎭			

	Goals	Year		Goals
R. Hunt, Liverpool	30	1965–66	M. Chivers, Southampton	30
R. Davies, Southampton	37	1966–67	D. Dougan, Leicester; Wolves	25
G. Best, Man United	28	1967–68	J. Hickton, Middlesbrough	24
R. Davies, Southampton	28			
J. Greaves, Tottenham	27	1968–69	J. Toshack, Cardiff	22
J. Astle, WBA	25	1969–70	J. Hickton, Middlesbrough	24
A. Brown, WBA	28	1970–71	M. Macdonald, Luton J. Hickton, Middlesbrough	24 24
F. Lee, Man City	33	1971–72	R. Latchford, Birmingham	23
B. Robson, West Ham	28	1972–73	D. Givens, QPR	23
M. Channon, Southampton	21	1973–74	D. McKenzie, Notts Forest	26
M. Macdonald, Newcastle	21	1974–75	B. Little, Aston Villa	20
E. MacDougall, Norwich	23	1975–76	D. Hales, Charlton	28
A. Gray, Aston Villa M. Macdonald, Arsenal	25 25	1976–77	M. Walsh, Blackpool	26

English League
Division 3

Division 3 (South)	Goals	Year	Division 3 (North)	Goals
J. Connor, Crystal Palace E. Simms, Luton G. Whitworth, Northampton	28 28 28	1920–21		
F. Richardson, Plymouth	31	1921–22	J. Carmichael, Grimsby	37
F. Pagnam, Watford	30	1922–23	G. Beel, Chesterfield J. Carmichael, Grimsby	23 23
W. Haines, Portsmouth	28	1923–24	D. Brown, Darlington	27
J. Fowler, Swansea	28	1924–25	D. Brown, Darlington	39
J. Cock, Plymouth	32	1925–26	J. Cookson, Chesterfield	44
D. Morris, Swindon	47	1926–27	A. Whitehurst, Rochdale	44
D. Morris, Swindon	38	1927–28	J. Smith, Stockport	38
A. Rennie, Luton	43	1928–29	J. McConnell, Carlisle	43
G. Goddard, QPR	37	1929–30	F. Newton, Stockport	36
P. Simpson, Crystal Palace	46	1930–31	J. McConnell, Carlisle	37
C. Bourton, Coventry	49	1931–32	B. Hall, Lincoln	42
C. Bourton, Coventry	40	1932–33	W. McNaughton, Hull	39
C. Pearce, Charlton	26	1933–34	A. Lythgoe, Stockport	46
R. Allen, Charlton	32	1934–35	G. Alsop, Walsall	40
A. Dawes, Crystal Palace	38	1935–36	R. Bell, Tranmere	33
J. Payne, Luton	55	1936–37	E. Harston, Mansfield	55
H. Crawshaw, Mansfield	25	1937–38	J. Roberts, Port Vale	28
G. Morton, Swindon	28	1938–39	S. Hunt, Carlisle	32
No competition		1939–46	No competition	
D. Clarke, Bristol	36	1946–47	C. Jordan, Doncaster	41
L. Townsend, Bristol	29	1947–48	J. Hutchinson, Lincoln	32
D. McGibbon, Bournemouth	30	1948–49	W. Ardron, Rotherham	29
T. Lawton, Notts County	31	1949–50	R. Phillips, Crewe P. Docherty, Doncaster	26 26
W. Ardron, Notts Forest	36	1950–51	J. Shaw, Rotherham	37
R. Blackburn, Reading	39	1951–52	A. Graver, Lincoln	36

Division 2	Goals	Season	Division 2	Goals
G. Bradford, Bristol	33	1952–53	J. Whitehouse, Carlisle	29
J. English, Northampton	28	1953–54	G. Ashman, Carlisle	30
E. Morgan, Gillingham	31	1954–55	A. Bottom, York	30
			D. Travis, Oldham	30
			J. Connor, Stockport	30
R. Collins, Torquay	40	1955–56	R. Crosbie, Grimsby	36
E. Phillips, Ipswich	41	1956–57	R. Straw, Derby	37
S. McGrory, Southend	31	1957–58	A. Ackerman, Carlisle	35
D. Reeves, Southampton	31			

Division 3 / **Division 4**

Division 3	Goals	Season	Division 4	Goals
E. Towers, Brentford	32	1958–59	A. Rowley, Shrewsbury	37
D. Reeves, Southampton	39	1959–60	C. Holton, Watford	42
A. Richards, Walsall	36	1960–61	T. Bly, Peterborough	52
C. Holton, Watford; Northampton	37	1961–62	R. Hunt, Colchester	37
G. Hudson, Coventry	30	1962–63	K. Wagstaff, Mansfield	34
A. Biggs, Bristol Rovers	30	1963–64	H. McIlmoyle, Carlisle	39
K. Wagstaff, Mansfield; Hull	35	1964–65	A. Jeffrey, Doncaster	36
L. Allen, QPR	32	1965–66	K. Hector, Bradford	44
R. Marsh, QPR	30	1966–67	E. Phythian, Hartlepool	23
D. Rogers, Swindon	25	1967–68	R. Chapman, Port Vale	25
R. Owen, Bury	25		R. Massie, Halifax	25
A. Dawson, Bury: Brighton	24	1968–69	G. Talbot, Chester	22
G. Jones, Bury	26	1969–70	A. Kinsey, Wrexham	27
G. Ingram, Preston	22	1970–71	E. MacDougall, Bournemouth	42
E. MacDougall, Bournemouth	35	1971–72	P. Price, Peterborough	28
A. Wood, Shrewsbury	35			
D. Horsfield, Charlton	25	1972–73	F. Binney, Exeter	28
B. Bannister, Bristol Rovers	25			
W. Jennings, Watford	26	1973–74	B. Yeo, Gillingham	31
R. McNeil, Hereford	31	1974–75	R. Clarke, Mansfield	28
R. McNeil, Hereford	35	1975–76	R. Moore, Tranmere	34
P. Ward, Brighton	32	1976–77	B. Joicey, Barnsley	25

Scottish League

Division 1	Goals	Division 1	Goals
1919–20 H. Ferguson, Motherwell	33	1933–34 J. Smith, Rangers	41
1920–21 H. Ferguson, Motherwell	43	1934–35 D. McCulloch, Hearts	38
1921–22 D. Walker, St Mirren	45	1935–36 J. McGrory, Celtic	50
1922–23 J. White, Hearts	30	1936–37 D. Wilson, Hamilton	34
1923–24 D. Halliday, Dundee	38	1937–38 A. Black, Hearts	38
1924–25 W. Devlin, Cowdenbeath	33	1938–39 A. Venters, Rangers	34
1925–26 W. Devlin, Cowdenbeath	37	1939–46 No Competition	
1926–27 J. McGrory, Celtic	49	1946–47 R. Mitchell, Third Lanark	22
1927–28 J. McGrory, Celtic	47	1947–48 A. Aikman, Falkirk	20
1928–29 E. Morrison, Falkirk	43	1948–49 A. Stott, Dundee	30
1929–30 B. Yorston, Aberdeen	38	1949–50 W. Bauld, Hearts	30
1930–31 B. Battles, Hearts	44	1950–51 L. Reilly, Hibernian	22
1931–32 W. McFadyen, Motherwell	52	1951–52 L. Reilly, Hibernian	27
1932–33 W. McFadyen, Motherwell	45	1952–53 L. Reilly, Hibernian	30

1952–53 C. Fleming, East Fife	30
1953–54 J. Wardhaugh, Hearts	30
1954–55 W. Bauld, Hearts	21
1955–56 J. Wardhaugh, Hearts	30
1956–57 H. Baird, Airdrieonians	33
1957–58 J. Wardhaugh, Hearts	28
1958–59 J. Baker, Hibernian	25
1959–60 J. Baker, Hibernian	42
1960–61 J. Harley, Third Lanark	42
1961–62 A. Gilzean, Dundee	24
1962–63 J. Millar, Rangers	25
1963–64 A. Gilzean, Dundee	32
1964–65 J. Forrest, Rangers	30
1965–66 J. McBride, Celtic	31
1966–67 S. Chalmers, Celtic	23
1967–68 R. Lennox, Celtic	32

1968–69 K. Cameron, Dundee United	27
1960–70 C. Stein, Rangers	24
1970–71 H. Hood, Celtic	22
1971–72 J. Harper, Aberdeen	33
1972–73 A. Gordon, Hibernian	27
1973–74 J. Deans, Celtic	24
1974–75 A. Gray, Dundee United	20
W. Pettigrew, Motherwell	20

Premier Division

1975–76 K. Dalglish, Celtic	24

First Division

1975–76 J. Bourke, Dumbarton	17
J. Whiteford, Falkirk	17

Home Internationals

Winners 1884-1977

Year	Champion	Year	Champion	Year	Champion
1884	Scotland	1914	Ireland	1956	England
1885	Scotland	1920	Wales		Scotland
1886	England	1921	Scotland		Wales
	Scotland	1922	Scotland		N Ireland
1887	Scotland	1923	Scotland	1957	England
1888	England	1924	Wales	1958	England
1889	Scotland	1925	Scotland		N Ireland
1890	England	1926	Scotland	1959	England
	Scotland	1927	England		N Ireland
1891	England		Scotland	1960	England
1892	England	1928	Wales		Scotland
1893	England	1929	Scotland		Wales
1894	Scotland	1930	England	1961	England
1895	England	1931	England	1962	Scotland
1896	Scotland		Scotland	1963	Scotland
1897	Scotland	1932	England	1964	England
1898	England	1933	Wales		Scotland
1899	England	1934	Wales		N Ireland
1900	Scotland	1935	England	1965	England
1901	England		Scotland	1966	England
1902	Scotland	1936	Scotland	1967	Scotland
1903	England	1937	Wales	1968	England
	Scotland	1938	England	1969	England
	Ireland	1939	England	1970	England
1904	England		Scotland		Scotland
1905	England		Wales		Wales
1906	England	1947	England	1971	England
	Scotland	1948	England	1972	England
1907	Wales	1949	Scotland		Scotland
1908	England	1950	England	1973	England
	Scotland	1951	Scotland	1974	England
1909	England	1952	England		Scotland
1910	Scotland		Wales	1975	England
1911	England	1953	England	1976	Scotland
1912	England		Scotland	1977	Scotland
	Scotland	1954	England		
1913	England	1955	England		

World Cup Finals
1930-74

Year	Venue	Winner		Runner-up	
1930	Montevideo	Uruguay	4	Argentina	2
1934	Rome	Italy	2	Czechoslovakia	1
1938	Paris	Italy	4	Hungary	2
1950	Rio de Janeiro	Uruguay	2	Brazil	1
1954	Berne	West Germany	3	Hungary	2
1958	Stockholm	Brazil	5	Sweden	2
1962	Santiago	Brazil	3	Czechoslovakia	1
1966	Wembley	England	4	West Germany	2
1970	Mexico City	Brazil	4	Italy	1
1974	Munich	West Germany	2	Holland	1

European Cup Finals
1956-77

Year	Venue	Winner		Runner-up	
1956	Paris	Real Madrid	4	Stade de Reims	3
1957	Madrid	Real Madrid	2	Fiorentina	0
1958	Brussels	Real Madrid	3	AC Milan	2
1959	Stuttgart	Real Madrid	2	Stade de Reims	0
1960	Hampden	Real Madrid	7	Eintracht Frankfurt	3
1961	Berne	Benfica	3	Barcelona	2
1962	Amsterdam	Benfica	5	Real Madrid	3
1963	Wembley	AC Milan	2	Benfica	1
1964	Vienna	InterMilan	3	Real Madrid	1
1965	Milan	Inter Milan	1	Benfica	0
1966	Brussels	Real Madrid	2	Partizan Belgrade	1
1967	Lisbon	Celtic	2	Inter Milan	1
1968	Wembley	Manchester United	4	Benfica	1
1969	Madrid	AC Milan	4	Ajax Amsterdam	1
1970	Milan	Feyenoord	2	Celtic	1
1971	Wembley	Ajax Amsterdam	2	Panathinaikos	0
1972	Rotterdam	Ajax Amsterdam	2	Inter Milan	0
1973	Belgrade	Ajax Amsterdam	1	Juventus	0
1974	Brussels	Bayern Munich	1	Atletico Madrid	1
			4		0
1975	Paris	Bayern Munich	2	Leeds United	0
1976	Hampden	Bayern Munich	1	St Etienne	0
1977	Rome	Liverpool	3	Bor Moenchengladbach	1

European Football Championship
(Nations' Cup)
Finals 1960-76

Year	Venue	Winner		Runner-up	
1960	Paris	USSR	2	Yugoslavia	1
1964	Madrid	Spain	2	USSR	0
1968	Rome	Italy	2	Yugoslavia	0
		(After 1-1 Draw)			
1972	Brussels	West Germany	3	USSR	0
1976	Belgrade	Czechoslovakia	2	West Germany	2
		(After extra time; Czechoslovakia 5-3 on penalties)			

European Cup-winners' Cup
Finals 1961-77

Year	Venue	Winner		Runner-up	
1961	Glasgow	Fiorentina	2	Rangers	0
	Florence		2		1
			4		1
1962	Glasgow	Atletico Madrid	1	Fiorentina	1
	Stuttgart		3		0
1963	Rotterdam	Tottenham Hotspur	5	Atletico Madrid	1
1964	Brussels	Sporting Lisbon	3	MTK Budapest	3
	Antwerp		1		0
1965	Wembley	West Ham United	2	TSV Munich 1860	0
1966	Glasgow	Borussia Dortmund	2	Liverpool	1
1967	Nuremberg	Bayern Munich	1	Rangers	0
1968	Rotterdam	AC Milan	2	SV Hamburg	0
1969	Basle	Slovan Bratislava	3	Barcelona	2
1970	Vienna	Manchester City	2	Gornik Zabrze	1
1971	Athens	Chelsea	1	Real Madrid	1
	Athens		2		1
1972	Barcelona	Rangers	3	Dynamo Moscow	2
1973	Salonika	AC Milan	1	Leeds United	0
1974	Rotterdam	FC Magdeburg	2	AC Milan	0
1975	Basle	Dynamo Kiev	3	Ferencvaros	0
1976	Brussels	Anderlecht	4	West Ham United	2
1977	Amsterdam	SV Hamburg	2	Anderlecht	0

UEFA Cup (Fairs Cup)
Finals 1958–77

Year	Winner	Score (aggregate)	Runner-up
1958	Barcelona	8–2	London
1960	Barcelona	4–1	Birmingham C
1961	AS Roma	4–2	Birmingham C
1962	Valencia	7–3	Barcelona
1963	Valencia	4–1	Dynamo Zagreb
1964	Real Zaragoza	2–1	Valencia
1965	Ferencvaros	1–0	Juventus
1966	Barcelona	4–3	Real Zaragoza
1967	Dynamo Zagreb	2–1	Leeds United
1968	Leeds United	1–0	Ferencvaros
1969	Newcastle United	6–2	Ferencvaros
1970	Arsenal	4–3	Anderlecht
1971	Leeds United	3–3	Juventus
	(Leeds won on away goals)		
1972	Tottenham	3–2	Wolves
1973	Liverpool	3–2	Bor Moenchengladbach
1974	Feyenoord	4–2	Tottenham
1975	Bor Moenchengladbach	5–1	Twente Enschede
1976	Liverpool	4–3	FC Bruges
1977	Juventus	2–2	Atletico Bilbao
	(Juventus won on away goals)		